TABULA GRATULATORIA

Family History Section of la Société Guernesiaise

Francesca Galloway (Asian textiles), 31 Dover St., London, W1S 4ND

Messrs Maggs, antiquarian booksellers, 50 Berkeley Square, London, W1J 5BA

Messrs Bernard Quaritch, antiquarian booksellers, 8 Lower John St.,
Golden Square, London, W1F 9AO

Matthew Adams

John C. Allez

Martin J. Bienvenu

Mark Andrew Bisson

M.J. Boden-Heaume M.A., M.Ed.

R.N. Brehaut

Sylvia Brouard

Christopher Cormack

Marj Cowie

Alasdair Cross

Lt.-Col. and Mrs C.C. Davey

Mr W.A.C. Davey

Paul Davies

Jonathan Dawe

Brian R. de Jersey &
    Glennys de Jersey

Susan de Putron

Philip G. Domaille

Ann and Adrian Dorey

Jan Dyke

Jean H.E. Edwards

Kathi Edwards

Pauline England

Stephen Foote

Yvonne Gettings

Ken Gibbs

Gill Girard

David Gurney

W.C. Hill

Anne & Michael Hutchings

Heather Kirk (née Nicolle)

R.E. Le Bargy

R.F. Le Bargy

Anthony Le Conte

Jurat David Le Conte

George Le Page

Robert Macdonald

Chris Meinke

Karyn A. Norman

Jean-Clement Pommier

J.N. Razzak

Valerie Rowland

Marie Sillars

Maureen S-J

Jeremy C.S.F. Smithies

Charles Tracy

Maria van der Tang

Andrew I. Way &
    Margaret R. Goman

When discussing eighteenth-century Guernsey merchants, historians have tended to focus on Nicholas Dobrée and Carteret Priaulx. However, these *négociants* were clearly just two of a large number. Cox set out to identify the others and he here presents the results of his investigation. In some instances he has found enough detail to present biographical sketches. He also examines the merchants as a group. He has identified three important sets operating in St Peter Port: indigenous aristocrats; Huguenot refugees; and economic migrants from the continent, England and Scotland. He concludes that by the end of the eighteenth century St Peter Port had about the same number of *négociants* as Lorient. In terms of wealth the Guernsey merchants compared with those of Dunkirk. There were no 'merchant princes' of vast wealth, but many *négociants* with very comfortable incomes. The merchants specialised to a certain extent. Not all were supplying spirits, tobacco and tea to smugglers; several leading merchants were in the international wine business.

Cox has placed the merchants in their context and discusses the trade, cargoes, shipping, networks and geography of their mercantile world. Whenever possible, he has quantified his discoveries. His investigations demonstrate that a few Guernsey merchants participated in the slave trade more than was hitherto understood. He also reveals the extent to which the merchants became involved in the economy of Catalonia. In the course of his investigation he has made some unexpected discoveries: Jacobite links in the wine-trade, for example, and the reason why a town in Guyana is called Port Mourant.

Gregory Stevens Cox was born at Ilchester (Somerset) and educated at Beaminster and Netherbury Grammar School. He was awarded the Canon Goodden prize by Dorset Education Committee and won an open exhibition to St John's College, Oxford, where he read Classics and Oriental Languages. He was subsequently awarded the degree of M.Ed. with distinction by Exeter University for research into teaching and learning history; and a Ph.D. by Leicester University for research into Guernsey history. The Royal Historical Society recommended the publication of his thesis, which appeared under the title *St Peter Port, Guernsey, 1680-1830* (Boydell & Brewer, 1999). He contributed several entries to the *Oxford Dictionary of National Biography*. He edits *les îles de la manche* – an occasional journal devoted to articles about Channel Islands history.

Cover illustration
'Prospect of St Peter's Port & town in the Island of Guernsey taken from Castle Cornet' [Bastide del., W.H. Toms sculp., printed and sold by John Tinney, Golden Lion, Fleet Street, London, early 1740s]. Reproduced by kind permission of the Priaulx Library, Guernsey.

Marguerite, 1758-1828, daughter of Elisha Tupper (jurat-merchant) and wife of
Isaac Carey, merchant (from a miniature, reproduced by kind permission
of Sir deVic Carey).

THE
GUERNSEY MERCHANTS
&
THEIR WORLD

in the Georgian era

an investigation

by

Gregory Stevens Cox

with a foresay by

Sir deVic Carey, Q.C.,

(Bailiff of Guernsey, 1999-2005)

2009

Published by the Toucan Press, Guernsey

ISBN 978-0-85694-603-5

© Gregory Stevens Cox 2009

Set in Plantin

 Printed by Creeds Telephone: **01308 423411** Web: **www.creedsuk.com**

for

Naomi,

Luke,

Matilda,

&

Alice

ACKNOWLEDGMENTS

Some of the material used in this volume was collected when I was researching *St Peter Port 1680 – 1830*. I repeat my thanks to all whom I there acknowledged – and I trust that they will forgive me if I do not here name them all again. Since the publication of that volume I have incurred further obligations. Research has taken me to Spain and Professor Valls Junyent was most helpful in discussing the eighteenth-century commerce of Catalonia. I thank the archivists in Barcelona and Tarragona for their patience with my faltering command of conversational Catalan. Mrs Moore has appeared at moments when I required help with translation. Pepe Romanillos and his family in Spain have been attentive and sympathetic hosts. Likewise, Ian Young proved an informative guide in the Languedoc. On my way home from Barcelona I spent several agreeable days studying Dobrée papers at Nantes; I thank the staff at the *Archives municipales* for their assistance, Veronique Guitton (Directrice), Mlle Elizabeth Guillaume, Mme Michele Mary and Mme Lydie Naud. In London the Royal Society, the British Library and the National Archives have provided a swift and efficient service. I found the National Library of Scotland a most pleasant environment in which to carry out research. I have received encouragement from several scholars and academics abroad and I thank Professors Cullen, Duguid, McCusker and Richardson in particular. Brigitte Brauch-Velhorn was helpful in locating books in German university libraries. Amanda Bennett, Tony Pawlyn, Derek Morris, Kenneth Cozens, Frank Botten and David Jones have likewise assisted in various ways.

This is an appropriate place to express my thanks to several of my old schoolteachers (whom I encountered recently at an 'Old Boys & Old Girls' re-union): Mr Barrett (who made valiant efforts to teach me Mathematics); Mr Fox (to whom I owe an enthusiasm for Geography); Mr and Mrs Cummins (who taught Science and English); and Mr Carpenter (thanks to whose teaching of Latin I find it reasonably easy to read Catalan).

At home in Guernsey I have received valuable assistance from the Island Archive Service and I thank Dr Ogier for his kindly interest in my work. He has saved me from more than one egregious error. The Greffe, the Priaulx Library and the Guille-Allès Library have, likewise, been more than helpful.

I thank Guernsey Museum, the National Maritime Museum, the National Library of Scotland, the Guildhall Library, the Priaulx Library, Messrs Christie's, Messrs Bernard Quaritch, Messrs Maggs, Francesca Galloway, the estate of the late Professor Parkinson, and several private collectors for permission to use illustrations. Likewise, I thank Mr Richard Hocart, editor of the *Transactions of La Société Guernesiaise* and author of *Peter de Havilland* for copyright permission to use certain quotations. I thank Margaret White and Deputy Guille for answers to my questions and their permission to make use of their research findings. Professor Seecharran of London Metropolitan University was most helpful in answering questions about Port Mourant and Guyana.

I owe many thanks to Blanchelande Girls' College. I am grateful to the Trustees, Governors, Principal and Vice-Principal for their help. Colleagues on the staff – Yvonne Browning, Karen Higgs, Cora Lee, Karyn Norman, Carole Perrott, Linda Rowe, Sarah Tribe, Jenny Wylie, Jeremy Smithies, Jeffrey Bailey, Christopher Claxton, David Merifield, Peter Izat and the school secretaries (past and present) – have all given encouragement and help (not least with computers!).

I have delivered some lectures about the Guernsey merchants and I thank the audiences for their perceptive questions. Julian Stockwin, Michael Walden and Peter Tagart have been similarly helpful. In travelling to and from The National Archives I have been looked after excellently by The Clarence Hotel, Weymouth, and by Mrs Kitchen in Kew. I thank John Collings and Jonathan Voak for hospitality in London. I am grateful to Mr and Mrs Malpas for sundry kindnesses. Anthony Payne has very kindly read proofs and has made valuable suggestions. I thank him also for having found some rare books for me (as has Hugh Bett). Simon Radcliffe, at Creeds the Printers, has patiently corrected proofs as has Mark Diment. I thank them and all their colleagues.

I thank Sir DeVic Carey for his kindness in granting permission to use material from *The Careys of Guernsey*. I am honoured that he, a descendant of the leading merchant family of eighteenth-century Guernsey, has written a *Foresay* to the volume.

Finally, I would like to express my gratitude to Emma, Andrew, Rosemary and Naomi who have journeyed with me to some of the ports discussed in this book. I hope that it will go some way to explaining my obsession.

Gregory Stevens Cox

CONTENTS

FIGURES

TABLES

PLATES

(frontispiece; and following p. 235)

XVIII St John's, Newfoundland; Quebec

XIX Custom House negroes at Rio de Janeiro; Rio de Janeiro

XX The brig *Collingwood* of Guernsey; the schooner *Aurora*

ABBREVIATIONS

(See also p. 173)

Actes	*Actes des Etats de l'île de Guernesey, 1605-* (Guernsey, 1851-)
BL	British Library
BSJ	Bulletin of the Société Jersiaise
COf	Constables' Office, St Peter Port
Duncan	J. Duncan, *The History of Guernsey* (London, 1841)
Dupont	G. Dupont, *Histoire du Cotentin et de ses Iles*, 4 vols (Caen, 1885)
EC	Ecclesiastical Court archives (housed at the Greffe, Guernsey)
l.t.	Livre tournois (see p. 210)
Ordonnances	*Recueil d'Ordonnances de la Cour Royale de l'Isle de Guernesey* 1553- (Guernsey 1852-)
PRO	Public Record Office, London; now styled TNA
[Q]RGS	[Quarterly] Review of the Guernsey Society
TC	Town Church, St Peter Port, Guernsey
TSG	Transactions of *La Société Guernesiaise* (Guernsey Society of Natural Science and Local Research before 1922)
Tupper	F. B. Tupper, *The History of Guernsey and its Bailiwick* (Guernsey, 1854)

CONVENTIONS

Dates are rendered as in manuscripts (i.e. old style before 1752).

Place names are frequently rendered as in the documentary source:

Cette = Sète; Gottenburg = Gothenburg; Monte Video = Montevideo; Salo = Salou.

Personal names: it should be noted that there were two branches of the de Sausmarez family, one branch spelling the name de Saumarez.

CURRENCY & MONEY

The Guernsey currency in the eighteenth century was the livre tournois (divided into 20 sols which, in turn, were divided into 12 deniers). Jamieson 1986, p. 479, gives a conversion rate for the eighteenth century of 'about thirteen or fourteen livres to the pound sterling'.

Comparing British and French currencies, F. Crouzet in *La Guerre économique franco-anglaise au XVIIIe siècle*, Paris, 2008, pp. 35-36, gives a conversion rate of £1 sterling = 24 *livres tournois*.

Nicholas Reserson's account refers to several currencies. Helpfully, he sometimes expresses an amount in two currencies, providing the following rates:

£1 sterling = 10.5 Brabant florins [*f*] (see p. 122)

£1 sterling = £C 9.1 [Catalan] (see p. 124).

Reserson also refers to *piastres courantes*. Contemporary Franco-Spanish documents give a conversion rate of 1 piastre = approximately 5 livres 6 sols. From this, and following Crouzet's conversion rate, £1 sterling = 4.5 piastres.

Assignats were paper money issued by the National Constituent Assembly during the revolution in France. Too many were printed and this led to hyper-inflation. *Assignats* were replaced by *mandats* which similarly lost their value.

There are frequent references in Nicholas Reserson's account to bills of exchange. A bill was a written order by the *drawer* to the *drawee* to pay money to the *payee*.

FOREWORD
By Sir de Vic Carey, Q.C.
(Bailiff of Guernsey 1999-2005)

This work is a fascinating sequel to Dr Gregory Stevens Cox's previous monograph entitled St. Peter Port 1680-1830. By concentrating on the individuals who formed Guernsey's merchant class he brings to life that exciting era which developed during the eighteenth century and prospered until the first half of the nineteenth. He has also included a great deal of detailed research on the economic activity, which generated the great wealth that was so tightly held within the relatively small number of families who comprised the merchant class.

Having always lived with the architecture of our magnificent Regency town and seen the extent of the warehousing along the front I have always been aware that the Island enjoyed a golden age two hundred years ago. [In a further two hundred years perhaps a similar legacy will be visible in the form of all the fine office blocks erected to serve the financial services industry in the latter part of the twentieth century] As a descendant of several of the merchants featured in this erudite but very readable work, my eyes have been opened for the first time to a detailed understanding of what they were about and the wide extent of their activity

These merchants travelled widely abroad, all over the world in fact in small sailing ships and stagecoaches. In England their wealth and spending power would bring them into contact with the upper echelons of English Society both landed gentry and those who began to generate serious wealth during the industrial revolution. They could never compete with and claim to be social equals of the real English aristocracy, who had prospered from and gained their social standing from substantial holdings of land built up over the centuries. Although by local standards there were large landholdings in Guernsey, and as the author points out some of these generated capital for the enterprises of the merchants, none of the local land owners could claim that the level of their activity and the size of their estates put them on the English social scale above the rank of yeoman farmers. However the merchants attained a higher status on the international stage. Although their success stemmed from trade, they could as a result of the respect and security the majority of their families had enjoyed as leaders of island society for many years hold their heads high when confronted by those who had suddenly acquired their wealth.

Many parallels can be drawn between the trading activities of two centuries ago with that of the financial services industry today. In both situations the insular authorities were on occasion put under much pressure from the Westminster government and others, who perceived that the Island's success was engendered at their expense. Then as now England taxed its inhabitants heavily and there were always those in England who would offer assistance to their fellow citizens to avoid such taxes, In the eighteenth century the main part of the tax avoidance industry was directed to organising the smuggling of dutiable goods ashore at quiet locations on the English coast. Policing frontiers was even more difficult then than it is today. It was natural that the British Government tried to lean on little Guernsey, whose merchants were on the face of it perfectly entitled to sell their wares to whoever set foot on the quayside, but in practice were a major source of supply to what was termed the illicit trade.. By 1800 we see that the position from London's point of view was no longer tolerable and the island suffered from the imposition of an effective curb on the supply of goods for smuggling to England.

One sees time and again through the Island's history enterprising individuals devising schemes to exploit the more restrictive laws of the larger jurisdictions around us and thereby gaining an advantage for themselves and their customers resident in those jurisdictions. All runs smoothly and no one complains or is inspired to take action until the level of activity reaches a level when it begins to hurt the interests of the larger jurisdiction.

Looking at the history of the merchants one soon realises that the success derived from much of their activity is not engendered from exploiting some fiscal loophole to the disadvantage of another jurisdiction. Their success resulted in the main, from commercial contacts built up outside the island, the availability of funding, their own expertise and the Island's geographical position. As is natural with all small jurisdictions the absence of bureaucracy and regulation encouraged a fleetness of foot that enriched all levels of the community. Above all there was a willingness to take risks.

Unlike the majority of today's entrepreneurs, the merchants traded without the benefit of limited liability, often incurring substantial losses when trading conditions turned against them. It is interesting to note how success or failure became a matter of family honour. Fathers and others lent their support and there was a reluctance to let bankruptcy raise its head. This reluctance to default no doubt helped the whole merchant community as it built confidence in the minds of foreign trading partners. One of the factors assuring financial survival was the pooling of fortunes by dynastic marriages. A study of our family records shows that marrying a first or second cousin was a fairly frequent occurrence in the late eighteenth century.

Notwithstanding its small geographical size Guernsey enterprise in the days of the Merchants reached all quarters of the globe, just as the financial services industry does today. Today business comes to the Island through external contacts and reputation and the expertise and probity of its institutions. One difference between now and then is that the Island has not been able to escape the need for international standards of regulation and oversight of those who are operating here.

With those members of my family whom I recall as a young man and who were born in the late Victorian age there was, I fear, a certain reticence in acknowledging that the source of the wealth of which they were still enjoying the fruits had been fairly recently acquired and came from trade. Business suddenly became looked down upon and the descendants of the merchants began to pursue more socially acceptable careers in the professions, the army or the church. Reading the biographies in the History of the Careys of Guernsey the few lines expended on many of the important merchants.

The history of my own branch of the family illustrates this trend. We read herein of my forbears Thomas, Isaac and de Vic and their well-connected wives. What is not the function of the Author to record is that de Vic put most of his sons in the services, no doubt paying hefty sums for their commissions. His eldest de Vic Francis (1831-1908) entered the Bengal Horse Artillery retiring with the rank of Major General at the age of 50. He became a respected Jurat, being one of the first to address the States in English! Again his eldest joined the Army dying young from maladies picked in the South African War. The next son, Victor became an Advocate provoking his father to tend his resignation as a Jurat, an offer that was not accepted. Victor's son and grandson followed in his steps at the Bar.

I commend this well written and richly illustrated volume. I congratulate Dr Stevens Cox on his industry and scholarship. The production of a work adds a valuable resource for all students of local history and we look forward to further monographs from this stable. I hope that his work will serve as an inspiration to future historians to produce works of similar quality.

INTRODUCTION

In 1999 Boydell & Brewer, on the recommendation of the Royal Historical Society, published my monograph *St Peter Port 1680-1830*. That was an urban study in which I addressed questions posed by urban historians. I attempted to quantify the volume and value of the maritime trade of St Peter Port and to relate these economic data to the demographic, social and physical evolution of the town. The present volume has a different focus. It is, first, an investigation in which I have tried to identify the Guernsey merchants of the Georgian era. Hitherto Nicholas Dobrée and Carteret Priaulx have been taken to exemplify the merchants, Nicholas representing the first half of the eighteenth century, Carteret the second half. But who were the other merchants? How many were there? What did they do? Secondly, this is an investigation in which I have tried to establish the trade networks of the Guernsey merchants operating in the Atlantic economy. There is, necessarily, some overlap with the *St Peter Port* monograph. For example, there is a direct and obvious correlation between the volume of port wine imported into Guernsey ('Cargoes') and the frequency of shipping arrivals from Oporto ('Foreign ports'). In order to obviate lots of cross-references I have integrated chapter 2 of *St Peter Port 1680-1830* (and some related appendices) into the present study. At various junctures this has allowed me to extend and develop what I originally wrote. In particular, I have quoted extensively from the report written by Stiles about his visit to Guernsey in 1800. Parts of this are known from Tupper's *History of Guernsey* but I have incorporated 'new' material from a manuscript housed at the National Archives. I have also included substantial extracts from the writings of F.B. Tupper. He was not only a historian, he was also a member of a leading merchant family and worked abroad on family business. His writings about Guernsey trade in the early nineteenth century constitute primary, rather than secondary, evidence. Although historians do not regard it as best practice to use lengthy quotations I have ignored that convention for two reasons. First, Tupper's writings are not to be found in many libraries. Secondly, this study is more in the tradition of *textes justificatives*; there is, I trust, some value in presenting a corpus of texts and data to underpin future study.

A work such as this embraces three topics: first, people – the merchants; secondly, a location – Guernsey; thirdly, transport technology – shipping. These topics overlap, but are not congruent. This is best expressed in terms of a Venn diagram.

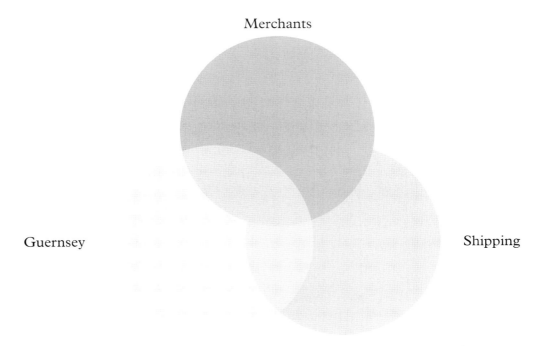

Fig. 0.1: The interlocking spheres of people, place and procedure

Many of the Guernsey merchants were based in the island; some, however, worked abroad as agents and factors. Guernsey merchants based in Catalonia frequently imported wheat from Quebec to Barcelona and traded with other Mediterranean ports. Moreover, some of the merchants intimately associated with the development of St Peter Port as an entrepôt were aliens normally resident outside the island (e.g. Archibald Stewart, based in London, who organised the shipping of wine from Guernsey to destinations such as Cuba). The Guernsey merchants maintained a fleet and looked after much of the shipping of cargoes to and from Guernsey; however, many foreign vessels regularly brought cargoes to the island (particularly neutral ships during wartime). We thus have foreign merchants, employing foreign shipping, using St Peter Port as a convenient focal point for their commerce. Finally, some of the island merchants, although based in Guernsey, were involved in trades centred not on Guernsey but on foreign ports. Examples of this are the 'trucking' of brandy in the Mediterranean and Atlantic; the slave trade; and the Newfoundland trade.

Throughout the eighteenth century the Guernsey merchants developed St Peter Port as an international entrepôt. The entrepôt trade was the foundation of their prosperity; even during war-years commerce made a valuable contribution, particularly when neutrals shipped scarce commodities from enemy ports to Guernsey for bulk-breaking and onward distribution to the British Isles. Much fruit arrived at English markets during the Seven Years War and the American War of Independence thanks to the workings of the Guernsey entrepôt. The French were in no doubt about the source of Guernsey's wealth – tea and brandy bought from the French and sold to English smugglers; and textiles, tobacco, lead and tin sold to French smugglers:

> La source de ses richesses vient du grand commerce que font les Habitans en *Thé*, & *Eau-de-vie* qu'ils tirent de France pour les envoyer en fraude en Angleterre. Une autre branche de leur négoce, est la contrebande *d'indiennes*, de *tabac*, de *plomb*, *d'étain*, de *draperies*, qu'ils font passer en France. (Pidansat de Mairobert, 1756, pp. 51-2).

An entrepôt offered distinct commercial advantages. Bulk-ordering brought economies of scale. Commodities could be purchased cheaply in seasons of abundance, stored, and sold later when demand increased. Moreover, a large stock stored in warehouses was an insurance against the interruption of supplies or adverse price movements. A merchant with a warehouse could take his time to find a buyer. In the case of some commodities (such as wine) warehousing gave time for maturing (with a subsequent sale at a higher price). Some goods such as tobacco were cleaned and processed at the entrepôt and sold on, with 'value added'. Finally, the entrepôt offered a service in which much of the capital belonged to others. Cargoes owned by foreigners could be handled on a commission basis. Cargoes often arrived and departed in foreign ships, the freight charges being paid by strangers. Running an entrepôt, the Guernsey merchants did not have to invest in all of the shipping and cargoes.

Large quantities of cargoes were sold to French and English smugglers. The reader will find relatively little about smuggling activity in the present volume. The reason for that is simple. As the Guernsey merchants pointed out in the eighteenth century, smugglers broke English and French laws, not Guernsey laws. The act of smuggling occurred on the French and English coasts. Smugglers were very important customers of the Guernsey merchants and, as such, are properly part of the Guernsey story. However, their clashes with English excise officers are not. Smuggling stories are, doubtless, exciting but tend to shift attention away from the activities of the Guernsey merchants. The island merchants sometimes engaged in fraud, passing French wine off as Spanish, in order to avoid the high excise payable on French goods. They also played fast-and-loose with the Navigation Acts. However, a great deal of the trade of the Guernsey merchants was open and lawful, both at the port of origin (St Peter Port) and at the ports of destination.

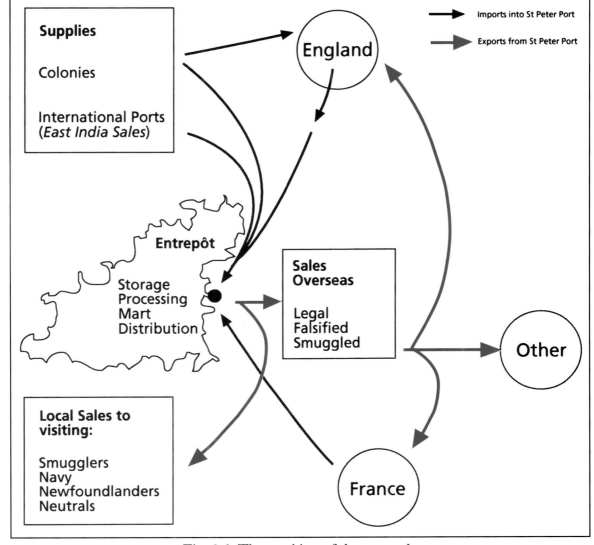

Fig. 0.2: The working of the entrepôt

Just as there is little about smuggling, so too there is little about privateering. Privateering brought wealth to some merchants; but it was a wartime activity and made no contribution to peacetime trade. Moreover, even in wartime, privateering was only *one* source of income. Large quantities of commodities from the countries of the belligerent powers were brought to Guernsey by neutral ships and redistributed through the entrepôt. This activity was as valuable as privateering. In 1792 John Guille wrote to his son:

> I wish you would write to all your friends in France to recommend me to them, because this island must become a general entrepôt – we lie so handy in mid Channel & so near the Coast that we must expect to see a vast & extensive business while the War lasts. English ships will be wanted for the French, we can furnish them (IAS, Stevens-Guille papers, John Guille to George Guille, 1 May 1792).

Privateering has tended to dominate the maritime history of the Channel Islands, just as it became the legend of St Malo – a town for decades known as a *ville corsaire*. In recent years French historians have paid much more attention to the ordinary commerce of the Breton port. They have also come to realise that St Malo was quite deeply involved in the slave trade. Patient research has brought a more balanced and nuanced tone to the historiography of the port.

In the last twenty years historians have become increasingly interested in the 'Atlantic economy'. There is an awareness that the old paradigm of the British Empire as a "hub-and-spoke" affair that ran from the "metropolis" to the "peripheries" is inadequate. Historians have generated more complex models. David Hancock, for example, in his study of the Madeira wine trade, argues that it was not managed from any centre:

> 'actual strategies, choices, and decisions were made in an ongoing set of decentralised negotiations between men and women on both sides of the Atlantic, in at least four or five places. Rather than rigid, the trade and its practitioners were flexible – protean men, working in an uncertain and porous environment, with an opportunistic approach to everyday business. Innovation was more the order of the day than was any passive imprisonment to inherited traditions and resources; these preindustrial people were enormously dynamic – witness the turnover of businesses, the development of new commodities, and the derivation of new socially significant uses' (Hancock, 2005, pp. 60-1).

Coclanis neatly summarises Hancock's thesis : 'patterns in many trades were much more open, adaptive, nonlinear, unpredictable, and contingent than scholars believe. In these trades multifocality, porosity, and cross-imperial economic assignations were the rule rather than the exception. In such trades, then, the proper metaphor, in Hancock's view, is not the hub and spoke but rather the spiderweb' (Coclanis, 2005, p.xiv). It will be found, I think, that the following chapters confirm Hancock's view.

The lay-out of this book is as follows: Chapter 1 offers an over-view of the trade of the merchants, outlining the phases of its evolution. Chapter 2 summarises the volumes of certain cargoes traded through the entrepôt. Chapter 3 examines links between Guernsey and other parts of the 'British Isles'. Chapter 4 surveys the foreign ports involved in the trades of the Guernsey merchants. Chapter 5 discusses the merchants and takes a closer look at five of them. Chapter 6 investigates the types of shipping used by the merchants. Chapter 7 summarises a series of voyages made by Captain Le Lacheur and draws attention to the frequency with which he dealt with Guernseymen in England, Canada, America and Spain. Chapter 8 is a register of the merchants that I have identified and offers, where possible, an indication of their activities.

This book summarises my investigations. It constitutes a beginning, not an end. Having now a better understanding of the *dramatis personae*, I hope to publish a series of monographs and articles exploring certain themes in greater depth. Volumes in active preparation include: *Guernsey shipping 1712-1786*; *Trade, War and Privateering 1776-1783; Guernsey merchants in Spain.* In a work of this nature it is inevitable that there are errors and omissions. I would be grateful to receive communications about such matters.

1
Trade

The Guernsey economy

Guernsey was not well endowed with land or capital and there was a constant threat that agricultural output would fail. Fishing increased the supply of food and left a surplus for export. During the mediaeval period Salerie, just to the north of St Peter Port, was developed as an éperquerie for the drying and curing of conger. Guernsey conger, mackerel and herring were regularly sold in France. Fishing was further developed in the sixteenth century when the merchants of St Peter Port participated in a triangular trade. They sent vessels to fish off Newfoundland; the catches of cod were shipped to Portugal, Spain and France; and the Guernsey vessels returned home with cargoes such as wool and iron. The Newfoundland fish paid for the imports. The balance of trade of the island further improved when the St Peter Port merchants developed a stocking export industry.

Had its fortune been dictated solely by the factors of production, the economic history of Guernsey might well have been limited to small-scale trading exchanges. However, the island profited from a favourable geographical location and from political decisions made by foreign powers. Guernsey, situated close to the coast of France, was well placed to engage in Anglo-French trade. Such opportunities were enhanced when a papal bull of 1481 confirmed an Anglo-French agreement that Guernsey would be regarded as neutral in any future conflict. This was advantageous to the islanders and to English and French merchants. The Queen of Hungary (as regent of the Netherlands) complained in 1544 that the English made use of the neutrality of Guernsey for bartering freely with the French as often as they liked without hindrance or restriction of any sort. In 1544 the import of French goods into England was prohibited; but, as the interdiction did not apply to the Channel Islands, French wine could be shipped to Guernsey and re-exported to England.[1]

The development of St Peter Port as an entrepôt

The trade of Guernsey with foreign ports was seriously disrupted by the English Civil War. From c.1660, however, the merchants of St Peter Port were able to benefit from a number of factors which, in combination, led to the rapid growth of St Peter Port as a major international entrepôt. These factors were: the development of the Atlantic economy; the location of Guernsey; the trading privileges enjoyed by the islanders; and the high tariffs associated with mercantilism.

In the late seventeenth and eighteenth centuries British and French trade increased considerably, thanks in part to a growing demand for American and Asian colonial products. This was accompanied by a demand in Europe for British re-exports of colonial produce. Britain also found an expanding market in her American colonies for British manufactures and re-exports of Asian and European goods. In this developing Atlantic economy major British ports, led by Bristol and Liverpool, as well as port cities of northern and western France, found opportunities for trading on a greatly increased scale. St Peter Port was excellently situated in relation to the principal shipping lanes of this Atlantic economy. First, the town was well located on the north-south axis to serve as an entrepôt in Anglo-French trade. Secondly, being at the western end of the Channel, St Peter Port was ideally positioned to engage in the Atlantic trade. In contrast to London the western outports were one or two weeks 'closer' to the West Indies and during wartime these outports benefited even more.[2]

Traditionally Guernsey had enjoyed considerable privileges in its trade with England. Relying on ancient practice the islanders saw themselves as free and discharged from all customs, tolls and subsidies, 'as well in the Island, as elsewhere, in Her Majesty's Dominions'.[3] Apart from 'some trifle for keeping their piers and harbours in repair' goods could enter Guernsey as into a free-port.[4] This was of considerable significance during the age of mercantilism, when national economies were protected by high tariff barriers.

The Guernsey merchants were well placed to ignore the provisions of the Navigation Acts. Under this legislation the Channel Islanders' shipping was regarded as English built, but no exception was made in regard to their commerce. Although the islanders could trade directly with any of the ports of Spain and Portugal or with those of the Azores, Madeira or the Canaries, they were not supposed to deal directly with the English colonies, or to bring colonial raw materials into English ports.[5] In practice the St Peter Port merchants ignored the Navigation Acts and invoked customary privileges. The customs authorities at the English ports were often confused. In 1744 the Treasury cleared up some of the misunderstandings by ruling that 'no one should bring from the Channel Islands into any port of the kingdom products from the English colonies, because not first taken on at the place of their origin'.[6] The implementation of this ruling led to an increase in the amount of colonial produce smuggled from Guernsey to England.

Throughout the eighteenth century the English authorities found it practically impossible to enforce the Navigation Acts in Guernsey. The regulations relating to the nationality of carrying vessels were regularly ignored. In 1777 (during the American War of Independence) John Guille of St Peter Port commented: 'We have had part of our brandy in French bottoms from Spain to avoid the high insurance & the Americans; tho' it is against the Act of Navigation no one has taken any notice of it. The bills [of] lading were made for Dunkirk.'[7]

The importance of St Malo to the Guernsey merchants

The rise of St Peter Port in the second half of the seventeenth century was linked to the flourishing commerce of the nearby French port of St Malo. Writing from Guernsey in 1667 Colonel J. Atkins commented: 'It is a rare thing now to hear from England, and 'tis as hard a matter to send thither, for St Malos is the place they all send to'.[8] This observation is confirmed by a 1678 listing of sailings from St Peter Port.[9] Of the 149 sailings recorded [28 August 1678 – 11 December 1678] 95 were to France and of these nearly a quarter were specifically identified as being to St Malo (no other named port, French or English, had a higher ranking).

St Malo was enjoying its golden age. To the south the Malouins made fortunes in Cadiz, trafficking in silver. There was also an extensive trade between St Malo and England. Textiles, lace, oil, soap, port, hemp, cordage and honey were exported from St Malo to England; in return the Malouins imported draperies, tin, lead, coal, slate, hides, beef, herring, sardine and other fish, and tallow. Most of this Anglo-French trade was conducted by strangers as the Malouins distrusted the English 'qu'ils disent estre infidels'. Analyses of the port movements of St Malo demonstrate that many vessels arrived in ballast in St Malo and left with merchandise, especially for the Channel Islands. The shipping patterns of St Peter Port and St Malo in the second half of the seventeenth century suggest that the Guernsey merchants were established as trusted middlemen in the St Malo – England trade. [10]

Malouins visited St Peter Port where they spent gold and silver on contraband goods, tobacco in particular. Trading links were maintained with the French even during wartime and despite British acts specifically forbidding such trade.[11] In September 1712 Mr John Sherwood reported to the English customs: 'the French merchants are here in great numbers … bring in wine, brandy, linen, cloth, salt and wares of diverse sorts … They carry from us coal, soap, rosin, wool, tobacco, East India goods and what not.'[12]

Trade with the Malouins flourished with the restoration of peace. In 1713 we find that le sieur Thomas le Mesurier of Guernsey made accord with Jean Heilly to command *l'Aigle* of St Malo, a vessel of 220 tons. Thirty-five men were engaged in Guernsey to serve as crew. The projected journey was a triangular voyage to Guinea – Jamaica – Guernsey.[13] It is not clear whether the expedition took place but there is good evidence of a joint venture soon afterwards. In 1716 a Guernsey ship at St Pierre, Newfoundland, had Malouins as its principal officers and crew fishing from its sixteen boats.[14]

The Malouins were active in developing trade with South America from where some cargoes reached St Peter Port. C.1716 a Frenchman from St Malo 'lately arrived from the South-Sea' came to Guernsey 'to traffic', bringing with him 'three small branches of a tree which he said was the tree that bore the Balsam of Peru'.[15] When St Malo declined as a great port in the 1720s, the St Peter Port merchants continued to trade there but they increasingly developed their links with Nantes and other ports involved in international commerce. For their part French merchants were attracted to St Peter Port where they could buy British colonial produce, principally tobacco and East India goods.[16] Between c.1720 and c.1750 the Guernsey merchants developed St Peter Port as an entrepôt. In the next section we shall examine the ways in which they improved the facilities of the port.

The improvement of port facilities

As there were no bonded warehouses in England in the early eighteenth century for the storage of wine, English merchants found it convenient to have cargoes shipped to Guernsey in bulk and then sent across to England in smaller consignments. In this way they avoided having to pay down one large sum in English duty. Thus in 1719 we find Abraham Eyre and his partners in Southampton explaining that they did not have the cash to pay the duty down for the whole cargo of Bordeaux wine shipped to Guernsey and so they let part of the cargo remain in the island until they were 'more in cash'.[17]

Eyre complained that 'by the hotness of the weather and the badness of their cellars which are above ground' his wines in St Peter Port had turned and were hardly fit for distilling. Between 1719 and 1747 new – and, apparently, better – warehouses were built. Several young men of the island sold their small estates 'and turned the money into building of warehouses for wine and brandy'. They regarded those who had it in their power but did not follow this method of trade as 'slothful and stupid'.[18] By c.1747 the merchants and 'the monied men' of the island had built some twenty or thirty 'magazines' (i.e. warehouses) which could be reckoned 'among the most magnificent and spacious in England'.[19] In 1751 Dicey eulogised St Peter Port as having 'the best vaults in Europe'. He claimed 'that all wines (especially Lisbon or white wines) kept at Guernsey but a very few months, do actually imbibe, or receive a peculiar flavour, and are mended in quality, to what the same species of wines have, when immediately imported here from Portugal or any part of Spain'.[20] The new warehouses represented a significant improvement in the entrepôt facilities. The St Peter Port merchants could handle large consignments of wine for English merchants *and* trade extensively on their own behalf.

The status of St Peter Port as an entrepôt was enhanced by harbour improvements. In the late seventeenth century the harbour consisted of a single pier which could shelter 'about 20 or 30 sail of small vessels'.[21] In 1684 the States decided to enclose the harbour by building a north pier. The work was started but there were interruptions and financial difficulties. In 1724/5 the leading merchants of St Peter Port and other inhabitants raised six to seven thousand livres tournois by a voluntary subscription. There were further grants in 1728 and by 1730 the pier was almost complete.[22] Altogether the townsfolk subscribed about twelve thousand livres tournois to the project. It was money well invested. St Peter Port harbour was rendered 'more easy of access'; its shipping was sheltered from storms; and trade considerably increased. Prior to the improvements the farm of the pier had been reckoned at six to seven hundred livres tournois per annum; by the 1750s it was valued at three thousand livres tournois.[23] The pride that Guernsey merchants took in their harbour improvement was soundly based. By the 1750s more – and larger – ships were visiting St Peter Port from European and American ports.[24]

The waters around Guernsey posed navigational hazards, especially to foreigners. This problem was solved in part when in 1746 Nicholas Dobrée (senior), a St Peter Port merchant, published charts of Guernsey and the other Channel Islands based on his own survey. The charts were considered 'very accurately done' and were issued with an accompanying booklet of sailing directions printed in French and English. The maps were republished in 1762, 1779, 1786 and 1794.[25]

OBSERVATIONS

SUR LES

CARTES

Des ISLES de

GUERNESEY, AUREGNY, SERCQ, HERM, & JETHOU;

Levées & dreſſées

Par *NICHOLAS DOBREE*, Ecuyer;

Agent de l'Admiraute;

Et miſes au net d'après les Desseins Originaux par M. *Thomas Carey*.

A LONDRES:

Chez J. Brotherton, a l'Enſeigne de la *Bible*, proche le Caffé de *Thomas* à *Cornhill*.   M,DCC,LXII.

Fig. 1.1: Title page of *Observations on the Charts* - by Nicholas Dobrée, a booklet issued in French and English to accompany Dobrée's charts.

The St Peter Port entrepôt at its zenith

From the mid-eighteenth century, and especially after the suppression of smuggling from the Isle of Man (1765), St Peter Port became one of the principal commercial entrepôts in the Atlantic economy. The merchants enjoyed a good reputation among the French who saw them as 'riches marchands qui font un grand commerce'. They were like the merchants in Jersey, but traded on a greater scale and were 'plus honnêtes'.[26] St Peter Port, with its improved harbour and purpose-built warehouses, had become an entrepôt in the fullest sense of the word. Cargoes, generally of goods that attracted high tariffs in the normal course of international trade, were brought to St Peter Port, which served as a storage centre, distribution point and mart.

The supplies came to St Peter Port directly from colonies; via major ports engaging in *le grand commerce*; and from the sales of East India goods in England, France, Holland, Denmark and Sweden. The Guernsey merchants sometimes acted for overseas clients and handled goods on a commission basis; but much of the cargo landed in St Peter Port had been bought by the St Peter Port merchants and was intended for re-sale either in bulk, wholesale, to another merchant (*négociant*) or in smaller lots to retailers (*marchands*). Some cargoes (e.g. wines) were held in St Peter Port for a considerable length of time before being forwarded; and wine and tobacco were often 'processed' in St Peter Port.

Many cargoes were sold in St Peter Port. Spirits and tobacco were bought by smugglers who sailed across to the town. A wide variety of goods was sold to vessels sailing for Newfoundland: tea, silks, muslins, calicoes, India goods of all kinds, French brandy, molasses, French and Dutch linens and woollens, French nets and lines for fishing, Dutch cordage, utensils, provisions and all sorts of wines.[27] Some English vessels bound for New England and Quebec, after clearing in Great Britain, took on 'great quantities' of goods in St Peter Port contrary to the Navigation Acts.[28] British naval vessels departing on voyages similarly stocked up in St Peter Port.[29] During wartime 'considerable purchases' of British manufactures were frequently made by neutrals who touched at the island.[30]

Some of the entrepôt goods were shipped openly and legally to their next destination. This was generally the case with bulky cargoes such as wine and fruit. Some cargoes were shipped openly to the British Isles but were furnished with false bills of lading. For example, French wine was described as of Spanish origin to evade the high duties on goods of French origin.[31] 'Considerable quantities' of tea, brandy, gin, wine and tobacco were shipped from Guernsey to Alderney. That island, being a little closer to England, was more convenient for English smugglers.[32] Sometimes Guernsey mariners ran contraband cargoes across to the English coast; but it was more commonly the case that the cross-channel smuggling was conducted by the English.

By the second half of the eighteenth century many commodities were handled in the St Peter Port entrepôt. The major items were spirits, wine, tobacco, East India goods, tea and fruit. The volume of cargoes handled by the St Peter Port merchants is discussed in Chapter 2.

Underpinning the development of St Peter Port as an international entrepôt was the establishment of a network of connections at strategic commercial points throughout the world of the Atlantic economy. As the nineteenth century historian Lukis observed: 'Parents, whose sons were intended for commercial pursuits, would send them to Spain, France, Holland and other countries, and there they established themselves as agents for their Guernsey relations'. Guernsey agents abroad were able to understand their local markets, buy on good terms, and organise the shipping of cargoes to Guernsey.[33]

The Guernsey merchants enjoyed good business relations with a number of foreign *négociants*. The excellent links with the merchant houses of St Malo have already been mentioned. Other important contacts included the Swedish, Danish, Dutch and French merchants who acted as agents at the various European sales of East India goods each year. Examples of such agents were Arfwidson & Sons at Gothenburg who bought for their Guernsey clients at the Swedish India sales; Fabritius & Wever of Copenhagen, who attended the Danish India sales; and Chenard, Giraudais & LePage who attended the sales of *La Compagnie Française des Indes* at Lorient.

For much of the eighteenth century there were several merchant bankers of Guernsey origin working in London – Bonamy & Samuel Dobrée, Dobrée & Aubin, Perchard & Brock and Paul Le Mesurier. These merchant bankers handled many financial transactions for their fellow islanders, negotiating bills of exchange, investing money, acting as shipping and insurance agents, securing letters of marque during wartime, and collecting rents from land held in England. The Guernsey connection gave these merchant bankers an unrivalled understanding of the entrepôt trade, privateering and French trade. Paul Le Mesurier set up a commercial house in Normandy in 1785 in partnership with his brother Havilland (based in Guernsey) with a view to developing trade with Tobago.[34] Paul was elected Lord Mayor of London in 1793, the first Guernseyman to achieve this distinction. He was also a Member of Parliament and was active in arguing in defence of the Channel Islands' interests. Another English MP, Mark Gregory, although not an islander by birth, was a friend of the St Peter Port merchant family of Guille and was a part of the Guernsey 'connection' in London. Gregory was a merchant and belonged to the governing body of Lloyds. He had interests in Turkey and Spain and set up a trading house in Barcelona in partnership with Guille. Much of the brandy shipped from Catalonia to Guernsey in the second half of the eighteenth century was handled by the partnership of Gregory & Guille.

Despite the growing importance of British shipping, many imports to St Peter Port continued to be carried in foreign shipping throughout the second half of the eighteenth century. Much of the gin, coffee, tea, silk, handkerchiefs, calicoes and chintz from Holland and Sweden arrived in ships belonging to the Danes, Swedes and Dutch. This is independently confirmed by cases heard in the *Cour d'Amirauté* at St Peter Port and by depositions recorded in the Dobrée protest book. Baltic shipping brought goods from the north on the outward voyage and sometimes carried southern produce to St Peter Port on return voyages from the Mediterranean. The true destination – St Peter Port – was frequently concealed, a policy dictated through a desire to thwart the Navigation Acts; to deceive insurers; or to protect the cargo during wartime. In 1778, for example, the St Peter Port merchant John Guille ordered a cargo of tea from John George Ekman of Gothenburg and gave instructions that the captain and crew were not to know 'they are to unload here'. If the vessel was seized, Ekman was to claim from the insurers, representing the cargo as his property.[35]

The fact that foreign vessels regularly delivered cargoes to St Peter Port had important implications for the Guernsey merchants. They were able to handle a greater volume of commodities than could have been carried by the island's shipping. The merchants employed their own vessels in a variety of profitable trades that served the entrepôt. Guernsey shipping carried wine, brandy, cottons and linens from France; rum from the West Indies; tobacco from Maryland and Virginia; and traded to Newfoundland and Africa. A clear pattern emerges. The Guernsey vessels concentrated on the Channel and transatlantic trades which were sheltered from foreign competition by the Navigation Acts. The northern trade with the Baltic – which demanded shipping with excellent manning ratios because of Dutch competition – was essentially left to foreigners. Guernsey vessels also participated in 'bulk-breaking', a characteristic activity at entrepôts. The cargoes brought in large foreign ships to St Peter Port were re-shipped in the smaller island vessels to London and the English outports.

From the late sixteenth century Guernsey fishermen went to Newfoundland to fish for cod. This developed into a triangular trade, the fish being taken to Newfoundland and sold in Spanish and Portuguese ports; cargoes such as wine were loaded there and transported back to Guernsey. In the late seventeenth century some four to six Guernsey vessels were engaged in the trade. Although several of the St Peter Port merchants maintained interests in Newfoundland during the eighteenth century, the level of activity was relatively low. It is possible that the competition of the West Country and Jersey 'Newfoundlanders' had some influence. Also, other mercantile ventures probably proved more profitable to the Guernsey merchants.

In the mid-eighteenth century some St Peter Port merchants participated in the notorious 'triangular trade', taking slaves from West Africa to the West Indies and returning to Europe with Caribbean cargoes. It is difficult to assess the extent to which the Guernsey merchants were involved in the trade. Nineteenth-century Guernsey historians denied that the islanders had ever participated in slaving voyages. However, a number of cases heard in the *Cour d'Amirauté* in St Peter Port provide evidence of several such voyages. Most expeditions of Guernsey ships to the West Indies in the second half of the eighteenth century appear to have been direct, the raison d'être of the voyages being the return cargo of rum from Barbados, Jamaica or Santa Cruz. On the West Indies run the Guernsey merchants used their own vessels which tended to be lightly manned. The Guernsey merchants also traded at Madeira, bringing brandy and taking away Madeira wine (which they often sold in the Americas).

French Revolutionary War

The outbreak of war between Britain and France in 1793 disrupted the normal patterns of trade. American vessels carried cargoes between belligerent countries; Hamburg became an important entrepôt; and vast quantities of wines and spirits were deposited in Guernsey. Writing to James Yates in 1796 the Guernsey merchant Guille advised that a cargo of cheese at Brest could only be shipped by 'applying to a house in Hamburgh, or other neutral place, to purchase it in their name and order the shipping of it for a neutral port, with a secret agreement to deliver it here, if there is a sufficient parcel to freight a vessel, as I am not clear that it can be imported direct to England. We have no kind of intercourse with Brest – from Bordeaux we have nearly weekly arrivals with brandy for your market and it is easy to get goods from thence by the Americans thro' the medium of Hambro'.[36]

This picture is confirmed by the historian Tupper:

> Moreover, the disturbed state of France, during the revolution, naturally induced the exportation of goods from that country to a place of security; and wines, brandies, &c., were brought over to Guernsey in such quantities, that the vaults and warehouses, numerous and capacious as they are, were totally inadequate to their lodgment, so that some cargoes were stored in fields, under temporary coverings. A single merchant received, for account of one firm in London, 2,491 hogsheads and 17 cases of Claret and Hermitage, by American vessels from Bordeaux, in 1795. About the same time the pier of St Peter-Port was frequently crammed to the very mouth, and there were some twenty or thirty vessels in the roadstead waiting to enter. (Tupper, 1854, p. 439).

British Intervention

The large volume of spirits, wine and tobacco passing through St Peter Port inevitably attracted the attention of the British authorities. They were alarmed at the losses sustained by the government and wished to curb the trade of the Guernsey merchants with English, Welsh and Irish smugglers. In the summer of 1800 the Privy Council and the Lords Commissioners of the Treasury sent an official, Stiles, to the Channel Islands to meet the Bailiff and Jurats of the Royal Court. Their Lordships in England were conscious that the islanders had been 'eminently loyal' and were reluctant to upset them during wartime. It was Stiles' duty to explain fully and clearly all the points detailed in the papers that he took across; and he was to listen to any observations made in consequence of such communications. Stiles was an experienced official. He had been sent to Guernsey thirty years earlier 'on a special service, by order of the Commissioners of the Customs' and had submitted a report on 3 Nov 1770. It was no youthful clerk who sailed across from Weymouth on board the revenue cutter *Hind* (Captain Bray). Stiles walked into a tense situation when he arrived in Guernsey on 23 August:

> The Merchants concerned in the supply of goods to the smugglers having been apprized of my coming, and at the same time acquainted (though without foundation) that Government designed to put an immediate stop to the fraudulent trade of the island, they instantly proceeded to discharge several hundred coopers, who, as well as their families, were before constantly employed and maintained in making kegs for the reception and smuggling of spirits into this kingdom.
>
> This measure, depriving so many individuals of their bread, created an alarm and apprehension not to be described, and was the cause of much ill humour and discontent amongst the lower orders of people; five or six hundred of whom assembled on the pier to await my arrival; what were their views I knew not, as they offered no kind of insult or outrage when I landed, though many of them followed me to, and remained together some time at, the door of my lodgings, which were at the house of the Serjeant to the Royal Court; but he soon afterwards informed me, the mob threatened to attack the house and break his windows, as a punishment for having received me. This report I considered however as unworthy of attention, especially as the Serjeant stated, that he could of his own authority immediately call out the guard in case of a riot, and the mob having had notice, that they would be fired on, if they presumed to commit any depredations, they thought fit to retire. Prior to my landing, but after my arrival in the Road, the same impression and alarm occasioned no less than ten smuggling cutters and luggers to get under way, and leave the island in my presence, in great hurry and confusion, altho' the weather was bad, and the winds not fair for that part of the coast of England to which several of them were known to be bound, and even before some of them had completed their cargoes. (TNA T64/153).

Stiles duly visited the Lieutenant-Governor and the Bailiff, who, in turn, relayed messages to the jurats and merchants. Stiles received no further insults from the lower orders of people and was treated with respect:

> Indeed all the merchants and principal inhabitants, with whom I occasionally conversed, repeatedly expressed their grateful acknowledgments to government for its moderation and favourable disposition towards the island.

Stiles sent to the bailiff the outlines of the principal regulations proposed. These were to be submitted to the Guernsey Court. Stiles took the opportunity to visit Jersey, sailing on the 13 September and returning to Guernsey on the 27th. Letters were exchanged and on 1 October the States of Guernsey assembled. Eventually Stiles learnt:

> They hope that Government will have the goodness to indulge them in some compensation in trade; by leaving to the islands a full right of remaining ports of deposit or entrepost, and receive favourably such suggestions as they may hereafter offer.

Some of the merchants mentioned that it would be highly beneficial to the island if the British government permitted ships to go from Guernsey 'direct to the British West India Islands, and to return in like manner with the produce of those islands to Guernsey'. Stiles rejected the suggestion immediately:

> The mischief that would arise to this country from such an indulgence is so obvious that I conceived it was my duty to tell them, that it was impossible the idea could be entertained for a moment.

The merchants had a further proposition 'That the articles of tobacco and snuff may not be prohibited to be exported from the island'. This concession was 'repeatedly urged and solicited in the most earnest and impressive manner' and was supported by the following arguments:

That in peacetime, the importation of these articles caused a great accession of wealth to the island, without the smallest prejudice to Great Britain. That in the course of sixteen months previous to hostilities no less than 2343 chasse-marees came from, and carried to Britanny and Normandy, tobacco and snuff to the amount of £105,000 sterling, all which was received in specie. That above one thousand of the poorest men, women and children were employed in manufacturing the articles in question, and that it was remarkable that during that time the hospitals (or poor houses) had in them only cripples and old people. That this intercourse with the French was productive of a still more general good, as they brought with them large quantities of provisions of all kinds.

That as the vessels employed to bring tobacco from America belonged to the merchants of the island, it also afforded a nursery for seamen.

That very little tobacco and snuff were purchased by the English smugglers, and that if the measure proposed against the exportation in general, should be enforc'd, it would prove detrimental and ruinous to the inhabitants, and deprive them of a trade perfectly harmless in itself to England.

Stiles was unable to verify the figures for the sailings as 'the officers of the customs stationed at Guernsey have not kept any account of the vessels which arrived at, or sailed from thence' but was inclined to believe that the trade was highly beneficial. However, Stiles was disturbed by some wartime developments:

Ships belonging to the island in time of peace might have been employed as the merchants assert in importing tobacco from America, but since the war it is evident that a number of American, Swedish, Danish, and other neutral ships has been so employed contrary to law. Two or three of such foreign vessels arrived whilst I was there, but were prevented from landing their cargoes by order of the Commisioners of the Customs. And it appears that two foreign ships were lately seized by the Collector of Liverpool for having been so employed, the prosecution of which is now pending.

Stiles included calculations in his report:

Table 1.1 An account of the total quantities of the following articles seized in the Out Ports between the 5th of January 1798 and the 5th of January 1799; with an account of the Customs and Excise to which the same would have been liable viz:

	Gallons actual	Gallons estimated	Loss actual	Loss estimated
Brandy	56,624	56,6240	£23,805 -1-3-6	£238,050
Rum	10,987	109,870	£3,685-4-4	£36,850
Geneva	210,740	2,107,400	£88,598 -12-2	£885,980
Wine	2,026	20,260	£574-16-7	£5,740
Compounds	1,053	10,530	£563-7-1	£5,630
	Pounds			
Coffee	6481	64,810	£462-9-5	£4,620
Tea	698	6,980	Ad valorem	
Snuff	114	1,140	£16-3-0	£163
Tobacco	81,870	818,700	£6,645-2-4	£66,450
			£124,351-8-5	

The Guernsey merchants gave Stiles an account of their trade:

> The foreign trade carried on by the inhabitants is in the importation of wines, brandy, and fruits from France, Spain, Portugal, Madeira, and Italy; rum from the West Indies; tobacco and grain from America; and fish from Newfoundland. The exportation is in such brandies and wines to America, Quebec, and the West Indies; large quantities of these liquors are intended to be exported to Great Britain and Ireland; the tobacco is destined for Hamburg, Embden, and the Baltic, exclusive of what is sold to smugglers. We subjoin the exact particulars of such trade. Many brandies are exported to Madeira and America. At the first place they are bartered for wines, which are carried to the West India Islands, and again bartered for rum and other produce, which is sometimes carried to Quebec in exchange for provisions to be carried to Newfoundland, and there bartered for fish, which is shipped to Portugal and the Mediterranean, whither we also export cargoes of pilchards from Cornwall, for account of the inhabitants who have large concerns in that fishery; the brandies carried to America are bartered for corn, rice, and staves, and brought hither. Several assorted cargoes, and especially prize wines, are annually exported direct to the West India Islands, where they have entry, and some to those islands which only admit those goods from England, where they are accordingly first landed, and also to Quebec, and there they are bartered for wheat and flour, which are imported into this island, or for provisions which are carried to Newfoundland, and there bartered for fish for the above named markets, or these islands.

> But a great part of our trade consists in the deposit of goods brought hither, to be regularly re-imported into Great Britain and Ireland, from France, Spain, and Portugal: this occupies our warehouses, built at great expense, and gives bread to coopers and labourers, and freight to many of our own and British vessels in the legal transportation of such goods to all parts of the United Kingdom; and the freights paid here for the goods are a considerable source of circulation and benefit to the island, as it is calculated that above one quarter part of the amount of such freight is paid in the island in wages to the crews, and in provisions, repairs, and necessaries for the vessels, and otherwise laid out here in the purchase of different articles, most of which are of British manufacture. We also beg leave to observe, that many of the tobaccos brought hither are purchased by such masters of neutral ships, as adventures, when bound to their own country, besides what is brought here by the crews. And, in the year before the war, the quantity of manufactured tobacco brought hither by the French amounted to above £150,000, which they smuggled back into Normandy and Brittany. In this manufacture, many indigent boys and girls are employed.

> The whole of this deposit trade facilitates the operations of the fair trader in the United Kingdom, as the merchants order their goods by parcels as they want them, and for such ports as may be most advantageous. But Hamburg has, during the whole year, carried away about one half of the deposit trade of brandies designed to be re-imported into Great Britain, and which might be limited to this island instead of throwing the profit to foreigners, and indeed to the advantage of the mother country, as it would keep considerable sums at home, favour the rate of exchange with the continent, and not leave British property exposed to the chance of events, and to sequestration and confiscation in foreign ports. The quantity of goods, however, exported from this island must, in a great measure, be known to you, and it must be very considerable, as the three undersigned [*Robert Porret Le Marchant, Daniel De Lisle Brock, William Le Marchant*] have alone shipped, since the 1ˢᵗ of October 3,325 pipes, and 983 hogsheads of brandy and wine, and the war has generally increased the several branches of trade. (Tupper, 1854, pp. 387-8).

The Napoleonic Wars

After a brief peace (1802-3) war resumed. Napoleon and the British pursued aggressive economic strategies and the authorities in London decided that they could no longer afford to forego the excise and customs dues evaded by English smugglers. Acts of parliament were introduced in 1805 and 1807 to suppress smuggling. The function of St Peter Port as an entrepôt was greatly reduced and there was considerable unemployment. The merchants looked for new markets and turned towards Brazil and St Domingo where most of the cheap articles of India goods found a ready sale. The merchants developed new voyage patterns. As in the past they carried cod from Newfoundland to Spain; but then they loaded wine and brandy, not for Guernsey but for South America; they returned from Rio de Janeiro with sugar, coffee and hides for northern Europe. There were also opportunities for trading commodities essential to the enemy. The historian F.B. Tupper provides a useful description:

> …the Peninsula was soon after driven into a war against France, and its ports, as well as those of its immense colonial possessions, were opened to British enterprize, and our merchants were not slow in availing themselves of the advantage. Many of their vessels were most profitably employed, from 1808 to 1815, in carrying codfish from Newfoundland to Spain, where, owing to the destruction and waste of the armies, it rose from fifteen shillings, its usual peace price, to sixty shillings nett per cwt. From Spain, these vessels usually took a cargo of wine, brandy, &c., to Rio de Janeiro, or the River Plate, returning home with sugar, coffee, and hides; and so lucrative was this traffic occasionally, that, as we learn on good authority, upwards of nine thousand pounds were cleared by a brig of about one hundred and fifty tons burthen, in one of the circuitous voyages we have described. We must add, however, that she ran without insurance and without convoy, an immense saving, when it is considered that the risk from American privateers was so great as to raise premiums to 15 and 20 per cent. for a voyage across the Atlantic, without convoy. The Guernsey vessels, sailing well, usually ran without convoy, and very few were captured, but when insured, the high premiums were a great drawback to their profits, as few of the voyages in those days were unprofitable.

> The island was also greatly benefited during the last three or four years of the war, by what was termed the license trade, Napoleon then relaxing his anti-commercial decrees, and permitting various goods to be exported from, and imported into, France, in vessels under a neutral flag. His chief motive was to obtain Peruvian bark and other drugs, of which his armies were in great need, and although the British government refused at first to allow of their exportation, yet they willingly sanctioned the traffic in many other goods; and at last removed their prohibition as to drugs. Guernsey was the principal mart of this licensed interchange of commodities between two nations, which had been for nearly twenty years waging war against each other, "*almost to the knife,*" and although the traffic was carried on amid many restrictions, risks, and difficulties, constantly varying as the caprice, or jealousies, or wants of either power prompted, yet it was very lucrative, and it was of essential service in introducing corn into the island, which at the time was much wanted, the northern ports being closed against us. (Tupper 1837, pp. 309-310).

Peace

With the coming of peace in 1815 the Guernsey merchants were well positioned to consolidate and develop their trade. They established themselves in South America, in Rio de Janeiro, Bahia and Montevideo. Guernsey houses in the Mediterranean – at Barcelona, Tarragona, Valencia, Alicante and Trieste – despatched goods to South America and received return cargoes. Although some of the voyages originated from, or ended in, St Peter Port, many of the voyage 'legs' were between foreign ports. Catalonia and Rio de Janeiro became the commercial centres for the Guernsey merchants who were now operating a carrying trade rather than running a home-based entrepôt business.

Captain Thomas Guilbert reminisced:

> The harbour at that time was full of ships of different sizes; there were letters-of-marque (privateers) and prizes lying idle. After a while trade revived and vessels were fitted out for the foreign trade. Partnerships were formed; these (*sic*) were also several individual ventures; the owners were also merchants, buying their own cargoes. Guernsey vessels generally left in ballast and proceeded, some to Oporto, Cette, Terragone, or Messina, to load wine for the Brazils or River Plate, some to Cadiz, Cagliari, or to the Cape de Verde Islands to load salt; others went to Newfoundland to load codfish dried for the Brazil market. Cargoes sold well in those days; when discharged they took in coffee or sugar for Europe, calling at Guernsey for orders. The principal markets were Hamburg, Bremen, Antwerp; also Copenhagen and the Baltic. When sent to the Mediterranean, Gibraltar was the port of call; but nine times out of ten the orders were: Trieste. It was a free port and less expensive. Return cargo thence was sometimes flour or steel bars and olive oil; or [*ships might*] leave that port in ballast for Sicily or Sardinia and load a cargo of salt. Some vessels loaded jerked beef (dried beef, without salt or bones) for Havannah. This was to feed the slaves, and sometimes it took three months before the cargo was out, on account of having to retail from the ship; when ready, the ship loaded a cargo of coffee or sugar, sometimes both, and proceeded for Trieste.
>
> In those days the Quarantine laws were strict, especially in the Mediterranean ports. Coffee in bags was loaded by the crew on the Quarantine wharf, then carried on a long track; 14 bags weighing one ton. Poor Jack Tar had to drag the load! Then every bag had to be emptied by the sailors in separate heaps, in rows with a passage between; the men from shore had a pair of tongs to stir about the coffee and take out anything they saw that might, by any possibility, carry contagion, such as a piece of rag, thread or twine, & c., and that was laid aside to be taken on board with the bags. Then the coffee was put into new bags by shore labourers and carted to the merchant's warehouse. Sugar in boxes from Havannah was bound with stripes (*sic*) of hide, as a substitute for iron hoops, and we sailors had to strip the boxes before landing them on the Quarantine ground; with great trouble and patience we had to burn the hide, and it was a tiresome job! (The Star 2 Feb 1901 'Recollections of an old sailor Captain Guilbert, aged 92').

By the 1820s the Rio trade was in full swing. In the eighteen months from January 1825 to June 1826 there were forty-three arrivals in Rio of twenty-six Guernsey vessels. A detailed account of these arrivals was published in 1827 (see pp. 88-90). For a while the trade flourished. In 1835 Inglis commented:

> The commerce of Guernsey consists chiefly of the carrying trade. Vessels are fitted out for a port in Spain, or the Mediterranean, there to take in cargoes of wines, with which they proceed to South America. The cargoes being disposed of, the vessels are then re-loaded with sugar, coffee, &c. With these new cargoes, the vessels probably return to Guernsey for orders, for it seldom happens now, that their goods are stored in Guernsey. They are then perhaps despatched to the north, - as to Antwerp, Rotterdam, or Hamburg; or possibly to the Mediterranean again. If to the former ports, they bring back corn, which terminates the voyage; or if to the Mediterranean, the cargoes are discharged; and another trip with wines then commences to South America.
>
> It is evident, that this is a somewhat precarious trade,- the merchant who chiefly navigates his own vessels, being dependent for his profits on the turn of the different foreign markets;

for he has neither an inland market at home, to depend upon; nor, like the Jersey ship owners and merchants, establishments in British colonies, affording a ready market for all the commodities applicable to civilized life. (Inglis, 1835, p. 229).

Tupper analysed some of the reasons for the precarious nature of Guernsey's trade:

The carrying of codfish terminated with the peace of 1815, and from about 1834, when there were serious losses by the sudden fall of colonials, many of the Guernsey vessels were employed on freight, for which however they were ill adapted, as being of little burthen from their size and sharpness: indeed, they were always much too small for profit. Up to 1835, the island vessels were constantly engaged in carrying wine, brandy, &c., from the Mediterranean to the Brazils and the River Plate; but this trade gradually declined, and has now entirely ceased. The race of speculative merchants, such as carried on business in Guernsey during, and several years after, the war may be said to have become extinct about the year 1845, a large commercial establishment at Rio de Janeiro, the partners in which held two-ninths of the shipping engaged in the foreign trade in 1836, having been abandoned in 1842. Fortunately, several small capitalists in Guernsey, about 1835, turned their attention to freights in the supply of London with fruits from the Azores, Spain, Lisbon, &c., and built many fast schooners in the island for that purpose. (Tupper, 1854, p. 444).

2
Cargoes

CARGOES

The principal cargoes associated with Guernsey's entrepôt trade were spirits, wine, India goods, tea and tobacco. These will shortly be studied in more detail. First, however, it needs to be recorded that the Guernsey merchants handled many varieties of commodities. The best evidence for this comes in an *ordonnance* of the States of Guernsey promulgated in June 1765. This imposed small port dues on entrepôt goods which were then enumerated.

Table 2.1 Entrepôt goods

beer, cider, perry, brandy, gin, sugar, coffee, cassia, rice, tobacco, indigo, cocoa, gunpowder, bullets, liquorice, nails, beef, porkfat grease, tallow, candles, soap, lard, pepper, figs, grapes, currants, plums and other dry fruit, juniper, anise, linen, small nuts, chestnuts, almonds, oranges, lemons, iron, steel, copper, lead, hemp, cordage, tanned or green leather, silk muslin, oils, rosin, pitch, tar, wax, turpentine, dry/salt fish, gums, sumac dye, wood, cork, sheets, wool, cambric, muslin, canvas, handkerchiefs, stuffs, silks, cotton, yarns, twine, paper, ironmongery, shoes, boots, furs, feathers, hops, butter, honey, pottery & china.

Source: Ordonnances, 1852, pp. 399-400 (translated from the French and summarised)

Partial confirmation of this list is to be found in lists of commodities (and countries of origin) compiled by the English customs authorities who investigated the Guernsey entrepôt in the mid 1760s (see map below).

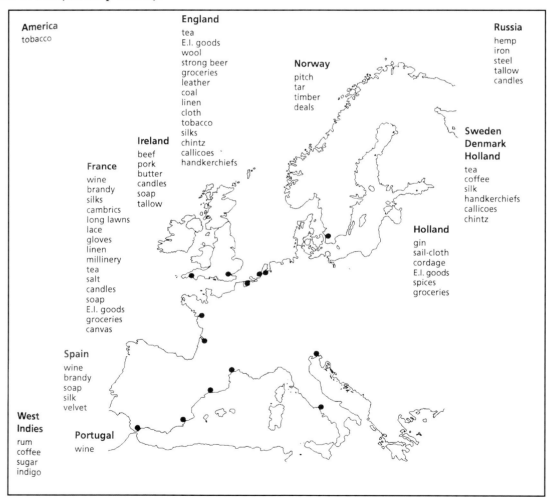

Fig. 2.1: Commodities sent to the entrepôt (and the location of Guernsey agents in Europe).
(Source for commodities: BL Add Ms 38463)

Tobacco

Tobacco was an important commodity to the St Peter Port entrepôt from the late seventeenth century onwards. Some was smuggled back into England but the main customers were the French. The establishment of the tobacco monopoly in 1674 in France made smuggling an attractive proposition. Professor Jacob Price has remarked that from the Channel Islands 'every variety of tobacco, even that of St Domingue, could be smuggled into France.'[1] Price's calculations suggest that perhaps 25,000lb of tobacco were required per annum for the needs of the islanders of Guernsey and for legitimate sales to visiting ships. The quantity of tobacco exported from England to Guernsey frequently ran far above this level and, by inference, was sold mainly to French smugglers. During the War of the Spanish Succession the annual average export from England to Guernsey was approximately 75,000lbs.[2] The volume rose considerably in the decade 1713-22 to an average of 357,768lbs. Tobacco continued to be exported from England to Guernsey in quantities larger than necessary for island consumption. On the eve of the American Revolution (from 1769-76) the annual average re-export from England to Guernsey was 291,438lbs. The quantity shipped from England fell after the American War of Independence. However, in the *post bellum* era Guernsey merchants imported not only from England but also intermittently from Scotland and directly from the U.S.A.[3]

After the defection of the American colonies the relevance of the Navigation Acts to trade between America and Guernsey was not clear. The island merchants profited from this uncertainty and imported much greater quantities directly from America. A total of 5,198 hogshead were brought into the island in 1789 and 3,144 hogshead in 1790. The bailiff calculated in 1791 that the island was handling five thousand hogsheads of tobacco annually, and that this earned above one hundred thousand pounds sterling 'on a moderate computation.' The French came in small craft to buy the tobacco, taking 15 to 30 hogsheads per vessel.[4] *Circa* 1802 it was estimated that the amount of tobacco imported into Guernsey was five thousand hogsheads (the hogshead measuring 1,200lbs); this gives a total of six million lbs of tobacco. During the four winter months of 1806-07 it was assessed that 350,300lbs of tobacco had been shipped out of Guernsey (see table 2.6).

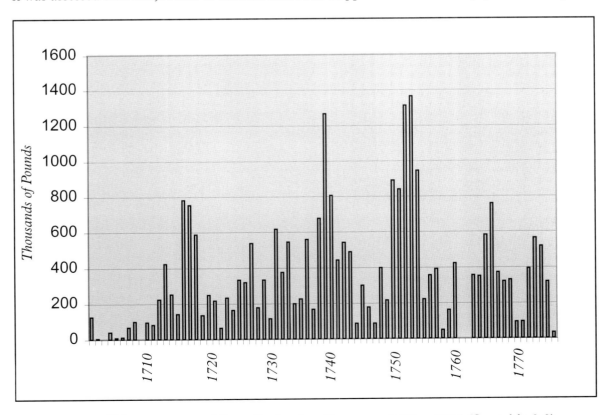

Fig. 2.2: Tobacco exported from England to Guernsey, 1701 – 1776 (See table 2.2).

Table 2.2 Tobacco exported from England to Guernsey, lbs weight, 1701 – 1776.

1701	124,930	1727	534,921	1753	1,361,386
1702	4,172	1728	174,565	1754	942,434
1703	--------	1729	330,506	1755	219,891
1704	37,846	1730	113,359	1756	354,465
1705	7,338	1731	614,844	1757	388,028
1706	11,009	1732	372,938	1758	47,323
1707	64,671	1733	542,459	1759	159,243
1708	96,686	1734	196,104	1760	421,002
1709	--------	1735	222,524	1761	--------
1710	94,179	1736	556,412	1762	--------
1711	78,663	1737	164,803	1763	353,231
1712	221,915	1738	674,081	1764	348,716
1713	419,877	1739	1,262,308	1765	579,632
1714	249,003	1740	803,842	1766	755,353
1715	140,233	1741	439,753	1767	369,798
1716	778,351	1742	539,605	1768	317,220
1717	750,300	1743	486,673	1769	326,577
1718	585,414	1744	84,063	1770	91,347
1719	133,622	1745	297,209	1771	94,854
1720	245,231	1746	174,761	1772	391,537
1721	214,962	1747	84,980	1773	562,944
1722	60,689	1748	396,826	1774	515,894
1723	229,332	1749	214,072	1775	316,119
1724	159,975	1750	886,734	1776	32,233
1725	330,999	1751	837,197		
1726	316,661	1752	1,308,956		

Sources: TNA Cust 3; Price, 1954.

East India Goods

East India goods were traded by the St Peter Port merchants in some quantity after the Treaty of Utrecht. In the years 1713-16 forty-five different types of East India fabrics were exported from England to Guernsey, the principal varieties being chintz, chelloes, cuttanees, romals, soosays and 'Stuffs Guiney' (See table 2.5). In the 1720s and 1730s tea consumption in Europe increased following the development of direct trade between Europe and China. In 1732 Henry Mauger reported that several merchants had imported into Guernsey large quanitites of tea from France; a quantity weighing 150lbs had been found hidden in a barn.[5] In 1734 Mauger complained that the St Peter Port merchants daily imported all sorts of India goods both from Holland and France: 'within these few days several of them are gone to Nants to be at a sale, so that in all likelihood many cargoes of Tea & other foreign commoditys will soon be imported here to the great detriment of the trade of Great Britain.'[6]

Tea and East India goods were frequently despatched from London to Guernsey *via* Southampton. [7] A 'very great quantity' of the tea (and some coffee) exported to the Channel Islands was run back to England. The year 1744 saw an exceptionally large volume of tea exported officially from England to Guernsey (90,724lbs from London, 73,482lbs from the outports). [8]

Customs reports in 1764 refer to East India goods 'of all sorts' imported into Guernsey from England, France and Holland. The merchants in Guernsey 'have India goods from Port L'Orient and Holland and have agents that attend the sales at these places.' [9] In the 1770s and 1780s teas were bought from England, France, Denmark, Sweden and Holland.

On 10th August 1780, Peter Lihou organised a joint order to Gothenburg for teas:

Table 2.3 Tea from Gothenburg

MERCHANTS	ORDER	DRAWING ON / LONDON
Elisha Tupper	30-50 chests Bohea tea Small quantity of Hyson, Tonkey, Suchong	Bonamy Dobrée
Jersey & De Lisle	20-30 chests Bohea. Small quantity of Congo, Tonkey, Hyson	Abraham Le Mesurier
Thomas Priaulx	20-30 chests Bohea.	Abraham Le Mesurier
Peter Lihou	21-32 chests Bohea, some Souatchon, Tonkey, Songlou, Hyson	William de Jersey
John Brock } John Le Marchant }	20 chests Bohea	William de Jersey

Source: Priaulx, Lihou Letterbook

The ratios correspond with the general trend of English tea imports - black tea accounted for 80% of English imports. Bohea was the most common type of black tea and was very popular in Europe. What do the volume and value of this order represent? The *Griffin*, an H.E.I.C. ship of about 600 tons, carried a cargo of 3,967 chests (Goddio, 2002). A chest held approximately 60 lb. The Guernsey merchants were ordering 110 + chests of Bohea, plus small quantities of other varieties. If we value the ordinary tea at 5 shillings per lb wholesale, the order was worth perhaps approximately two thousand pounds when the small quantities of choicer teas were included.

Table 2.4 Types of tea

Black	*Green*
Bohea: the most common type	Gunpowder: a Hyson of superior quality
Congou: a common type	Hyson: rare and expensive
Souchong: finest and strongest black	Songlo: common variety
	Twankay/Tonkey: common variety

Table 2.5 Quantities of prohibited East India goods re-exported from England to Guernsey since the peace of Utrecht to Christmas 1716

	1713	1714	1715	1716
Allibanes	-	65	-	-
Anjengos	-	-	30	-
Bafts	-	20	30	-
Chelloes	3	212	-	30
Cheradarees	-	20	-	31
Cherconees	7	57	55	90
Chints	179	1443	435	678
Chuckleas	17	10	-	-
Cloths long blew	-	-	20	-
Culjees	27	-	-	-
Cuttanees	21	72	24	19
Damasks	49	7	-	10
Elatches	-	-	-	51
Gorgoroons	15	4	-	6
Goshees	-	5	6	-
Hankerchiefs	26	-	-	-
Hannos	-	3	-	-
Hawkins	6	-	-	-
Humhums	-	-	110	-
Longeeshera	-	70	-	-
Mackbanees	20	-	-	-
Neganepants	-	-	10	-
Night gowns	-	2	-	-
Nilleas	-	13	-	-
Pallampores	3	39	10	-
Paunches	8	93	-	2
Pelongs	46	-	10	-
Peniasoes	-	38	-	-
Petticoats	4	-	-	-
Persians	-	-	-	2
Photays	12	67	35	-
Quilts	32	65	-	-
Romals	25	575	388	343
Salampores	-	60	-	-
Satins	3	-	-	1
Seersuckers	-	-	-	25
Shalbafts	17	16	-	-
Shawls	-	-	-	1
Silk brocaded	11	3	-	1
Soosays	11	166	33	144
Stuff guiney	-	120	1260	24
Taffaties	104	60	4	5
Tapsiels	-	12	-	-
Tepoys	22	10	-	-

Source: TNA CO 390/8 ff 238-240. (See H. Yule and A.C. Burnell, *Hobson-Jobson* (London, 1985 reprint, for definition of most of the terms).

Table 2.6 British government estimates of spirits and tobacco traded
by the Guernsey-Alderney merchants

(a) Summary of BL Add Ms 38759 f 105v - 106r; estimate c. 1802 - 3

Spirits

60 vessels supposed to be employed in bringing Geneva into the island from Holland (under licence), calculated @ 150 tuns spirit in each:	2,268,000
Brandy 28,000 pipes brought into the island @ 120 gallons each	3,360,000
Rum 500 puncheons, 100 gallons each	500,000
	6,128,000
The quantity is increased at least 1/6 part by water mixed with spirits in the island	1,022,000
	7,150,000
	1,000,000
The quantity of spirits consumed in the island, what is shipped for other countries, what is lost, cannot exceed.	6,150,000

Tobacco £475,000

5,000 hogsheads of tobacco annually brought into the island - duty on
1,200lbs per hogshead @ 1/7 per lb

(An alternative calculation of the spirits smuggled)   6,750,0009
150 vessels at least employed in smuggling, on average 15 trips annually,
bringing 500 tubs; tubs contain 4-9 gallons, computation made on 6 galllons.

(b) Summary of An account, presented to the House of Commons, of the number and names of vessels cleared out from Port of Guernsey, in the months of November and December 1806, and January and February 1807: with the amount of the excise and custom duties thereon (London, 1807), p. 10 in Parliamentary Papers, House of Commons, Accounts and Papers, session 27 June - 14 August 1807, iv, <57>, pp 85 -95.

Spirits and tobacco exported from Guernsey, Nov. 1806 - Feb. 1807

[Lost duties]	Customs	Excise
400,560 gallons brandy	£29,471-15-2	£302,923-10-0
49,570 gallons rum	£2,244-8-4	£25,714-8-9
109,395 gallons gencva	£7,429-14-10	£82,729-19-4$^{1}/_{2}$
350,300lbs tobacco	£11,165-16-3	£27,732-1-8

(Pipe of brandy - 120 gallons; pipe of rum - 115 gallons; pipe of geneva - 120 galllons; cask of tobacco - 1000lbs)

Spirits

The late seventeenth and early eighteenth centuries witnessed a rapid acceleration in the production of distilled drinks in the western world. This was partly production-led, thanks to the improvement of distilling techniques and the increasing availability of raw materials, and partly consumer-led, as urban society acquired a taste for new tipples. Guernsey merchants in France took an active part in developing the Cognac brandy trade. Professor Cullen observes that in the second decade of the eighteenth century these Guernseymen were the main impetus behind shipments destined for London, the largest and most discriminating spirits market in England.[11] St Peter Port merchants supplied brandy to the English market throughout the eighteenth century. They imported principally from Nantes, La Rochelle, Bordeaux and Sète in France; and, increasingly, from Spain. Small quantities of the brandy were shipped openly to England but most of the sales were to smugglers.

The St Peter Port merchants appear to have become interested in the rum trade c.1730.[12] In 1738 the quantity of rum shipped from Guernsey to Southampton was 1,724 gallons; in 1740 it amounted to 5,062 gallons. When the British government gained greater control over the Isle of Man in the 1760s, Manx traders shipped rum from the Danish West Indies to Guernsey.[13]

The scale of the spirit trade at the end of the eighteenth century can be quantified with some precision. In the eight months from January to August 1796 some 6,975 pipes of French brandy, 2,354 pipes of Spanish brandy, 1,507 pipes of gin and 88 pipes of rum were brought into Guernsey. This amounted to 10,924 pipes and was all for British accounts. It was not possible for a precise figure to be given of the imports for the accounts of island merchants but it was estimated that they had received about 15,000 pipes.[14]

An estimate made c.1802/3 suggested that annually 60 vessels from Holland imported 2,268,000 gallons of gin to Guernsey and Alderney. The quantity of brandy imported was reckoned at 28,000 pipes (3,360,000 gallons) and the rum imported was estimated at 5,000 puncheons (500,000 gallons). According to the calculations the alcohol was increased at least one sixth in volume by water added in Guernsey. The British allowed one million gallons for what was consumed on the island, or shipped elsewhere, or lost. This left an estimated 6,150,000 gallons which entered Britain from Guernsey, mostly illegally. (See table 2.6).

In the four months from November 1806 to February 1807 the vessels observed clearing Guernsey carried cargoes which totalled 400,560 gallons of brandy, 49,570 gallons of rum and 109,395 gallons of gin. Had all of this been smuggled into England the lost excise duties would have amounted to £411,367/18/1½, the lost custom duties £39,145/18/4 (See table 2.6).

Wine

It has been mentioned earlier that St Peter Port merchants were involved in the shipping of French wine to England from the mediaeval period onwards. During the eighteenth century the island merchants continued to trade in French wines (from the Bordeaux area in particular) but they increasingly dealt in Portuguese and Spanish wines, especially port. This reflected the swing in English fashion away from French wines towards Iberian produce. British legislation and tariffs were directed against French goods on the one hand; and trade links with Portugal were strengthened on the other. In 1762 the Consul and Committee of the British Oporto Factory complained to the Earl of Egremont that the Portuguese were shipping 'several thousand pipes' of wine to Guernsey, Plymouth and Portsmouth in their own vessels: 'large quantities of their wines are deposited in the Island of Guernsey which are afterwards fraudulently introduced into England as British property.'[15]

In 1763, in the exceptional conditions of wartime, the Guernsey merchants shipped 1,869 tuns 2 hogsheads 15 gallons of Portuguese wine to the English outports and 718 tuns 2 hogsheads

29 gallons to London. The following year Warren Lisle reported to the London Customs Board that many of the merchants had laid out great sums of money in making vaults and magazines 'for receiving of port wines which is now at an end and greatly lessens the burden here.'[16] In fact the Guernsey merchants continued to handle considerable quantites of Portuguese wine. Thanks to a British concession Guernsey merchants were allowed 12% 'leakage' on foreign wines that they handled for English accounts. A certificate was required and the shipper in the island had to declare, *inter alia*, that the wines had received no mixture since their landing in the island, that the wines had been imported in British bottoms only, and that the wine was the property of British subjects only.[17] During the following two decades quantities of between three to six hundred tuns of Iberian wine were shipped annually from Guernsey to England. Considerable quantities of French wines were traded by the St Peter Port merchants, particularly during the years of the French revolutionary wars.

André Simon observed that at the end of the eighteenth century:

'there was a short but brilliant period of prosperity in England when gaiety, optimism and extravagance were at their highest. It was then that we hear for the first time of French Champagne shippers coming or sending agents to England to sell their wines, Jean Remy Moët, from Epernay, and François Ruinart, Vicomte de Brimont, from Reims, were the two pioneers who laid the foundations of the fortunes not merely of the firms of Moët et Chandon and of Ruinart Père et Fils, but of the modern Champagne trade as we know it to-day.

'Naturally, trade between England and France was bound to be most grievously affected owing to the unsettled political outlook during the short periods of so-called peace which characterized the first fifteen years of the nineteenth century, although some Champagne was shipped now and again direct to some English Ports and fairly regularly indirectly via the Channel Islands.'[18]

The Guernsey merchants continued to handle considerable quantities of wine after the end of the Napoleonic wars and well into the ninteeth century. Inglis commented: 'The trade of Guernsey, in wine and spirits, is still very large. During the year, ending with October 1833, there were imported 264,201 gallons of wine, of which 112,500 gallons were re-exported; and of brandy, there were imported no less than 240,913 gallons, of which, however, I find only 53,057 gallons re-exported'. [19]

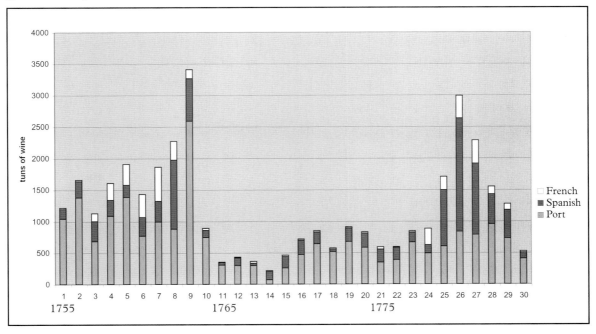

Fig. 2.3: Wine imported into England from Guernsey and Jersey, 1755 – 1784 (See table 2.7)

23

Table 2.7 Wine imported into England from Guernsey and Jersey (In tuns - hogsheads - gallons) [*Source*: TNA T64/274 document 138]

		PORT	SPANISH	FRENCH	RHENISH
1	**1755**	1044-1-10	151-2-37	21-1-00	
2	**1756**	1381-3-30	253-2-31	23-2-56	2-2-26
3	**1757**	687-1-34	315-1-14	126-2-48	0-3-39
4	**1758**	1088-3-51	256-2-61	267-1-07	0-3-23
5	**1759**	1386-0-36	192-0-59	327-0-51	2-0-37
6	**1760**	772-3-40	294-2-19	364-2-61	0-3-45
7	**1761**	993-0-42	330-0-48	537-0-13	0-2-27
8	**1762**	880-1-19	1093-0-58	296-1-12	
9	**1763**	2589-3-34	675-3-40	140-3-02	2-1-08
10	**1764**	748-1-54	111-3-34	32-1-54	
11	**1765**	305-1-54	37-2-49	11-3-45	
12	**1766**	296-2-50	122-2-09	14-2-36	
13	**1767**	295-2-14	38-1-28	31-1-34	
14	**1768**	70-2-04	128-0-13	15-0-00	
15	**1769**	258-0-28	181-1-18	21-0-54	
16	**1770**	472-1-24	229-1-57	16-0-13	0-0-12
17	**1771**	642-0-43	188-2-03	19-3-19	0-0-04
18	**1772**	515-3-21	42-0-53	16-0-34	0-0-25
19	**1773**	677-2-56	213-2-15	18-2-17	
20	**1774**	584-1-06	225-0-08	20-1-05	
21	**1775**	345-3-49	209-2-12	35-3-53	
22	**1776**	386-3-44	194-2-14	13-0-32	
23	**1777**	666-1-14	157-1-29	21-3-19	
24	**1778**	490-2-16	130-3-08	262-2-61	0-0-19
25	**1779**	600-3-48	895-2-08	209-0-16	
26	**1780**	836-2-56	1789-1-61	361-3-41	
27	**1781**	784-0-47	1128-3-45	369-0-18	0-2-42
28	**1782**	952-1-55	474-3-30	121-1-59	10-1-40
29	**1783**	731-3-12	446-1-54	97-1-04	33-1-13
30	**1784**	404-2-12	96-2-20	22-0-3	1-1-26

Fruit

The Guernsey merchants frequently dealt in fruit from France and the Mediterranean. There were particularly good opportunities during the War of the Austrian Succession and the Seven Years War for profitable trade in this sector. The year 1763 was exceptional with over two and a half thousand tons of fruit being imported into London and the English outports from Guernsey. The fruit was shipped in bulk to Guernsey and then carried in smaller vessels to England. Entries in the Bristol port books illustrate the Guernsey – England stage of the trade.

Table 2.8 The quantities of fruit and wine imported into England from Guernsey, 1733-1745

	PRUNES	RAISINS	LEMONS & ORANGES	WINE
	cwts/qts/lbs	cwts/qts/lbs	number	Tuns/hogsheads/gallons
1733	40.0. 0	62.0.10	2000	228.2.49
1734	142.0. 9	397.1.12	-	224.0.60
1735	514.0. 5	10.0. 0	-	338.3.36
1736	568.0.10	-	-	364.1.9
1737	290.0.19	-	500	377.1. 3
1738	60.3.26	-	-	420.3.24
1739	203.1.19	-	-	576.1.49
1740	128.3. 4	3565.0. 5	-	1913.0.30
1741	360.0. 7	0.0.27	24250	603.3.41
1742	561.1.16	-	7250	374.1.24
1743	208.2.19	-	10250	787.0.58
1744	62.3.11	297.3.25	16500	847.1.15
1745	-	378.2.17	-	925.0.21

Source: TNA 64/274, documents 128, 129

Table 2.9 The quantity of fruit imported into England from Guernsey, 1763

	to London quantity cwts/qu/lbs	to the English outports quantity cwts/qu/lbs
	---	---
currants	6973-3-14	1644-2-8
prunes	1518-3-10	
raisins		
denial	30229-2-11	3775-2-11
lyord	1297-3-5	
Malaga	8-0-20	
Solis	4803-2-23	2395-3-6

Source: TNA CUST 3/63

Table 2.10 Shipping from Guernsey to Bristol, June 1763

June	Vessel	tons	master	crew	cargo
1	*Elizabeth*	20	John Little	m + 2	wine, raisins, cork
8	"		Thomas Hammong	m + 3	raisins, oil, cork
9	*Mary*	25	Andrew Morell	m + 2½	raisins, wine, oil, cork
15	*Jenny & Mary*	12	John Snow	m + 2	wine, cork & c.
17	*Nancy*	30	Nicholas Enuf	m + 3½	raisins, cork

m = master, ½ = boy

Source: W. Minchinton, *The Trade of Bristol in the Eighteenth Century* (Bristol Record Society, 1957) pp. 43-45

The American War brought renewed opportunities for the Guernsey merchants to supply fruit to the English market. In the year 1780 twenty thousand five hundred oranges and lemons were supplied to the English outports, eight thousand to London. Other fruits are tabulated below:

Table 2.11 The quantity of fruit imported into England from Guernsey, 1780

To outports	**cwts / qu / lbs**
Almonds, sweet	113-1-26
Currants	2450-1-24
Prunes, French	1063-1-14
Raisins, Denia	288-0-0
Lexia	938-3-16
Malaga	1070-0-0
Solis	2663-0-1
To London	**cwts / qu / lbs**
Currants	1260-1-21
Figs	1138-3-11
Prunes, French	3452-1-4
Raisins, Denia	11514-3-16
Malaga	2010-1-14
Lexia	1932-1-0
Lipari	116-3-14
Portugal	605-3-14
Solis	5056-3-21

Source: TNA CUST 3/80

3
Northern Isles

Jersey

There was a certain amount of trading between Guernsey and Jersey but little trace of it remains in the records. The maritime and commercial history of Jersey was significantly different from that of Guernsey. Throughout the eighteenth and nineteenth centuries Jersey was deeply involved in the Newfoundland trade, with some thirty and more vessels regularly voyaging there each year; Guernsey, on the other hand, sent only a few. In the late seventeenth century (and early eighteenth century) Jersey benefited from its close proximity to St Malo and derived trading advantages. Moreover, Jersey supplied large quantities of tobacco to French smugglers throughout the eighteenth century. However, Jersey was situated too far south to attract English smugglers; Guernsey – and Alderney even more – enjoyed the better geographical situation for supplying the south coast of England. The English smugglers had an appetite for brandy, gin, rum, and tea. The Guernsey merchants were also able to supply tobacco to French smugglers.

At a relatively early date the merchants of Guernsey settled in St Peter Port. Writing in 1685 Dumaresq commented:

> As to their trade and manufacture, it is much the same as that of Jersey but differ in that their whole trading lies in the Town; where, by the conveniency of the Harbour, all the men of Estates and note dwell; whereas in Jersey they are spred up and down the Island; nether *(sic)* have they that proportion of shipping or seamen as Jersey bigness for bigness.[1]

In Jersey the merchants were scattered across the island, they were still in part farmers who also traded. Concentrated in St Peter Port, the Guernsey merchants were able to share news, check credentials, organise joint expeditions, assemble cargoes and solve problems with much greater ease. The merchants developed the urban institutions that, in time, underpinned St Peter Port as an international entrepôt. In the eighteenth century Jersey was riven by factional feuds which compromised the development of commerce. It was in this context that the Jersey chamber of commerce was established in 1768.[2] Guernsey endured no such difficulties and it was only in 1808 that the merchants founded a chamber of commerce. They did so in reaction to pressure from the British government, not because of insular disputes.

Alderney

Alderney formed part of the bailiwick of Guernsey but, in practice, enjoyed its own freedom. Throughout the eighteenth century Alderney had members of the Le Mesurier family serving as Governors of the island. The Le Mesuriers had strong ties with Guernsey and this helped to promote the interests of both islands. Lying to the north of Guernsey, and closer to England, Alderney served as a 'counter' visited by English smugglers. The merchants of Alderney worked closely with their Guernsey counterparts. Cargoes of goods to be sold to the smugglers were sometimes shipped direct to Alderney but often arrived *via* Guernsey. The leading Alderney merchants in the late eighteenth century included: Joseph Laurany, Thomas Olivier, John Patourel and Nicholas Robilliard. When Stiles made his journey of investigation in 1800, Peter Le Mesurier, the Governor of Alderney observed:

> Alderney is about four miles in length, and from one mile and three quarters, to two miles in breadth; that there is no roadstead for vessels safely to remain at anchor more than for one tide only, before they enter the pier, which is incapable of receiving vessels above the burthen of one hundred tons; that there are about two hundred and fifty families in the island, and its population upon the whole, including all descriptions of persons may be computed at thirteen hundred, and that all those capable of labor, except his own family, he said, were employed in making kegs for the smugglers.[3]

This account corresponds with that given a few years later by Samuel Carden. He stated that he had been deeply engaged in the illicit trade carrying on in the island of Alderney – that he made, in the course of eleven months, (previous to his vessel being taken), three voyages to Holland for spirits and French goods; but in the performance of a fourth his vessel was taken, when he made his escape in the long boat. Carden told Leabon:

> That he generally made two voyages a week to the English coast, taking over each time from six to seven hundred eight-gallon kegs of spirits, besides lace and other French articles.

> That the one hundred and seventeen kegs of spirits detained by me [*George Leabon*] on the second of March, 1809, (and for which I was tried before a garrison Court of Inquiry,) were his property, and that, on the same night, he shipped off a large quantity from another part of the island.

> That there were about six hundred coopers constantly employed in the island making kegs – that on an average each man would make seven in a day – that a duty was paid of one shilling upon every keg containing eight gallons. [4]

Travel between Guernsey and England, 1776-1782

1776 July 15: I left London in company with Mr La Serre, his nephew, Mrs Perchard of London & her daughter and Peter Le Marchant. Embarked at Southampton in the *Montague*, Capt. Priaulx, the 19th inst. Put back at Alderney and got here the 23rd inst. Wind contrary the whole passage. N.B. I had been in London 15 months in Mr Perchard's compting-house. E. Dobrée.

1777 July 2nd. I left Guernsey on board Capt Priaulx – was chas'd by a ship supposed to be an American privateer – got next evening to Yarmouth – lay there and sail'd next morning at six and reached Southampton by nine. Next day, got to London – the 5th inst Saturday night.

1777 Augst 8th. I left London. Next day sailed from Southampton on board the *Ceres*, Judas – put into Yarmouth – remain'd there until the 13th – then sailed and got the 15th inst to Guernsey.

1778. June 1st. I left Guernsey, sail'd on board the *Montague*, Capt. Priaulx, and arrived next day at Southampton – took coach next day and got to London at Night. I left London June 13th arrived at night at Southampton – left next day and travelled through Ringwood, Wimbourne, Blandford, Dorchester & Bridport to Lyme; from whence I sailed Monday night the 15th and arrived in Guernsey next day the 16th June 1778, on board the *Infant*, John Harding, master.

1782. I left Guernsey February 14th on board the *Express* packet Capn Wood – wind N.E. next day made the Needles, endeavoured to get in, but the wind increasing was obliged to put into Portland Road, where we lay all night. Next day got on shore at Chissell – walked to Weymouth, thence took a post chaise to Blandford & lay there the 16th. – Next day pursued our route to Salisbury – thence took stage-coach and got to London the 18th at noon.

March 13th.-I set out in the stage coach on my return arrived at Southampton at night – next day at 12 o'clock embarked on bd. the *Express* packet wind at N.N.E. a fine breeze, went thro' the Needles about 3 o'clock. Next morning at 8 o'clock landed safe in Guernsey, thank God.

Source: Priaulx, McCulloch ms., 'copied from Elisha Dobrée's journal'

Trade with England and Wales

In the late seventeenth and eighteenth centuries Guernsey's trade with England and Wales was based on London, the ports of the South West, and the coal ports of Newcastle, Sunderland, Swansea and Llanelli. Southampton handled a great deal of Guernsey's trade. During the war years 1710-12 nearly half of the vessels clearing from English ports for Guernsey sailed from Southampton. With the return of peace (1713-17) the total volume of traffic between England and Guernsey increased and Southampton's share dropped to just below 30%, although the number of sailings from Southampton actually rose during those years (See table 3.2). Southampton continued to serve as a 'staple port' to Guernsey throughout the eighteenth century. High-priced goods from London were frequently despatched to the island via Southampton, especially during wartime, when the London – Guernsey voyage was endangered by enemy privateers. By 1807 Southampton was forwarding goods from London, Manchester, Birmingham and Sheffield to the island.[5]

The port books record a large number of vessels sailing from Newcastle and Swansea to the island. These statistics in part represent the fact that the Guernsey merchants were involved in the export of coal to France. English and Welsh coal transported by sea to the west coast of France was 'cheaper there than French coal, which had to be carried great distances overland.'[6]

From 1697 onwards official figures exist for Guernsey's trade with England.[7] These have to be interpreted with care as commodities were valued at fixed prices selected at the beginning of the eighteenth century. The statistics therefore suggest the physical volume of foreign trade rather than the value. Moreover the figures make no allowance for smuggled goods. Nevertheless, if analysed with caution the statistics do reveal the growth and changing patterns of Guernsey's trade.

English imports from Guernsey consisted principally of:

(a) island produce: cider, cattle, salt, lobsters, stone and knitwear;

(b) entrepôt goods: wine, fruit, salt (French), textiles, iron and a variety of other goods.

During the early eighteenth century the major constituent in the value of imports into England from Guernsey consisted of the woollen garments knitted on the island. The stockings alone sometimes accounted for almost half of the total value of all imports. By the second half of the century this had changed. A much larger volume of entrepôt goods was being imported into England, while the volume of island produce rose only slightly. Although less Guernsey knitwear was imported into England, there was a big increase in the quantity of granite shipped from the island to London.

The exports from England to Guernsey can be classified as follows:

(a) goods for the Guernsey domestic market (principally food, textiles, building materials),

(b) goods destined for the international entrepôt trade (including colonial re-exports such as tobacco);

(c) materials required to operate the entrepôt trade (glass, timber, iron).

During the course of the century the quantity of commodities required by the Guernsey domestic market rose. This was due, first, to the increase in population which needed more food, clothing and heating (= more flour, textiles and coal). Secondly, the growth in prosperity stimulated a demand for more fashionable luxuries (= more expensive textiles). Thirdly, a building boom in the last quarter of the century led to the shipping of more limestone, bricks, pantiles, slabs, steps, quoins and slates. Larger quantities of goods were also sent from England for the entrepôt market. Moreover the merchants and coopers needed more glass, bottles, wooden staves and hoops to package their alcohol and tobacco. The busier the harbour became, the greater was the demand for sailcloth, cordage and the ironmongery of the chandler's trade.

Having broadly characterised the nature of England's trade with Guernsey, it remains to examine the trade statistics, always bearing in mind that we are dealing with volume rather than value, and that the trade figures represent only the legal trade. Between 1697 and 1801 the volume of exports from England to Guernsey was commonly in excess of the volume of imports into England from Guernsey. There were 37 years in which this was not the case: 1701-11, 1746-48, 1755-59, 1761-63, 1770-73, 1777, 1779-81, 1783, 1796-1801. The terms of trade improved for Guernsey in these years because the volume of her exports to England increased. It is immediately apparent that these were almost all war years. The merchants of St Peter Port benefited because, with the disruption of international trading patterns, they were able to take over some lucrative business. The exports from Guernsey to England during wartime also included some prize cargoes. During the course of the eighteenth century the aggregate volume of legal trade between England and Guernsey (i.e. imports + exports) increased tenfold.

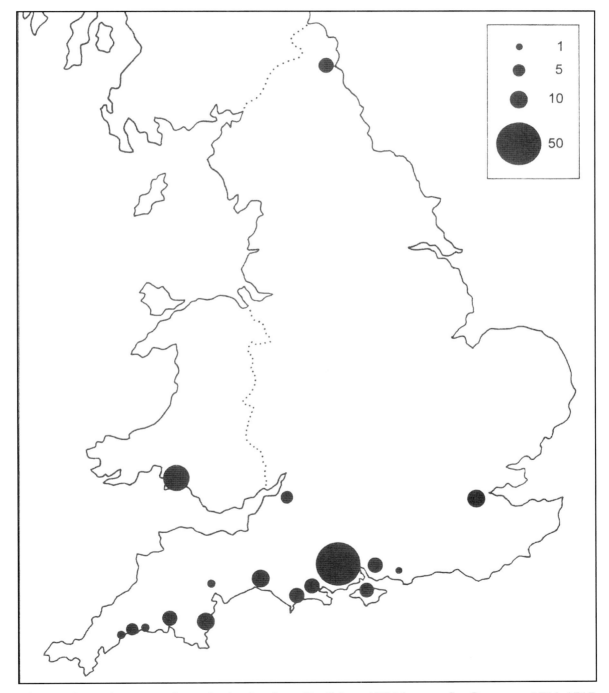

Fig. 3.1: Annual average of vessels clearing from English and Welsh ports for Guernsey, 1710-1717
(*Source*: See Table 3.1)

Table 3.1 Ships clearing from English and Welsh ports for Guernsey, 1710-1717

	1710	1711	1712	1713	1714	1715	1716	1717
London	2	2	3	3	6	5	23	13
Sunderland	2			1		1		1
Newcastle	5	3	3	8	4	5	3	3
Deal							1	
Chichester		4	3	2			1	
Portsmouth		1	4	3	8	5	3	12
Southampton	35	39	48	40	55	52	45	53
Cowes	2	2	2	11	11	8	6	2
Poole	4	14	8	9	4	4	2	1
Weymouth	2	2	6	9	2	4	4	6
Lyme Regis	3	3	4	8	15	7	6	8
Exeter	3	2		1	2		3	1
Dartmouth	3	4	7	2	4	8	11	19
Plymouth	2	4	8	1	5	7	4	14
Looe				1	2	4	1	5
Fowey		3		3	4	10	8	8
Truro							1	
Penryn	1	2	3	6	5	4	2	3
Falmouth		2	1		2	1	1	3
Gweek								1
Penzance				2	1			
St Ives					1			
Padstow			1					1
Bideford		1		1			1	
Minehead								1
Bristol			1	5	3	2	8	8
Neath								1
Swansea	1		3	8	33	35	17	17
Llanelli							1	2
Milford				2	1			

Source: TNA CO 388/18, TNA CO 390/8

Trade with Scotland

During the eighteenth century the Scots greatly enjoyed drinking French claret; for some it was a rejection of port – the English drink – and hence an affirmation of Scottish independence. French wines, however, were the subject to heavy duties and so the Scots looked to entrepôts such as St Peter Port for their supplies. French wine could be shipped from Guernsey to Scotland as Spanish or Portuguese wine, Iberian produce attracting a smaller duty than French at the Scottish port of entry. In 1751-52 and 1760- 61 almost all of the French wine landed at Leith was from Guernsey. Other produce imported from Guernsey included French prunes and, occasionally, walnuts, chestnuts and salt. There are some rare references to Scottish exports to Guernsey. Between 1741 and 1744 James Watson, merchant of Greenock, shipped roll and leaf tobacco in trusses on board the *Endeavour* of Wexford and the *Mary* of Waterford to the island. However, the total quantity of tobacco shipped to Guernsey seems to have been relatively small.[9]

In general it is very difficult to quantify the scale of trade between Guernsey and Scotland in the first half of the eighteenth century. There is better evidence for the volume of trade in the second half of the century. Customs returns show that generally the volume of imports into Scotland from Guernsey was greater than the volume of exports from Scotland to Guernsey. The imports into Scotland included small quantites of a considerable number of goods, some of Guernsey origin, the rest foreign. In 1775 the list of imports included anchovies, apples, capers, cork, nuts, oil of cloves, olives, pickles, rosin, brandy, vinegar and wine.[10] During the French revolutionary wars large quantites of wine were imported from Guernsey (e.g. 412 tuns 1 hogshead 23 gallons of Spanish wine and 41 tuns 2 hogsheads 45 gallons of French wine in 1799).[11] There was a regular export from Scotland to Guernsey of small quantities of coal, bottles and green glass. In some years large quantities of tobacco were exported to Guernsey and this altered the terms of trade in Scotland's favour (e.g. 1766: 490,400lbs of tobacco to Guernsey; 1789: 233,477lbs).[12]

Trade with Ireland

There was considerable trade between Guernsey and Ireland in the eighteenth century but it is not easy to quantify before 1782-83. In 1765 the parliament of Bordeaux forbade the mixing of Spanish wine with local claret, a mixture esteemed in Ireland and previoulsy exported there in great volume. About 8,000 tuns of claret were shipped yearly from Bordeaux to Ireland, according to William Le Marchant. In consequence of the ban on the mixing of wines, the claret and Spanish wines were shipped separately to Guernsey, mixed in the island and forwarded to Ireland. The St Peter Port merchants made a profit of above £3,000 on this transaction; and in 1766 the Bordeaux parliament reversed its ban on mixing.

Trade between Guernsey and Ireland seems to have been stimulated during the American War of Independence. In February 1782 Henry Budd complained to the Lieutenant Governor about the considerable quantities of salted beef and port brought from Ireland to Guernsey by Captain Cullen, master of a brigantine from Waterford. These shipments were for Mr Khae, an Irish merchant who had been resident of the island for some months. Some of the provisions were destined for the 'iniquitous traffick of conveying from hence salt provisions for the equipment of the enemy's fleet'.[13]

In the last two decades of the eighteenth century Irish exports to Guernsey consisted principally of meat and dairy products (beef, pork, ham, bacon, butter) together with items manufactured from animal fats (candles, soap, tallow). Irish exports were usually shipped from the ports of south-east Ireland (from Dublin round to Cork), but there were occasional shipments of linen from Belfast.[14]

Guernsey exports to Ireland consisted of a variety of goods but the main value resided in wines. The volume of trade increased during the French wars, with 966 tuns 1 hogshead 33 gallons of French wine being exported from Guernsey to Ireland in the year ending 25 March 1796; just over 90% of this was for the Dublin market. Exports from Ireland to Guernsey also ran at a higher level during war years 1793-1800.

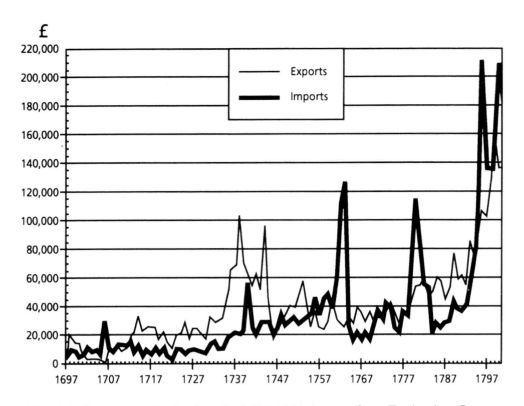

Fig. 3.2: Guernsey - England trade, 1697-1801 (export from England to Guernsey, imports from Guernsey into England).

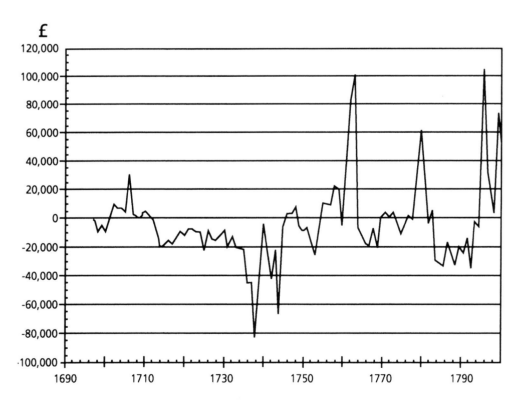

Fig. 3.3: Guernsey - England, balance of trade (positive figures indicate a balance in Guernsey's favour). Note the favourable trade balance during many war years (Seven Years War, American War, French Revolutionary War).

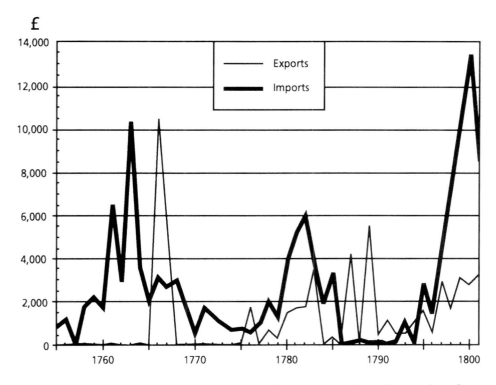

Fig. 3.4: Guernsey - Scotland trade, 1755-1801 (exports from Scotland to Guernsey, imports from Guernsey into Scotland).

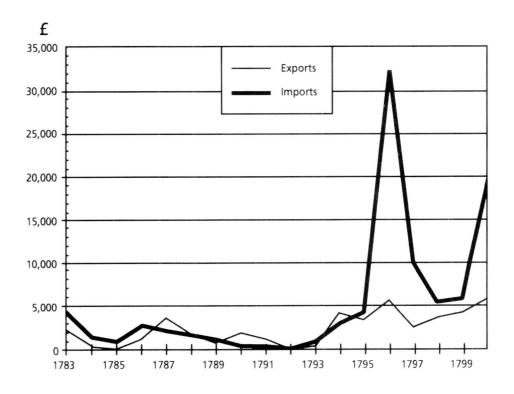

Fig. 3.5: Guernsey - Ireland trade, 1783-1800 (exports from Ireland to Guernsey, imports from Guernsey into Ireland).

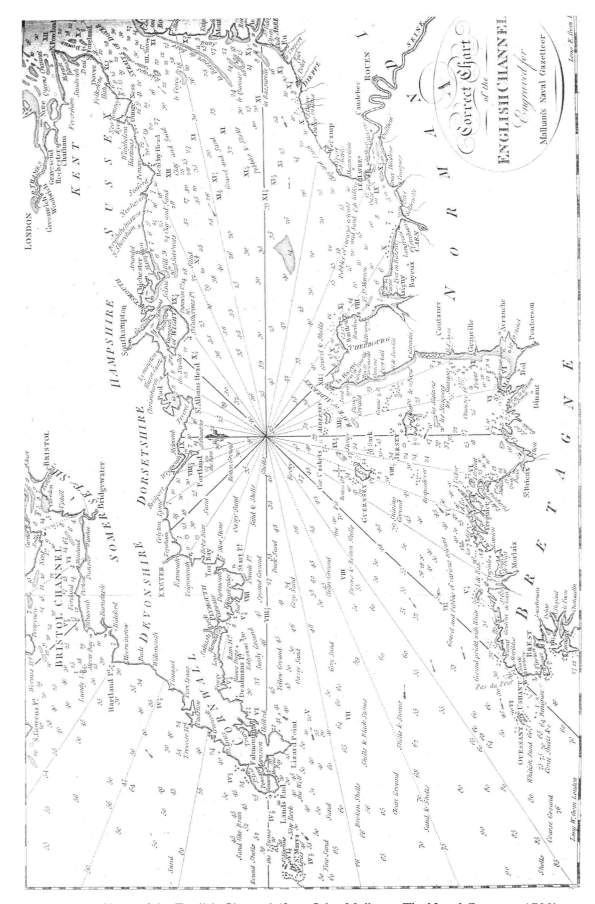

Fig. 3.6: Chart of the English Channel (from John Malham, *The Naval Gazetteer*, 1799)

4
Ports

of which were funk, and 1 ftranded; her Cargo of Sail Cloth expected to be faved.

The Vrow Elizabeth, Dirks, from St. Martin's to Amfterdam, laden with Salt, Brandy, Wine, &c. is on Shore at Bantham in Bigbury Bay; 17 Cafks of Brandy, and 1 Hogfhead of Claret are faved..

The Penelope, Walker, from Quebec for Jamaica, &c. was taken the latter end of December, near St. Kitts, by the Britton, French Privateer of 40 Guns, and carried into Cape François.

The Ann, Geives, from Guernfey for London, with Fruit and Wine, is ftranded near Pool.

The Quebec, Smith, from St. Euftatia, arrived at Jamaica, has carried in with her two Prizes, bound from Port Au Prince to Carracou, laden with Sugar, Indigo, Coffee, and Cotton.

Barbadoes, 17th Feb. On the 12th Inftant arrived the Andromeda, and Convert Men of War, with 31 Sail of Ships from England, and the Day following arrived the Phœnix Man of War, Sir Hyde Parker, with 105 Sail from ditto.

Dartmouth 21. Yefterday arrived the Dart Privateer, Captain Yeoman, with L'Age D'or, Captain Pierre, from Martinico for Marfeilles, with Sugar, Coffee, &c. valued at 15,000l. after an Engagement of three Glaffes, in which the Dart had two Men killed, and three wounded; the French had three killed and fix wounded; fhe failed from Martinico with four Sail, without Convoy, and was taken the 4th Inftant, in Latit. 35 6. Longit. 10, 30. Weft.

The Clarendon, Parr, from Jamaica, is on Shore in Leverpool River, but are in Hopes of getting her off.

The La Vulture Prize to the Pallas Privateer of Leverpool, is totally loft in Ireland, and feveral of the People drowned.

Gravefend ——— arrived from
21 Mar. Lacanto Colftallo, Belvino Leghorn
    Scanderoon Galley, Loutidge Lifbon
22 Caftor, Straker Gibraltar
    Pomona, Rutherford ditto
23 Ceres, Barker Gibralter
    Watcomb, Reed Guernfey
    Ann & Sufanna, Carr Jamaica
——— Sailed for
21 Refolution, Peters St. Auguftine
    Ewreto, Featonby Montreal
22 N. S. Da. Conceicao, Marquis Oporto
    Houghton, Godfhall ditto

Beaver, Powell Montreal
Ann and Elizabeth, Fowler ditto
23 Love, Mann Lifbon
    Portfmouth, Hunt Quebec
    Detroit, Inglis ditto
    Montreal, Gibfon ditto
    Befley, Boyd Montreal
Lancafter ——— arrived from
    Abby, Court Jamaica
Leverpool ——— arrived from
    Juliana, ——— Jamaica
    Anfon, Ball ditto
    Britannia, Thompfon dit.o
    Rawlinfon, Daggers ditto
Briftol ——— arrived from
    Potowmack, Mitchel Jamaica
Southampton ——— arrived from
21 Chichefter, a Cartel St. Maloes
    Torrington ditto Cherburgh
23 Dove, Lancy St. Maloes
    Little Jenny, Woodman Chichefter
——— Sailed for
23 Montague, Lefevre Guernfey
Portfmouth ——— arrived from
22 Good-Intent, Davis Cherburgh
    A Dutch M. W. St. Euftatia
    St. Laurence, Arvedo Oporto
    St. John Evangelift, Antonio ditto
    Mars, Kentifh Jamaica
Dover ——— arrived from
    London, Richardfon Jamaica
    Baltimore, Glafby ditto
    Ellis, Watkins ditto
Downs ——— arrived from
21 Charon M. W. Jamaica
    St. George's Planter, Peacock ditto
    Morant, Carter ditto
    Fullerton, Johnfon ditto
    Diamond, Gradara Zant
    Brilliant, ——— Portfmouth
    Experiment, ——— ditto
23 Paxhoufe, Wood Jamaica
    John, Smith ditto
——— Sailed
    Eolus M. W.
    Fairy Sloop
    With feveral Coafters
——— Remain for
23 Mathew and Ann, Colnes Limerick
    Lenox, Hay Jamaica
    Pallas, Warring ditto
    Diana, Cleveland ditto
    Wefton Hall, Howfon ditto
    Nathaniel Baily, Morfe ditto
    George and John, Dear ditto
    George and Sufannah, Angus ditto
    Nottingham, Curtis ditto
    Lady Juliana, Stevenfon ditto
    Lady's Adventure, Cooper ditto
    Afhley, Caftle ditto
    Mary and Ann, Junis ditto
    Charming Molly, Gill ditto
    Jamaica Planter, Thompfon ditto
    Auguftus Cefar, Fowler ditto
    Olive Branch, Trew ditto

Lord Howe, Francis ditto
Old Harbour, Power ditto
Princefs Royal, Ruthwin ditto
Samuel, Weftback ditto
George, Trenham ditto
Henry, Richardfon ditto
Effort, Hewfon ditto
Afhton Hall, Sheppard ditto
Nancy, Magnefs ditto
Elliot, Brown ditto
Kingfton, Read ditto
Mary, Gilftone St. Kitts
Rowley, Power ditto
Douglafs, Crombie ditto
Matthew, Slegg ditto
William, Flannery ditto
Dorfetfhire, Waddy ditto
Maria Catharina, Archdeacon ditto
Britannia, Wheatly ditto
William, Luce ditto
Brothers, Tomlin ditto
Lamb, ——— ditto
Henry and Ann, Hart Nevis
London Mercht Davis ditto
Worcefter, Whitehead Barbadoes
Rachel, Henry ditto
Free Mafon, Mansfield ditto
Betfey and Sally, Peters ditto
Lord North, Jordain ditto
Three Brothers, Brenan ditto
Britannia, Leech ditto
George, Philpot ditto
Mary and Ifabella, Morris ditto
Polly & Charlotte, ——— ditto
Thomas, Sydes Lifbon
Dublin, Ryder Dublin
Free Trade, Stringer ditto
Betfey, Galloway Cork
Matthew and Mary, Smith ditto
Thomas, Bruce Antigua
William and Elizabeth, Young ditto
Betfey, Kidd ditto
Good-Intent, Brown ditto
Nancy, Keys ditto
Harriot, Lufby ditto
Ceres, Howe ditto
Montferat Packet, Ryan Montferat
Thomas, Baird Madeira
Two Sifters, Smith ditto
London, M'Cullock ditto
Active, Mafkall ditto
Peggy, Miller Tobago
Ware, Roxborough ditto
Ocean, Ewin New-York
Mary, Stuart ditto
Centurion, Hepburn Halifax
Young William, Haftings ditto
Alexander, Bell ditto
Dunmore, ——— ditto
Bell, Oldrice Quebec
Lizard, Max ditto
Nautilous, Henderfon ditto
Nancy, Creighton ditto
Two Brothers, Young St. Lucia
Bermuda, Nafton Bermudas
Veftal M. W.
Mercury ditto
Dromemary ditto

Warwick, ditto

WINDS at DEAL
21 SW 22 NW 23 S

Cork ——— arrived from
11 Mar. William, Cofgrove Portfmouth
14 Laurel Frigat ditto
    Rhemus, (a Prize) Newbury
——— Sailed for
11 Two Brothers, Bafs Youghall
13 Richmond, Patrick Glafgow
    Four Brothers, Smith Waterford
    North, Cowan Dublin
    Concordia, Srytgen Bourdeaux
    Ann & Elizabeth, Allen Campveer
Oporto ——— arrived from
    Lovely Amy, Taverner Pool
Hamburg ——— arrived from
    Endracht, Janfen Guernfey
Amfterdam ——— arrived from
    Lady Ann, Dick S. Euftatia
    Courier of St. Euftatia, Dick ditto
Guernfey ——— arrived from
    Jan & Peter, Akkes Rotterdam
    Vrow Alida, Peters Spain
    ———, Onaman Nantz
    Neptune, Ottendale Barcelona
    Genaemt Forgwick, Bogena Bourdeaux
Oftend ——— arrived from
    Efperance, Wallis Nice
    Hawke, Slater New-York
Barbadoes ——— arrived from
    Polly, Pratt London
    Royal Charlotte, King ditto
    Randolph, M'Nabb ditto
    Breffet, Parker ditto
    Ceres, Pine ditto
    Tabitha, Spence ditto
    Britannia, White ditto
    Jupiter, Young ditto
    Sally, Hardy ditto
    Experiment, Bruce ditto
    Loyal Briton, Young ditto
    Generous Friend, Livermore ditto
    Nelfon, Hayes ditto
    Tobin, Cruden ditto
    Exchange, Tyrrel ditto
    Thomas, Mann ditto
    Betfey, Richardfon ditto
    Warners, Martin ditto
Jamaica ——— arrived from
    Governor Dalling, ——— Clyde
    Jamaica, Fletcher Leverpool
    Lord North, Webb Briftol
    Chambers, Langley ditto
    Hawke, Small Africa
    Quebec, Smith St. Euftatia
    Petersfield, ——— Briftol
Penfacola ——— arrived from
    Thomas, Birch London
    Earl Bathurft, Anthony ditto
    Brown Hall, Nefbit ditto & Cork
    Earl of Denbigh, Crockat ditto ditto

LONDON: Printed by JAMES PHILLIPS, George-Yard, Lombard-Street.

Fig. 4.1: Lloyd's List N° 1148 (Friday, 24 March 1780). This issue records the arrival in Guernsey of ships from Rotterdam, Barcelona, Spain, Nantes, Bordeaux (column 4); and news of the *Ann* 'from Guernsey for London, with Fruit and Wine' (column 1).

The port books of Guernsey were destroyed during World War Two. The loss of such an important archive is frustrating, not least because it was not studied prior to its destruction. However, the gap can, to a certain extent, be filled by information gleaned from elsewhere. Dr Jamieson (1986) used the 'seamen's sixpences' archives to illustrate some voyages made by Guernsey-owned vessels. The archives of Lloyd's of London can be used to illustrate the rôle of St Peter Port as an entrepôt. It is to these records that we now turn.

From 2 January 1740 onwards Lloyd's issued a news-sheet twice a week, on Tuesday and Friday. An archive of these has survived, covering most years between 1740 – 1826. The first page of the sheet generally carried financial details (the exchange, annuities and similar). The second page provided information about the arrivals of vessels at ports in the British Isles and abroad. The ship and the name of the master were usually given, together with the port whence the vessel had sailed. From this it is possible to build up tables of shipping arriving at St Peter Port (see pp. 41-43).

Before we examine these, however, it is essential to emphasise the limitations of the data. The Lloyd's listings were far from comprehensive. Hardly once, between 1750 and 1826, did they record an arrival in St Peter Port from St Malo and yet we know that there were regularly hundreds of such visits in a year. The Lloyd's authorities were not interested in small craft and cabotage, their concern was with larger, insured, vessels. The tables accordingly show us aspects of *le grand commerce*, of international trade. The Baltic ships carrying wine and brandy from Catalonia to Guernsey were regularly recorded; but the locally-owned sloop bringing a similar, but smaller, cargo did not warrant notice when it arrived in St Peter Port. It follows that the tables present an *incomplete* picture.

Secondly, the data concern ships arriving in St Peter Port. The data tell us about the entrepôt, not about Guernsey shipping. Some of the vessels listed were Guernsey-owned; but a great many more were foreign-owned. Much of the activity of Guernsey-owned vessels passed unnoticed. We must also remember that ships frequently made triangular voyages. Guernsey vessels regularly went to Newfoundland; most then proceeded to Spain. If such a ship appears in the record, it is as a return from the Basque coast or Catalonia. Some vessels did come straight back from Newfoundland to Guernsey and these are to be found recorded under Newfoundland. These ships constituted a minority, they did not follow the traditional triangular route.

Finally, I have presented my analysis not numerically but in a visual format. To give numbers would be to engage in a spurious - and potentially misleading - precision. One ship of 350 tons burden could carry more than three smaller vessels. Moreover, we cannot be sure whether vessels arrived wholly or partially laden (or in ballast). I have therefore employed a technique that aims to convey a general impression of trends. One asterisk represents the arrival of one, two or three vessels, two stars indicate the arrival of four, five or six vessels, and so on. We should infer nothing from the 'nil' returns; but we are entitled to notice what *did* happen.

The most striking feature of the first table (Table 4.1) is the role of Bordeaux and Oporto. Wine came from these ports on a regular basis. From the very beginning of St Peter Port as an entrepôt, wine was central to the islanders' trade. The Guernsey merchants also imported wine from Faro, Lisbon, Alicante, Cadiz, Malaga, and the Canaries. This is independently confirmed by the *Livre de certificats*. It was after 1765 (and the suppression of the Isle of Man as a supply base for smugglers) that Guernsey became a great mart for spirits. St Peter Port was really significant as an entrepôt in the last quarter of the century. From 1775 onwards there was a marked increase in the number of recorded ship arrivals. There was a greater demand for spirits – brandy, gin, rum – and tea. Brandy came from Charente and Cette in France, from Barcelona and Salou in Spain; gin came from Rotterdam; rum came principally from St Croix in the West Indies. After the American War tobacco was increasingly shipped directly to Guernsey. The East India Companies based at Copenhagen, Gottenburg, Amsterdam and Lorient supplied tea.

Table 4.1 reveals changing patterns of trade. There were close ties with Barbados in the mid-eighteenth century but in the 1760s St Croix emerged as Guernsey's principal West Indian contact. This switch can be explained, independent evidence corroborates the data of the Lloyd's Lists (see p. 84). The table also illustrates the function of St Peter Port during the war years 1779-1783. Neutral ships (Danish and Swedish) brought cargoes from Spain and France and these imports were then trans-shipped from Guernsey to Britain. Ten years later the French Revolutionary Wars had a major impact on trade patterns. St Peter Port, Rotterdam – and then Hamburg – cleared cargoes shipped by neutrals between belligerent countries. Contemporary references demonstrate that large quantities of brandy were shipped from Spain to Guernsey in 1795 – 1796. This is vividly confirmed by the table.

Although the table tells us about St Peter Port as an entrepôt (receiving shipping), it occasionally provides 'echoes' of other trades. The Guernsey merchants took cargoes of wine from Madeira to the Americas; some vessels, however, returned directly from Madeira to Guernsey and this is captured in the table (see p. 70).

The French Revolutionary Wars (1793-1802) were profitable for the Guernsey merchants; the Napoleonic Wars (1803-1815) brought a crisis and this is reflected in the data. The British government clamped down hard on smuggling in 1805 and in 1807. The Guernsey merchants co-operated and the table shows very few ship arrivals in St Peter Port during the years 1805 – 1809. Old trades came to an abrupt end, there was suddenly no tobacco from Virginia, no rum from St Croix and St Thomas, no brandy from Salo. However, as Britain and her allies gained an ascendancy over Napoleon, so trade resumed. Some old patterns re-emerged, some new enterprises were established. The Guernsey merchants quickly realised that there were opportunities in the Mediterranean, at Trieste in particular; in the Caribbean, carrying sugar from Cuba; and in trading with South America. This new order is well illustrated. Rio de Janeiro became the new centre. Priaulx and Tupper and other Guernsey merchants based themselves in Brazil and despatched coffee, sugar and leather to northern Europe.

Tables 4.1 and 4.2

Lloyd's Lists do not survive for 1745, 1746, 1752, 1754, 1756, 1759 and 1778. During the years 1744 – 1754 there are records of some twenty-nine arrivals at Guernsey from Amsterdam, Barbados, Bordeaux, Cette, Copenhagen, Malaga, Newfoundland, Oporto, Rhode Island, Rotterdam and Salou. Nearly half of these arrivals were from Oporto.

Key:

*   arrival of 1 - 3 vessels;

**   arrival of 4 – 6 vessels;

***   arrival of 7 – 9 vessels;

and then by similar increments.

See Endnotes (pp.213-214) for a further discussion of these lists.

Table 4.1 Vessels arriving in St Peter Port, 1755-1792, based on Lloyd's Lists

Port	1755	1757	1758	1760	1761	1762	1763	1764	1765	1766	1767	1768	1769	1770	1771	1772	1773	1774	1775	1776	1777	1779	1780	1781	1782	1783	1784	1785	1786	1787	1788	1789	1790	1791	1792
Northern Europe																																			
Amsterdam																																*	*	*	
Copenhagen	*				*															*		*	*	*	*	*								*	*
Emden								*																											*
Gottenburg					*	*														**	*	**	**	**	*	***		*	*	*	**	*	*	*	*
Hamburg																						*			*								*		
Ostend			*			*																***	***	*	*	*	*	*	*	*	*	**	*	*	**
Rotterdam				*		*																**	****	*	*										**
France																																			
Boulogne		*				*	*															*	****		*		**	*	**	**	*	*	*	*	*
Bordeaux	*	*				*	*		*								*			*		*	*	**	**	*	**	*	******	****	*	*	**	*	*
Cette								*		*									*	*	*		*	*	*	**	**	**	*	****	**	*	**	*	*
Charente																				*	*		*		*	*	*		*	*	*	*	*		*
Lorient																					*		*												
Nantes																																			*
Roscoff																														*		*			
Toulon																														*					
Portugal																																			
Faro															*	*							*												
Lisbon	*	**	**	*	*	*						*				*		*	*	*		*	*	*	*	*	*	*	*	*	*	*	***	*	*
Oporto	*	**	*	*			*					*		*	**	*	**	*		*		*	**	**	*	***						***			
Spain																																			
Alicante		*	*			*				*					*				*	*	**		****	***	**		*		*	**	*	***	*	*	*
Barcelona																									*								*		*
Cadiz							*	*															***	***	*				*		*				*
Malaga			*			*																	*												*
St Lucar		*	*			*																						*					*		
Salo	*							*			*	*		*									*					*				*			*
Valencia																							*												*
Basque Road							*																*	*			*						**		*
Spain																				*			*		*	**	****	*	**	**	**	*	*	**	*
Atlantic																																			
Canaries	*																		*				*												
Gibraltar																														*					
North America																																			
Newfoundland										*															*			*	*		*	*	*		
Quebec				*							*	*	*														*								*
Virginia			*		*					*					*									*											****
Caribbean																																			
Barbados			*	*			*																			*			**				*	*	*
Granada				*																									*			*	**	*	*
Honduras											*																				**				*
St Bartholomew			*								*																								*
St Croix											*				*						**		*							*	**	*	**	*	*
St Eustatia																							*											*	
West Indies	*																			*			*	*										*	*
OTHER	*		*	*	*	*	*	*	*	*		*	*		*			*		*			*	*			*	*						*	*

Table 4.2 Vessels arriving in St Peter Port, 1793–1826, based on Lloyd's Lists

	1793	1794	1795	1796	1797	1798	1799	1800	1801	1802	1803	1804	1805	1806	1807	1808	1809	1810	1811	1812	1813	1814	1815	1816	1817	1818	1819	1820	1821	1822	1823	1824	1825	1826
Northern Europe																																		
Altona				*	*		*																											
Antwerp																						*	*	*					*	**	*	***	***	**
Copenhagen								*																				*	*	*	*			
Danzig						*	*	*																							*	*	*	*
Emden						**	**	**																										
Gottenburg	**		**	**		*		*									*	*			***	**	*							*			*	*
Hamburg		**	*	*	*	*	**	**	*													*				*			*	*	*	*	*	
Norway																						*	****										*
Ostend																						*												
Riga													*									*												
Rotterdam	*****	*******	*	*	*	**		*			*											****	****	**	**	****	*		*	*	*		*	*
Stockholm													**	*								**	*							*				
France																																		
Bordeaux	*	*	******	***	*		*	***	**	*	*											**	*	*										
Cette	*		*								**												*				*				**			
Charente			*			*	***	***	*	*												*												
Portugal																																		
Lisbon					*	*	*	*	*	*							*	*	*	*	**	*	*											
Oporto	*	*	***	*	*	**	*****	***	****	**	**	*	*	*			*	*	***			*	*						*					
Spain																																		
Alicante		*																						*										
Barcelona	*	*				*	*		*											*	*	*												
Cadiz			*		*	*	**	**	*		*			*			*		*	*	*		*											
Malaga		*				*	**	*	*		*							*																
Salou	*	*	***			*	**	*			*																							
Tarragona																			*			**	**			*				*			*	*
Valencia			*						*		*	*								*		*	*											
Villa Nova																				*	*	*												
Basque Road																					*	**	**											
Spain	**	*****	*****	*****		*	**	***	***	*	****																							
		*****	*****	*****							***																							
		*****	***																															

Table 4.2 Continuation

	1793	1794	1795	1796	1797	1798	1799	1800	1801	1802	1803	1804	1805	1806	1807	1808	1809	1810	1811	1812	1813	1814	1815	1816	1817	1818	1819	1820	1821	1822	1823	1824	1825	1826
M'terranean																																		
Majorca																			*	*	*													
Malta																				*	*									*				
Messina																																		
Naples		*							*	***	***	*										*	*	*										
Sicily										*	*									*														
Trieste																													*				*	
Atlantic																																		
Canaries																							*	*			*							
Gibraltar			*	*			*	**			*	*					*		*	****	*	*	*		*									
Madeira		*		*	*		*	*			*			*				*	*					*		*					*			
North America																																		
Quebec			*	*				*						*											*							*		
New York	*		*	*			*	*										*											*					
Virginia	*	**	*	**	**	**	*	*			**	****	***	**	**																			
Caribbean																																		
Cuba																				*	*	****	****	**	*	***	*	*	**	*	*	*	*	**
Grenada			*								*																				*			
Hayti																		*						*										
Honduras																									*									
St Bartholomew								*																										
St Croix				*			*							*	*						*	*	*											
St Domingo															*	*																		
St Eustatia	*																																	
St Thomas		*		*			*	*			*	*	*	*												*	*				*			
West Indies		*		*																**				*										
South America																																		
Bahia																						*	*	*	*	*	*	*	*	*	*	*	*	*
Brazils																					*	*	*	**										
Buenos Ayres																	*	*	*	*	*	*		**	*	*	*	*	***	*		*	*	*
Demerara															*				*				**	*					*					
Montevideo																	*	**	**			**	**	**	***	****	***	**	****	****	****	****	****	**
Rio de Janeiro																					*	**	**		***	****			**	**	****	**	***	***
OTHER	*	**		*	**	*	*	*	*	*	*	*		*	*				*	**	**	***	***			**	**	*	*		*		**	**

THE ORIENT

In the course of the eighteenth century significant quantities of textiles, tea and china were imported from India and China to Europe. The trade was managed by six East India Companies based in Lorient, London, Ostend, Amsterdam, Copenhagen, and Gothenburg.

The calendar of the trade was dictated by the climate. Because of the monsoons it was easier to sail eastwards in the Indian Ocean between April and October. This meant that the East India ships had to leave Europe between October and the beginning of April. They crossed the equator well to the west of Ascension Island, coming close to the coast of Brazil, and then swung eastwards, around the Cape of Good Hope. Once in the Indian Ocean there were three routes: between Madagascar and Africa, northwards, then eastwards; to the east of Madagascar, northwards; or eastwards, then northwards (see map). The ships arrived at India some eight to ten months after their departure from Europe.

The ships that sailed on to China went *via* Malacca or *via* the Philippines. They loaded cargoes at Canton in the late autumn/winter and aimed to depart between January and April, arriving at the Cape of Good Hope before the end of May. Once in the Atlantic they sailed north, touching sometimes at Ascension, then keeping to the west of Cape Verde, arriving at their home ports in Europe between July and September. As soon as the ships had safely returned, 'flyers' were sent out to advertise the auction sales of East India goods. These sales took place in the autumn. The Guernsey merchants regularly purchased tea at these auctions. (Tea was heavily taxed in England and the merchants found a ready market supplying smugglers.) The island merchants sometimes bought directly at the sales but often used a local merchant as an agent.

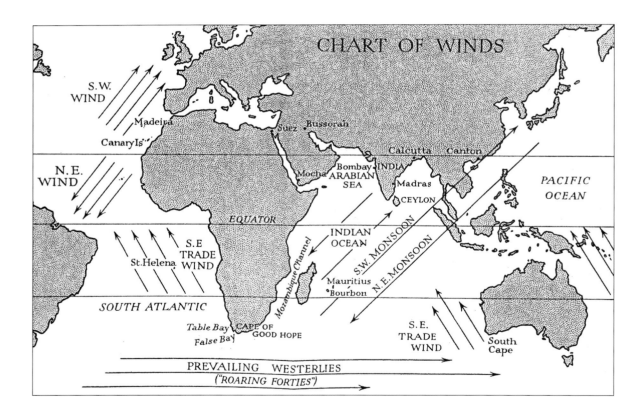

Fig. 4.2: Prevailing winds dictated the calendar of the East India companies.

The links between Guernsey and the Orient were not confined to cargoes. In 1750 Nicholas Dobrée (jr) visited Canton and wrote home to his grandfather, Nicholas Dobrée (sr). After thanking him for his kindness over the years, Nicholas continued: 'Mr Stuart who was here lately informed me that he had been at your house, & that you was in perfect health, which gave me a great deal of pleasure, as I really was afeared you was not well, having heard nothing from you during this long voyage. Cap. Le Geyt of Jersey is here, & has behav'd to me with a great deal of Complaisance' (IAS, 2Q-7-14 letter no 172, Dobrée to Dobrée, Canton, 25 Nov 1750). It is remarkable that Dobrée should have bumped into both Stuart (see p. 105) and Le Geyt (Captain of an H.E.I.C. ship) on the other side of the world.

Several Guernsey merchants invested in the H.E.I.C. Peter Dobrée (jun) invested in Company stock in 1767. Other investors included John and Peter Le Mesurier (Thomas, 2002, p. 40). Paul Le Mesurier was appointed as a director of the H.E.I.C. in 1784. There were also Guernsey men who served in the H.E.I.C. John Dobrée (b. 1766) initially gained experience in the West Indies. He then entered the service of the H.E.I.C. In 1785/6 he served on the *Ponsborne* as 6th mate. By 1791/2 he had risen to the rank of 2nd mate. In 1795/6 he served as Captain of the *Busbridge* and in 1802/3 as Captain of the *Carmarthen*. The ships were not directly owned by the H.E.I.C., the Company commissioned them. The records show that when John Dobrée was Captain of the *Busbridge* the principal managing owner for the voyage was Samuel Dobrée. Another Guernseyman who served in the H.E.I.C. was Frederick Le Mesurier (b. 1751). After serving as a seaman on the *Two Brothers* on a voyage to Honduras he entered the H.E.I.C. and served as midshipman on the *Neptune*, as 5th mate on the *Calcutta* (2); then, aged only twenty-one, as 3rd mate on the *Alfred*; as 2nd mate on *Lord Holland* (2); 1st mate on the *Colebrooke*. In 1779/80 he was Captain of the *Ponsborne* (Farrington, 1999).

The East India Company was not only a trading organisation, it also had an army. The Guernseyman Joshua Ahier (1775-1803) joined the 14th Battalion Native Light Infantry of the East India Company's Military Service and saw service in the East. He wrote home and his letter provides an interesting insight into his thoughts, ideas and values. Ahier, like Nicholas Dobrée, met islanders in the east (see next page).

Fig. 4.3: Hongs on the waterfront at Canton, where Europeans traded. (Aquatint, published Calcutta, 1802, James Moffat the artist.)

Malacca,

26th November, 1797

My dear Mother,

You will receive this by a ship which is expected here from China and goes direct to England from hence. The letter I wrote to you from the Prince of Wales Island, I hope, has reached you long ere this, with accounts of our disappointment respecting our Mahratta expedition. It has been a very great expense to the Company in embarking troops and taken ships at a very heavy expense. Admiral Rainur who commanded the Navy had sailed from Madras with the second division of our Army, when despatches arrived overland with news from Spain (next day, previous to the Consul sitting, a ship was sent after the Admiral to call him back) and to our great surprise, next day, a ship of war arrived at the Prince of Wales Island to recall the Army.

Our Regiment was ordered to proceed to Malacca and Amboyna. My Company was to have been sent to the latter place, but my having been ill there, I had the good fortune to meet with an exchange with another officer of the same corps. I have now been stationed here twice, and I think it is one of the best situations I know. Madras is a much prettier place but far more expensive, and of course, a subaltern ought, if it was in his power, to prefer a garrison, where he can live comfortably on his pay. I believe I told you in my last letter of my having met a number of Guernsey lads. Mr Mauger was here about a week ago and came ashore and dined with Larani and myself. I never was so happy as then. You know, my dear mother, when countrymen meet, which is so seldom, how happy it is for them to converse about Guernsey matters. Mr Mauger was at school with me at Mr Matthew Guerin's. He is now Second Officer of the "Sybille", a beautiful ship. Larani and I go and dine on board tomorrow. Don't be much astonished to hear some of these days, of my having taken a wife to myself. I find it's the only way to enjoy happiness and it also makes a great difference in the housekeeping way. I have seen a great deal of it at Pondicherry. An Officer who married the other day at that place to a French lady, told me, that he lives on what he could not do before, on his bare pay. I would not at the same time marry a girl that came from England. They never turn out to any good; too much extravagant are their ideas that a fortune could hardly maintain them, no, if ever I marry, it will be at Pondicherry to a French lady. They are so much like our own ladies in Guernsey, which makes me partial to them. I have not had a single letter from home these two years past. They went to Amboyna, and after my leaving it, they were sent back to me at Madras, and now being there, I suppose I shall have them by the time I receive other letters from you. A soldier does not know one hour where he will be the next. I should wish much to hear how Uncle Malby is coming out – I suppose as usual. What will become of him, I cannot imagine.

Mr Falla who came from England lately informed me that he saw him previous to his leaving it, and that he was the same way. Our ladies on that little island don't seem to get married; this is the country for those who wish to have a husband. The first thing they do when they arrive at Madras, is to dress handsomely with the latest fashion and then to the public room they go and show off their elegant figure in dancing in the best manner possible. Next evening they are sure to get a beau, and that beau never quits her till the knot is fast.

I understand, by the by, that our ladies have not behaved lately at all to their credit. Am told they are too partial to the red-coated gentlemen. It's all over with them when they form an idea of that kind in their giddy heads.

I shall conclude to assure you that I am,

 My dear mother,

 Your dutiful and affectionate son till death,

 Joshua Ahier.

P.S. Send kind compliments to my many friends. A happy Christmas to you and family, I wish I were one of the number. J.A

Source: Priaulx Library, transcript in Ahier family file

NORTHERN EUROPE

In the seventeenth century the Malouins handled large quantities of cargoes from the north. In the eighteenth century the Guernsey merchants did the same. **The Baltic** was important for a range of products. Norway produced pitch, tar, and timber. Russia gave hemp, iron, steel, candles and tallow (used for lighting, making soap, in tanning and as a lubricant). Sweden, Denmark and Holland each had East India Companies which offered tea, coffee, silk, handkerchiefs, calicoes and chintz at their auction sales each autumn. In addition, Holland produced gin, sail-cloth, cordage, and groceries.

Gothenburg was the headquarters of the *Svenska Ost-Indiska Compagniet* (1731 – 1806) which traded almost exclusively with China The greater part of the goods brought back to Gothenburg were re-exported 'to the level of almost 87% according to sources of the period' (Soderpalm, 2000, p. 99). The Guernsey merchants regularly bought through the agency of Arfwidson at Gothenburg.

Copenhagen was the headquarters of the *Dansk Asiatisk Kompagni* (1732 – 1830), which traded with India and China. The main cargo imported from China by the DAK was tea. Eckman acted as agent for Guernsey merchants at the Danish auction sales. According to Lukis, John Le Marchant's eldest son was established at Halsingborg – close to the Sound and to Copenhagen (Priaulx, Lukis ms. p. 27).

Hamburg developed as a leading international entrepôt in the late eighteenth century. During the American War some of the prize cargoes sold at St Peter Port (Guernsey) were dispatched to Hamburg. The merchant Rudolph Uttermark, of Hamburg, married into the Dobrée family at that time. During the French Revolutionary Wars Hamburg was used by neutrals to transfer cargoes between belligerent countries (see p. 8). De Boisgelin refers to its commerce as 'immense', Hamburg being 'the staple for all the merchandizes sent to the north of Europe' (De Boisgelin 1810, vol.1, p.55).

Amsterdam was the head quarters of the VOC (*Vereenigde Oost-Indische Compagnie*, 1602 - 1800) and the Guernsey merchants bought at their sales, sometimes through the agency of James Le Marchant. He established a house at **Rotterdam** in the mid-eighteenth century and shipped large quantities of gin to Guernsey. The business survived into the nineteenth century. Le Marchant also had a house in Amsterdam (Priaulx, 29109/408C, Lihou letterbook, 20 October 1779). Roche and Lihou of Guernsey established a partnership in Holland in 1776 (Nantes, AM, fonds Dobrée 2-A-20, Dobrée to Dobrée, 11 Nov 1776: 'Mr Roche & Mr Lihou notre voisin senvont s' etablir en Hollande en société ensemble'). James Bowden, Collings, and a member of the Maingy family also set up trading houses in Holland (Priaulx, Lukis ms. pp 25-27; private collection, Harvey letters, for the partnership of Collings and Bowden).

The Guernsey merchants had several links with **Ostend** in the 1780s. This port enjoyed a neutral status during the Anglo-Dutch War of 1780-1783 and it was proclaimed a free port in June 1781. The town experienced an economic boom: 'By 1782 over 50 foreign firms were settled there and 1,173 new 'burghers' had been officially registered. The population of Ostend increased spectacularly by 65 per cent from 6,000 to 10,000 inhabitants in the space of two years' (Parmentier, 1997, pp. 207, 209). Large quantities of foreign commodities (spirits, tea, tobacco etc) were shipped between belligerent countries, *via* Ostend, by neutral vessels. French and English merchants opened houses there, together with the Irishmen David Michael Gallwey (with connections in Bordeaux and Nantes), Edward & Philippe Connelly, and Murdoch & Co. The Guernsey merchants Reserson and Tupper opened a house at Ostend in 1781 (see p. 115 *et seq.*).

FRANCE

The Guernsey merchants acquired a large range of goods from France: wine, brandy, silks, cambrics, long lawns, lace, gloves, linen, millinery, tea, salt, candles, soap, East India goods, groceries, and canvas. For most of the eighteenth century Britain imposed a high tariff barrier against French goods. This led to fraud, French wine was shipped from Guernsey to England in pipes/*barriques* previously employed in the Spanish trade. In this way French wine was disguised. The Guernsey merchants engaged in cabotage with several Norman and Breton ports. In *le grand commerce* their interests centred on Bordeaux, Charente, Cette (Setè), Lorient, Nantes, Roscoff, and St Malo. They occasionally traded with Toulon (for brandy) and Marseilles (for soap).

Bordeaux was the leading French port in the eighteenth century, outstripping Marseilles, Nantes and Rouen. Between 1720 and 1790 Bordeaux's trade with the French colonies multiplied eight-fold. Bordeaux drew sugar, coffee, indigo, cacao, cotton, and rum from the colonies and became an entrepôt serving northern Europe. Products exported from Bordeaux included wine, textiles and manufactured goods. There was an important community of foreign merchants in the city.

Guernsey merchants had traded with Bordeaux from the medieval period. The island merchants sold coal and stockings there in the late seventeenth century and in the eighteenth century they bought wine and brandy (de Sausmarez papers; C. Huetz de Lemps *Géographie du Commerce de Bordeaux à la fin du règne de Louis XIV*, 1975, pp. 235, 419, 429, 432, 440, 447, 448, 530). Jean Martell and Jean Fiott (both of Channel Islands origin) set up a house at Bordeaux in 1723 and had a correspondence with at least ten Guernsey houses. 'Fiott and Martell were buying Margaux wine at 350 livres: in other words they had dealings at the top end of the London market (Haut Brion and Margaux). Wine was consigned directly to Elisha Dobrée in London. The house was big enough to have two clerks; and having two they had to decline to employ a son of one of the Le Febvres in 1725' (Cullen, 1998, p. 202).

In 1771 the Guernsey merchant Le Marchant recorded:

> There are about 8000 tons of claret (so called) shipped yearly from Bordeaux to Ireland. In those clarets it is usual at Bordeaux to mix nearly one-fourth of Spanish wines. The wines will not do for the Irish market without this mixture. The parliament of Bordeaux, nevertheless, thinking such practice lessened in proportion the exports of their own wines, prohibited those mixtures under severe penalties . The consequence was, that both clarets and Spanish wines were brought to this island (Guernsey); the mixture was performed here, and we profited thereby above 3000l. But after this experiment, the parliament of Bordeaux seeing their cellars and warehouses empty, and their people unemployed, prudently rectified their error the very next year. (Le Marchant, 1771, p. 57).

William Carey of Guernsey was resident in Bordeaux for eighteen years, eleven of those in business (BL Add Ms. 38389 f 144r, 15 Mar. 1786). He was in partnership with Galwey (IAS, Price papers refer to Galwey and Carey) and was part of the Hennesy clique (Cullen, 2000, p. 123). In the 1770s Guille of Guernsey had contacts with the Irish house of Johnston at Bordeaux. Johnston was part of 'a tight-knit Protestant coterie' much involved in the wine trade (Lyons & O'Connor, 2008, p. 99). A correspondent writing from Bordeaux to de Sausmarez (Guernsey) 29 Nov 1773 commented 'there is two or three Guernsey gentlemen here…a Mr Hemery, Mr Tupper & a young gentleman named Chepmell' (Sausmarez Manor archives, box 68K). Mr Hemery was, in fact, from Jersey (Jamieson, 1986, p. 315).

Cette (Sète) was the port that served the Languedoc. It exported textiles, wine and brandy. In August 1733 le Sr Pierre Bonamy, master of the vessel *le Goodfriend*, found himself in trouble over 3 *bariques de vin de frontignan* and 5 *bottes* of brandy left at Cette; the cargo had been bought by Mess Fressinet for Le Sr Jean Le Roy (CdA, vol. 10, p. 175, 11 Aug 1733).

Fig. 4.4: Bordeaux, an engraving designed by N.-M. Ozanne, published *circa* 1776.

Fig. 4.5: Cette, an engraving designed by N.-M. Ozanne, published *circa* 1776.

Fig. 4.6: Lorient, an engraving designed by N.-M. Ozanne, published *circa* 1776.

Fig. 4.7: Nantes, an engraving designed by N.-M. Ozanne, published *circa* 1776.

Cette supplied wine and brandy to Guernsey throughout the eighteenth century. In 1764, at the age of seventeen, Peter de Havilland was sent to Cette, to the house of Marc Fraissinet, a merchant with several Guernsey correspondents. Fraissinet treated him well and de Havilland remained there three years but returned to Guernsey to pursue a legal career, (Hocart, 1997, p. 5). The Guernsey merchant Brock was at nearby Montpellier in the early nineteeth century (see p. 203).

Cognac and Charente

Jean Martell from Guernsey joined Augier in partnership in 1718 in Cognac and supplied brandy to Guernsey merchants. At first the business boomed. 'At the end of 1720, in estimating the trade with Guernsey, he put the quantity variously at 1,200 to 1,400 pieces, and at more than 1,500 pieces. His estimate of his turnover (which suggests a rough 5,000 barriques) implies that he handled virtually all the business for Guernsey in 1720, and in October 1721 he stated that he was the only person loading for Guernsey and Jersey' (Cullen, 1998, p. 198). The years 1721 and 1722 were equally successful. Professor Cullen comments: 'the buoyancy of the Guernsey market, combined with the uncommon weakness of Dutch demand, turned Martell for a time into the most important house on the banks of the Charente' (*op. cit.*, p. 200). When Martell moved to Bordeaux in 1723 to join Jean Fiott (from Guernsey) in the wine export trade, the Cognac business was left in the hands of Anthoine Le Mesurier (from Guernsey). The Le Mesurier family may have been the first Channel Island family to have settled in Cognac, prior even to Martell (Cullen, 1998, p. 201). There was a crisis in the brandy trade in 1726 and Martell went bankrupt. Martell's network based on Cognac-Guernsey-London broke down, possibly through jealousies (Cullen, 1998, p. 204). Brandy was increasingly shipped to England *via* Dunkirk. However, the link between Charente and Guernsey became important again later in the eighteenth century (see Table 4.1).

Lorient was founded in the late seventeenth century as a naval port. Subsequently it became the official headquarters of the French *Compagnie des Indes*, trading with the Orient. When ships arrived home, the Company sent out a notification of the cargo. Then, two months before the sale, there was a second 'flyer' announcing the date of the auction. The sales were held in the autumn. Mignot de Montigny left a vivid description in 1752: 'The sales take place in an enormous room in which all the merchants are ranged in an amphitheatre. The auctioneers, seated at a desk opposite, conduct the bidding and declare the result by hitting a dish with a stick. These settlements take place very swiftly and in grand style. In a morning you can see goods selling for two or three million. A twenty-five-million sale lasts a fortnight or three weeks at most' (Haudrère, 1989, vol. 2, pp. 430 – 431, translated).

The Guernsey merchants sometimes bought directly at the Lorient sales. Often, however, they worked through French agents, quietly shipping their purchases to Guernsey. It follows that the official statistics of the French Company under-represent the Guernsey purchases. The letterbooks of Guille and Priaulx leave the impression that the India sales at Rotterdam, Copenhagen and Gothenburg were preferred by the Guernsey merchants. Prices at those auctions could be cheaper; and there was always a steady stream of Swedish and Danish shipping ready to bring a cargo to St Peter Port.

Nantes was too far up the Loire to be accessible to large ships. This brought about the establishment of small satellite ports nearer the sea. Nantes was deeply involved in the slave trade, in this regard ranking second in France behind La Rochelle. It conducted much trade with the French colonies, importing sugar, coffee, indigo, and rum. Exports included salt, wine, sail canvas, cordage, and printed cottons. Wealth led to the building of fine houses, many of which belonged to the important group of foreign merchants (Dutch, German, Swiss and Irish) resident in the city. During the eighteenth century there was a certain amount of trade between Nantes and Guernsey (e.g. the shipping of tea and brandy to St Peter Port); the links were strengthened when Pierre-Frédéric Dobrée settled there (see pp. 107-110).

Roscoff became infamous in the 1760s. The English authorities clamped down on smuggling from Guernsey; this did not deter the smugglers, it just diverted them from St Peter Port to the French harbour. British and Guernsey merchants then settled there to supply the smugglers. Le Marchant described the episode vividly in 1771:

> an unknown, an unfrequented port, the resort only of a few fishermen, has arisen upon our ruin, and now raises its head; so that from small hovels, it has now, in this short time, sundry good houses, and large warehouses, occupied by English, Scotch, Irish, and Guernsey merchants. These, on the one hand, give every incitement to the English and Irish smugglers to resort there; and on the other hand, the French government, ever attentive to catch at every national advantage, gives every encouragement to those merchants (Le Marchant, 1771, p. 34).

A different perspective was offered by Stiles when he reported in November 1770:

> The merchants of Guernsey having spared no pains to propagate an opinion, and induce a belief, that the smuggling formerly carried on from thence was wholly transferred to the free ports in France, I thought it my duty, during my residence in that island, to use every prudent precaution my favourable situation afforded me, to ascertain the state of the smuggling trade at Roscoff. From that enquiry I was satisfied, the accounts which had been given of it by many of the Guernsey merchants were partial and exaggerated; but nevertheless it did appear by the evidence of competent and disinterested persons that such commerce had greatly increased at Roscoff, that many English and Irish smugglers had resorted thither; that the rents of houses and warehouses were in consequence enhanced; and that every encouragement and indulgence were given by the French government to the illicit traders. It was moreover agreed on all hands that the goods were purchased by the smugglers with English guineas which were immediately forwarded to the mint at Paris.

> That the merchants of Guernsey to the number of twenty five, had entered into partnership and opened a house at Roscoff to carry on the business, and that an opulent and capital dealer in the island (whose name I then mentioned) had likewise established a house there for the same purpose; but that I was assured he had lost money by the enterprise, and that the great company (as they were called) had not profited by it. (TNA T64/153 Stiles report).

St Malo, on the north coast of Brittany, grew rich in the second half of the seventeenth century through its trade with the Baltic and Cadiz. Because the Malouins disliked the English, the island merchants carried cargoes to and from England for them. In the Augsburg War the Malouins took enthusiastically to privateering. The islanders had little option but to follow their example. When peace returned in 1713, the Guernsey merchants rapidly resumed friendly links (indeed, there is some evidence of collaboration between St Malo and St Peter Port even during the war years). Throughout the eighteenth century there was steady commercial intercourse between the French port and Guernsey. The research of Delumeau, Lespagnol and other French scholars has demonstrated that between 1716 and 1777, annually, there were somewhere between two hundred and five hundred departures from St Malo to Guernsey, and some four to six hundred arrivals at St Malo from Guernsey (Raban, 1986, p. 154).

Leading Guernsey merchants such as Thomas Priaulx, the Dobrées, and John Guille were well acquainted with their Breton counter-parts. Pierre Marin **Beaugeard** (1727-1792) was known by the Dobrée family. Beaugeard was one of the wealthy armateurs of St Malo, annually fitting out a dozen vessels for voyages to Africa, the Far East, and the Newfoundland fisheries. His business house was directed by his nephew Louis **Blaize de Maisonneuve**. Beaugeard's fortune was estimated at 1.800.000 livres when he became *trésorier général des Etats de Bretagne* in October 1776. He was a freemason, belonging to the lodge Triple Essence at St Malo and Parfaite Union at Rennes (Foucqueron, 1999, vol. 1, pp. 110-111).

Fig. 4.8: Roscoff, an engraving designed by N.-M. Ozanne, published *circa* 1776.

Fig. 4.9: St Malo, a postcard issued *circa* 1890.
This scene was only slightly different in the eighteenth century.

Fig. 4.10: A Newfoundland fishing vessel, of about 100 tons, from St Malo
(after an engraving in *Traité Général des Pesches* by H.-L. Duhamel du Monceau, Paris, 1782).

Fig. 4.11: St Servan (St Malo), with *Terreneuviers* in the harbour, from a postcard *circa* 1890.
This scene looked little different a century earlier.

Sebire l'aîné was a correspondent of Thomas Priaulx. This was Dominique François Sebire de Longpré, (b. 1717). Sebire was a *négociant* and *armateur*. He served as deputy for St Malo in the States of Brittany in 1769, 1771 and 1783; and was elected *maire de St Malo* on 17 February 1786. In 1789 he was created president of the *Conseil permanent* (Foucqueron, 1999, vol. 2, p. 1438).

The following five *négociants* were all correspondents of John Guille. François Pierre **Chenard de la Giraudais** (1725-1775) joined his father's business in 1732. He led a very active life, privateering and sailing to the Newfoundland fisheries. In 1757 he was received as merchant-ship captain by the *Amirauté* at St Malo. He became acquainted with Bougainville on a voyage to Canada. In 1760 he clashed with Byron in the St Lawrence (Foucqueron, 1999, vol. 1, pp. 343-4). Guille corresponded with his widow. **Dupuy-Fromy** (fl1763-1792) was one of the greatest of the St Malo armateurs, with a particular interest in fishing (Roman, 2001, p. 59). **Marion Brillantais** was a timber merchant, and shipbuilder for the French Royal Navy: *Il peut fournir 100.000 pieds cubes de bois aux chantiers de Brest et conserver 80.000 autres à Saint-Malo, ce qui represente un capital de 400.000 livres.* He was also a privateering *armateur*. On the eve of the Revolution his captain Landolphe took possession of the isle of Borodo (Foucqueron, 1999, vol. 2, pp. 1054-5). Denis Francois Robert des Saudrais called Robert le Jeune (signed as **Mennais Robert** and other styles) (1744-1829) was another *négociant* known to Guille (Foucqueron, 1999, vol. 2, p. 1344). Pierre Jacques **Meslé du Grand-Clos** (1728-1806) was one of the most influential *armateurs* in St Malo and also one of the wealthiest. He was one of only two Malouin *armateurs* to make a fortune during the Seven Years War. This allowed him to build up his business so that it became the leading house of St Malo. In the course of just over thirty years he sent out thirty-five ships to the slave trade, thirty to the Antilles, several to the Orient. At the height of his activity he owned more than ten ships at sea in one year. His address book included more than seven hundred names, with addresses stretching from Canton to the West Indies (Roman, 2001, pp. 65-66). In December 1793, during the Revolution, he evaded arrest by escaping from his bedroom, making his way to the quays, and then, *via* St-Coulomb and the Channel Islands, he reached Southampton and London (Foucqueron, 1999, vol. 2, p. 1078).

The Guernsey merchants were dealing with some of the wealthiest merchant families. Meslé de Grandclos, Dupuy Fromy père, Mennais Robert fils, and Blaise de Maisonneuve ranked among the twelve richest Malouins in 1790 (Roman, 2001, p.205). They – and their colleagues - were importing 'luxury' products from the Americas – sugar, coffee, and cotton. And yet they often left the re-export to others. Roman comments: 'An examination of the departures from St Malo in 1775-1776 offers the proof. Malouin vessels are almost absent from this traffic. Small caboteurs from the Channel Islands (e.g. *les Deux Frères* of Guernsey, 9 tons) made ten to twelve trips annually, guaranteeing a veritable shuttle-service of tea, sugar, and coffee between St Malo and Dunkirk' (Roman, 2001, p. 86, translated). Guernsey shipowners were serving the Malouins much as they had in the seventeenth century – as trusted 'middle-men'.

GUILLE'S TOUR OF FRANCE

In the summer of 1787 a member of the Guille family (probably George) made a business tour of France. From his manuscript journal (Priaulx Library) we can infer that he was interested in meeting merchants and that he wanted to develop his stocking export trade. He kept a note of the merchants that he met and he frequently recorded the names of those who had provided introductions. Three aspects immediately emerge. First, he owed introductions to at least nine Guernsey merchants: Carteret Priaulx, Mathew De Carteret, William De Jersey, Thomas Dobrée, Peter Frère, Nicholas Guille, Richard Guille, M. Métivier, and Peter Mourant. These merchants had connections throughout the west of France. Secondly, the St Malo merchants were helpful in providing introductions. Thirdly, some of the contacts were prominent Protestant bankers. We note in particular the Dutch banker Vandernyver; the house of Girardot Haller (formed by the partnership between Emmanuel Haller and Jean Girardot de Marigny, the official bank for the French government); and the Swedish bankers Ferbere Frères (Swedish bankers who settled in Paris in 1782). These influential bankers were part of *la banque protestante en France* analysed by Luthy.

Guille's notebook reveals what interested him. In a minor way we get to see eighteenth-century France through the eyes of a Guernsey *négociant*. The following is a summary of his tour. (It should be noted that all of the comments were made by Guille, there are no editorial interpolations.)

Guille crossed from Guernsey to Jersey and arrived at **St Malo**. At **Chateauneuf**, 3 leagues from St Malo, Guille saw a citadel with garrison room for 1800 troops and camping space for seven to eight thousand. The citadel was camouflaged by trees. Guille surmised that it had been built to serve as a safe retreat in the event of an invasion of Brittany. At **Rennes** he observed that the manufacture of cloth was very considerable. At **Josselin**, he admired 'gros draps qui sont bien bons'. He was not impressed with the state of commerce at **L'Orient** 'le commerce nous a paru fort peu de chose'. He opined that the interests of Nantes, la Rochelle, and Bordeaux were hostile to the privileged position of the *Compagnie des Indes* at Lorient.

At **Nantes** he found plenty of business, despite the failure of nine or ten houses. Guille noted the slave trade, sugar, coffee, indigo and cargoes from West Indies; the manufacture of printed cottons. He also observed that it was an entrepôt where foreign cargoes destined for the Guinea coast could be deposited without having to pay dues to the *fermiers généraux*. Guille saw this as prejudicial to French producers as they could not be as competitive as the Swiss and English (who supplied fabrics). Guille admired the women of Nantes for their business skill, they were often in charge of enterprises.

Guille considered **la Rochelle** unhealthy because the arcades prevented the free circulation of air. The chief commerce was the slave trade (30 or 40 expeditions to the Guinea coast with return cargoes of sugar and coffee from the West Indies). The town had a considerable interest in faïencerie but Guille thought that it would suffer from English competition, English goods being better and cheaper. At **Rochefort** ('port du roi') Guille observed much construction, but there was little business with foreigners (apart from the sale of some brandy). Guille noted that foreigners (if not English) could see the fortifications. The town was unhygenic because of the marshy ground of the province of Aunis.

Guille commented that twenty thousand pieces of brandy were exported annually from **Charente**, much to England. He found the river very pretty, there were always 18 feet of water. **Sainte**, the capital of Saintonge, he considered a 'petite ville' with a population of five to six thousand. The inhabitants produced brandy which was passed onto Charente. The manufacture of serge employed 100 to 150 people and there was a hospital which manufactured cottons and basins. He looked at the ruins of an ancient amphitheatre. Part of the journey to Bordeaux was by boat. As he waited in his carriage, Guille looked out at some French women who were soaked to the skin by a rain shower.

At **Bordeaux** Guille admired the architecture and lay-out of the city, particularly the statue of Louis Le Grand on a superb horse. He believed that the Eden Treaty would not hurt Bordeaux; since May some 600 to 700 *thonneaux* of wine had been sent to England. Guille found **Toulouse** a fine town suitable for business but felt that the inhabitants did not make much effort to realise the potential. He saw some dessicated cadavers at the Eglise des Cordeliers. Guille admired the Canal du Midi and its lock system at **Beziers. Cette**, the only sea-port of Languedoc, had considerable commerce, with 150 to 200 shipments of wine and brandy for England, Holland, Flanders, and the Baltic. The locals transported wines and brandies in their ships to the Americas, returning with tobacco for the *férmiers*.

There was much business at **Montpellier** in cotton, verdegris, crème de tartare. Guille found the air healthy and he considered the promenade one of the most handsome in France. He liked the bronze statue of Louis xiv on a horse and the *chateau d'eaux*. **Nisme** boasted a fine silk manufacture; the town had a population of two thousand, two thirds of whom were involved in the manufacture of silk stockings. Guille admired the superb Roman monuments. **Beaucaire**, a small town, hosted a great fair (22 July – 30 July) attended by merchants from all over France, and by Spanish, Genoese, Italians and Neapolitans. The fair had been in decline for some years. It was visited by between one hundred thousand and three hundred thousand people.

Guille admired the planning of the new town at **Marseilles**; the port was one of the best in France, holding six to seven hundred large vessels. Guille noted the activity of the *Compagnie des îles* and the manufacture of soap. From Marseilles to **Toulon** Guille travelled on horse-back. He found this tiring but he enjoyed the fine mountain scenery. He noted the trade in brandy and oil at Toulon. At **Aix** Guille felt that he had some hope of supplying stockings from Guernsey. He commented on the fine olive oil made in the vicinity.

Lyons had a population of three hundred thousand, two hundred thousand of whom were involved in silk working. Guille saw the advantage of two rivers and the usefulness of the rapidity of the Rhone for powering mills. He found the interior of the city dirty and unhealthy (because of the dyes). He admired the fine houses on quays and noted that the Jesuits had in Lyons one of finest libraries in Europe. However, he regretted the lax morals of men and women (prostitutes and decent women) bathing together in the river Saone. And so to **Paris,** where he went sight-seeing. He admired the porcelain manufactured at **Sèvres** and reflected on the perils risked by those who travel to China. **Versailles** impressed Guille with its gardens, fountains and labyrinth.

At **Rouen** Guille observed that eighty thousand of the population (of one hundred thousand in total) were employed in textile manufacture. He felt that the Eden treaty, recently signed, would hit Rouen badly. The French minister who negotiated the treaty ignored the advice of the French chambers of commerce. Guille contrasted the English character with the French. The English industrialist did not despise the business that brought him wealth *(Un fabriquand qui a gagné une fortune par ses fabriques ne daidaigne pas son premier établissement)* whereas in France the man who had amassed the equivalent of three, four or five thousand pounds sterling withdrew from business. The French minister should have realised that the French could not compete, especially given the English use of large machines in the textile industry, producing goods preferred in European markets and elsewhere in the world.

GUILLE TRAVELS FROM GUERNSEY TO SPAIN

In September 1791 the merchant John Guille travelled to Barcelona with his sons George and Williám. He made brief notes of his travel expenses and from these it is possible to reconstruct some aspects of the journey. I have expanded Guille's rather bald document by quoting details from a contemporary travel guide to France: *The Gentleman's Guide in his Tour through France*, London, 1787. These additions are given within square brackets, in italics.

Before leaving Guernsey Guille made an inventory of the clothes that he took: 12 shirts, 3 night shirts, 9 cravats, 12 silk handkerchiefs, 3 cambric handkerchiefs, 12 pairs silk stockings, 6 pairs of cotton stockings, 7 pairs of breeches, 2 pairs drawers, 7 waistcoats, 4 undercoats, 3 coats, 1 great coat, 2 pairs of shoes, 1 pair boots. He was armed with bills of exchange and 200 gold guineas. [*Into a small trunk I would have you put a dozen of shirts; they ought to be much coarser than the English in general wear them; otherwise, their slovenly manner of washing (which is by beating them with a board against a stone in cold water) will soon oblige you to buy others; half a dozen pair of shoes; a pair of boots, and buckskin breeches, would be requisite; as the French leather is not proof against water: your stockings should be silk, which is the fashion of France, even among the meanest mechanics.*]

They left on 29 September 1791. The passage from Guernsey cost 5 guineas and Guille tipped the sailors 5 shillings. At Portland it cost 3 shillings to be ferried ashore. Supper, bed, breakfast and servant at Portland came to 9/2. The following day they made their way to Weymouth by cart. The chaise from Weymouth to Dorchester cost 5 shillings and 6d, the fastening of the luggage involved another 6d for the postillion.

The fare from Dorchester to London in the mailcoach, luggage included, came to £4-18-0. Dinner at Blandford was 7 shillings. By 'dinner' Guille understands our 'lunch'. Supper was taken at Wolverton.

On arrival in London there were expenses of 4 shillings at the *Swan and Two Neck*. 2 October was a busy day. George required the services of Dr Cline (2 guineas). George received a further £1-8-6 (16 shillings being for stockings, 2 shillings for a book). There were some coach journeys in London (1 shilling; and 4 shillings and 6d), a knife cost 6d, sealing wax and an inkstand another 1/6, washing 2 shillings. The major expense was 'cost of coach 59.15.6' – this coach took them from London to Barcelona, for we hear no more references to the hire of coaches or the paying of fares; instead we meet payment for horses and turnpikes.

On 6 October the party set out from London and travelled *via* Dartford to Rochester where they took supper (12/6). Breakfast on 7 October came to 2/6. There were changes of horses for Sittingbourne (£1-4-6), then for Canterbury (1-16-6); and finally for Dover (£1-16-6). When they arrived at Dover they took dinner at Payne's Hotel. Embarking the carriage cost 18/6 and the passage on 8 October was £2-5-0 with a further payment to Captain Mailors of 7/-. Disembarking the coach at Boulogne came to only 7/6 but 5 shillings had to be spent mending it. Ever the conscientious book-keeper, Guille noted that he had spent 'as far as Boulogne' £27-11-7 (not including the purchase of the coach in London).

On 8 October they travelled *via* Samers - Cormont - Montreuil - Nampont to Bernay where they ate supper. On 9 October they proceeded *via* Nouvion - Abbeville [*a neat pretty town, and not far distant from the sea; well inhabited by people of fashion*] - Ailly le haut Clocher -Flixcourt - Pecquigny - Amiens [*very disagreeable in the autumn, or in winter, as it rains most of the time*] - Hebecourt - Flers - Breteuil. During the course of the day they bought jelly at Abbeville, dinner at Flixcourt, grapes at Amiens and finally supper at Breteuil.

On 10 October they went to Vavigny - St Just - Clermont - Chantilly [*it is well worth your while to stop at Chantilly, and visit the palace, park, and gardens of the Prince of Conde…. you will frequently see in the road, several miles distant from this terrestrial paradise, hares, partridges, and pheasants, enjoying, with the most undaunted assurance, the happy protection of this absolute prince*] and on to Paris.

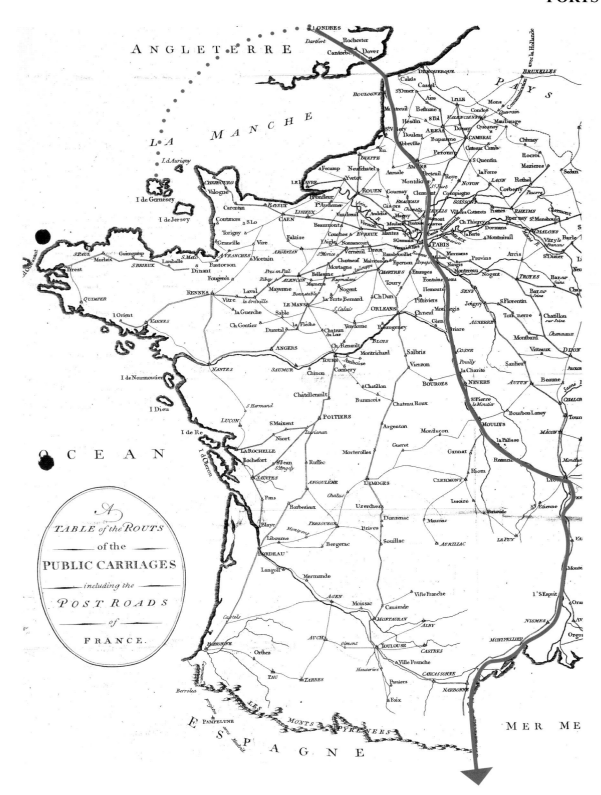

Fig. 4.12: Guille's route from Guernsey to Spain
(map from *The Gentleman's Guide in his Tour through France*, London, 1787).

The next day in Paris was very busy, with money spent at the hairdresser, on books, at a play, in a coffee-house, mending the carriage, buying a hat for George, paying for washing, tea, breakfast, dinner, suppers. William visited an apothecary. They lodged at the *Grand Leon*.

The following day, 12 October, they headed south [*this road by the Bourbonnois is firm and flat, and you travel faster than on the other through Burgundy, except in winter or very wet weather, when you have the resource of the pavement on the latter*]. They ate 'fowl and grapes on the road' and supped at Nemours. The 13 October saw them dining at Puit la lande and arriving for supper at Briare [*a little town on the Loire… remarkable only for the canal of communication from the Loire to the Seine. There is a pleasant walk between this canal and the river. The roads are very fine on the banks of the Loire*]. On 14 October there was *bouillon* at Cosne, supper at Nevers [*a considerable town, prettily situated on the Loire, over which is a handsome bridge; the approach from Moulins is magnificent*]. The next day (15 October) they made the passage across the Loire and ended the day at Moulins [*capital of the Bourbonnois, on the river Allier, in a pleasant fertile plain, almost in the centre of France. It has a considerable commerce in cutlery wares*]. On 16 October they went to Roanne [*in an extensiver plain. Here the Loire begins to be navigable to its mouth*]. On the 17 October they took *bouillon* at Tarare and reached Lyons where they stayed for a while.

At this juncture Guille omits dates and we get only a sketchy notion of the journey. There were expenses on the Rhone and so it appears that they travelled south, with their coach, on a boat [*You will find the Diligence par eau equally as commodious as the last you was in; it stops to dine, sup, and lie; and for eight livres will conduct you thither in great safety in three days; so that you may easily judge of the rapidity of the Rhone, as no sail is made use of, except now-and-then, to avoid a shoal: when you get a little below Lyon, you will be highly delighted with various and beautiful prospects; the hills on each side are immensely high; castles on the very summit of several of them, which, though barren in themselves, are made (by industry and hard labour) as fertile as the island of Calypso: here peaches, figs, almonds, plums, nectarines, pomegranates, and, in short, all the fruit that can flatter the taste, or please the eye, are in the greatest abundance; and vines heavily loaded under their purple produce, artfully hanging in festoons from tree to tree, and imposing on their more sturdy neighbours a fatigue which their own weakness renders them incapable of supporting*].

At Montpellier they saw a play. Thence they travelled on to Narbonne and Perpignan, where William required the services of a surgeon; – supper at Roanne.

By 27 October they had reached the custom house office at Jonquierra where they paid a toll and supped. On 28 October they dined at Figueres and supped at Colduvol. They reached Mataro on 30 October. The last day of the month saw them arriving safely at Barcelona, home of the firm of Gregory & Guille.

(*Source:* manuscript notes, private collection.)

SPAIN

In the seventeenth and early eighteenth centuries the Guernsey merchants regularly carried their catches of Newfoundland cod to the Basque coast. Having sold the fish there, they returned to Guernsey/England with cargoes of wool, iron or wine. When St Peter Port was being developed as an entrepôt in the mid-eighteenth century, this pattern changed. Guernsey vessels increasingly took fish, and later wheat, to the Mediterranean coast of Spain, to Barcelona in particular. There were valuable cargoes to be loaded in Spain - wine, brandy, soap, silk, and velvet.

Several Guernsey merchants set up trading houses in Spain to make the best of the opportunities. Nicholas Guille from Guernsey joined Mark Gregory of London to establish the house of Gregory & Guille at Barcelona; William de Vic Tupper and Nicholas Reserson, both from Guernsey, set up the house of Reserson & Tupper in the same city. In the late eighteenth century they – and others – shipped large quantities of brandy and wine to Guernsey. This trade was disrupted by wars between Spain and Britain. However, neutral shipping – mainly Danish and Swedish – carried cargoes from Spain to Guernsey during these years.

In the early nineteenth century, at the height of the Napoleonic Wars, the trading patterns changed yet again. The Guernsey merchants employed their ships to take Spanish (and Mediterranean) produce to South America. A young generation of Guernsey merchants – Tuppers, Careys, Kennett, Métivier and others - settled in Spain to make their fortunes. Most of their activity centred on Catalonia (Barcelona and Tarragona) and this is considered below. First we shall notice other Spanish ports linked to the Guernsey trade.

The Guernsey merchants handled a large volume of wine from **Malaga**. They bought both white wine (known as 'mountain') and red (known as 'tent', a corruption of *vino tinto*). In the 1770s – 1780s the Guernsey merchants William Bell, Jean Carey (senr), J. & T. Le Marchant, T. Le Marchant (fs James), Wm Le Marchant, James Lihou, David Thompson, and E. Tupper were supplied by Clies & Babington, Warre & Calvert (Culverts), Oliver Becket & Co, Patricks & Escott, Etty Offly & Co, Bearsley & Webb, Bowman & Franklyn, Askell Marsh & Co, Fitzpatrick & Escott, A. Marsh, Henry Child, Kirkpatrick & Escott (*Livre de certificats*).

The Guernsey merchants were importing wine from **Alicante** by the 1740s. In November 1748 Cornelius Huisson, master of the Dutch vessel *Degert Ferlereedes*, was actioned to pay custom on brandy brought from Alicante and unloaded at Guernsey (CdA vol. 12, 19 Nov 1748). John Guille (jr) received a small shipment of white wine in August 1776 from Fletcher Rodd of Alicante (*Livre de certificats*). On 16 Feb 1791 Jean Guille wrote to his son William that Maingy, de Jersey, Mourant and others were receiving brandy from Alicante (IAS Stevens-Guille papers). Carey & Co established a house here in the 19th century.

Cadiz, famous for its sherry, supplied Guernsey from time to time. In the 1770s – 1780s William Bell, Jean Carey (senr), David Thomson and Elisha Tupper bought from Jesson Welsh, John Welsh, Duff and Welsh, and Thomas Ryan (*Livre de certificats*).

In the 1790s Guernsey merchants were active in 'trucking' brandy from **Valencia** (see p. 70). Price, Tupper & Co. were established here in the early nineteenth century and corresponded with Carteret Priaulx (see p. 203). The Careys set up a house here in the post-Napoleonic era.

Ships occasionally arrived in Guernsey from **St Lucar** (San Lucar), a port near Cadiz. San Lucar produced a form of malmsey wine, sherry-style wine, and a red wine called vino carlón (J. Jeffs: *Sherry*, 1982, p.235).

CATALONIA

During the second half of the eighteenth century Barcelona relied heavily on the importation of wheat and fish. Even in the best seasons the region could not supply a quarter of its needs. Wheat had to be imported from abroad – from Canada, Virginia, Maryland and England. Vilar comments that during the period 1784-1790 the monthly average importation was 32,770 quarters, vessels under the 'English' flag shipping 30.8% of the total (Vilar, 1977, vol. 3, p.108).

Catalonia imported foodstuffs because the province had been turned over to vineyards, for the production of wine and brandy. Townsend recorded that Catalonia 'furnishes thirty-five thousand pipes of brandy, and two thousand of wine, besides thirty thousand bags of nuts containing three bushels each at twenty shillings the bag. Of the above, about four thousand pipes of brandy and some silk go to Guernsey and Alderney and the rest to France, all to be smuggled into England' (Townsend, 1792, vol. 1 pp. 150 - 151).

Guernsey merchants such as Reserson, Tupper and Guille were directly involved in the Catalan economy, shipping wheat and fish to Barcelona and exporting wine, brandy, fruit and some textiles. As war approached in the mid-1790s, the export trade became more difficult. The British consulate at Barcelona reported to Sir Ralph Woodford on 15 May 1795: 'as British ships are become scarce in these seas, several Danish & Swedish vessels are at present loading for that island' (Guernsey) (TNA FO 638/1). This is amply confirmed by the Lloyds Lists which record such arrivals in Guernsey. Some Channel Islands ships - the vessels listed below, for example, - visited Barcelona flying American flags.

Table 4.3 Channel Islands vessels flying American flags

Vessel	Master	Cargo for Guernsey
Liberty	Giffard	440 pipes of brandy
Sophia	Thomas Chiles	
Daphne	John Mahy	273 pipes of brandy
The Adventure	U Carrey	236 pipes of brandy
Phoebus	Ph Le Ruez	340 pipes of brandy
Nancy	James Toine	155 pipes of brandy

Source: TNA FO 638/1, 16 Jan 1796

The amount of brandy stored at Guernsey rapidly increased. The merchant Borràs at Reus explained that the high price of brandy (transported in Swedish and Danish vessels) in Catalonia in 1796 was principally due to the English smuggling trade, he had heard that over six thousand pipes of brandy were stored by the sea-side at Guernsey. (Segons el comerciant Borràs de Reus, <El precio exorbitante que tubieron nuestros aguardientes desde Diziembre de 1795 hasta fines de Julio del presente – 1796 – se debe en la mayor parte al grande contrabando que en todo aquel tiempo hicieron en ellos los Ingleses, pues aunque las expediciones salieron de estos puertos en barcos suecos y dinamarqueses con despachos para Hamburgo, han descargado generalmente en la costa y plazas de Inglaterra y mucho más en la isla de Guernsey, donde se dice existen todavía escondidos dentro del agua, cerca de las playas sobre 6.000 pipas de aguardiente'(J. Andreu, cited by Valls Junyent, 2004, p. 265. Borràs' observation is independently confirmed by other sources – see p. 42).

BARCELONA

In the 1770s the firm of Ford Curtoys supplied brandy, wine and silk handkerchiefs to the Guernsey merchants Thomas Dobrée, Elisha Tupper, Abraham Le Mesurier, Jersey and De Lisle, Nicholas Le Mesurier, John Carey jr., John James Macullock, John Harvey (Barcelona, AHCB, Fons Comercial, A79, A80). At the same time Joseph Morris & Comp of Reus were supplying the following Guernsey merchants: Henry and William Brock, Carey jr, Charles Carteret, Edward Collings, Paul Grut, Daniel de Jersey, Leonard Jehan, Lihou, Peter Mourant, John Perchard, John & Joshua Priaulx, Nicholas Reserson, Elisha Tupper; and Jos Laurany, Thomas Olivier, John Patourel and Nicholas Robilliard of Alderney (Barcelona, AHCB, Fons Comercial, B11).

The *Livre de certificats* shows that William Bell, Jean Carey (sr), Jean Carey, Pierre Frère, Jean Guille (jr), Eliza & Jean Le Mesurier, Duncan McBride and E. Tupper were buying wine from Barcelona during the years 1768-1788; they were supplied by Robert Herries & Co., Pratt Marti Baldich & Fuster, Gregory & Guille, Ford & Curtoys, Greene Ford & Curtoys.

The centre of the brandy production was Reus: 'a market is held there every Monday, to which come the brandy-makers of all the neighbouring villages, to sell their spirits, the most highly rated in all Catalonia...some of the leading business houses in Barcelona have their own premises at Reus to treat the spirits and other produce of the vast, fertile country of the Tarragona plain' (Segarro Blasco, 1994, p. 113, citing Lipp; translated from the French).

There were several small ports and harbours in Catalonia and the shipping of brandy and wine was frequently conducted from these outports – Benicarlo, Cambrils, Mataro, Salou, and Villanova. Salou presented problems. There was little more than a beach there and the pipes had to be ferried out to the ships lying off shore. Bad weather and poor sea conditions frequently made loading a long and tedious affair. In the early nineteenth century Tarragona completed its port improvements and took over from Salou as the principal shipping port.

GUERNSEY MERCHANTS in Catalonia

Eighteenth century

Nicholas **Guille** was partner with Mark Gregory in the firm of *Gregory & Guille*. This operated in Barcelona between 1769 and 1794, with a war-time break. (See pp. 66-67 for fuller details about Gregory & Guille). After the breakdown of the partnership Nicholas Guille continued in business, and was succeeded by his son John (IAS Stevens-Guille papers).

Nicholas **Reserson** went to Barcelona c. 1771; between 1775 and 1789 he was in partnership with William de Vic **Tupper,** in the house of *Reserson & Tupper*. The whole sorry story of this partnership is to be found on pp. 115 – 135. After his bankruptcy in 1793 Reserson remained in Barcelona. In 1819 he was recorded by the British Consul as a *negociante* of 48 years' residence living at *Calle Sn Sablo 54, Barcelona*. William de Vic Tupper traded for some years in Barcelona after his partnership with Reserson was dissolved. He returned to Guernsey and was killed in a duel in 1798.

Nineteenth century

The **Carey** family became very energetic in Spain in the nineteenth century. We find John Carey exporting wine in the early 1800s (Segarra Blasco, 1994, p. 135). In 1819 the British Consul recorded Devic Carey as a *negociante*, resident for four years in Barcelona, dwelling in *Calle de la Merce* (TNA FO 639/8). Devic Carey started to sign as proconsul in Barcelona in October 1824 (TNA/FO 638/3). Frederick Carey was styled 'clerk of the house of Messrs Kennett Carey & Co merchants in this city' in December 1818 (TNA FO 639/5). In 1819 he was listed as a *negociante*, resident for five years in Barcelona, dwelling in *Calle de la Merce* (TNA FO 639/8).

The Careys established a house at Tarragona *circa* 1813. In 1825 Kennett & Carey and Tupper & Co were respectively the first and third business houses in Tarragona exporting wine (Valls Junyent, 2004, p. 353).

Dobrée

P.B. Dobrée (= Peter Bonamy Dobrée) was in Barcelona in 1814, importing codfish from Newfoundland (TNA FO 639/4). He was recorded as a merchant in 1819, living in *Calle Nueva,* Barcelona (TNA FO 639/8).

Guille

John Guille (son of Nicholas Guille, see above) was active in Barcelona in the early nineteenth century. In 1811, as war raged in Spain, he transferred to Palma, Majorca. On 14 February 1812 he wrote to his uncle (John Guille) in Guernsey and explained that there was a ready market for wheat, flour, and rice 'Catalonia is starving & takes off in small boats whatever cargoes arrive here' (IAS, Stevens-Guille papers). On 22 December 1813 Guille sent out from Tarragona a printed letter explaining: 'The repaired Fortifications of this place now again affording the desirable Security to Trade, the operations with the Coast of Catalonia carried on since two years thro the medium of Mayorca, have resumed a direct Course, and concentrate here as formerly. Mayorca thus ceasing to offer any advantage in a Commercial View, I have removed to Tarragona my late establishment in that Island, the better to attend to my property in Catalonia.' (IAS, Stevens-Guille papers).

Kennett

Daniel Vardon Kennett arrived in Catalonia *circa* 1803; he was at Tarragona, 1808-9, importing cod from Newfoundland and exporting brandy, wine, cork and fruit to Guernsey and England (TNA FO 639/3). In 1809 he moved to Minorca (Tarragona municipal archives - Arxiu Històric de Tarragona, notarial record 2437[3]). By 1813 he had entered into partnership with the Carey family, trading as Kennett & Carey, in Tarragona (TNA FO 639/4). In 1819 he was recorded as *negociante* of 16 years' residence, dwelling at *Puerta Ferisa,* Barcelona (TNA FO 639/8). On 16 Dec 1833 Kennett wrote from Barcelona to Métivier that the house of Kennett Carey & Co had that year shipped the 'extraordinary' quantity of 13 or 14 thousand pipes of wine and brandy (Priaulx Library, Kennett papers).

Métivier

William Métivier was at Valencia working with the Careys by 1814. He worked in partnership with Kennett and the Carey family. In the early 1820s he moved to the new partnership of Métivier, Betts and Carey at Trieste.

Tupper

Having served at Valencia, Peter Carey Tupper served as British Consul for Catalonia 1815 – 1825, residing in Barcelona (TNA FO 639/5). He traded at Barcelona, *inter alia* importing wheat from Trieste, sugar and logwood from Havannah, pilchards and sardines from Ferrol and Carthagena (TNA FO 639/4). See chapter 8 (register) for full biography.

William de Vic Tupper (so named after his uncle) was unable to obtain a commission after the peace of 1815 and spent two or three years in Catalonia (Tupper, 1862, pp 38-9). It is possible that William de Vic was involved in commerce during his years in Catalonia.

The house of John Elisha Tupper & Co was working at Reus in the 1820s (TNA FO 638/3 f 202 v, British Consulate to J. E. Tupper, 10 Jan 1824).

Table 4.4 Passports issued/endorsed at Barcelona to Guernsey travellers

Date	*for*	*to travel to*
Mar 1785	W. Guille	Cette
Dec 1785	Charles Price	Alicante
Apr 1786	Nicholas Guille & Son	France
Dec 1790	Wm de Vic Tupper & servant	Cadiz
Mar 1791	George Guille Esq	France
May 1791	George Guille	France
Nov 1791	George Guille	France
Mar 1792	Charles Guille, William Guille	France
May 1793	Irving Brock	Madrid
Jan 1794	John Thompson	Madrid
May 1819	Wm Métivier	Guernsey
Apr 1821	Jos Brock	Tarragona
	Albert Carey	Valencia & Alicante
	Saumarez Carey and wife	Valencia & Alicante
	D. V. Kennett & lady	Marseilles
Dec 1822	Brock Tupper	England
July 1824	N. Reserson	Guernsey
Sep 1824	I. Carey	Alicante
Sep 1825	Brock Tupper	Guernsey
Apr 1826	D.V. Carey	England
Sep 1826	D. V. Kennett & family	St Quintin
Oct 1826	J.V. Métivier	
	J. Priaulx	
Oct 1826	Nicholas Carey	Alicante
Dec 1826	J.V.Métivier	Tarragona
Apr 1827	D.V. Carey	Tarragona
Sep 1828	Arthur MacCulloch	Valencia
Feb 1829	Devic Carey	Tarragona
Feb 1830	Devic Carey	England
Oct 1830	J. Carey, wife, two children	Alicante
Nov 1830	Chs Thos Brock	
Nov 1830	Hy Fk Brock	
Sep 1831	John & De Vic Carey	Guernsey
Aug 1832	Saumarez Carey	Alicante

Source: TNA FO 639/2, 639/8

The partnership of Gregory & Guille, Barcelona

The partnership of Gregory & Guille, Barcelona, was set up in 1769. The firm was founded by Mark Guille of London and Nicholas Guille from Guernsey. Details of the firm are to be found in some Scottish litigation. Charles Dempster, merchant of St Andrew's, brought an action against Gregory of London for negligence in the sale of a cargo of fish. The Assignees of Mark and Thomas Gregory and Company of London, and of Gregory and Guille, merchants in Barcelona, responded by outlining the history of the two companies. William Gregory was nephew of Mark Gregory.

...The petitioner, in some of his papers, was pleased to represent Mr Guille as an insignificant *foreigner*, and a mere *nominal* partner, whom Mark and Thomas Gregory had assumed into the concern merely to enable them to change the name of the company, for the purpose of drawing and redrawing. But the fact is this, Mr Guille is a *British* subject. He and *Mark* Gregory went to Barcelona many years ago, and established a house there, in which they had an *equal* concern, under the firm of *Gregory and Guille*. Afterwards Mr *William* Gregory, the present consul at Barcelona, was admitted a partner; and from that time the firm has been *Gregories and Guille*. The constituent members of the company of Gregories and Guille, therefore, were Mark and William Gregory, and Mr Guille.

On the other hand, the house in London consisted originally of Mark and *Thomas* Gregory, and a Mr Turnbull, who, just about the commencement of their correspondence with Mr Dempster, withdrew from the house, on getting some contracts from government, in which Mark Gregory could have no concern, being a member of parliament. This alteration was communicated by letter to the petitioner, with the signatures of the remaining partners, Mark and Thomas Gregory, which in future was to be the firm of the house. [May 31. 1785].

Although, therefore, the circumstances of *Mark* Gregory being a partner in both houses naturally made the house in London do all their business at Barcelona, and other places in the neighbourhood, through the medium of Gregories and Guille, and the house at Barcelona to correspond at London with Mark and Thomas Gregory and Company, in preference to any other house, and perhaps occasioned a more intimate and confidential connection between the two houses than would otherwise have happened, yet it is perfectly clear, that the two houses were not naturally and reciprocally partners, or one and the same: on the contrary, their correspondence, although confidential, was carried on with the strictest mercantile regularity. Their concerns were kept perfectly distinct; each house had vast concerns in different parts of the world, of which the other had no kind of knowledge, and in all their transactions their profits and their losses were entirely independent of each other. Of this many persons have very substantial knowledge; for the house of Mark and Thomas Gregory and Company of London have since failed; and neither the respondents, their assignees, nor any one of their creditors, (except the petitioner), ever thought of coming upon Gregories and Guille of Barcelona, as partners of the house in London; which they would have been most happy to do, if they could, as the latter house remains to this hour one of the most substantial in the Mediterranean...

Source: National Library of Scotland, Edinburgh: Session Papers (BCL. D2840).

February 11.1796 Answers, Assignees of M & T Gregory, to Pet.- Charles Dempster

Answers for the Assignees of Messrs Mark and Thomas Gregory and Company of London, Merchants, and Gregory and Guille, Merchants in Barcelona, and their Attorney, Pursuers, to the petition for Charles Dempster, Merchant in St Andrew's, Defender pp 4-5.

See also: 10 June 8. 1796 PET. – CHARLES DEMPSTER against INNER-HOUSE Interlocutor Mr Sinclair, Clerk. Geo. Tod, Agent. Unto the right honourable The Lords of Council and Session, the Petition of Charles Dempster, Merchant in St Andrews.

In fact the house of Gregory & Guille, Barcelona, was dissolved in 1793, although at least one of the partners continued to trade. What happened is set out in a quasi-legal letter written by John Guille in 1816:

…My uncle John Guille of St George in 1791 purchased in the name of his son George or rather George purchased of William Gregory for I suppose £st 2500 the half of Mark Gregory's property in the house of Gregory & Guille which William Gregory had just then bought of Mark for £st 5000. The admission of George Guille as partner was announced to the publick by a circular but without further explanation & as the transaction above mentioned was of the private interest of George Guille & William Gregory without any alteration of the capitals the books have continued the property in Mark Gregory's name & as to my father or myself we have no proof or document to evince George Guille's rights as above tho' no doubt he or my uncle must at the purchase have taken from William Gregory a formal notarial document of that cession. The failure of Mark Gregory and other misfortunes which occasioned the dissolution of Gregory & Guille in December 1793 have been followed by an unfortunate & litigious liquidation which to this day presents both William Gregory and George Guille debtors under the subsisting account of Mark Gregory with very uncertain prospects of how far the claims of the society still outstanding may become productive. The balance of the house & state of its concerns have been regularly communicated to my uncle & particularly explained by letter 21 March at his request and in reply to which he proposed to me that to terminate every concern between us relative to the accounts of Gregory & Guille for the concern of George Guille above expressed the family would give me a full discharge of the same & all claims value or not value on my making over to them the rents & sums I have in their hands & of which here annexed you will find a note so far as known to me…(IAS, Stevens-Guille collection).

The house of Gregory & Guille, Barcelona, was successful for most of its life. The Barcelona cadastre records the firm for the years 1769 – 1779 and from 1783 to 1795 (the gap was occasioned by an Anglo-Spanish war). R. Fernandez Diaz has calculated that it ranked third among the foreign business houses established in Barcelona and in eleventh position in the ranking of all businesses, Spanish and foreign (R. Fernandez Diaz, La burguesia commercial barcelonesa en el siglo XVIII. Tesi doctoral. Lleida: Estudi General, 1987, pp. 509 – 510, 533 – 534).

Much of its work revolved around the import of wheat, flour and fish to Barcelona. The vessels often left Barcelona in ballast and took on cargoes – brandy, wine, fruit, cork, salt - at other Spanish ports: Alicante, Benicarlo, Cadiz, Carthagena, Denia, Malaga, Mataro, Murviedo, Palamos, Rosas, Salou, Tarragona, Tortosa, Valencia, Vinaros. The ships then proceeded to Guernsey, and England (Plymouth, London, Hull). Other shipping went to Sète, Marseilles, Nice, Genoa, Leghorn, Palermo, Zante, Smyrna, Quebec, New York and Philadelphia. It may be presumed that Gregory & Guille arranged some, if not all, of the export cargoes. Source: TNA FO 639/1

THE MEDITERRANEAN

During the Napoleonic Wars the Guernsey merchants developed markets in the Mediterranean. Carteret Priaulx supplied fish to **Leghorn**; and pilchards (from Cornwall) and cod (from Newfoundland) to **Naples** (Priaulx, Carteret Priaulx papers). John Maingy, H. Dobrée and others established themselves at Naples (Priaulx, Lukis ms. p 27). Priaulx corresponded with Rigaud, Brock and Maingy (see p.203). In 1809 Ferdinand de Lisle, thinly disguised as a Dutchman, was in business in Naples (Hocart, 1997, p. 76).

Trieste emerged as an important market for the Guernsey merchants. Trieste was a freeport which served as an entrepôt for the Austrian Empire. In December 1819 the acting British consul at Trieste reported to his superior at Vienna: 'From 1815 to 1818 inclusive British vessels were sought for Odessa, Smyrna, Alexandria and to ports in Spain & Portugal: the returns to England from hence were principally in grain and pulse: many ships were chartered to carry fruit to Amsterdam, Hambro' &c and to fetch produce from the Brazils and the Havannah' (Private collection, letterbook, Brymer to During, 3 Dec 1819). Guernsey shipowners participated in the carrying trade from the Brazils and Cuba, bringing mainly coffee and sugar to Trieste and taking away cargoes of wheat and olive oil. The Guernsey merchants Métivier, Betts and Carey established a house at Trieste c. 1822 (Priaulx, Kennett letters).

Accident at Trieste, 1821

A dreadful accident happened on Thursday last. Captain Mahy of the ship *Caledonia* of Guernsey working in the hold, a case of sugar fell upon him & broke his leg, the bones of which were crushed to splinters & the fleshy parts shockingly bruised & torn – being in quarantine, it was some time before he could receive medical assistance: at my request the Board of Health admitted him to pratique though but just arrived from Brazil (the quarantine of which is 28 days) and he was transported on Friday to the quarters lately occupied by Holman in the Dogana Vecchia: the amputation could not be effected until yesterday at noon: I was obliged to be present at the operation, which the poor man supported with great constancy – I am sorry to say he is not yet out of danger. [*Private collection, Trieste letterbook, H. Brymer (Trieste) to George During (Vienna), 29 April 1821.*]

Fig. 4.13: Trieste in the early 19th century (after a print in an album, private collection; source not identified but probably from a continental book).

PORTUGAL

Throughout the eighteenth century, thanks to the Methuen Treaty, the English enjoyed an advantageous trading relationship with Portugal. Portuguese wine was fashionable in England; it was patriotic to drink port, unpatriotic to drink French wines (with their Jacobite associations).

From the 1740s onwards the Guernsey merchants shipped large quantities of wine from Portugal, some from the Algarve (Faro), Figueira and Lisbon, but much greater quantities from Oporto. The wine was shipped in Portuguese and British vessels. Wine carried to Guernsey in British bottoms for British merchants was recorded in Guernsey in a *Livre de certificats*. However, it is important to remember that the *Livre* did not record wine carried to Guernsey in Portuguese ships (nor wine carried for non-British merchants). The full story of the exports to Guernsey is to be found in the national archives at the Torre de Tombo, Lisbon.

No Guernsey merchants appear to have established themselves in Portugal (although John Lemprière in the Algarve bears a Jersey surname). The Portuguese wine trade was so highly developed, and so many English houses had been established, that there was probably little point in a Guernsey merchant trying to enter into competition there.

Table 4.5 Merchants in Portugal supplying wine to Guernsey merchants

---

Algarve

John Lemprière supplied William Bell and E. Tupper. (John Lemprière, a merchant in Lisbon, was appointed consul in Faro in 1761: See Shaw, 1998, p. 52).

Figueira

Tidswell, Richards, Tidswell supplied E. Tupper.

Lisbon

Branfill Goddard & Co; Stev Clark & Stephens; Clies Babington; John Fitzgibbon; Fowke Evans; Stephen(son) Holford; Thomas Horne & Co; Mayne & Co; John O'Neill; Robert & John Pasley; Richard Stert, SUPPLIED William Bell, Jean Carey (senr), T. Le Marchant, William Le Marchant, David Thompson, E. Tupper.

Oporto

Bearsley & Webb & Sandford; Oliver Becket; Bell Woodman & Babington; Bell, Woodmass & Babington; Bowman & Franklin; M R Braga; Clies & Babington; Clies & Baily; John Collings; Etty Offly; Etty Offly Campion; John Fitzgibbon; Ford Curtoys; Harris & Archdeacon; Hitchcock & Wood; Holdsworth Olive & Newman; Lambert Kingston; John Meckler; John Nevel & Co; Thomas Ryan; Stafford Cooper & Champaine; Stafford Cooper & Smith; Stafford, Tulk, Cooper, Smith; Stephenson & Searle; Swarbreck & Lambert; R & S Thompson; Thompson Croft; Tidswell senr/junr; Turner & Bayley; Warre & Culverts; Wells & Co; John Welsh; Wine Co Alto Douro; Francis Young; Townshend & Wettenhall SUPPLIED William Bell, Brock & Co, Jean Carey senr, Matthieu de Saumarez, William Le Marchant, Thomas Le Marchant fs James, Henry Le Mesurier, James Lihou, James Lihou jr, Peter Mourant, E. Tupper, David Thompson .

(Greffe, *Livre de certificats*).

ATLANTIC

Gibraltar

Thomas Lihou & R. Robinson from Guernsey established themselves at Gibraltar (Priaulx, Lukis ms. p 27). Robinson and Lihou (Gibraltar) wrote to Carteret Priaulx (Guernsey) on 29 May 1805: 'we sincerely regret the capture of your ship *Sarnia* by a Spanish privateer within sight of our port the 14th day after the departure from your island. The *Sarnia* was well defended and could have been saved by one of our cruisers in the harbour but they frequently allow British property to be captured. It is very damaged and will be costly to repair. If it goes cheap we will have her purchased for your account' (Priaulx, Carteret Priaulx papers). Gibraltar became important in the nineteenth century as a port at which ships' masters would receive instructions about the next leg of their voyage.

Madeira

Professor David Hancock has demonstrated that in the eighteenth century the merchants of Madeira developed an important wine export trade. They fortified their wine with brandy. Guernsey merchants became involved in this trade in two ways. First they carried wine cargoes from Madeira to destinations such as America. Secondly, they carried brandy to Madeira for the fortification of the wine. The Madeira merchants preferred high quality brandies such as Cognac and Armagnac; they considered Spanish brandy 'trash' and 'Channel Island stuff much worse'. However, during the war years of the 1790s the Guernsey merchants were able to dominate the brandy trade "trucking" low quality brandy from Guernsey and Valencia (Hancock, 2000, p. 145). Thomas Lihou & R. Robinson from Guernsey were also to be found at Madeira (see Gibraltar *supra*; Priaulx, Lukis ms. p 27).

Canary Isles

The Canary Isles were famous for sack wine. The Guernsey merchants Jean Carey senr and Thomas Le Marchant fs Jas are recorded in the *Livre de certificats* as buying wine from Robert Pasley there. In 1776 a group of Guernsey merchants petitioned the British authorities, objecting to changes concerning the importation of Canary wine into the British Isles. The merchants argued as follows:

> …For that several of the Newfoundland ships who sell their fish in the Canary Islands either bring their returns in such wines or get a freight of such wines for their ships for account of the British merchants, which wines having no other market than Great Britain & Ireland, the being deprived of such markets must put a total stop to the advantages accruing from that branch of their trade. And of late years the people of the Canary Islands have taken to the making of a dry wine called Vidonia wine, which tho' it falls short in quality of the best Madeira wine, yet is now brought to that perfection that a great quantity thereof has of late years been imported into Great Britain; and as the first cost thereof does not exceed for the best qualities twelve pounds per pipe, and that Madeira, Lisbon, and Sherry wines are purchased at or near 50 per cent higher, the encouraging of the consumption of the said Vidonia, Canary Wine, in Great Britain and Ireland must occasion a saving to the nation equal to the difference of such first cost.

> And as such Vidonia wine is mostly carried into the outports, none of which ports can take off a whole cargo at a time, the landing of such cargoes into the said islands of Guernsey and Jersey, and importing them thence into the ports of Great Britain and Ireland in small parcels is a great convenience to the merchants and must, as your petitioners humbly conceive be of no small advantage to the revenue, as well as to the British navigation, seeing moreover that by the Act of Parliament the 8th of His present Majesty's reign Chapter 23d no wine imported from this and the island of Jersey into Great Britain or Ireland can be entitled to the 12 per cent allowed for leakage, unless Certificates on oath are produced to the officers of the customs in Great Britain and

Ireland of such wines having been imported therein for British account and in British shipping.... (TNA TI / 520 / 59-61, 20 March 1776).

Maio (Mayo)

Maio was a 'salt island', with rich deposits available free: 'salt-loading operations at Maio were efficent, prompt, and frequent, and they involved large quantities' (Bentley Duncan, 1972, p. 185). Maio was visited both by some Guernsey 'Newfoundlanders' and by vessels on the South American run.

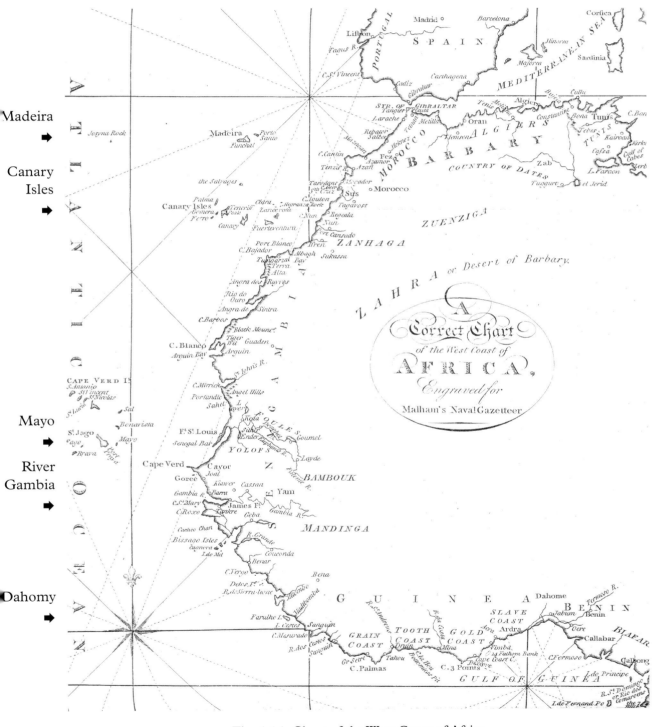

Fig. 4.14: Chart of the West Coast of Africa
(from John Malham, *The Naval Gazetteer*, London, 1799*)*.

AFRICA

The Guernsey merchants became involved in African trade in the mid-eighteenth century but it is not easy to assess the extent of that involvement. Much of the evidence comes from cases heard in the *Cour d'Amirauté*. The entries are brief and we shall try to tease them out.

The first episode concerns the **Anne Galley**, le Sr Thomas Ebsworthy master. The *armateur* of this expedition was Pierre Dobrée. He actioned Ebsworthy to make restitution for what he had received at Barbados from Messrs Morecraft & Co. It was alleged that Ebsworthy had acted contrary to a contract signed on 6 January 1740/41 and he was asked to pay £216:1:0½ Barbados currency, of the sum achieved by the sale of eight negroes at Barbados. Ebsworthy claimed that seven belonged to him and the eighth to the surgeon. Apparently Ebsworthy was allowed only four. For his part Ebsworthy made a counter-claim against Mr Nicholas Dobrée jr for a *botte* of rum. Witnesses called included Mathieu Bernard, Pierre Bailleul, Jaques Bienvenu, Manuel Perel, Henry Robert, Pierre Garcelon, Daniel Naftel, Jean Henry, Pierre Bonamy, David Sale, and Jean Martin. These men were presumably members of the crew; and the surnames of most herald a Guernsey origin.

On 20 February 1742 Ebsworthy declared that he did not have the bill of sale; Dobrée demanded the Mediterranean pass; Ebsworthy actioned Dobrée for a balance of £70 st; Dobrée demanded delivery of 25 elephants' tusks and a piece of camwood. The case was brought back to the court on 15 May 1742. Ebsworthy was variously charged with the misappropriation of some merchandise taken from Europe (presumably to Africa, for trading purposes); of acquiring seven slaves in Africa and selling them on his own account; of muddling merchandise; of signing the *livre de commerce* long after the appropriate time; and of failing to sign the *livre* about the dead slaves until 15 days after leaving Barbados (CdA, vol. 11).

Raban identified the *Anne Galley* as a letter-of-marque trading ship. It was commissioned in December 1739 when it was described as being of 180 tons (14 guns, 30 crew), the owners being P. Dobrée, N. Dobrée (sr), N. Dobrée (jr), W. Brock, H. Brock, J. Brock, Daniel Falla and P. Stephens (Raban, 1986, p. 146).

Contemporary with this case was that of the **Charles**. James Seaborn (the master) was actioned to render accounts of the voyage made in the *Charles* to the coast of Africa; Seaborn sued Mr Charles Mauger over a quantity of rum placed in Mauger's cellar. In the summer of 1742 James Le Marchant, Daniel Le Febvre, Thomas Le Marchant de la Plaiderie and Charles Mauger, previous owners of the *Charles*, actioned Seaborn over the commission at 5% on the proceeds of 6200 lbs of ivory; Seaborn's rum was to be sold.

Ebsworthy and Seaborn were both masters with Bristol connections. Seaborn was master of the *Amoretta* which went on a voyage from Bristol to Africa and South Carolina in 1731; in 1733 he was master of the *Lively* and went from Bristol to Africa and Barbados (where the slaves were sold). The *Lively* was apparently lost on its home run; Seaborn did not lack experiences (Richardson, 1987, vol. 2, pp. 15, 45). A Guernsey master associated with the slave trade was John Mauger. In November 1748 he was issued with a pass to take the snow **Cumberland** (50 tons) to Africa and America (TNA ADM 7/135 pass 434). Then in January 1749/1750 he received a pass to take the ship **African** to Guernsey and Guinea (TNA ADM 7/135 pass 1366). There is independent confirmation of the voyage of this ship. On 13 November 1750 Lloyd's List (no 1561) recorded the arrival in Barbados, from Africa, of 'a Guernsey Ship, Majorey'. In issue no 1567, 4 December 1750, a more accurate listing appears: '*African*, Mauger'. A contemporary manuscript gives details of the auction of the slaves transported by the *African*: one hundred and five slaves were sold at Speight Town, Barbados (see p. 83).

In 1751, the *Cour d'Amirauté* considered the agreement of Pierre Ougier to serve on *l'Africain* (Elizée Tupper armateur) to the Gambia on the same terms as le Sr William Coutart, captain of the **Gold Coast Galley** (CdA, 24 Aug 1751). This latter ship appears in the colonial shipping returns. It was of 135 tons (6 guns, 14 men) and had been built at Boston in 1744. It was registered at Guernsey on 20 August 1750 and belonged to William Brock. It left Jamaica on 14 March 1752 with a cargo of sugar, rum and pimento (TNA CO 142/15 f 124v). Lloyd's List (no 1730) for 19 June 1752 records that Captain Coutart arrived in England from Jamaica on 10 June 1752. In 1753 the *Cour d'Amirauté* heard a case involving le Sr Wm Coutard (sic) and Marie Guerin, widow of le Sr Wm Foster, over £30 sterling Jamaica currency, that being the sum entrusted by the late Foster to Coutard, the product of the sale of a slave at Jamaica (CdA, 4 June 1753). The fragments of evidence suggest that Coutart took the *Gold Coast Galley* on a triangular voyage to Africa – Jamaica – London.

To return to the *African*. It was a ship of 180 tons (TNA ADM 7/135 pass 1366) and was involved in more than one triangular expedition. On 21 July 1752 Lloyd's List (no 1739) noted the arrival in the Gambia of 'Affrican, Pinaux' from Guernsey. On 19 December 1752 List no 1779 carried the small news item: 'Capt Pineaux arriv'd at Gravesend from Barbadoes, spoke with the Dolphin Dewar, from London for Philadelphia, the 30th of October in Lat. 27 Longitude 54, all well'.

In 1986 Dr Jamieson drew attention to some letters-of-marque of the late 1770s concerning Guernsey vessels involved in African voyages (see table 4.6). The proposed routes point unequivocally to the triangular trade and the size of the vessels is compatible with slaving. The late Professor Minchinton analysed slave-trade shipping and observed: 'During the first three quarters of the eighteenth century, vessels of not more than 160 tons proved to be appropriate carriers in the trade for a number of reasons. Such a tonnage limited the capital investment involved; it restricted the number of slaves that could be carried by the vessel and hence decreased the amount of time spent off the west coast of Africa, where there were few harbours and the teredo worm posed a threat to the hulls of vessels; and it facilitated the disposal of slaves, particularly where the markets were limited' (Minchinton, 1989, pp. 61-62). The manning ratios are, in some instances, above average for slave expeditions but compatible with privateering.

Table 4.6 Guernsey vessels proposing triangular voyages

Name	Tons	Masts	Master	Crew	Owners	Proposed Voyage	Ref
Hunter	55	2		25	John Wood Richard Guille	Africa, West Indies	TNA HCA 26/62/50
Tartar	70	1	William Le Mesurier	40	Henry Le Mesurier, Peter Morant, Nicholas LeMesurier, William Chepmel	Africa, Barbados, Guernsey	TNA HCA 26/62/121
Tiger	80	2	Peter Tocque	80	John Wood, Richard Guille	Africa, West Indies	TNA HCA 26/64/16
Tartar	80	1	Cornelius Gosselin	40	Henry Le Mesurier, Nicholas LeMesurier, Peter Morant, William Chepmel	Africa, Barbados, Guernsey	TNA HCA 26/65/74
Revenge	80	2		60	Daniel Vardon jr, N. Maingy & Sons, John Wood, John La Sarre, Richard Guille	Africa, West Indies, Guernsey	TNA HCA 26/65/151

In 1792 the *Hester* 'left Bristol with 32 crew and took on 4 additional men at Guernsey between 3 November and 7 December 1792' (Richardson, 1996, p. 214). It was not uncommon for British ships to touch at Guernsey on their voyage out to Africa; St Peter Port provided cheap alcohol and other commodities suitable for bartering. On 6 April 1791 Jean Guille (Guernsey) wrote to his son William and made reference to a Mr Culla 'agent to a society for the Guinea trade, they send their ships once or twice a year in this Island for goods which comes from Holland for them to the address of Mr Bell'(IAS, Stevens-Guille papers). At about this time Mr Bell was subscribing for two copies of *The History of Dahomy* by Alexander Dalzel, a defender of the slave trade. Other subscribers included Paul le Mesurier and Havilland le Mesurier.

See p. 214 (below) for a further discussion about the slave trade.

NEWFOUNDLAND

By the late seventeenth century some four to six Guernsey ships were annually visiting Newfoundland. At this time Channel Islanders fished in Bay de Verde, New Perlican, Trinity, St John's, Cap de Raz, Renouz, Harbour Grace, Carbonear, Bonaventure, Trinity, and Salmon Cove. Under the terms of the Treaty of Utrecht (1713) the south coast of Newfoundland was ceded by the French to the British. There is evidence of at least one French crew being raised in the St Malo region at this time to serve on a Guernsey ship bound for Newfoundland. It may well be that a French crew, with experience of the south Newfoundland waters, was considered especially valuable by a Guernsey captain better acquainted with other fishing grounds (*vide supra*, pp. 3-4).

In 1716 Peter Carey and William Le Mesurier (owners of the vessel *l'India Prince*, Jean Chamberlain master) made use of a '*habitation*' at St Peter's belonging to William Taverner; years later he actioned them for payment of £14 sterling for the use of the *habitation* and two boats belonging to him (CdA, vol. 10, p. 186). In the 1720s, Peter Carey rented a 'plantation' at Grand Burin on the south coast of Newfoundland. On occasion Jean Lenfesty made use of the facilities without the permission of Peter Carey. Jean Lenfesty was actioned by William and Abraham Le Mesurier, previous owners of a habitation at Grand Burin on the south coast of Newfoundland, for the use thereof during the fishing seasons of 1728, 1730 and 1731 (CdA, vol. 10, f 188). Jean was also in trouble for the year 1729 when it had been let out to Mr Pierre Carey. Abraham and William Le Mesurier also acted against Mr Pierre Carey de la Brasserie for rent due for a *habitation* at Grand Burin in 1732 (CdA, vol. 10, f 191). Pierre Careye '*du marché*' was in court in 1733. Marguerite, wife and 'procuratrice' of le Sr James Hubert, master of the brigantine *le Blessing* actioned Careye for £50 st because he had failed to put on board the said vessel the people he was to send from Newfoundland to Guernsey after the fishing in 1733 (CdA, vol. 10, f 212).

Some of the voyages were distinctly unhappy. Apart from the hazards of the sea, there could be incidents involving the crew. In 1734 le Sr Pierre Perchard, master of *Le James*, proceeded against Jean Bouteiller (previously *contre-maitre*) claiming that Bouteiller should forfeit his wages because of his outrageous behaviour. On occasion Bouteiller was not fit to go fishing in the chaloupe and, when reprimanded, called Perchard a *bougre de chien*. (Elderly Guernsey folk remember that this was still a disgusting form of abuse in the early twentieth century.) Bouteiller's misdemeanours included taking Perchard's sword, upsetting food and neglecting his duty at Lisbon (CdA, vol. 10, f 196v).

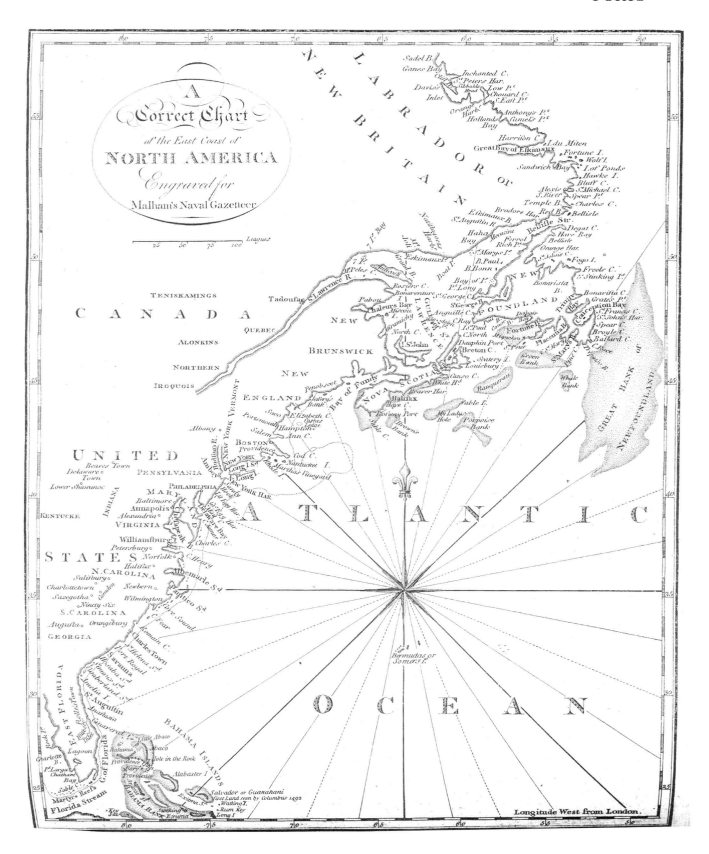

Fig. 4.15: Chart of North America
(from John Malham, *The Naval Gazetteer*, London, 1799).

Fig. 4.16: Fishing Platform
(from an engraving in *Traité Général des Pesches* by H.-L. Duhamel du Monceau, Paris, 1782).

In the seventeenth century cod had regularly been taken to the Basque coast but by the 1730s we find cargoes designated for Spain's Mediterranean coast. A court case reveals that Thomas Mancel, master of *le Wm* (i.e. Thomas Mansell, master of *William*), loaded 536 quintals of dry cod to take to Alicante or Barcelona (agreement signed by Mancel 15 September 1733; CdA, vol. 10, 207). In the second half of the eighteenth century, and in the nineteenth century, Guernsey vessels regularly took cod to Catalonia. The Guernsey merchants also transported considerable supplies of food, drink and tools to the fisherman and settlers at Newfoundland.

Fishing at Newfoundland

...The fishing season is from spring to September, and the principal business is done on a very large bank, near 150 leagues long and 50 broad, in the gulph of St Lawrence, near the island; this is called the great bank, and there are many others less considerable, which serve for the same purpose.

The fishing is of two kinds, fixed and moveable; the moveable fishery is that carried on by vessels that come to Newfoundland every spring, and return in autumn with the fish they have taken. The fixed fishery is that which is carried on all the year by the inhabitants of the island, and other parts of North America.

The cod is also prepared two ways; one way is to salt it on board the vessels that take it, and carry it into Europe, without touching at Newfoundland, and then it is called green cod. Of this sort we bring home very little, but dispose of it either in the bay of Biscay or the north of Portugal. The other way is to carry the fish on shore in shallops as it is taken, head it, gut it, scale it, and salt it, upon stages or scaffolds, which are erected for that purpose on the coast; then to spread it on the strand to dry. Thus dressed it is called dry cod, and is the subject of a very considerable trade, which is also of two kinds; the most simple is that which is carried on by the fishers themselves: They generally go out from Biddeford, Pool, Dartmouth, Barnstaple, or some other port in the west of England, in vessels which have nothing on board but provisions, salt, and fishing tackle, and they reach Newfoundlands early in the spring. In the other trade it is not necessary for the vessels to arrive so soon; but they are exposed to many dangers by the bad weather which happens in the latter season. They are freighted with merchandize and provisions of various kinds, which they barter with the inhabitants for cod that is already dried, and they pay in bills of exchange for the surplus. These bills of exchange have seldom more than two months to run, and are generally paid with great punctuality; and it sometimes happens, that the inhabitants of Newfoundland freight vessels on their own account.

An able cod-fisher will take from 350 to 400 in a day, but this is the most, and the weight of the fish, with the extreme cold that prevails on the Great Bank, makes it a laborious and painful employment. The vessels employed in this trade are from 100 to 150 tons burthen, and the crew is from 20 to 25 men. Those who deal in the green cod return to Europe as soon as they have 30,000, or at most 35,000, for they do not venture to stay for more, least those first taken should spoil.

The principal part of the cod that we take is transported to Portugal, Spain and Italy, or to Barbadoes and the rest of our American islands; and it is said, that at these different markets we dispose of 200,000 quintals of cod, which are supposed to produce 138,000 pounds sterling, net money, exclusive of the freight; a prodigious sum, which is all clear gain; for the oil and the offal of the fish, which we sell at the Antilles to feed the negroes, pays the whole expence of the voyage...

Source: Gentleman's Magazine, May 1750

CANADA

ISLE MADAME – ARICHAT – CAPE BRETON

Guernseymen were fishing at Arichat by 1764. After the American War of Independence the Jersey family of Janvrin was busy there. The Arichat & Gaspé Society was founded with Philip and Francis Janvrin in partnership with the Guernsey merchants Carteret Priaulx and Co, William Peter Price, Daniel Tupper, John Elisha Tupper and members of the de Lisle family. The Guernseymen Le Rossignol, Mr Paint, Peter de Lisle and Ferdinand B. Tupper acted as agents at Arichat in the post - Napoleonic era.

The Guernsey partnership of Thoume, Moullin & Co, in operation between 1817 and 1836, had a strong interest in Cape Breton. Ten of their fleet of twelve vessels were built there and engaged in trade in the West Indies, South America, the Mediterranean and Northern Europe. The partners were James Thoume, Daniel Moullin, Nicholas Paint and John Brehaut (Sarre & Forbrigger, 1991, pp. 173-181).

NOVA SCOTIA

A court case provides evidence of what may have constituted a typical cargo for the Canadian market. On 23 September 1761, at Halifax, Thomas Burnett (Commander of his Majesty's ship *Rochester*) seized cargo from a snow called the *Two Brothers*, Nicholas Le Masurer master, 'for clandestine and illicit trade having imported at the Isle of Bic in the River St Lawrence a quantity of wine and other goods..not having been shipped in England'. James Major, supercargo, appeared on behalf of James Le Ray, merchant of Guernsey, and claimed the cargo except thirty one hogsheads of white wine, one case of capers, one case of olives, four bales of almonds, nine hogsheads of red wine, one box of hungary Water, six small barrels of March, three butts of cider, fifty dozen pairs of hose – as own property. The snow was declared the property of James and John Le Ray and the snow and cargo were forfeited. The snow sold for £400, and the cargo for £2960-2-2 (Little, 1959, pp. 6-7).

QUEBEC

The Guernsey merchants developed a considerable trade with Quebec after its capture by the British in the Seven Years War. They took wine and spirits there and loaded wheat which they delivered to Spain. The letterbooks of Guille, Priaulx and Le Lacheur (*Pomona*, see pp. 150-170) and the records of the *Cour d'Amirauté* refer to the Quebec merchants Mr Brehaut, Louis Dunière, Gregory and Gill, and Charles Le Marchant.

Pierre Brehaut (1764 -1817) has been well researched by Stanley Brehaut Ryerson (*Dictionary of Canadian Biography online*). Brehaut sailed from Guernsey for Quebec *circa* 1788. 'Soon after his arrival he was hired as a cooper by businessman Louis Dunière. From 1792 on, he practised his trade independently. He operated a shop close to Quebec's port facilities, where the import-export trade was centred, and engaged now and then in sales of wines and spirits imported from Guernsey and the West Indies…on 19 Nov. 1800 he acquired for £3,250 Dunière's properties at the foot of Cap Diamant: a 200-foot river-front lot with wharf, warehouse, two sheds, and a stable. He was then able to set on foot a wholesale trading enterprise that opened the way to capital accumulation. In 1802 Peter Lemesurier joined the firm…under the name of Peter Brehaut and Company the partners specialised in the grain trade and the import of wine and spirits…Through commercial connections with Samuel Dobrée and company of London and Janvrin and company in Jersey, the firm reached new overseas markets in Ireland, Portugal and the West Indies'.

Marjorie Wilkins Campbell, writing in the *Dictionary of Canadian Biography online* throws light on **John Gregory** (b.*circa* 1751 in England – 21 Feb 1817). She suggests that Gregory may have been connected in Britain with Mark and Thomas Gregory, 'a London firm that had entered the fur trade shortly after the conquest'. Elsewhere (pp. 66-67, 136-138), we see that Mark Gregory had very close trading links with the Guille family in Guernsey and he was in partnership with Nicholas Guille in Barcelona. It fits neatly if Guernsey merchants were in correspondence with a relation of Mark Gregory in Canada. The *Dictionary* continues: 'He came to North America in 1773 and that year formed a partnership with the fur trader James Finlay, who had considerable experience in the field, having been one of the first British traders to reach the lower Saskatchewan River by 1766. Little is known of Gregory's life as a trader, but he did spend some time on the Sturgeon River (Sask.)..... It would appear that during the 1780s Gregory had begun spending most of his time in Montreal.'

Charles Le Marchant: an action brought in the *Cour d'Amirauté* by le Sieur William Richardson (master of *St George*) in 1777 refers to lumber loaded at Quebec in July 1775 by Mr Charles Le Marchant, acting for Thomas Dobrée. It was sent to Barcelona to Messrs Curtoys & Co, agents of Mr Dobrée, and was a substitute cargo replacing 100 *tonneaux* of wheat (CdA, vol 16, 14 Jun 1777).

Louis Dunière (1723-1806) see pp. 155-156.

Settlement - Newfoundland and Canada

Marion Turk has done a great deal to illuminate the way in which many Guernsey folk were early settlers in Newfoundland and Canada. The Guernsey merchants arranged their transport and subsequently helped to supply them. Turk calculated that some thirty percent of **Newfoundlanders** are thought to be descended from Channel Islanders. Newfoundland rings with the surnames of fishermen and settlers from Guernsey:- Allez, Bienvenu, Blondel, Bonamy, Carey, de Carteret, Collinette, Corbin...

Nicholas Paint (b. Guernsey *circa* 1790) became M.P. for **Cape Breton.** He promoted a town named Guernsey at Point Tupper. The streets had Guernsey names such as Saumarez, Tupper, Guille, Dobrée, Le Marchant, Mander and Paint.

Prince Edward Island (formerly the Isle of St John) was settled by the British in the late eighteenth century. *Circa* 1806/7 a shipload of 73 people from Guernsey, led by Henry Brehaut and his wife Elizabeth, landed at Charlottetown. 'Guernsey' place-names such as Carey Point, Fort Amherst, Amherst Cove, St Peter's Harbour, and St Andrew's abound.

When Bishop Charles Inglis visited **Gaspé** in 1789 he recorded that there were several brothers called Le Mesurier there 'natives of Guernsey. They generally catch from 10,000 to 12,000 quintals of fish every year and sometimes bring over 100 fishermen from Guernsey for the season' (a quintal is 112 lbs).

To thank Isaac Brock for his valiant defence of Canada in 1812 'the Canadian Legislature granted to Major-General Brock's four surviving brothers 12,000 acres of land in Upper Canada, **Ontario,** and in addition they were allowed a pension...The four surviving brothers were Daniel Delisle, William, John Savery, and Irving. The four brothers came to Canada in 1817 to see their land. There were 6000 acres in East and West Falmborough at the head of Lake Ontario, 1200 acres at Murray on Lake Ontario... The brothers sold most of their land, or gave it away to relatives'.

Sir John Gaspard Le Marchant (b. 1803, Guernsey) served as Lieutenant-Governor of **Newfoundland** from 1847 to 1852; he then served as Lieutenant – Governor of Nova Scotia (1852 – 1858).

Source: M.G. Turk, *The Quiet Adventurers in Canada*, 1979

NORTH AMERICA

The Guernsey merchants maintained a steady trade with America. They regularly bought vessels made in the colonies (see Table 6.3 and p. 144). They also traded with the colonials. Shipping returns reveal that they had a particular interest in Maryland, Virginia and South Carolina from the 1730s onwards. These colonies were abundant in timber, 'naval stores' and plantation crops such as tobacco and rice. The merchants carried rice, pitch, tar, turpentine, mahogany planks and staves from South Carolina; tobacco, staves, and planks of walnut and oak from Virginia; and tobacco, flour, flax, staves and planks from Maryland. The cargoes taken inward were varied. Several Guernsey vessels went to Virginia carrying rum, sugar and molasses from Barbados; at least one brought salt from Isle Mayo; other cargoes delivered in Virginia consisted of salad oil, Canary wine, 'Portugal wine', Spanish soap and cambric. Cargoes for South Carolina were equally varied: Madeira wine, port, 'Portugal wine', claret, brandy, soap, butter, rum, salt, Jesuit's bark, steel axes, necklaces, British beads, a box of hats.

The shipping returns are incomplete but they suggest that two or three Guernsey vessels a year were trading to and from the colonies. James Le Ray emerges as the major Guernsey merchant active in this sphere.

Table 4.7 Guernsey vessels visiting South Carolina, Maryland, Virginia, 1734-1764

Name	Type	Master	Tons	Crew	Owners
Alexander	brig	Wm Coutart	90	9	Isaac Dobrée, Wm Coutart
Dolphin	sloop	Daniel Perchard	30	7	James Le Ray
Dolphin	brig	Thos Le Page	70	10	James Le Ray
Economist	brigantine	William Rivoire	100	-	John Rivoire
Friendship	snow	Philip de Carteret	100	10	John Le Mesurier
George Galley	ship	Thos Le Mesurier	130	14	James Le Ray
Guernsey	brigantine	Thos Naftel	50	8	Thos Dobrée; Isaac Dobrée, John Carey
Hope	snow	Peter Ougier	100	10	James Le Ray
Hope	snow	Daniel Roland	150	15	James Le Ray
John	snow	N. Guille	60	8	Nicholas Guille & James Le Ray
James & Mary	brig	Henry de Jersey	80	9	James Le Ray
Kitty	snow	William Carey	150	11	William Carey
Mary	brig	Peter Bailleul	60	9	Henry Brock & Mary Brock
Mary	snow	Peter Bailleul	100	11	James Le Ray
Mary	ship	Robert Gover	130	12	Robert Gover
Mary	ship	James Falla	150	17	James Le Ray
Matthew	snow	Samuel Bonamy	60	9	James Le Ray & Jonathan Perchard
P/Wales	snow	Robert Gover	90	11	Robert Gover & James Le Ray
P/Wales	ship	Robert Le Viscont	150	15	Isaac Carey & Co
Rodney	schooner	Joshua LeGeyt	50	6	Lewis De Fraise
Southampton	ship	Hilary Mauger	60	9	Peter Carey & Daniel Perchard
Telemachus	ship	James Ballein	180	22	Wm & Thos (Le) Merchant et al
United Society	brigantine	William Solbé	120	10	William Solbé & Co
Two Brothers	snow	Nicholas Le Mesurier	100	10	James Le Ray, John Le Ray
Wm & Thos	—	Peter Olliver	20	5	Thomas Picot & Co

Source: TNA CO5/509-510, CO5/750, CO5/1443-1450

After the American War of Independence the Guernsey merchants became increasingly involved in the tobacco trade. When William Le Lacheur bought in Virginia he dealt, among others, with Peter Coutart (of Guernsey origin). Coutart was joined there by John Chepmell, probably also of Channel Islands origin. Gregory & Guille (Barcelona) imported wheat, flour, staves and rice from Baltimore, Chester, Philadelphia and Virginia in the late 1780s.

THE WEST INDIES & THE CARIBBEAN

The West Indies offered sugar, rum, coffee, and indigo. Several Guernsey merchants became involved in the slave trade and carried Africans across the Atlantic to work on the West Indian plantations. At least two Guernseymen acquired a plantation; others settled and worked as factors. During the Napoleonic era a 'secret trade' developed, the British government licensed vessels to trade British merchandise to the Spanish colonies from the Channel Islands, Gibraltar, Malta, Portugal and Spain (and to import Spanish goods). The Caribbean became a hot-bed of smuggling and of new trading possibilities.

ANTIGUA

The Englishman Sir Christopher Codrington established a plantation in the late seventeenth century and the island was soon given over to the cultivation of sugar. The Guernsey merchants bought rum here.

In 1730 Nicholas Dobrée, father and son, Charles Mauger and Henry Brock were involved in a dispute with le Sr Helier Le Pelley, master of the ship *la Marie*. Le Pelley had bought a cargo of rum at Antigua and had paid 3d per gallon more than if he had bought at Barbados. In turn the master actioned the merchants for payment of the freight on 13799 gallons of rum at the rate of £4 st *par tonneau*. (CdA, vol. 10, p. 42, 19 Dec 1730). Not long afterwards we find that Mr James Le Marchant ordered Louis Lambert master of *la Marie* to buy rum at Antigua. Lambert kept a *barique* of 119 gallons (CdA vol. 10, p. 206). In 1740 Wm Brock 'contre maitre' of *le Clapham Galley* proceeded against Pierre Ougier, master, for wages for his last voyage to Antigua, 19 March 1739 to 15 July 1740, @ £2:12:6 st per month (less one month and 15 pots of rum @ 15d per pot). The length of the voyage suggests that it may have been a triangular expedition (CdA, vol. 11, 4 Oct 1740).

At a later date George Betts settled on the island as an agent (Priaulx, Lukis ms. p 27).

BARBADOS

Barbados was colonised by the English in the seventeenth century and was developed as a major sugar-producing island. The Barbados shipping register covering the years 1729-1736 shows that it was regular for Guernsey vessels to arrive at Barbados, usually in ballast, and take cargoes of rum north to the Newfoundland fisheries (see table 4.8).

From a case heard by the *Cour d'Amirauté* in St Peter Port in September 1733 we learn that Jean Holland had had to pay a caution to the Barbados customs because Wm Warren, part-owner of *le Wm & Margueritte* (Holland previously master) had permitted a negro named Jacko to be hidden on the said vessel and taken from Barbados to Guernsey ('pour avoir le dit Warren permis qu'un certain nègre nommé Jacko ait été caché au bord du dit navire & emmené hors du dit lieu de la Barbade en cette Isle' (CdA, vol. 10, 17 Sept 1733, f 179).

Daniel Tupper and William Le Mesurier settled on the island at some time in the first half of the century. In 1750 William paid £702-0-0 for 22 men and 5 women at an auction of slaves held at Speight Town (see p. 196 for details of William). Daniel Tupper purchased an old slave for £15 (see p. 83).

In 1751 Daniel wrote from Barbados to Thomas Price (a Guernsey merchant) giving favourable news of the crop, quoting terms for rum, and commenting on a terrible *ouragon* that had wrought havoc to the cane plants on the adjoining islands (IAS, Tupper to Price, 16 Oct 1751, AQ 49/12-09).

Jean le Mesurier (1713-1792) was a plantation - owner in Barbados. In his will he left his plantations, slaves, houses to Mary, the widow of his brother Nicholas. See p. 196.

Table 4.8 Guernsey vessels visiting Barbados, 1729-1736

Date	Ship	Tons	Master	Owner	From	Cargo	Next Port	Cargo
31.i. 1729	*William*	50	J. Dobrée	_	Guernsey	ballast		
22.3. 1729	*M & Thom*	50	Thos Le Mesurier	James Le Ray & master	Madeira	20 pipes wine		
10.v. 1731	*Two Brothers*	80	Thos Le Mesurier master	James Larey, Peter Rabey	Southampton	21,000 bricks, hoops	N'land	rum
30.iv. 1733	*Two Brothers*	80	Thos LeMesurier	James Le Ray, Peter Rabey	Guernsey	In ballast	N'land	rum
7.v. 1733	*William*	50	Nicholas Bonamy	Nicholas Dobrée senr	Guernsey	In ballast	N'land	rum
10.v. 1733	*William & Margaret*	30	J Holland	Samuel Dobrée	Guernsey	In ballast	N'land	rum
2.vi. 1734	*Charles*	50	Eleazar de la Rue	Charles Mauger	Guernsey	In ballast	N'land	
26.iv. 1735	*William*	50	Nicholas Bonamy	Nicholas Dobrée senr	Guernsey	In ballast	N'land	rum
15.v. 1735	*Providence*	60	Rawlin, Le Vesconte	Peter Guignon & master		In ballast	N'land	rum
19.iv. 1736	*Wm & Jane*	50	Saml Thoume	William Ahier	Guernsey	In ballast	Guernsey	rum

Source: TNA CO 33/16-17

Table 4.9 Slaves sold at Barbados, in 1750, cargo of the *African*

To William Le Mesurier, 22 men and 5 women	£702-0-0
John Bailey, 3 men	78-0-0
William Williams, a girl	15-0-0
Richard Barker, a woman and boy	51-0-0
Matt. Philips, a girl	20-0-0
Joseph Salmon, a boy	27-10-0
John Carter, 2 boys and 1 girl	63-10-0
Roger Leader, a boy and a girl	48-0-0
John Bayley, 3 boys	78-0-0
Jacob Skinner, a woman	24-0-0
Abel Clarke, a boy	22-10-0
Thomas Selman, 3 boys and a girl	60-0-0
Thomas Codagan, a boy	25-0-0
William Trotman, a woman	23-0-0
Thomas Niblet, a girl	20-0-0
Domin Lynch, 8 men and 5 women	299-0-0
Domin Lynch, 4 men	80-0-0
Benjamin Mellows, a boy	12-0-0
Dan Tupper, an old man	15-0-0
John Bayley, 3 women	45-0-0
After giving further details of sales at Speights Town, the document continues:-	
Brought over	55-0-0
Thomas Denny, a girl	17-15-0
William Harris, a man	16-5-0
Thomas Denny, a boy	23-5-0
Alex Ross, a woman	17-0-0
Will Harris, a girl	20-10-0
SICK NEGROES	
To Thomas Rust, a boy	10-15-0
Sir John Yeomans, a woman	13-15-0
Hugh Edwards, a girl	7-15-0
Thomas Denny, 1 girl	11-5-0
Edward Bishop, a boy	7-5-0
Thomas Thomas, a girl	5-0-0
	£2,232-5-0
Commission at 4%	89-5-9½
	£2,142-19-2½

Source: Guernsey Evening Press, 18 April 1930 (details supplied to the Press by a bookseller who had discovered the manuscript account tucked in a book).

The DANISH ISLANDS

The Danish West India Company took possession of **St Thomas** in 1672. In 1718 it also took **St John** and in 1733 it purchased **St Croix** from the French West India Company. In 1753 the three islands became Danish state property. The islands were given over to sugar plantations worked by African slaves. Raw sugar was shipped back to Denmark and the merchant Niels Ryberg described the three islands as 'the finest jewel' in the Danish crown (Jespersen, 2007, p. 126).

In the second half of the eighteenth century **St Croix** became a major supplier of rum to the Guernsey market. How this came about is to be found in a report written by Lutwidge. He explained that the Manx smugglers had imported rum but, on the sale of the Isle of Man, they shipped it to Guernsey.

> 'By an Ordonnance subsisting in Denmark the quantity of Rum to be imported from their sugar islands is limited, and no vessel is allowed to bring home more than one third of her cargo in that commodity. The reason for this probably is to lay the inhabitants of those islands under the necessity of exchanging the remainder of their rum for provisions. Accordingly the whole of this rum formerly was carried to our colonies in North America in return for provisions and lumber; till the late war, when the traders of the Isle of Man fell upon the means of importing it here for the purpose of smuggling in return for provisions sent from Ireland. Since the purchase of this island certain Manks smugglers continue in like manner to import this Danish rum into Guernsey. There is a vessel at present bound from the Isle of Man to Sancta Cruz, upon this trade, and one Taubman a capital smuggler in this island lately commissioned 20,000 barrels of beef to be made up in Cork in order to be sent to Sancta Cruz whence he has already imported into Guernsey two cargoes of rum and proposes soon to land many others, having stationed one Parr a notorious smuggler as his agent there'. (TNA TI 445, 24 Nov 1766).

Abraham Le Mesurier settled on the island and supplied Priaulx, among others. The Guernsey captains Maingy, Puirvaux, Allez, and Lauga were all at St Croix in December 1775 (Priaulx Library, Priaulx letterbook); and in 1776 we find captains Breadthaft, Le Messurier, and Jehan arriving at Guernsey from St Croix (Lloyd's Lists, 21 June, 6 Aug, 6 Sep, 1 Nov). On the outbreak of the American War it became hazardous for Guernsey vessels to venture to the West Indies. Lloyd's List reported on 22 Oct 1776 that the 3 vessels captained by Naftel, Moulpied and Ahier (bound from St Croix to Guernsey) had all been taken by the Americans. Thomas Priaulx hatched a plan to send Captain Kennett to St Malo to mount an expedition to St Croix. There would be a French captain and about two thirds of the crew would be French. The ship would pass as French (and would not, therefore, be seized by the Americans). Priaulx instructed Mess Veuve Chenard Giraudais & Le Page of St Malo to buy provisions. In fact the voyage ended up with Kennett selling provisions at St Thomas. In 1778 Priaulx arranged for rum to be shipped on a Danish vessel (Priaulx, Priaulx letterbook, p. 397).

St DOMINGUE – HAITI (HAYTI)

In the eighteenth century St Domingue was one of the richest colonies in the French empire. It was known as the 'pearl of the Antilles' and outstripped the British West Indies colonies in the production of sugar and coffee. After Dessalines' *coup d'état* in 1804 it became an independent republic known as Haiti. Petion ruled in the south, Christophe in the north. In 1811 Christophe was declared King Henri. The Guernsey merchants Thomas Price and Hannibal Price established themselves at Jacmel in Haiti in 1805-1807. They installed a beam engine and sugar mill there. *Circa* 1815 one of the Price brothers was back in England. Elizabeth Ham wrote:

> …about this time Mary Mansell visited Scotland and England in company with some cousins of her husband. Mr Price had been settled as a merchant in the Island of

Hayti. He was now at home, and, as he wished to take his sister with him on this tour, he prevailed on Mary to accompany them…..Mary then told me, before her husband, and of course by his approval, that Mr Price having talked to her in confidence of some children left in Hayti to whom he was warmly attached, and very unhappy about the idea of their being left without mental culture or education of any sort. His great wish was to have them brought over to England and placed under the care of some Lady who would be a mother to them, and that the expense would be no object to them. Mary had mentioned me, and he had seized on the idea with avidity, and she now asked me if I were willing to undertake such a charge. I knew nothing of the opinion of the world on such matters. I only thought how interesting it would be to train up these poor little Indian children in my own way with no one to interfere with me. And then, to have useful occupation and comparative independence, the prospect seemed quite delightful. The father was on the eve of returning to Hayti, where he was on very intimate terms with King Christophe, and wished to hear my decision as soon as possible….I soon got a letter to say that Mr. Price was delighted that I had accepted the charge, and that all necessary preliminaries should be settled when he got back to Guernsey. In the course of two or three weeks a letter came to say that, as soon as this arrangement had transpired, Mr. Price's family had been so indignant at the idea of his sending his children home, and had said such ill natured things to Henry and Mary about it, that Henry had at once declined in my name, my having anything to do with it. (Ham, 1945, pp. 192-3).

SANTO DOMINGO
Santo Domingo was a Spanish colony. The Guernsey merchants found an outlet here for cheap India goods in the early nineteenth century (TNA CUST 105/102, 27 Jan 1810, Guernsey to Commissioners).

CUBA
Cuba was a Spanish colony from the fifteenth century until 1902. The British held Havana for some ten months during the Seven Years War, but gave up the town under the peace terms (1763). Archibald Stuart was involved in the export of wine from Guernsey to Havana at that time (see pp. 105-106). In the early nineteenth century Cuba became a leading producer of sugar; the Guernsey merchants became seriously involved in carrying cargoes from Cuba *circa* 1814 (see pp. 13, 43).

GRENADA
Grenada was a French colony ceded to the British in 1763 by the Treaty of Paris; it was captured by the French in 1778/9 but restored to Britain by the Treaty of Versailles, 1783. It produced sugar, rum, and nutmeg. Vessels arrived in Guernsey from Grenada from time to time (see Tables 4.1, 4.2).

ST BARTHOLOMEW (St BETHELEMY)
The Swedish king acquired this small island in 1784 from the French. The Swedes established a settlement which 'reached its peak during the Revolutionary and Napoleonic Wars, when it served as a neutral free-harbour for the warring parties'. (Jespersen 2007, p. 119).

ST EUSTATIA (ST EUSTATIUS)
A Dutch colony, played a similar rôle during the Napoleonic wars. Vessels from St Bartholomew and St Eustatia arrived occasionally in Guernsey (see Tables 4.1, 4.2).

HONDURAS
Honduras was a Spanish colony until it declared its independence in 1821. In the eighteenth century mahogany was shipped from Honduras. Jamieson (1986, pp. 375-6) noted passes issued in 1765, 1767 and 1768 to Guernsey vessels bound for Honduras.

SOUTH AMERICA

Demerara (now Guyana)

Britain gained control of Demerara in 1796. This colony produced sugar, cotton, rum and coffee. Carteret Priaulx (Guernsey) dealt with the Guernsey merchants Mourant and De Lisle at Demerara. In April 1802 the cargo of the *Nancy* (of Guernsey) which unloaded at Demerara included wine, beer, butter, cheese, salmon, sausages, barley, pickled greens, boxes of ironmongery, seventy bundles of shovels, three large boxes of clothing and three boxes of men's handkerchiefs' (White, citing Priaulx to Mourant, De Lisle 3 April 1802) White infers that Mourant and De Lisle had a plantation. There is confirmatory evidence.

Mourant and De Lisle were signatories to a petition of planters, merchants and other inhabitants, 23 Nov 1803 (TNA CO 111/5); Stephen Mourant was signatory to a declaration about prices (of flour, rice, beef, pork, sugar, rum, Madeira, port, nails, tar, pitch, white lead) 9 May 1805 (TNA CO 111/6 f 52); and Thos De Lisle was signatory to a memorial of planters and merchants in 1809 (TNA CO 111/9 f 11).

Where was their plantation? Port Mourant, Guyana, is located at 6° 15' north, 57° 20' west, in the East Berbice – Corentyne region of Guyana. It is about one metre above sea level. The Mourant -Delisle plantation was, presumably, the origin of this settlement. The area was described by Bolingbroke in 1809 'The same field for speculators and adventurers presented itself here, as in the other colonies. The west coast was first put in cultivation, and in 1799 that to the eastward of the river, as far as the Devil's creek, attracted notice, and was quickly transformed from an heavy impenetrable forest to a field of cotton trees. This coast was surveyed, and was cut into two parallel lines of estates with a navigable canal between the two lines, for the convenience of water carriage; behind this second row of estates, runs the stream of the river Canje, the banks of which on both sides are cultivated with sugar, coffee, and plantains. The estates are thus denominated; that line facing the sea are the coast estates, the second line the canal estates, and the other are the Canje' (Bolingbroke, 1809, p. 56).

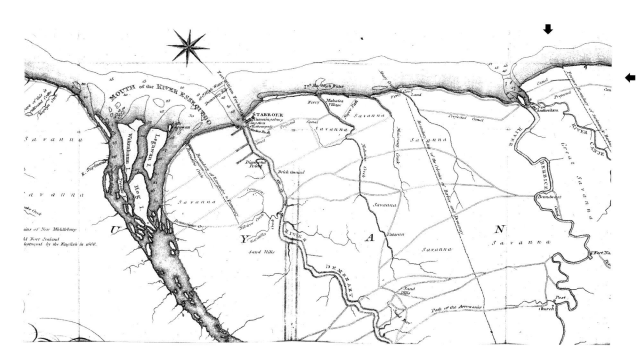

Fig. 4.17: Port Mourant's location is near the River Canje and the sea
(detail of map in Bolingbroke, *A Voyage to the Demerary*, 1809).

Brazil

In the nineteenth century the Guernsey merchants found new opportunities in the trade between the Mediterranean and the newly independent Brazil. LeBreton, Lihou & Co established themselves at Bahia. At Rio de Janeiro were to be found P.Bonamy, Miller, and Mr G. Collings and Priaulx, Tupper & Co. (Priaulx, Lukis ms. p 27; Carteret Priaulx papers). The house of Priaulx, Tupper & Co traded until 1844 when, on the death of Thomas Priaulx, it closed. The main commodities exported from Brazil were sugar and coffee. Some figures survive for the volume of trade of Priaulx, Tupper & Co:

Table 4.10 Priaulx, Tupper & Co exported

		1827	**1828**	**1829**	**1830**	**1831**
Coffee:	bags	28322	27265	47326	39350	47805
	barrels		321	233		
Sugar:	cases	529	1314	472	2175	1950
	boxes			5		
	bags	567	1414	560	751	929
	barrels	65				
Hides		1296	573	5728	3399	13026
Horns		2000	21708			
Tobacco in rolls					114	

Source: Priaulx Library, Priaulx papers

F.B.T. (= F.B. Tupper) visited Rio de Janeiro in November 1826. He wrote an account that was published ten years later in *The Guernsey and Jersey Magazine*. He was shocked by the scenes of slavery there, 'at seeing his fellow-creatures employed as beasts of burthen, and particularly at hearing their agonizing shrieks while suffering under the lash of punishment. The annual importation of slaves into this port alone is now estimated at nearly thirty thousand…' When Tupper returned home to Guernsey he took action: 'I sent out instructions that a black servant should be made free. On receiving his freedom, he resolved on coming to Guernsey to thank me personally for it, and actually performed a long voyage of upwards of 5,000 miles for that purpose, arriving in Guernsey on the 14th June, 1833. I sent him back again, as he wished to return; he cried bitterly on taking leave, and said that he would never see me more; and I am not ashamed to confess, that I was affected even to tears by his artless and grateful conduct. ('Remarks on the slave trade at Rio de Janeiro. – 1827' by F.B.T. *The Guernsey and Jersey Magazine*, edited by Jonathan Duncan, 1836 vol. 2, July 1836, pp. 9-12).

It is probably thanks to Tupper that *The Star* (a Guernsey newspaper) published (6 Feb 1827) details of Guernsey vessels arriving in Rio de Janeiro between January 1825 and June 1826 (see Table 4.11 below).

Table 4.11 Guernsey - owned vessels arriving in Rio de Janeiro, January 1825 to June 1826

Vessel	arrived	from	cargo	sailed for
	1825			
St George	26-Jan	Genoa	19 pipes Olive Oil; 113 barrels wheat; 30 cases Tallow Candles; 28 cases and 94 bales Paper; 105 boxes Steel	Trieste
Duke of Gloucester	3-Feb	Guernsey	610 cases Geneva; 227 barrels and 40 bags wheat; 62 cases, and 100 cheeses	Guernsey
Enterprize	10-Feb	Bahia	77 pipes, 24 hogsheads, and 44 quarter casks redwine; 27 pipes olive oil, and 59 barrels wheat	Guernsey
Unity	14-Feb	Ancona	171 barrels and 132 bags Wheat; 54 bales Paper.	Guernsey
Blossom	15-Feb	Tarragona	20 pipes brandy; 224 pipes, 33 hogsheads, and 19 quarter casks red wine; 19 pipes olive oil; 150 bales paper and 147 boxes steel.	Guernsey
Collingwood	17-Feb	Tarragona	146 pipes, 30 hogsheads, and 20 qyarter casks red wine; 22 pipes olive oil; 4 cases tallow candles and 26 bales paper.	Guernsey
Mercury	17-Feb	Cette	32 pipes, 6 hogsheads, and 20 quarter casks brandy; 60 pipes and 20 hogsheads red wine; 374 barrels wheat 200 strings and bundles onions; 44 cases and 135 bales paper; and 114 boxes steel.	Guernsey
Laura	1-Apr	Guernsey	109 pipes and 30 quarter casks wine; 22 pipes vinegar; 14 pipes geneva; and 207 cases ale and porter.	Guernsey
Princess Charlotte	5-Apr	Tarragona	246 pipes, 48 hogsheads, and 60 quarter casks red wine; 19 pipes olive oil; and170 boxes steel.	Guernsey
Rachel and Mary	10-Apr	Cette	198 pipes, 40 hhd. And 29 qr. Casks red wine; and 89 boxes steel.	Isle of Mayo
Alexander	1-May	Tarragona	291 pipes, 70 hogsheads, and 62 quarter casks red wine; and 4 packages goods (not described)	Boa Pista
Three Sisters	21-May	Tarragona	30 pipes brandy; 268 pipes and 40 hogsheads red wine; 30 cases macaroni; and 138 boxes steel.	Trieste
Nancy	11-Jul	Sicily	4 pipes brandy; 150 pipes, 40 hogsheads, and 34 quarter casks red wine; and 60 pipes olive oil.	Trieste
Charles	18-Jul	Arichat	688 tubs and 833 barrels codfish.	Antwerp
Dolphin	18-Jul	Guernsey	32 pipes, 5 quarter casks, and 3 cases red wine; 3 pipes geneva; 16 cases ale and porter; 111 cases soap; and 59 coils cordage.	Trieste
				Guernsey
Two Brothers	25-Jul	Guernsey	32 pipes and 788 demijohns geneva; 124 cases ale and porter; 1036 bags wheat; and 20 hams.	Guernsey
Two Sisters	2-Aug	Guernsey	in ballast	Guernsey
Alexander	3-Aug	Buenos Ayres	with 4,877 hides.	Guernsey
Rachel and Mary	10-Aug	Buenos Ayres	with 4,160 hides, and 5 packages goods (not described).	Guernsey
Blossom	18-Aug	Guernsey	65 pipes red wine; 9 pipes olive oil; 188 barrels and 29 bags wheat; 157 hams; 5 tons potatoes; and 240 cases of soap.	Trieste
Venus	2-Sep	Guernsey	100 cases ale and porter.	Buenos Ayres
Alfred	16-Sep	Antwerp	96 barrels and 667 bags wheat.	Antwerp
St George	30-Sep	Tarragona	20 pipes brandy; 130 pipes, 16 hogsheads, and 15 quarter casks red wine; 20 pipes olive oil; 338 cases tallow candles; 10 bales paper; and 118 boxes steel.	Guernsey
Peace	1-Oct	Isle Mayo	48 moyos salt	Guernsey

88

Ship	Date	Port	Cargo	
Swift	7-Oct	Tarragona	10 pipes and 30 quarter casks brandy; and 181 pipes and 47 hogsheads red wine.	Guernsey
Collingwood	10-Oct	Guernsey	13 pipes and 6 hogsheads red wine; 4 pipes geneva; 50 cases ale and porter; 60 jars linseed oil; 126 cases soap; 17 coils cordage; and 9 cases glass.	Monte Video
Mercury	16-Oct	Guernsey	32 cases ale and porter; 250 bushels potatoes; and 293 bars iron.	Trieste
Caroline	24-Sep	Isle Mayo	6 pipes brandy, 6 pipes geneva; and 60 mayos salt.	Trieste
Louisa	15-Nov	Oporto	239 pipes, 36 hogsheads, and 56 quarter casks port wine; and 600 strings and bundles onions.	Trieste
Laura	28-Nov	Oporto	271 pipes, 36 hogsheads, and 64 quarter casks port wine; and 500 strings and bundles onions.	Guernsey
Hope	9-Dec	Gibraltar	24 quarter casks brandy; 86 pipes and 4 hogsheads red wine; 3 cases ale and porter; 41 pipes olive oil; 26 bags biscuit; 46 cases paper; 80 boxes steel; and 1 case hats.	Monte Video
Union	11-Dec	Oporto	195 pipes, 28 hogsheads, and 44 quarter casks port wine; and 600 strings and bundles onions.	Trieste
Duke of Gloucester	26-Dec	Guernsey	59 pipes and 5 hogsheads brandy; 150 pipes and 6 hogsheads red wine; and 46 cases ale and porter.	Guernsey
1826				
Three Sisters	25-Sep	Sicily	22 pipes, 14 hogsheads, and 4 quarter casks brandy; 173 pipes and 26 hgsheads red wine; 69 pipes olive oil; 86 barrels wheat; and 169 boxes steel.	Guernsey
Swift	26-Feb	Guernsey	152 pipes and 31 hogsheads red wine; 5 pipes and 14 hogsheads white wine; 20 cases ale and porter; 16 cases cider; and 75 coils cordage.	Trieste
St George	1-Mar	Guernsey	1 pipe and 1 hogshead brandy; 155 pipes and 12 hogsheads red wine; 20 pipes and 111 demi-johns geneva; 220 jars linseed oil; and 1½ tons potatoes.	Guernsey
Reward	5-Mar	Oporto	307 pipes, 20 hogsheads, and 188 quarter casks port wine; and 24 cases ale and porter.	Guernsey
Two Brothers	12-Mar	Tarragona	30 pipes and 24 quarter casks brandy; 195 pipes and 30 hogsheads red wine.	Gibraltar
Dolphin	18-Mar	Trieste	30 pipes olive oil; 149 barrels and 352 bags wheat.	Guernsey
Blossom	12-Apr	Tarragona	30 pipes brandy; 215 pipes, 28 hogsheads, and 20 quarter casks red wine; 20 pipes olive oil; 26 cases currants; 308 cases tallow candles; and 160 boxes steel.	Trieste
Charles	5-May	Tarragona	15 pipes and 10 hogsheads brandy; 202 pipes, 20 hogsheads, and 50 quarter casks red wine.	Trieste
Alexander	24-May	Tarragona	60 pipes bransy; 277 pipes and 35 hogsheads red wine.	Guernsey
Collingwood	17-Jun	Guernsey	258 barrels and 59 bags wheat; 8 caseas soap; 1 case tallow candles; and 18 dozen brooms.	Hamburg

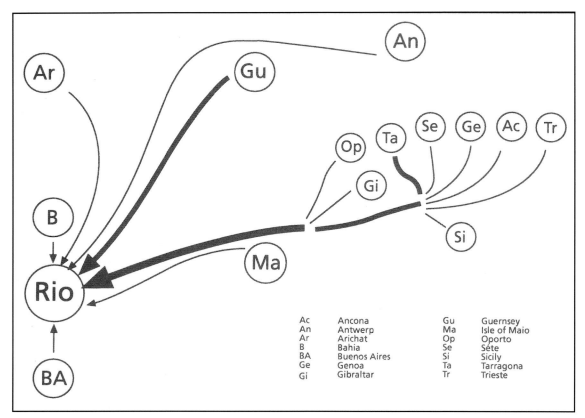

Fig. 4.18: Ports of departure of Guernsey vessels sailing to Rio de Janeiro,
January 1825 to June 1826. (Schematic, not geographical representation.)

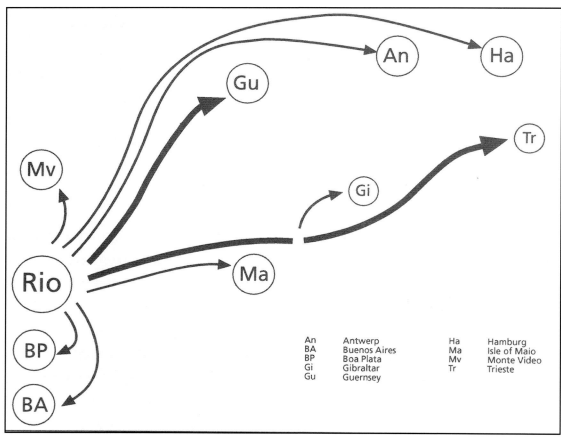

Fig. 4.19: Ports of destination of Guernsey vessels clearing from Rio de Janeiro,
January 1825 to June 1826. (Schematic, not geographical representation.)

90

5
Merchants

MERCHANTS

In important essays published in the *Transactions of the Société Guernesiaise* Meg White and Richard Hocart have presented detailed studies of Carteret Priaulx and Nicholas Dobrée. Subsequently these two merchants have been taken to exemplify the Guernsey merchants; the other merchants have remained in obscurity. Part of the reason for this arises from the difficulty of identifying them. There are no directories for eighteenth-century Guernsey, with neat, alphabetical lists of 'leading merchants and traders' (as exist for some English and French ports). There are, however, a number of manuscript sources that identify merchants, either explicitly or implicitly. These are now examined.

There are three sources that cover the 1720s and early 1730s. [1] The letterbook of Jean **Martell** contains the names of ten Guernsey merchants supplied with brandy and/or wine in the 1720s. [2] This evidence is contemporary with that of the **Sun** Fire Insurance Company which provided cover for twenty-one merchants living in St Peter Port (1720s). [3] *Circa* 1732, J De Sausmarez wrote a note, apparently for English authorities, listing 'ye dealers in wine **brandy** in Guernsey' and offered the names of 'Peter Caryee (*sic*) ye brewer one of ye jurats of ye Royal Court, Samuel Bonamy one of ye jurats, Nicolas Dobrée, Charles & Elias Mauger, Michael and John Falla, Henry Brock, Peter Coutard advocat of ye Royal Court, James Le Ray, Samuel and Daniel Le Febure, Abraham Le Mesurier' (ten families represented). He continued: 'Theses (*sic*) are the names of ye chiefs forgot to observe if any evidence swear against them that their money & effect, part is in Mr William Dobrée marchand here living in Buloph Lane and Elias Perchard living at ye corner house of Cannon street and Abchurch Lane'. (It would seem that de Sausmarez had thrown in his lot with the English and was denouncing his fellow islanders.)

The second half of the eighteenth century is better documented and the number of merchants increased. [4] A petition about **wine** duty was signed on 15 September 1752 by fourteen Guernsey merchants (from eight families) and addressed to Lord de la Warr. [5] In 1764 thirty-four merchants (from twenty-four families) were involved in founding the *Société des Veuves*. The document issued at the time of foundation explicitly identified the occupation of each member. [6] On 20 March 1776, twenty-six Guernsey merchants (from twenty families) signed a protest against British restrictions on handling **Canary** wine. It cannot be inferred that all of the signatories handled Canary wine but they all had an interest in protesting the legislation. [7] Between 1768 and 1788 the Guernsey authorities kept a *Livre de certificats*, entries in which recorded the handling of wine carried in British vessels for British merchants. The *livre* records twenty-three Guernsey merchants (from sixteen families). [8] In 1779 twenty-nine 'principal merchants and traders' of Guernsey (from twenty-seven families) signed a petition to Lord **Amherst**, requesting that the convoys to Southampton be strengthened. Finally, [9] the account books of Zephaniah **Job** records eighteen Guernsey merchant houses supplying Cornish smugglers (see table 5.5).

These nine lists give a total of sixty-three families having one or more members working as a merchant in the eighteenth century. This constitutes the basis for the Register of merchants (chapter 8). In many cases it is appropriate to think in terms of 'merchant families' who engaged in trade for several generations. Such families are almost bound to be 'caught' by the lists. However, it is clear that none of the lists are truly comprehensive. In most instances leading merchants are named, lesser merchants are missing. To try to compensate for this, I searched the records of the *Cour d'Amirauté* (Greffe, Guernsey); Isaac Dobrée's notary book (Priaulx Library); letters-of-marque recorded by the High Court of Admiralty (TNA England); and wills recorded in the Ecclesiastical Court archives (Greffe, Guernsey). From these sources extra names were added to the Register.

How many merchants were there? A letter sent to French *négociants* in port towns in May 1792 was signed by 'soixante-deux négocians de cette île' (see Plate VIII) – sixty-two. A few, perhaps, were absent and did not sign In the late eighteenth century there were *268 négociants* at Dunkirk, 100+ at Le Havre, 145 at St Malo, 76 at Lorient, 400 at Nantes, 425-450 at Bordeaux (Le Bouedec 1997, p. 303).

Table 5.1 Guernsey merchants identified

	[1] Martell 1720s	[2] Sun 1720s	[3] brandy 1732	[4] wine 1752	[5] *Veuves* 1764	[6] Canary 1776	[7] *Livre* 1768-88	[8] Amherst 1779
Ahier								1
Anley					1			
Bell							2	1
Bonamy	1	1	1	1	2	1		
Bowden		1			1			
Brock			1	3	2		2	1
Carey	1	2	1	1	2	2	1	1
Cornelius				1	1	1		
Coutart		1	1		1			1
de Carteret					2		1	1
de Fraise					1			
de Havilland					1	1		
de Jersey		2			1	2		1
de Lisle						1		
de Quetteville	1	1						
de Sausmarez		1					1	
Dobrée	2	4	1	3	3	2	1	1
Falla	1		2					
Fiott	1							
Frère							1	
Grangerau		1						
Grut						1		
Guérin		1						1
Guille					2		2	1
Hubert						1		
Icemonger						1		
Jennings					1			
La Serre					1			1
Lageman							1	
Lauga					1	2		1
Le Cocq								1
Le Febure	1		2	1				
Le Lievre						1		
Le Marchant				3	2	1	3	2
Le Mesurier		1	1		1	1	3	1
Le Ray			1					
Le Roy		1			1			
Lihou					1	1	1	1
Ludlam								1
Maingy								1
Martin	1							
Massey		1						
Mauger	1	2	2					
McBride							1	
Mollet						1		
Mourant					1	1	1	1
Perchard					1			1
Priaulx					2			1
Price								1
Rivoire						1		
Robinson								1
Sheppard								1
Stephen		1						
Thomson					2		1	1
Tupper				1		3	1	2
Vardon								1
Watkins						1		

Who were the merchants?

It is possible to discern five groups.

(i) First and central, were some twenty and more merchant families of ancient Guernsey lineage: Bonamy, Brock, Carey, De Carteret, De Havilland, De Jersey, De Lisle, De Quetteville, De Sausmarez, Fiott, Guille, Le Cocq, Le Febvre, Le Lievre, Le Marchant, Le Mesurier, Le Ray, Lihou, Maingy, Perchard, and Priaulx. These families constituted a significant part of the insular aristocracy. They were almost all armigerous and over the centuries had supplied the bailiffs and jurats who governed the island.

Table 5.2 Jurats elected between 1680 and 1815

Family surname	no	
Le Marchant	12	M
Carey	8	M
Andros	6	?
Guille	4	M
Bonamy	3	M
De Beauvoir	3	?
De Lisle	3	M
Dobrée	3	M
Brock	2	M
De Havilland	2	M
De Jersey	2	M
Fiott	2	M
Priaulx	2	M
Tupper	2	M
M = merchant family		

Between 1680 and 1815 jurats were elected from twenty-nine families. Well over half of these families had members who were *négociants*. What is even more significant is an examination of the families who supplied two or more jurats (Table 5.2). There were fourteen such families, at least twelve of which could boast *négociants*. (The Andros and De Beauvoir families do not seem to have been involved in trade). This is significant. There was a congruence between political power and mercantile interest. The jurats enjoyed great power because they issued *ordonnances* regulating island life. Many of the jurats being *négociants* (or coming from merchant families) pursued policies consistent with their trading interests.

These merchant-families almost all had a history of sea-faring and trading. A wealth of practical experience had been handed down the generations. Several families owned ships and understood voyaging to France, England and Newfoundland. Many of these families were involved in privateering in the Nine Years War (1689 – 1697) and the Succession War (1702 – 1712). Privateering helped capital formation and introduced the Guernsey merchants to the supplying of prize cargoes to the English. Duncan commented:

> English merchants came over to purchase the French goods captured by the privateers, and particularly brandies, which met with a ready sale. When peace was restored, new ideas of trade gradually developed themselves among the inhabitants, who had now acquired some capital.

These families also owned land and derived an income by farming, or as rentiers, or by organising the stocking-knitting industry. In this fashion they had accumulated the capital necessary to become merchants. The Guilles are an excellent example. In the early eighteenth century we find Jean Guille on his estate at St George (Castel parish). There he farmed, produced cider, gathered in rentes, and helped to organise vessels and crews for the Newfoundland fishery. His son and grandsons became *négociants*, trading in spirits, wine, and tea. For Guille jr, living and working in St Peter Port, the farm at St George became a pleasant summer retreat, a home appreciated particularly by his wife who lived in dread of a fire in the town.

(ii) Not all of these families operated at the highest level. There was, rather, a spectrum with the Careys, Le Marchants and Le Mesuriers at the upper, wealthier end, and other families of lesser means at the lower end, operating more as traders, and blending with islanders of humbler origins. Hard work could lead to the acquisition of a small vessel, the owner-master trading between Guernsey and nearby ports. A fortunate man might accumulate enough capital to make the transition from master-trader to merchant (see chapter 8 - Daniel Rolland). These sea-farers are poorly represented in the archives but they were an important sector of the port economy.

(iii) Next we notice the Tuppers and Dobrées. These families arrived in Guernsey in the sixteenth century. They were of continental origin and left their homelands to escape religious persecution. They settled in the island, prospered and intermarried with the insular aristocracy. The fact that the Tuppers and Dobrées could boast jurats (see above) is eloquent proof that the families had been fully assimilated into the Guernsey establishment.

(iv) At the end of the seventeenth century – and in the early eighteenth century - there was a new wave of religious refugees, Huguenots from France. Some of these were sailors and artisans; others belonged to the merchant ranks: (de) Guérin, La Serre, Lauga, Métivier, Rivoire, and Vardon. The Huguenots of Guernsey were not wealthy but they had useful contacts among their co-religionists in London, Southampton, and the Devon ports. They also had a thorough understanding of the *mentalité* of the French authorities and the economic structure of France. This knowledge would have made them a valuable asset to the island merchants.

(v) During the course of the eighteenth century they were joined by economic migrants: Bell, Bett, Douglas, and Thompson from Scotland; Chepmell from Jersey; Affleck, Cornelius, Frecker, Harvey, Price, Robinson, and Sheppard from England; Frère, probably from the West Indies; Adam, Crousaz de Prelaz, Lagerman, and Uttermark from the continent. (Compared with many ports the ratio of alien merchants was relatively small, the Guernsey authorities had it easily within their power to control the extent of immigration).

By the late eighteenth century there were some forty families living in Guernsey, involved in international commerce. It is important to recognise that some families were quite given over to trade, with several members simultaneously in business (e.g. the Guille family), while other families could boast but one *négociant*. That was often the case with immigrant merchants of the first generation. But with the passage of time, marriage – and children – the single immigrant could become the head of a new Guernsey dynasty.

Their business

The word merchant can translate two French words – *négociant* and *marchand*. For many historians (e.g. Lespagnol) there was, in the eighteenth century, a divide between *négociants* and *marchands*. The former dealt wholesale, buying from businessmen and selling to businessmen; the latter were traders, frequently selling retail and operating at a lower level. In terms of maritime commerce the *négociants* were involved in *le grand commerce*, while the *marchands* operated *le petit cabotage*. In practice it is probably misleading to think in terms of binary alternatives, it is more plausible to understand that we are dealing with a spectrum which stretched from wealthy, aristocratic *négociants* at one end, through lesser *négociants* (with less capital) to 'leading traders' and ending with the humble trader handling two or three pipes of brandy.

At the 'top' end, the work of the merchant could be varied and might embrace one or more of the following activities: shipping, trading, factoring, planting, slaving, government contracting, commission work, and banking (Hancock, 1995, thus defines the work of his London merchants). The Dobrées, Le Marchants and Le Mesuriers engaged in these activities at different stages. Many of the merchants handled a wide range of cargoes. They were entrepreneurs, ready to deal in whatever seemed promising. However, some merchants tended to specialise in particular commodities. In the second half of the eighteenth century we find about a dozen who were interested in wine, buying from continental *négociants* and selling on to English, Scottish and American merchants. Other Guernsey merchants, however, made their living by selling high-duty goods to smugglers (see Table 5.5). This could be lucrative but several *négociants* steered clear of that type of trade. Thomas Dobrée, for example, actively disliked selling to smugglers; he much preferred 'big deals' with other *négociants*. He found the idea of a large-scale tea transaction with Le Mesurier of London more to his taste (see p. 109). The Carey family also seems to have shunned the West Country smugglers.

The immigrant merchants appear to have specialised more than the island merchants. They came to Guernsey with knowledge and experience of certain types of commodities. Frère understood the West Indies trade; Bell had served his apprenticeship learning about wine; Crousaz also understood wine. With their knowledge these merchants could make a positive contribution to St Peter Port as an entrepôt. By concentrating on their specialities they did not directly challenge the established merchants. On the contrary, they brought their own lists of correspondents and enhanced the reputation of the island as an international trading centre.

Wealth and rank

In the first half of the eighteenth century Guernsey designated rank in three ways. The upper échelons of society were styled *Mr – Monsieur*; below that came *le Sieur*; and at the bottom of the social pyramid were common people who were known simply by their name, without any 'handle'. These styles of rank were frequently used in documents and, when present, are valuable evidence. However, rank titles were not always employed, so some care is necessary. Nicholas Dobrée belonged to the upper rank and was often accorded *Mr*, but it is possible to find his name written without any designation. In the first half of the eighteenth-century relatively few merchants attained the status of *Mr*. In the second half of the century there was a form of 'inflation', with several families claiming a higher rank. The Guernsey system was modelled on that of *ancien régime* France and found itself in difficulties when confronted by English merchants and immigrants. The English *Mr* (i.e. mister) was used more promiscuously than *Monsieur* and devalued the French terminology. As a consequence, the late eighteenth-century office-holders (e.g. jurats) and certain armigerous families adopted the designation *écuyer* (esquire) in order to assert their social superiority.

The leading merchants of St Peter Port in the early eighteenth century compared with the 'second class' English merchants of King (1688) but, with the prospering of the entrepôt, the leading Guernsey merchants of the late eighteenth century came close to the 'first class' English merchants of Massie (1759). The Guernsey fortunes are not comparable with those of some of the East India merchants in London, nor with those of the millionaires of Nantes. Nevertheless several Guernsey merchants were wealthy and there were families whose combined wealth was significant. There was no one family of enormous wealth, but rather a small cluster of wealthy families above a larger group of middling and lesser traders. The pattern resembles that of several French ports 'le monde des négociants présente des hiérarchies impressionnantes où s'affirme un noyau de grands négociants, mais où se maintient un groupe de petits et moyens négociants' a duality illustrated at Bordeaux (Le Bouëdec, 1997, p. 305). The Guernsey merchants seem to have been on a level with those of Dunkirk [1].

Table 5.3 Taxes 1779

	Christian name	Surname	Status	Quarters	Capital £ st	Vingtaine	Rank
	Jean	Carey	Ec	1900	38000	Grande Rue	1
	Pierre	Mourant	Ec	1000	20000	Grande Rue	7
	Richard	De Beauvoir	Ec	950	19000	Grande Rue	9
	Henry	Brock	Mr	800	16000	Grande Rue	11
	Jean	Le Marchant	Ec	800	16000	Grande Rue	12
	Thomas	Carey sr	Mr	600	12000	Grande Rue	17
Mdme	V. Abraham	Le Mesurier		480	9600	Grande Rue	20
	Elizee & Jean	Le Mesurier	Messrs	380	7600	Grande Rue	32
	Nicholas	Le Mesurier	Ec	320	6400	Grande Rue	45
	Henry	Le Mesurier	Ec	320	6400	Grande Rue	42
Mdme	V. Thomas	Priaulx	Mr	320	6400	Grande Rue	46
Mdme	V. Pierre	Dobrée	Mr	260	5200	Grande Rue	54
	Pierre	Ludlam	Mr	250	5000	Grande Rue	61
	Wm	Pierre Price	le Sr	250	5000	Grande-Rue	63
Mdme	V. Pierre	Carey	Ec	245	4900	Grande Rue	64
	William	Chepmell	Mr	200	4000	Grande Rue	78
Mdme	V. Jean	Le Roy	Mr	200	4000	Grande Rue	72
	Thomas & fille	Le Marchant	Ec	1020	20400	Carrefour	6
	Henry	Le Mesurier senr	Ec	800	1600	Carrefour	10
Mdme	V. Isaac & enfants	Dobrée		600	12000	Carrefour	15
	Jean	Perchard & enfants	Ec	450	9000	Carrefour	24
	Thomas	Le Marchant	Ec	430	8600	Carrefour	26
	Nicholas & enfants	Dobrée	Ec	420	8400	Carrefour	28
Dlle	Judith	Dobrée		420	8400	Carrefour	27
Revd	Josue	Le Marchant		410	8200	Carrefour	29
	Pierre	De Jersey senr	Mr	370	7400	Carrefour	33
Mdme	V. Pierre	Le Pelley	Mr	360	7200	Carrefour	34
	William	Le Marchant	Ec	350	7000	Carrefour	39
	Jean	Tupper	Ec	350	7000	Carrefour	36
	Nicholas	De Lisle	Ec	330	6600	Carrefour	40
Mdme	V. Jean	de Sausmarez		320	6400	Carrefour	43
	George	Le Febvre	Ec	270	5400	Carrefour	51
	Thomas & enfants	Guille	Ec	260	5200	Carrefour	57
Mdme	V. Daniel	De Lisle jr		240	4800	Carrefour	65
Heirs	Jean	Brock	Ec	1320	26400	Pollet	3
	William	Bell	Mr	650	13000	Pollet	14
Heirs	Mathieu	De Sausmarez	Mr	460	9200	Pollet	22
	Charles (& belles soeurs)	De Carteret	Mr	450	9000	Pollet	23
	Daniel	De Jersey senr	Mr	400	8000	Pollet	30
	Thomas	Dobrée	Ec	350	7000	Pollet	38
	Jean	La Serre	Mr	320	6400	Pollet	44
	Pierre	De Jersey jr	Ec	300	6000	Pollet	48
	Pierre	De Lisle	Ec	300	6000	Pollet	47
	William	Brock	Ec	280	5600	Pollet	50
Mdme	V. Pierre	Perchard fs P.	Mr	250	5000	Pollet	60
	Tuteur James	Brock fs Wm		210	4200	Pollet	69
	Tuteur Henry	Brock fs Wm		210	4200	Pollet	68
	Wm (& fs de sa femme)	Le Mesurier	Mr	205	4100	Pollet	70
	Thomas Fouachain	Andros	Ec	200	4000	Pollet	77
	Pierre	Etienne	Mr	950	19000	Pilori-Eglise	8
	Richard	De Jersey	Mr	650	13000	Pilori-Eglise	13
	Pierre & fille	Lihou	Ec	600	12000	Pilori-Eglise	16
	Michel (& belle mere)	Robinson	Ec	450	9000	Pilori-Eglise	25
	Pierre	Bonamy	Mr	270	5400	Pilori-Eglise	52
	Jean	Carey senr	Mr	250	5000	Pilori-Eglise	59
	Salomon	Lauga	Mr	200	4000	Pilori-Eglise	75

Table 5.3 Taxes 1779 Continued

	Daniel	Vardon	le Sr	200	4000	Pilori-Eglise	71
	Nicholas	Maingy	Mr	1300	26000	Berthelot	4
Revd	Wm	Dobrée		270	5400	Berthelot	53
	Pierre	Maingy	Mr	230	4600	Berthelot	67
	Jean	De Havilland	Ec	200	4000	Berthelot	73
	Josue	Le Marchant	Ec	200	4000	Berthelot	74
	Elizee	Tupper	Ec	1850	37000	Cimetiere	2
	James	Hubert	Ec	520	10400	Cimetière	18
	Thomas	Priaulx	Mr	300	6000	Cimetiere	49
	Daniel	Tupper	Mr	250	5000	Cimetiere	58
	Nicolas	Reserson	Ec	500	10000	Fontaine	19
	Pierre Martin	Carey	Ec	355	7100	Fontaine	35
	Jean	Guille	Ec	350	7000	Fontaine	37
	Thomas	Price	le Sr	260	5200	Fontaine	55
	William	Coutart	Mr	250	5000	Fontaine	62
	Thomas	Mansell	Mr	200	4000	Fontaine	76
	Thomas	Olivier	le Sr	260	5200	Contrée-Mansell	56
	Nicolas	Gosselin	Mr	240	4800	Contrée-Mansell	66
	Pierre	Dobrée fs Elizée	Mr	1070	21400	Truchot	5
	Josue	Gosselin	Ec	480	9600	Truchot	21
Heirs	Wm	Le Marchant fs Eleazar Ec		40	8000	Truchot	31
	William	De Lisle	Mr	330	6600	Truchot	41

V=Veuve (widow)

In 1779 St Peter Port raised a *taxe*. For the purpose of the assessment £30 sterling annual revenue from the English funds was valued at 40 quarters, £1000 sterling 'en effets ou en espèces' (i.e. capital) was valued at 50 quarters. Table 5.3 above lists all of those who were assessed at 200 quarters and above (column 5). Column 6 gives the worth of the taxpayers in terms of capital (based on the criterion above). Column 8 gives rank in order of wealth. It will be seen that virtually all of these wealthier townsfolk were merchants, or belonged to merchant families. There were a few – de Beauvoir, Gosselin, le Pelley - who derived their income from *rentes* (or in some other fashion). It was previously understood that St Peter Port was a town of merchants; this table clarifies the extent to which this was the case. We find a handful of seriously wealthy merchants: John Carey in the Grande Rue (£38,000), Pierre Mourant also in the Grande Rue (£20,000), Elizee (Elisha) Tupper in the Cimetière-Beauregard vingtaine (£37,000), the heirs of John Brock in the Pollet (£26,400), Nicholas Maingy in Berthelot Street (£26,000), Pierre Dobrée in the Truchot (£21,400), Thomas Le Marchant at the Carrefour (£20,400). Beneath these came a small group worth between ten to twenty thousand pounds. There was then a sizeable cohort worth between £4,000 to £10,000.

The majority (63%) were to be found in three vingtaines at the heart of the old town, the Grande Rue, Carrefour and Pollet. Many dwelt here in ancestral homes, tall houses with medieval foundations. Buildings giving onto the harbour had cavernous cellars and were ideally located for receiving cargoes straight from vessels lying in the harbour. Some merchants lived further from the centre. Those in the Pollet and Truchot vingtaines were probably closer to the new warehouses built in the mid-eighteenth century. In the 1780s and 1790s many of the families living in the centre of St Peter Port moved out to the suburbs. They escaped the crowded streets and created fine new houses with gardens and lawns. Peter Mourant was probably the first merchant to make such a move.

By 1779 most wealthy merchants rejoiced in the designation Ecuyer, the French equivalent of Esquire. They claimed this privilege either because they served as jurats or because they came from armigerous families. We find only three merchants designated as le Sieur (the third rank, below Ecuyer and Mr) – the Prices and Vardon. They came of 'immigrant' families.

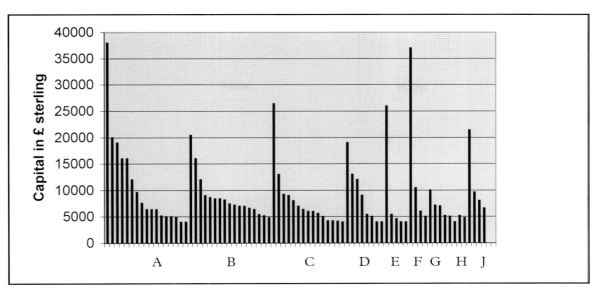

Fig 5.1: The seventy-eight wealthiest tax payers, arranged by vingtaines.

The vingtaines

A. Grande Rue

B. Carrefour

C. Pollet

D. Pilori-Eglise

E. Berthelot

F. Cimetière-
   Beauregard

G. Fontaine

H. Contrée-Mansell,
   Hauteville,
   Mt Durand

J. Truchot

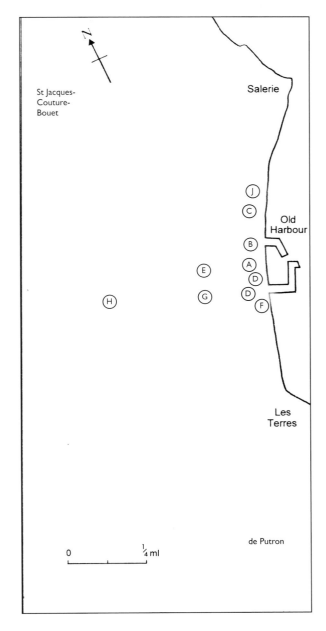

Fig 5.2: The vingtaines of St Peter Port.

Their lives

Many of the Guernsey merchants had town houses by the late seventeenth century. Dumaresq commented in 1685 that 'their whole trading lies in the Town; where, by the conveniency of the Harbour, all the men of Estates and note dwell...' (see p.28). This observation is confirmed by the archives of the Sun Fire Insurance Company which show twenty merchants (from fifteen families) taking cover for their homes and warehouses in St Peter Port in the 1720s. Quite apart from the harbour and the warehouses, the town offered various facilities. There was the *Cour d'Amirauté* which sat regularly and provided the chance to resolve a commercial dispute in speedy fashion. (It has to be admitted, however, that some Guernsey folk of the eighteenth century enjoyed litigation and there were cases that dragged on for years). In town could be found advocates and notaries. There were also merchants and gentlemen who could translate foreign languages. As St Peter Port developed its entrepôt trade, a command of foreign languages became increasingly useful. In the mid-eighteenth century we find Mr Nicholas Le Mesurier translating statements made by the captains and crews of Danish, Dutch, Finnish and Swedish vessels (the common language may have been Dutch); Mr John Le Marchant was an 'interpreter of the Dutch tongue' and Mr Daniel Roland was an 'interpreter of the Spanish tongue' (Priaulx, Isaac Dobrée's notary book, pp. 66, 69, 73, 78, 79, 80, 88, 89 for Le Mesurier; 27 May 1758 for Le Marchant, 5 June 1759 for Roland). Town was a place for hearing gossip and picking up information that might prove commercially useful. Town was a place for doing deals, for inspecting ships and cargoes, for strengthening friendships. Town housed the *Société de la Chambre*, an exclusive club frequented by members of the leading island families Between 1737 and 1766 we find - Le Marchant (10 members!), Carey (3), de Lisle (3), Dobrée (3), Fiott (3), de Sausmarez (3), Le Mesurier (2), Mauger (2), Andros (1), Bonamy (1), Brock (1), de Havilland (1), Reserson (1). Almost all of these members belonged to merchant families. Quite apart from conversation any merchant would have found it helpful that the club subscribed to newspapers (which were to be opened inside and not removed). Newspapers were of vital importance to eighteenth-century merchants.

Town contained the warehouses where coopers busily attended to wines and spirits. A good cooper was a precious asset to the merchant for he could 'nurse' wine and spirits into the best condition for sale. This not infrequently involved the mixing of 'good' with 'bad' wine. The cooper understood the properties of the woods used to make barrels. He was skilled at decanting French wine into Spanish barrels to deceive customs authorities. He knew how to calculate liquid measures (it is not simple to determine the capacity of a curved container). The cooper tested the alcoholic strength of spirits and knew what was appropriate for different markets. He sometimes travelled with a cargo and could repair damaged barrels. In short, the cooper was at the heart of the business and the wise merchant treasured him. John Guille and Richard de Jersey clearly valued cooper Corbin and invited him to become the third member of their partnership (see p. 183).

The streets of St Peter Port were busy with porters conveying barrels and sacks to and from the harbour. The harbour was a place of great activity. It was often packed with vessels, loading and unloading cargoes. Auction sales were held on the south pier. It boasted a 'globe' on which merchants (both residents and visitors) could place notices. In May 1729 merchant Anthoine La Grace used this facility to advertise the sale of 34 tonneaux 'de vin rouge de Grave de Bordeaux' which had arrived on the barque commanded by Joseph Townson. The two notices pinned up by La Grace were smeared with filth ('*entièrement couvertes d'ordure...excrément*'). La Grace suspected that le Sr Henry Brock sr had torn and defaced the notices to frustrate any sale. He appealed to the *Cour d'Amirauté* for justice.

Educating the young

After receiving an elementary education locally, the sons of the leading *négociants* were regularly sent away to complete their studies abroad. Henry de Sausmarez went to Holland, perhaps the finest venue for a mercantile education in the late seventeenth/early eighteenth centuries. Most boys, however, were sent to England, for English was well on its way to becoming the leading language in international commerce. A mastery of English was essential for the ambitious Guernsey merchant. Some English schools offered vocational subjects of utilitarian value to the apprentice merchant – practice in writing business-letters, keeping accounts, solving sums about weights and measures, calculating duties, subsidies, drawback, bounties, tariffs and imposts. (Towards the end of the eighteenth century there were schoolmasters delivering such lessons in Guernsey). When school studies came to an end, some young men were sent on a 'grand tour'. Others were immediately placed in the business-house of a relation, friend or correspondent, to gain several years of work experience as a factor abroad. In this way the Guernsey merchants built up networks. When Nicholas Reserson, for example, had spent some years working in a business-house in Barcelona, his father set him up in partnership there with a fellow Guernseyman, William de Vic Tupper. By the late eighteenth century the Guernsey merchants had relations working in England, Holland, Spain, Canada, America, and the West Indies. This 'network' underpinned the working of the entrepôt.

The sons of *négociants* were frequently given experience at sea, serving as junior officers. We find them also in the thick of privateering ventures. They had the hope of action, of a rich prize perhaps, and the expectation of cutting a dashing figure amidst the ladies when peace returned. Good marriages were important to *négociants*. A wedding brought together not just two people but also combined the financial resources of the two families. In this way marriage promoted capital formation. Not surprisingly, many merchant families were linked by marriage. Marriage alliances were long-term. The merchants also frequently entered into partnerships. These were often relatively short-term and for specific purposes.

In the rest of this chapter we shall look in some detail at five merchants: William Bell; Peter Mourant; Pierre-Frédéric Dobrée; Nicholas Reserson; and John Guille. These have been chosen partly because there is good evidence about their activities, partly because their careers represent different aspects of the Guernsey story. William Bell arrived in St Peter Port at the age of 23. He had strong connections with Scottish Jacobite sympathisers. With his excellent contacts he built up a prosperous business in Guernsey. Peter Mourant is a good example of an upwardly-mobile merchant. Trade and some privateering ventures brought him wealth and the opportunity to move to a fine new house on the outskirts of St Peter Port. Pierre-Frédéric Dobrée left Guernsey as a young man and succeeded in Nantes (all the while maintaining links with his Guernsey family); Nicholas Reserson, on the other hand, went to Barcelona and ended up bankrupt. John Guille quietly prospered.

Fig. 5.3: Transporting goods through St Peter Port -
a detail from a plate in William Berry's *History of Guernsey*, 1815.

Table 5.4 Guernsey merchants dealing with Zephaniah Job, 'the smugglers' banker', 1778-1808

	78	79	80	81	82	83	84	85	86	87	88	89	90	91	92	93	94	95	96	97	98	99	00	01	02	03	04	05	06	07	08
Jersey deLisle	–																														
Peter de Lisle										–	–	–	–	–	–	–	–	–	–	–	–	–									
De Jersey Corbin																															
John Guille & Co						–	–	–	–	–	–																				
DeJersey Guille & Co																															
Henry Brock		–	–	–																											
Peter Mourant		–	–	–	–	–	–	–	–																						
Mourant & Chepmell		–																													
Mourant & Combes		–	–	–	–	–	–																								
Peter Mourant & Co					–	–	–																								
Thomas Priaulx						–	–																								
Priaulx de Carteret & Co		–	–	–	–	–																									
De Carteret & Co						–	–	–	–	–	–																				
Nicholas Maingy & brothers																					–	–									
Brock-LaSerre-Maingy		–									–	–	–	–	–	–	–	–	–	–	–	–									
John Lukis														–	–	–	–	–	–	–	–	–	–	–	–	–	–	–	–	–	
Hillary Boucault & Co																						–	–	–	–	–	–	–	–		
Thoumine Moullin & Co																							–	–	–	–	–	–	–	–	

Source: Gleanings from the records of Zephaniah Job, of Polperro by F. H. Perrycoste (1929).

WILLIAM BELL

From humble beginnings, with the help of Archibald Stewart (q.v.), William Bell became a négociant, specialising in the wine trade. He settled in Guernsey in 1749 and married into the Le Marchant family.

William was born at Leith in 1726. On his father's death in 1738 he went into the counting-house of Archibald Stewart (q.v.) in Edinburgh and attended occasionally the vaults of Leith until 1740. In 1742 he went to Boulogne and remained there, working in the vaults and counting-house of Charles Smith. When war broke out between France and Britain he returned home. Then he went to London. In April 1745 he set off to Dover and Ostend for Ferrier in Zealand, where he arrived 1st May 1745; he made a trip to Amsterdam, Rotterdam and Antwerp. He saw the Stadtholder proclaimed and was two days in Bergen-ap-Zoom lines during the siege. He dined with Lord London. About 1st Nov he returned to Leith suffering from a tertiary Zealand ague which he only got rid of in the summer of 1748. He sailed from Leith for Hamburg but had to to put back on account of contrary winds. He journeyed from Leith to London on horseback. He left London and arrived at Guernsey 1st August 1748. After a stay of five weeks he returned to London and set off (5th Sept) on a journey to France, journeying from Calais to Dunkirk and Boulogne, Paris, Rheims, Beaune, Lyons, Avignon, Montpellier, Cette and by canal to Languedoc, from Toulouse to Bordeaux, where he saw peace proclaimed. From Bordeaux he sailed by the Captain Kelly to Guernsey where he arrived in May 1749. (Priaulx Library, Le Marchant family file, copied from 'Mr Cathcart's mss').

In 1755 he married Mary Le Marchant, a member of the wealthy, aristocratic family of Guernsey *négociants*. He was designated merchant-shipowner *temp.* Seven Years War. In the early 1760s he served as Constable of St Peter Port. The Tax registers show him as living in the Pollet at that time and he was assessed at 180 quarters *(CO Taxe)*. In 1772 he bought the house of Thomas Le Marchant, his brother-in-law, for one thousand pounds sterling (Nantes 2-A-18, Dobrée to son, 16 Nov 1772). He was designated as merchant-shipowner *temp.* American War but he does not seem to have been much interested in privateering. Bell traded in wine from the Algarve, Barcelona, Cadiz, Lisbon, Malaga, and Oporto *(Livre de certificats)*. His son, William jr, also traded in wine. Father and son were included in the list of leading merchants/traders in 1779. By the late 1780s he was assessed at 900 quarters. He did not rank with the wealthiest merchants but he was very comfortably off. William was a member of the *Society for the Encouragement of Arts, Manufacture, and Commerce* from 1787 to 1799 and subscribed to *The History of Dahomy* by A. Dalzel (London, 1793), purchasing two copies. In 1792 William sr left off business in favour of his sons William and George. In 1795 he lost his dearly beloved wife in London (6th March). She was buried in St Andrew's churchyard, Holborne. He died, 30 Sept 1805, aged 79 years.

Bell's connections are very interesting. In the 1740s he worked for Charles Smith. He was a prosperous Scottish merchant, based at Boulogne-sur-Mer in France. Smith was a Jacobite supporter and was active prior to the 1745 landing of Prince Charles Stuart in Scotland. Recent research has drawn attention to his significance. (Some of his correspondence is among the Stuart papers at Windsor Castle. Sir Joshua Reynolds painted his portrait in 1760; it is now at the City Art Centre, Edinburgh). Bell was placed with Smith by Archibald Stuart to whom we shall now turn.

Archibald Stuart / Stewart

In 1752 J Harris wrote to Ligonier, the Governor of Guernsey, stating:

> About four years ago, being then at Guernsey, I saw there Mr James Stuart, at this day ye greatest wine merchant in Europe, and tho' but just then broke from being Lord Provost of Edinburgh, for basely surrendering it up to ye Rebels in the late unnatural Rebelion in Scotland, yet he was frequently at Mr Strahans, about which time broke out ye refusal of

Fig. 5.4: Archibald Stewart
(after a portrait in *The Lord Provosts of Edinburgh*, Edinburgh, 1932,
reproduced by kind permission of The National Library of Scotland).

paying ye Duties on Wines &c. and tho' Mr Strahan was pleas'd in a letter to your Honour to fix that refusal upon Mr Isaac Dobrée as ye invention of a hot headed young fellow, yet it may be presum'd to be of Mr Stuarts invention, jointly with the other dealers in wines, and perhaps not without the privitty of Mr Strahan himself for he still hath a great regard for Stuart's clark by frequently inviting him to dinner, whereas this Stuart thus justly branded with infamy, might have been a motive sufficient for Mr Strahan to have shunn'd the man, but some men have oddities peculiar to themselves, and Mr Strahan's being yearly afflicted with a megrim upon the anniversary Inauguration, Coronation, and birth days of his Majesty's, and no bells then allow'd to be rung, for fear of increasing his pain, tho he lives a mile from the church, this may not be be accounted a very great oddity by some people, especially where self interest leads the van (BL Lansdowne Ms 657, f 24r – f 25r 1 Feb 1752 Harris to Ligonier. 'Stuart's clark' is probably a reference to William Bell).

Harris considered Stuart responsible for the scheme whereby Guernsey merchants imported wine into the island for British colleagues who thus evaded duty payable to the king. He described Stuart as being 'just then broke from being Lord Provost of Edinburgh' but 'at this day the greatest wine merchant in Europe'. Harris made a mistake about Stuart's Christian name. It was Archibald who was Lord Provost of Edinburgh in 1745.

Archibald Stuart was a successful Edinburgh wine merchant with warehouses at Leith. We catch a glimpse of his business in the State Papers. In May 1744 William Wood wrote that Archibald Stewart & Co had produced a licence to import thirty hogsheads of French wine but the ship's report showed that the cargo also included unlicensed wines. Wood asked whether the Commissioners of Customs would allow the wine to be imported (TNA SP 36/64 Wood to Stone, 25 May 1744).

In 1741 Archibald had entered parliament and in 1745 he became Lord Provost of Edinburgh. During the rebellion of 1745 a force of nine hundred men supporting Prince Charles Edward entered Edinburgh by night. Many suspected that the Lord Provost sympathised with the Stuart cause and that he had connived at the entry of the Jacobite army. He was arrested and eventually brought to trial. David Hume wrote a pamphlet in his defence – *A True Account of the Behaviour and Conduct of Archibald Stewart* - arguing that it would not have been possible to defend Edinburgh and that a siege would have brought disastrous consequences. Archibald was found 'not guilty' and sent some good Burgundy to Hume as a 'thank you'. 'The gift', said David, in his good-humoured way, 'ruined me; I was obliged to give so many dinners in honour of the wine' (Mackenzie, 1927, p. 172).

Archibald transferred his business to 11 Buckingham Street, London. From the 1760s he 'spent ever longer periods at his country villa in Mitcham leaving the responsibilities of business to his son John Stuart'. John was a remarkable man who 'combined business acumen with a flair for intrigue and a talent for writing political articles'. He was active in the East India Company, assisted Sir George Colebrooke and became a MP in 1771. Archibald died in 1780, John in 1781. (www.kuiters.org/wgi/history/botgardpaxton.html, 26/07/2007).

Stray references indicate that Archibald Stuart and his son made use of Guernsey in their wine trade. In July 1748 Archibald was ordered to pay Mr Jean Cornelius £221-10-6 st., outstanding on wine sold by Cornelius to Archibald Stuart (CdA, vol. 12 f 124 v). In 1762 Archibald Stuart and Edward Marjoribanks lodged a protest with a Guernsey notary. They had received orders from John Stuart of London to furnish (at Guernsey) a cargo consisting of one hundred butts Spanish wines either mountain or sherry, fifty pipes red wines, one hundred hogsheads ditto, one hundred thirty hogsheads wine to be drawn off in bottles & put in proper packages, three or four tuns of soap. This order was to be executed for Samuel Touchet, a London merchant. The cargo was to be loaded at Guernsey on board a ship called the *Royal Charlotte* (George Calbreath commander) and despatched to Havannah. The goods were made ready 'the wines bottl'd & packed up a considerable time before the ship's arrival in this island'. When Captain Calbreath arrived, they informed him of the quantity of goods they had to ship on board, 'upon which he told them his ship could not take in so much, she having taken in more goods in London than probably Mr Touchet had been acquainted with or words to the purpose'. Only part of the cargo was loaded by Captain Calbreath. Archibald Stewart and Edward Marjoribanks considered that some agreement had been made in London between Samuel Touchet and Captain Calbreath or his owners 'either verbal or written about the goods the said ship was to load here before he gave orders to provide the same and therefore they demand to protest' (Priaulx Library, Isaac Dobrée protest book).

What is interesting about this episode is that Archibald Stuart was in Guernsey, arranging the cargo. He was accompanied by Edward Marjoribanks. According to Debrett's *Baronetage of Britain*, Edward Marjoribanks of Hallyards & Lees, co Berwick, married Grizel or Grace Stewart, daughter of Archibald Stewart, Lord Provost of Edinburgh 1745 - Edward was Archibald's son-in-law.

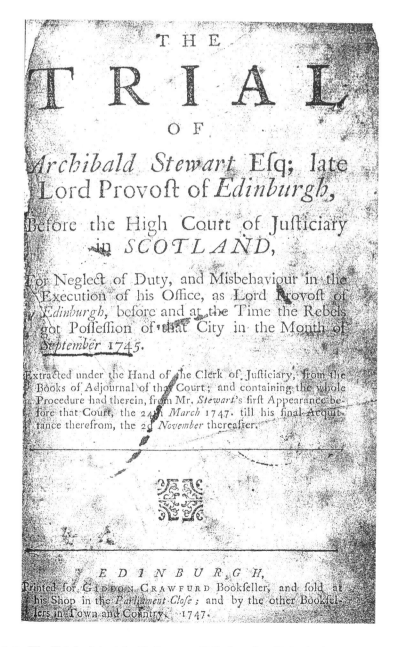

Fig. 5.5: *The Trial of Archibald Stewart*, Edinburgh, 1747 (private collection).

PIERRE-FREDERIC DOBRÉE (1757-1801)

Pierre-Frédéric received some elementary education in Guernsey and was then sent (20 April 1771) to Highgate Grammar School (London), where he learnt Latin, arithmetic and the correct pronunciation of English. In 1773 he returned to Guernsey for eighteen months. His father, Thomas, accompanied him to Lorient in September 1775 and introduced him to André Galwey (among others). Thomas Dobrée initiated his son into his mercantile procedures.

On 13 Nov 1775 Thomas sent Pierre Frédéric instructions about loading a cargo on the *Durell* (Capt Ph Dean, master). Twenty chests for Mr Elisha Tupper were to be marked Δ, ten of Mr La Serre marked ILS, five marked +H belonging to Mr Harvey, nine belonging to Cap Mourant marked SM. Pierre-Frédéric was to take care to make out a bill of lading & consign them to Mr Corn Vanderhoeven of Rotterdam,

> 'and you are to make the following insurances, if it comes to be done at Lorient write to Mr Berthault of Nantes to get the same executed but pray take care to do it as soon as the vessel arrives at Lorient, viz

£2000 on the five chests marked +H

 4400 on the 10 chests marked ILS

 4000 on the 9 chests marked SM

10400

> Those of Mr Tupper are not to be insured. The moment you have executed the above orders and that my friend Gallwey does not whant (*sic*) you, you may repair for Nantes as I fancy Messrs Meynert & Co must expect you by that time'.

PF soon moved to Nantes, where he worked for the German *négociant* Meynert (Meinert). He fell in love with Marie-Rose Schweighauser, the daughter of a wealthy German/Swiss *négociant*. There was a short engagement. At first the Schweighauser parents had reservations about the match. After negotiations the dowry was fixed at 150,000 livres and PF brought fifty thousand livres to the union (contract 21 June 1777). PF was soon incorporated as a partner in the Schweighauser business.

Throughout 1778 he maintained a steady correspondence with his father in Guernsey. It was an interesting and difficult time for a young Guernseyman newly established in Nantes. The marriage of a foreign youngster into a wealthy Nantes family was, perhaps, bound to generate some jealousies. There was the added complication of war, the American colonists were staging their rebellion against the 'tyranny' of George III. This led to the customary problems and opportunities attendant on international crises. In April 1778 PF investigated the navigation acts and their implications. In June he was of the opinion that speculation in tea was not a good idea, indigo, sugars, tobacco and rice were better, he favoured indigo. In August he was thinking of sending his father's wines to America. The following month PF reported news of the arrival of ships from the east and offered to attend the auction on his father's behalf. Maritime hostilities brought the opportunity to help Carie l'ainé, a merchant at Nantes; on his behalf PF asked his father to assist Mons Grandin, a passenger on the *Lynx* taken to Jersey by a privateer of that island. On the other hand PF was irritated by Channel Islands *armateurs* who asked him to interecede on behalf of their captains. If PF interceded, that would play into the hands of his enemies in Nantes: 'je donnerois beau jeu à mes ennemis car ce n'est pas un bonheur pour moi d'être natif de Guernesey'. Moreover, he was not inclined to help these captains because they had captured vessels carrying cargoes to Nantes ('car ils ont pris bien des navires qui nous étoient adressés', 12 Sept 1778). Twelve days later PF asked his father to intercede on behalf of Monsieur Le Breton of *l'Orphée*, PF wanted to prove himself to his French colleagues at Nantes. On 10 October he urged his father to speculate 'if I were there I would make a fortune sending to Hamburg and Rotterdam' and he relayed questions from the Chamber of Commerce at Nantes about the situation of French boats carrying American tobacco. Two days later he asked about Jean Jacob Schweighauser (nephew of PF's father-in-law) who had been a passenger on a ship captured by Guernsey privateers. On 16 October he again begged his father to tell Channel Islands *armateurs* not to trouble him about sailors taken prisoner. PF had envious enemies on the lookout for reason to harm him ('trouver quelque motif pour me nuire'). The next day he reported that Fischer intended to visit Guernsey to buy at the sales of prize goods. Fischer was reported as having credit on Mess Pierre Simon & Hankey and on Lewis Tessier, solid houses. At about the same time Mons Diodatti of Paris was enquiring about Guernsey affairs. PF recommended Diodatti as 'un de nos plus grands speculateurs' and 'très solide'.

In March 1779 John de Havilland wrote from Guernsey to PF, assuring him that his father had no concern in privateers, so PF would be able to refute the malicious aspersions of his enemies. There was also family chit-chat – news of Cousin Betsy's marriage with Mr Utermark of Hamburgh (1 Mar 1779). In June 1780 PF told his father about two Irishmen – a priest and a doctor – going to Ireland on a neutral ship; they might put in at Guernsey and, if so, would father protect them, please (20 June 1780). In August 1780 PF was of the opinion that the price of tobacco would fall, there being cargoes at Gottenburg, Amsterdam, and Rochelle. There was Jamaica rum to be found on two prizes at Bordeaux. He also recorded the visit of Beaugeard (*négociant* of St Malo) to Nantes to render his annual account to the *Chambre de Compte*.

In 1782 we find PF bemoaning the poor standard of French taught at Guernsey and suggesting that the college would do better to teach modern languages. This may have been an argument to squash the idea of an islander joining him in Nantes. In June 1782 PF suggested to his father that he should write to le comte de Belgiojoso, the Imperial ambassador in London, to get his recommendation, there being need of an Imperial consul in Guernsey. PF had written to Van Schoon & fils, bankers 'de la cour à Bruxelles' on the matter.

The return of peace brought quieter times. Thomas Dobrée attended the sales at Lorient and hatched an interesting idea. If he and his son acquired 1000 or 1200 chests of tea, would Paul Le Mesurier (a Guernseyman in the East India Company, London) take them on commission? Le Mesurier was open to the suggestion and mentioned 2 ½ % commission provided the Dobrées could purchase at the current prices and it did not appear that the buying had been the means of running the prices up to the prejudice of the English Company's orders (15 July 1785). It is not clear whether the deal went through. There were also transactions with another Le Mesurier. In June 1786 TD asked his son whether Mr Havilland Le Mesurier's house at Havre had taken the consignment of Madeira wine, he was anxious to have it sold (27 June 1786).

The autumn and winter of 1786 saw PF trying to secure his appointment as British consul at Nantes. In October 1786 TD reported that he had consulted Paul Le Mesurier about the matter. The appointment rested with the Marquis of Carmarthen, Secretary of State for the foreign department, by way of Lord Shelburn. Paul Le Mesurier had already been obliged to trouble his Lordship in favour of Mr William Carey, soliciting the place of consul at Bordeaux; and Paul's brother Havilland was trying to secure the consulship at Havre. In addition to his news about lobbying in high places, TD added some Guernsey news: 'Yesterday no less than two large vessels arrived here from Gothenberg'. Teas there had been sold 'very cheap... I dare say those of Lorient have been sold for much more as it is commonly the case that goods in general are sold dearer there than at the other sales'. At the end of October (30 Oct 1786) a letter from Paul Le Mesurier indicated that the consul must be a native of Great Britain and a protestant; 'one who has taken an oath of naturalisation to the French government and in consequence has been allowed to trade in his own name and on his own account to French colonies is debarred'. In December TD floated the idea that Sam Dobrée might help over the consulship application. Sam had lately married Miss Hankey, 'his connexions by his wife's side are very good, some of them in Parliament'. TD was able to add the promising news that 'Our Lt Gov has just now received a letter from Lord Hamhurst [= *Amherst*] who promises to do all he can to get thee appointed'. Thomas Dobrée, meanwhile, was trying to advance his own cause and become the French consul in Guernsey. On 7 Feb 1787 he explained to his son that he needed the recommendation of Madame La Duchesse de Polignac 'who by means of the queen can get all she asks'. He might have to travel to Paris.

Trade was slack in Guernsey: 'there is no trade here (except the smuggling business) worth carrying on, and the smuggling trade is such and so very hazardous that I don't chuse to have anything to do therewith, happy are those who have made their fortune' (15 Jan 1787). In June 1787 TD was thinking of buying brandy cheap, keeping it until the price increased, then selling it on the English market. He considered brandy of Cognac the best for this market 'D'autant plus que tant plus ils ont d'age et tant plus ils sont estimés'. He suggested that his son should send 100 pipes from Nantes to Guernsey. There was a lot of rum from St Croix at Guernsey but it was difficult to shift despite being offered @ 2 shillings the gallon. He recommened brandy, flour, butter, textiles from Laval and Brittany 'quelques pièces de Batide & La Canille' & silks as the best commodities for shipping to Madeira. In November 1787 TD was thinking of sending his vessel *le Success* to Nantes, either to sell it or to find employment for it. Later in the month he was forwarding *4 bottes* and *4 barriques* of excellent Madeira wine for his son to sell at Nantes. Pierre's mother wrote to him in the same month, announcing the marriage of Auguste Dobrée to Miss De Lisle. She thought that it would prove a successful match: 'il est bien assidu & elle bien économe'.

January 1788 saw TD dispensing commercial advice to his son. India goods were prohibited at Madeira, brandy answered best there. If Madeira wine could be sold at Lorient it was best to direct it there rather than send it to Charleston: 'It is better to go on a certainty than to rely on an uncertainty' (13 Jan 1788). The *Success* was to sale to Madeira with a cargo of 50 pieces brandy, 35 tons wheat, calicos, linens, cambrics, butter and then be sold.

February brought news of a slaving venture in which PF was involved. *La Véronique* had transported a cargo of 275 negroes across the Atlantic; 55 had been lost through dysentry, leaving 220 of whom 176 had already been sold (16 Feb 1788). On 23 Mar 1789 TD reported that tobacco from James Town was in demand 'les fraudeurs en font une consummation considérable' and he ordered 100 – 200 *boucauts* 'belle & large feuille' of 'bon odorat' (but NOT ordinary tobacco). PF was apologetic that he did not attend his sister's wedding. His father was very understanding: 'I think you are quite right in taking care of the main chance, business is the first thing (after our duty to God) that must be attended to' (9 July 1789).

On 23 Jan 1790 TD observed that a large number of boats had been arriving from France for salt and tobacco. It was clearly a boom time for tobacco sales and on 2 Feb 1790 TD recorded that in Guernsey alone not fewer than fifteen or twenty manufactories had been set up (for the cleaning and preparation of the tobacco leaves) 'and I dare say at Jersey they have three or four times that number'. In March 1792 TD wanted two or three hundred cubic feet of mahogany: 'I should imagine that you can easily find to freight at moderate price a bark or chasse-marée to bring these goods here'.

In June 1795 St Peter Port was overstocked with French wine. TD reported that the price of red port (if good) was 18 to 22 pounds sterling per pipe; old and excellent red port fetched as much as £25 or £26 per pipe. On 28 May 1795 TD estimated that R.P. LeMarchant & Mr Lauga had received on commission from Bordeaux about six or seven thousand tuns of wine but felt that they would turn out to be 'a bad account'. TD repeated his forebodings in August 1796: 'There is at present an immence (*sic*) quantity of brandies rum gin & French wines in the island, on which I am afraid there will be a considerable loss' (1 Aug 1796).

War interrupted trade and correspondence. Pierre-Frédéric was in the utmost danger on occasions, he was suspected of being a traitor or a spy. There is reason to believe that he did, in fact, provide valuable services to the British government. But that is another story that must await another occasion.

LE PORT DE NANTES
Vu du Chantier de Conſtruction de la Foſse

Fig. 5.6: Nantes, an engraving designed by N. M. Ozanne, published *circa* 1776, reproduced by kind permission of The National Maritime Museum.

PETER MOURANT

Peter was born in 1740, the son of Etienne/Stephen Mourant, a well established Guernsey captain. In his early career Peter was ranked as 'le Sieur' but later in his life he was accorded 'Esq'. He belonged to the *Société des Veuves*; signed the Canary wine petition in 1776; and was signatory as a leading merchant-trader in 1779. In the 1770s we find Peter importing wine (*Livre de certificats*). He dealt with Zephaniah Job either in his sole name (1778-1779) or in his partnerships: Mourant & Chepmell (1778-1783); Mourant and Combes (1782-1783); house of Peter Mourant & Co (1783-1784). When the American War broke out, Mourant engaged in privateering, in partnership with Chepmell. Their vessels *Swift* and *Tartar* captured valuable prizes – *Swift* to the value of £19,387 and *Tartar* £22,553 (Greffe, de Sausmarez manuscript).

Thanks to this success Mourant was able to move out of St Peter Port into the nearby countryside. At Candie he enjoyed extensive grounds with plenty of room for gardens. Candie House was built *circa* 1780-1781. In 1782, through the Dobrée bank in London, Mourant arranged an insurance on his new dwelling house. His Sun insurance policy provided six hundred and fifty pounds cover on the 'stone & slated' house and one hundred and fifty pounds cover on the household goods therein (Guildhall, Sun: policy 455953, 7 February 1782, volume 298, p. 648). In 1793 Mourant had greenhouses built – the first in Guernsey (Marr, 1984, pp. 193-194).

Mourant's business affairs for the years 1783-1790 are recorded in a large journal. *Négociants* had three principal working books for keeping their accounts: the waste book; the journal; and the ledger. First was the waste book, in which the merchant made an immediate record of each transaction. Next came the journal. William Richards explained its function in his manual *The Complete Penman*, London, 1747:

> The Journal is the next principal Book; and therein all the Transactions mention'd in the Waste-Book, are thrown into Method and Order. Here the Debtor and Creditor of every Parcel is declar'd, the Sum and Substance of the Transactions express'd, and the whole Skill of an Accomptant employ'd in making proper Entries, and placing the Terms, Debtor and Creditor, so as to balance every Account a-right...

In the final stage the merchant transferred information from the journal into the ledger, in which transactions were systematically recorded under the names of suppliers and clients. Thanks to Mourant's journal we know that he owned not just Candie but property elsewhere:

Table 5.5 Peter Mourant's properties

Vault under Peter Mourant's house in High Street	£40 rent
The tea room	£15
Cellars at Bordage	£21
Vault at Candie	£20

Source: Priaulx, Mourant Journal, p. 307

Insurance on the house in High Street was arranged through Perchard & Brock in London (Priaulx, Mourant Journal, p. 389). Some of Mourant's shipping insurance was arranged by B Dobrée of London.

The journal shows that Mourant dealt in spirits - brandy from Charente and Cette (suppliers: Augier & Co; Annibal Broussard & Ph Gernon; Falconnet Burnet & Delamarche) and from Spain (Gregory & Guille); gin from Rotterdam (Peter Roche and James & James LeMarchant); rum from Grenada and St Croix. He bought tea and china from Arfwidson of Gothenburg and imported tobacco from America. Sometimes he traded in almonds and cotton. There was a steady need for staves (from America) and iron hoops (from Peter Roche at Rotterdam) – to make barrels. Some coopering was carried out at Candie. Mourant paid John Rougier and William Blanchemain, his coopers, £30 each, per year (Journal, 1 Feb 1788, p. 420).

As we have seen above, Mourant, like most Guernsey merchants, worked in partnerships. He was also involved in shipping partnerships and had a major interest in several vessels in the 1780s. Valuable details are provided by the Journal.

Table 5.6 Peter Mourant's shipping interests

Copenhagen: Sarre (2007) speculates that this may have been chartered by PM.

Ceres: A British-built ship of 300 tons. It was bought at public auction for £2205st. Mourant had a $\frac{3}{8}$ interest (other owners included Daniel Lauga, Hilary Gosselin and F. Anquetil). It was employed on the West Indies run. The Journal records it carrying a cargo of 35205 ¼ gallons of rum, worth £4840-14-6 (Journal, p 214). According to Sarre it was reported lost at sea on a voyage from Guernsey to the West Indies, 12 Oct 1784.

Hope: Mourant had a $\frac{5}{8}$ interest in this ship (which was variously valued at £3000st and £2,500). It was employed on the West Indies run (to Grenada) and also took Cognac brandy to Madeira.

Three Sisters: a ship of some two hundred tons built at Hull in 1783; it cost £2451-19-10. The ship was used on the West Indies run (carrying rum from Grenada); and also made voyages to Toulon, Cette and Madeira.

Pomona: Mourant had a half interest in this ship built at Teignmouth in 1784 (valued at £1600 st.). In 1791 she was lengthened at Bursledon and sailed faster (now 270 tons). See pp. 150-170 for details of her voyages.

Unity: a brig valued at £500, employed on the West Indies run.

Swift: variously described as a sloop or cutter, built in 1787 at Ringmore, Devon; 46 tons; valued at £500 st. Mourant had a $\frac{5}{8}$ interest. She was employed on the West Indies run.

Fly: schooner, purchased from Francis Anquetil, Mourant had ¼ share. In March 1784 she was fitted out in Jersey for a Newfoundland voyage.

Hudibras: 170 tons, Dutch built, pass for Madeira and West Indies (L. Jehan master). (Mourant insured 21 May 1787).

Sources: Priaulx, Mourant Journal; Sarre (2007).

The journal contains inventories which detail the volume of stock carried and the utensils of trade (see table 5.8). We can reconstruct the counting house. There were six chairs – enough for Mourant and his partners to meet with other merchants. There was a mahogany desk. It was, perhaps, on this that rested four vital reference books: Salmon's *Gazeteer*; *Foreign Exchange*; Baldwin's *Survey of the Customs*; and *Lex Mercatoria*. (In 1796 he subscribed to Jones's *English System of Book-keeping by simple or double entry*). He was well equipped with stationery, sealing wax, weights and measures. The inventory shows that he carried a large stock of wine and spirits.

Peter Mourant's four children made good marriages, linking the family to prominent merchant dynasties. His son Peter married Miss Sophie Carey (daughter of Mr John Carey of the Bigoterie). Martha married Mr Bonamy Dobrée (issue: one son and six daughters); Mary married Henry F. Brock; and Ann married William Brock. There was much sadness in the latter part of Mourant's life. In 1798 W. T. Money visited Guernsey and he recorded the bereavements endured by the merchant.

> 'In the afternoon we dined with Mr Mourant, a polite, hospitable well-informed gentleman with much urbanity of manners, and a cheerfulness in conversation, which it was easy to discern he had borrowed for the entertainment of his company, under the pressure of severe calamity.
>
> Sick with the weight of care, he smiled Hope in his countenance while Grief sat at his heart.
>
> He, a few months ago, was deprived of his favourite daughter, married to Mr. Dobrée, and within these six weeks, it has pleased Providence to remove from him his wife, the fond companion of his youthful days, the faithful prop of his declining years. Poor Dobrée, our friend, too appears at times, ready to sink under his loss; he took me with him to the garden……
>
> In this garden every Saturday Mr. Mourant has his six mourning grand-daughters to pass the day with him. He amuses them with fishing, pleases them with flowers, treats them with his fruit, and in his Alcove sits and watches over them with a parent's delight.
>
> While we were at table we had the pleasure to see the Pacquet from Weymouth come into the roads, with a strong gale from the southward which forced a ship under Quarantine from her anchors, and obliged her to run through the Little Russell – the passage between the islands and the rocks to the north-east. At this time the smuggler who had taken in

his cargo yesterday, took advantage of wind and weather – to him a propitious gale – and the sunshine of his hopes under the very nose of the Men of War, with his three reefed longsails stood over for England. Sometimes he is obliged to return after an unsuccessful attempt to land – swearing there were too many rogues (Customs or Excise Cutters) on the Coast. (Carey 1931, 241).

Table 5.7 Inventory of the goods in stock of Peter Mourant & Co., 'the old partnership, supplied to present partnership, 1 Jan. 1785'.

8 pipes	Cette spirit	147-4-4
84 pipes	Cette Brandy	1193-6-6
70 pipes	Geneva	846-1-9
90 veltes	Jamaica Rum	31-10-0
47 veltes	Shrub	16-9-0
10 pipes	Brandy wash	50-0-0
12 pipes	Rum in the Tuns	178-1-5 ½
22 pipes	Brandy in the Tuns	248-17-7
38 pipes	Salou brandy ⎱	406-10-6
7 half hogsheads	" ⎰	
6 pipes	Cognac Brandy (Common)	76-17-7
26 pipes	Cognac Brandy (London)	362-9-4 ½
11 puncheons	Rum in the cellars	118-8-4
164 puncheons	" at Candie ⎱	1898-1-10
11 ¼ hogsheads	⎰	
10 hogsheads ⎱	St Drezeny wine	45-0-0
1 pipe		
6 hogsheads ⎰	Claret	65-0-0
2 tierces		
16 dozens of	St Drezeny wine	4-0-0
2 pipes	Sea Stock wine	12-12-0
11 dozens	" "	2-4-0
2375 lbs	sling stuff	19-0-0
2319 lbs	made slings	20-5-10
1340 lbs	spunyarn	10-14-5
60 dozens	bottles	5-0-0
15 pieces of	cloth for bags	63-7-6
15 ditto	oil case	3-4-9
28 double	½ hundred bags	3-10-0
85 double	¼ ditto	5-6-3
90 lbs	Lead in sheets	10-9 ½
19	cave bottles	19-0
6	juggs	6-0
20	empty puncheons	5-0-0
24	empty hogsheads	1-16-0
60	" "	4-10-0
65	" ½ "	6-10-0
566	ankers	56-12-0
109	half ankers	9-10-9
120	four gallon kegs	8-5-0
70	flaggins [sic]	3-10-0
32	six pound dollop bags	10-8
6	twelve pound " "	3-0
$\frac{5}{8}$ of the ship	*Hope* valued at £3,000	1875-0-0
½ of the ship	*Pomona* valued at £2,600	1300-0-0
30 pipes	of Cette Brandy sent to Madeira which are not comprehended in the Inventory and as we make the owners of ship *Hope*. Drs for the amount of the invoice we make this partnership Drs for them at the price as we charge the other Brandy Viz. 4231 ½ gallons @ 2/=	423-3-0

20 pipes	Cognac brandy sent to Madeira with the other 30 pipes Cette Brandy as above 2277 ½ gallons at 2/3	256-4-4 ½
¼ of	schooner *Fly* valued at £360	90-0-0
$\frac{5}{8}$ of £98-14-6	premium &c of insurance on ship *Hope* which has been charged	61-13-9
	To the old partnership	
		£9,937-7-4

UTENSILS IN TRADE

8 tuns valued at	£ 70-0- 0
Sundry coopers tools	3 - 7- 0
A large new beam	6 -0 -0
A large ditto & scale	2 -2 -0
A small beam & scales	6 - 0
Sundry weights	5 -0 -0
Candle sticks & scoops	5 - 0
Notes & bills of exchange	5- 0
A standard gold weight & scales	15-0
2 pairs of hand scales	1- 0 -0
A set of avoirdupois weight	7 - 6
Salmon's *Gazeteer*	6 - 0
Osnabrey's *Foreign Exchange*	10-0
A standard pair of candlesticks	18-0
A mahogany desk	2 -0 -0
6 chairs	12-0
Baldwin's *Survey of the Customs*	1 -1 -0
Lex Mercatoria	1 -7 -0
150 quills	6 - 0
300 paper bags	4 - 0
5 ½ reams of white packing paper	1 -2 -0
6 lbs thread	6 - 0
28 lbs twine	1 -5 -0
16 papers of Powder for ink	8 - 0
13 quires of writing paper	6 - 0
2 " of post "	1 - 0
2 reams of common "	1 -4 -0
4 reams of French "	1 -0 -0
A tackle & double blocks	1 -5 -0
2 Falls of cordage weighing 65 lbs at 42/= per 100w	1 -7 -4
2 spoons for lead	5 - 0
4 moulds for ditto	12-0
2 hand barrows	8 - 0
78 sticks of sealing wax	6- 6
	106-7 -4

£10,043-14-8

NICHOLAS RESERSON

Richard Hocart, in his study of Peter de Havilland, refers to the ill-fated partnership of Reserson and Tupper:

> De Havilland's brother-in-law Nicholas Reserson suffered financial disaster in 1793, when his son, also called Nicholas, who had been trading in Barcelona for over twenty years, became insolvent. Reserson senior had agreed to act as his son's guarantor and had to surrender his whole fortune, which de Havilland thought was between £10,000 and £12,000. De Havilland said that 'the blow has overwhelmed him, and he has fallen into a dejection out of which it is at present impossible to draw him'. His wife, a saintly woman who was already suffering from the wasting disease which eventually left her bedridden, had enough money to support them both. Neither was in a fit state to write to their son, so de Havilland wrote on their behalf. He urged Reserson junior to declare himself bankrupt rather than to come to an arrangement with his creditors, but Reserson ignored his advice and entered into a verbal agreement with William Tupper, the son of Jurat Elisha Tupper, then in business in Barcelona. Reserson undertook to work for Tupper who would in turn arrange a settlement of his debts. De Havilland wrote Reserson a stinging rebuke for ignoring his advice and entering into an unwritten agreement. Reserson remained in Barcelona and was said in 1796 to be the chief employee in another trading house in Barcelona (Hocart 1997, pp. 56-57).

The story of this failure is explained in a manuscript in the Priaulx Library. The account is written neatly in ink, in French, and fills one hundred and one pages. There is no statement of authorship and the account refers throughout to Reserson. However, some of the content would have been known to Nicholas Reserson alone, and to none other; moreover, Reserson was almost certainly the only person who would have possessed an over-arching understanding of the story. Finally, the account serves as an *apologia* for Reserson. It is not easy to conjecture who else would have had a motive for writing the document.

Reserson may have chosen to write in the third person to achieve a certain 'distance' and objectivity in the account. In choosing to use the third person Reserson had plenty of precedents to guide him. Caesar's *Commentaries* were well established in the Georgian educational curriculum; and notarial depositions may have accustomed him to the practice. In making a translation of Reserson's account I have turned his *oratio obliqua* into *oratio recta*. Thus, all the *third* person references to Reserson become *first* person. This makes the account more immediate and personal. It reminds us that the account is an *apologia*. Finally, it renders many sentences more immediately intelligible. (An English sentence such as ' Smith told Jones that he regretted his behaviour' is potentially ambiguous. 'I told Jones that I regretted my behaviour' avoids such a problem).

Reserson had a tendency to write long sentences with a sequence of subordinate clause. In my translation I have often broken down such sentences into shorter units. Although the document is in French, Reserson occasionally quotes letters written in English. I have transcribed such passages in italics.

We learn something about the Barcelona trade of Reserson & Tupper from shipping returns. They handled imports of fish and wheat; and managed the export of brandy, wine and fruit. The pattern was very similar to that of Gregory & Guille (Barcelona), but on a smaller scale (see p. 67).

NICHOLAS RESERSON'S STORY

The misfortunes that I experienced as a merchant at Barcelona have induced me to record the contributory causes. I have not sought to hide any mistake that I may have made and I have, above all, stuck to the truth of the facts.

William de Vic Tupper and I, both of Guernsey, established a business house at Barcelona in 1775, trading as 'Reserson and Tupper'. This house was set up thanks to the resolve of our respective parents. William and I had not had the opportunity to get to know one another. I was almost always absent from Guernsey during the nine years prior to the setting up of the partnership, the last four of those years in a house at Barcelona. My father, the worthiest of parents, saw in this partnership only the great advantages that might come to me by way of the considerable fortune of William's father and the extent of his commercial contacts – who has not made a mistake?

A partnership between two young men, one not yet twenty-two years old and the other nineteen, of quite opposite characters, could hardly prosper. I liked calmness, William was passionate and liked everyone to yield to his wishes. This brought him several unpleasant quarrels. He would have liked me to have embraced all his disputes but that was contrary to my temperament, I was satisfied to suffer silently, uncomplainingly, hoping that time would bring some remedy. William could not easily forgive me for not siding with him in all his personal squabbles - which for the most part were caused by his own fault.

In setting up a business, prudence dictates that one should proceed carefully and control ambition. I was not swept along by the desire to make a huge fortune. I did not want the house to engage in speculation; rather it should stick to solid commissions and, especially at the beginning, expenditure should be kept within the strictest control. Immediately after our arrival in Barcelona I went to Reus for several days to make arrangements with an agent there for the purchase of brandy etc. During my absence William left the tavern where we were lodging, rented a house, engaged a cook and other servants, and employed two clerks in addition to the man appointed before I left for Reus. This episode is mentioned solely to show that William wanted to do whatever seemed good to him and to appear in everything as head of the house.

It would take too long to go into detail about all the troubles that I experienced in connection with the business of this house, I was often obliged, despite myself, to submit to my partner's will to avoid a break-up. Unfortunately I was the victim of the respect that I always wished to maintain for the arrangement that my father had made for me. I will quote just two examples to show that the house could not succeed, given the manner in which it was run.

Our correspondents in London proposed that the Barcelona house should take a one-third interest in a cargo of grapes and nuts, which we would ship to Bristol, two houses there would take the remaining two-thirds interest. I would not have agreed but William was in favour, the result was most disastrous. The cargo arrived safely and sold at a good price; but not a penny was made from our one-third interest. The Bristol merchant in charge of handling the cargo had a business failure and a legal case between him and someone else in England prevented the winding up of his affairs. The case had only recently started and, given the countless years that have elapsed since the shipment made in 1777, the transaction can be regarded as a total loss.

The other transaction was even more unfortunate, if that is possible. We received, very late in the season, that is to say towards spring, a small order for some raisins. Our agent at Valencia wrote to us that the order could not be fulfilled unless quite a considerable quantity was taken, the owner wishing to part only with his entire stock. There was no reason to hesitate, the order should have been declined. William insisted on buying the complete stock and, having fulfilled the order, sent the surplus speculatively, on the house's account, to London.

The cargo arrived quite damaged, costs were not covered and the resulting loss for the house was far in excess of £1000 st. It does not take many deals like that to go broke.

We continued our business under the same designation of Reserson & Tupper until 1778 when, France and England being at war, we deemed it appropriate to put the house under the name of George Henri Rollfsen, a German employee. This could have been postponed but William was in a hurry and straightway left for England, leaving me in Barcelona. I remained there until the following year, 1779, that is to say as long as was possible for me. War having broken out between Spain and England, I was obliged to leave Spain and return to Guernsey, where William now was. The business at Barcelona remained under the control of Rollfsen.

When war broke out between England and Holland in 1780, William and I (along with several other merchants who had houses in Spain) were obliged to use a house at Ostend to carry on our business and to conceal the identity of friends who wished to place orders with us. In 1781 William and his parents asked me to set up a trading house at Ostend. I agreed, but with some reluctance, given that I would much have preferred to stay at home. The house was established at Ostend in September 1781 by myself, William de Vic Tupper and Jean Kirkpatrick, the first two having $\frac{5}{12}$ shares each, the third $\frac{1}{6}$, under the name of Reserson, Tupper, Kirkpatrick. The principal and sole aim was to facilitate the business of the Barcelona house and it was regarded as just a temporary expedient.

A few weeks after setting this up, William departed for London, leaving the burden of work to me and the other partner. We gave the house all our attention and busied ourselves unceasingly, our principle was to enter into nothing speculative. The result was that towards June 1782, when William returned, we had accumulated a goodly sum. There would be no exaggeration in calculating the profit at 30 – 35,000 Brabant florins, with no bad debt and the happy situation of being able to settle all our accounts immediately.

After William's arrival at Ostend, I was minded to go home to Guernsey for a holiday that I needed after the hard work of the previous months. At the same time I wanted to sell some of the brandy that Rollfsen had – without orders – shipped on some Guernsey-bound vessels, to complete their cargoes. I went to Guernsey *via* England, in the strong conviction that the Ostend house would follow the business plan adopted at the beginning. The success of this had been so favourable that I had correspondingly more reason for my expectation. When in England William had written to me, strongly recommending that I should not undertake any speculations such as those being made by several Ostend houses chartering neutral ships to bring cargoes from Tobago and Grenada.

During my stay in Guernsey I sold the brandy in question. I learned that since my departure from Ostend much was being done by *société d'assurance* and that the house was also taking risks. I wrote very firmly that, as far as I was concerned, I wanted no involvement in such business. At last, in January 1783, I left Guernsey to return to Ostend. On my arrival in England I learnt that peace had been made between the belligerent powers. I went to Bristol to try to sort out the sorry business already discussed but there was no way of resolving it. When I arrived in Ostend, William keenly pressed me to go as soon as possible to Barcelona to watch over our common interests. This I did immediately and so I did not have time to examine the state of affairs at the Ostend house.

After my departure from Ostend, William went to England and to Guernsey and arrived in Barcelona in September 1783. The house then took up its former name of Reserson & Tupper. It was a little after this era that I began to become aware of the huge losses that the house at Ostend had sustained, after the flourishing state in which I had left it, as has been said. The greater part of these losses arose from the freighting of ships as speculative ventures to transport cargoes from the West Indies. With the coming of peace the very high freight costs were cut by at least a half. I had the more reason to be surprised by these transactions after William had expressly recommended not getting involved and that, during the time that they were undertaken, not a sole word was written to me about them. Quite the reverse, William's letters had always given me to understand that the affairs of the house were in good order.

During the years 1785 and 1786 Mr E. Tupper (William's father) and his elder son Daniel seemed quite sure that I was in no way to blame for all the setbacks experienced by the Ostend house. In a letter written to me on 14 June 1786 the father said to me *inter alia* '*For I am entirely of your opinion that instead of forming New Houses*' (referring to a house that GDT spoke about establishing in London) '*that of Ostend should be dropt, at least the affairs liquidated, and you may depend that I have long insisted with him to do it*' and in another paragraph '*I am really vexed that he should have undertaken so much to make you and the Families so uneasy*'. In his letter of 26 August Mr Daniel Tupper wrote as follows to me (I was asking for news about the state of affairs): '*These sums together will reduce my Fathers property very much and it makes him I assure you very uneasy, he is as well as myself sensible that the fault don't lay with you, I know speculations can only have brought the House to this dilemma*'.

As a consequence of all the losses sustained by that house in the short space of a few months it found itself so embarrassed in the year 1784 that the house at Barcelona was obliged to prop it up. This inflicted considerable harm on its own business and the Barcelona house could not have continued to do this without the help of Mr E. Tupper of Guernsey who advanced very considerable sums. Although the house at Barcelona had done some considerable business during the war, it had gained almost nothing, the expenses of G.H. Rollfsen and other causes having swallowed up all the profits and when the said Rollfsen left the house he owed £C 5,800, none of which was recovered, apart from a trifle due to him in Barcelona.

In December 1784, William left Barcelona for Ostend under the pretext of taking some measures relating to the latter house since there was much question of war between the Emperor and Holland. This trip resulted only in a very serious quarrel at Ostend with William placed in prison, to the great prejudice of both the business and the credit of the house, of which he was then the only director. Mr Kirkpatrick was not then at Ostend, having set out on a short journey; and Pierre, my brother to whom an interest in the said Ostend house had been made, had not yet returned from a tour that he had been making in the south of France and at Barcelona to convalesce. What then does one judge the discomfort that I was bound to feel on receiving such news, for it is difficult to express it? Eventually PR reached Ostend, steps were taken, the trouble was partially resolved and William came out of prison.

William stayed at Ostend until the beginning of 1786. From there he crossed to England, for his entertainment and for some personal business, and he did not return to Barcelona until towards September 1787. He was so little interested in the business of the house that he failed to give me essential information and he thought only of debauchery, about which he later boasted. During his absence of almost three years, seeing with pain the continuing embarrassment of the Barcelona house caused by the Ostend house, I wrote to him several times expressing my wish to see the Ostend business wound up and the house closed, but to no avail.

In the end the dissolution was decided upon. I was doomed to have all the trouble. I left Barcelona in May 1788 and went to Ostend. Having found Kirkpatrick a little indisposed I decided to go on to Guernsey. Having spoken with Mr E. Tupper on the subject of the liquidation of the partnership at Ostend, it was agreed that the elder son, Daniel Tupper, would travel with me to Ostend to help to carry this out.

We left London together for Ostend and on our arrival I seriously busied myself in the affairs of the house. After carefully examining the books I found to my great regret that the house was in the most deplorable financial state, much worse than I had ever imagined, for I was very far from being in the know about all the Ostend matters. William was much better versed in them, partly because several contracts had been entered into while he was in charge (during his stay at Ostend before the peace), partly because he had lived there in 1785, and finally through the correspondence that he had maintained with Kirkpatrick in 1786 and a large part of 1787 (when William was in England). Apart from the ruinous speculations already described, other equally bad undertakings had been mindlessly entered into – there is no point in chronicling them here – but it is worth observing that when I was in charge, and everything was going well, expenditure had been kept within very strict limits; it grew significantly when William was in charge and business affairs were going disastrously wrong.

The house owed Mr E. Tupper the sum of £8,000st or thereabouts for the advances that he had made (as already explained), Reed and Parkinson at London (guaranteed by Tupper) were owed about £1,900st, the other creditors were owed but a trifle. To settle these two considerable sums what was found after balancing the books? Several bad debts that would never be recovered, some other debts which might yield some return in time, some furniture and finally some merchandise worth very little.

In such circumstances how was I to act? Certainly the wisest course for me, and the one that I should have followed if I had just consulted my own interests, was to render the house bankrupt. For that I would have had the best motives to plead, chiefly that the house was totally unable to discharge its debts. But bearing in mind that Mr E. Tupper was effectively the sole creditor, and flattering myself that I would meet with understanding, I thought that it was more honourable not to contemplate such a step, but rather to try to recoup at Barcelona what had been lost. This is why, when Daniel Tupper proposed a bond in favour of his father payable in two years, each for our respective proportion, I made no difficulty over signing it and it was also signed by Kirkpatrick.

While I was busy at a task as unpleasant and disagreeable as was bound to be the balancing of the accounts of the unhappy establishment at Ostend, what was William doing at Barcelona? He thought only of amusing himself, without any embarrassment over the extraordinary costs that he had caused at Ostend, half of which I had to underwrite. William courted a lady and found it convenient to install her at the house with her husband. Expense was not spared, as may be imagined; it was parties and feasting, all paid for by the partnership. At the very moment that I was devoting my time and efforts to resolving the unhappy business to which I had not contributed, I was dragged into useless costs which, in fairness, were not my responsibility. Besides, it should be observed that, on the eve of my departure for Ostend, William judged it right, without there being any necessity, to rent a new house at a high price. By doing this without consulting, he increased expenditure.

I never charged any personal expenses to the house account and consequently had more cause to complain at having to pay for William's high living. When I judged it appropriate to have a horse, I paid from my own purse not only the maintenance but also the stabling expenses etc. Sometimes I had the mortification of enduring the quibbles and reproaches of William about some petty expenses paid for essentials for the house, real misery, it's not worth talking about, this compared with his conduct demonstrates his despotism and the extent to which my patience was tested. A little before my departure from Barcelona for Ostend, there were some differences between William and me and after that he bore me much ill-will in several of his letters and threatened me with a dissolution of the partnership.

Edmond Connelly, having worked about two years in a house at Barcelona, had left it and was in Dunkirk when I passed through that town, travelling from Ostend to England and back. Connelly expressed to me his wish to join the house at Barcelona and be remunerated at a level commensurate with his services. I wrote about the matter to William, proposing that Connelly be incorporated in the house but, before a reply could reach me, I received a letter from William indicating that he had decided to dissolve the partnership, I could fix the day for the separation.

It was then that I started to see the fix I was in through having signed the bond, the separation would render me unable to discharge it, for a long time at least. Nevertheless, seeing no remedy, I wrote to William that as he was bent on the separation it could be effected on 31 December that year.

I still had the power to evade payment of the bond, by declaring the impossibility (given my situation) of completion by the due date but the same motives that impelled me to sign checked me and, in the confidence that I would not be troubled (in view of the manner in which I had acted), I determined to do business on my own behalf in Barcelona after the separation, hoping that with time and hard work I would succeed in recovering the losses made and find myself in a position to discharge the bond that I had contracted. So I told Connelly what William had written to me, and my intention to work on my own account, and I agreed with Connelly to take him. I communicated this to William.

Connelly and I left Dunkirk together in December 1788 and arrived in Barcelona in January 1789, hindered on our journey by bad weather. I must pay Connelly the credit he deserves for his conduct in the affair of the separation – Connelly said to me several times that he advised avoiding a separation with William if it was possible and that if, to attain this goal, it was necessary to abandon him, that was no obstacle since he would look for a position elsewhere. However matters sorted themselves out. It was agreed that Connelly would enter the house and would 'have the signature' just like Mr Guillaume Almgren who had been there for four and a half years; the trading name would become Reserson, Tupper & Co. This was effected on 1 April 1789.

It is clear from later events that it was never the intention of William that this new partnership would be permanent, he even acknowledged to some individuals (as was learnt later) that his goal was to lull me into a false sense of security, the better to play his game and execute his scheme.

In practice the partnership did not last long, one thing that certainly wasn't worth the trouble was the excuse for the winding-up. William having gone to Reus, Connelly one day asked me if the house was in the habit of granting to the Cadiz houses with which it was linked part of the commission on consignments that they could procure. I replied 'Yes' and so Connelly offered to give a proportion to a Cadiz merchant, one of his friends to whom he was busy writing. I agreed. The upshot of this approach was that the Cadiz merchant secured a cargo of corn for the Barcelona house. Connelly and I told William that this resulted from the letter Connelly had written to his friend and to whom part of the commission was owed. William replied that before doing this we should wait until the Cadiz merchant suggested something, as though our word given was not sufficient title by itself. William went off again to Reus, for he was ever restless. During his absence the house received a letter from the Cadiz merchant requesting a prompt reply. There was no way of avoiding telling him what was credited to him for his share in the commission on the cargo of grain.

William came back from Reus. Casting an eye over the letterbook and spotting what had been written about the commission, he gave vent to anger and insisted on a separation, despite my doing all that I could to calm him, even offering personally to underwrite the share of the commission that had been given. All in vain, it was clear that William was just looking for an excuse and, if that had been lacking, he would have found another. A few days later it was decided that the separation would take place on 31 July 1789.

I was not able to resist any longer the dismay and grief that I had endured for a long time. I fell dangerously ill and was kept in bed by one of the most violent fevers. I only began to get back into things at the time appointed for the separation. Meanwhile, let's cast an eye over the state of affairs of the Barcelona house.

We have already seen that nothing was gained while Rollfsen was in charge and, from that time on, it was continuously troubled to subsidise the Ostend house. This rendered it incapable of pursuing its business with all the advantage that would have followed had the situation been different. William, heedless of the circumstances and without considering that the house had no reason to praise him as a result of several pieces of business undertaken solely at his whim, sometimes complained about my failure to enter into speculations. It was all very well to be willing to talk without thinking, he should have realised that during his long absence from Barcelona and while he was busy enjoying himself, I was doing enough to prop up the two houses by my work. Besides, when I was inclined to undertake some speculations, even those most attractive in appearance, how could I have done it? Funds did not permit, it was continuously necessary to use all possible resources to help the Ostend house and this one goal was enough fully to occupy my attention.

The funds of the Barcelona house consisted of advances that Mr E. Tupper had made to his son on several occasions. Mr Tupper was also the guarantor for some credit at London. In 1785, while William was away from Barcelona, finding myself in straitened circumstances, mainly for the reason already given (propping up the Ostend house), I drew in the name of Reserson & Tupper on Mr Perchard of London on my father's account and, after having made some remittances to Perchard, there was a credit balance for my father of £586-17-11 st. which remained in the house.

After the setting up of the partnership of Reserson, Tupper & Co in April 1789, William said to me one day that he no longer wished to allow any bill to be placed under his father's guarantee, hitherto the practice of the house. Finding it needed money and the only resource being forbidden, hoping to preserve peace and quiet, I undertook to draw further in the name of the house on my father's account at Perchard and Brock in London in April and May to the value of £726 st. In the June following I drew on my own account £527-1-6 st., from funds they had in hand of my deceased brother and also some funds that my father had given me. After the Perchards had remitted me the account of these funds there was still a balance in my favour of £189-5-3 st. for which I had an understanding with them some time after.

Balancing the house books down to 31 July 1789, the day appointed for the dissolving of the partnership, there was not enough to re-imburse Mr E. Tupper for his advances plus interest (which mounted to a considerable sum) nor my father for the bills drawn on his account. Even so, it would have been possible to realise all the assets of the house. Some debts could not be recovered immediately, and among others the sum of about £C 9,500 for some corn sold to two people was not very secure. During my absence the affairs of the said debtors were in a very bad state, although there was hope of retrieving something over time.

As soon as the separation was decided on, having foreseen that it would not be possible for the house to repay Mr E. Tupper immediately, I wrote to my father on this matter. He replied that he had spoken to Mr E. Tupper who had no intention of troubling me and that he would write to his son William. Nevertheless, straight after the separation William insisted that I should repay him immediately half of his father's advances to the house (deducting what had been drawn for the account of my father) which amounted for the said half to about £C 21,000 in consequence of what could not be realised at the moment.

Still convalescing and wishing as far as possible to avoid fuss, I did not know what to do to preserve the peace. Eventually I decided to draw on Perchard and Brock in my own name on the account of my father for £859-4-8 st. and on Mr Samuel Dobrée (also of London) for £1,386-16-8 st. by which means I paid the sum in question in August to William. The bills were cleared but Mr Dobrée wrote to me that those that I had made on him would be placed to my own account in consequence of what my father had written to Dobrée.

The liquidation of the affairs remained with me, that is to say the work and the trouble, for William judged it appropriate to keep to himself tasks from which some benefit might arise, particularly the sale of a cargo of cod that had arrived, consigned to the house a few days before the separation phase. William disposed of it of his own accord, without my ever seeing the bill of sale (which was rendered by William) and I contented myself with what William wished to give me some time after for my part of the commission but it must be observed that William had demanded that I should pay out my proportion of the dues. I even have some reason to suspect that William did not scruple to appropriate some commissions given to the partnership before the dissolution was determined.

My new business started, then, on 1 August 1789 under the title of Reserson & Co, my associates being Edmond Connelly and Guillaume Almgren, who had both been in the earlier company. It is true that this new house did not start under favourable auspices since I did not find myself in a state to introduce funds immediately and my father was not in a condition to help me, considering that I had been obliged to draw on his account, as has been observed. My sole resource for the moment was in my share of the recoveries made from the debtors and the other effects of the preceding company and some credit that I could have in London &c. However, I had room to hope that I would get funds through some friends as soon as I could make a trip. I could not do this immediately, being charged with the liquidation of the old business and this kept me busy. As far as the two other associates, there was no question that they would furnish funds. The agreement I made with them was for 3 years with G. Almgren, averaging a sum fixed annually, and with E. Connelly for 6 to 9 years, that is to say: two years averaging a fixed sum and thereafter he would be due to receive either one quarter of the profits or a fixed sum, at his option.

Messrs J. Reed & J. Parkinson of London, old friends of the house of Reserson & Tupper, were connected to William thanks to his father and they procured lots of business for him. I could not boast a similar support, nevertheless I had no cause to complain about the business I procured, quite a lot of which came through my partner E. Connelly and his friends in Dunkirk. Had the affairs of France not become more and more chaotic, entirely disrupting commerce, there is every reason to think that, despite all the disadvantages attending the foundation of my new house, I would in a little time have amassed a sum sufficient to clear myself of the bond contracted at Ostend etc., which was my sole aim.

However, at the beginning of this new house, busy with the affairs of the new company and with the liquidation of the old, I had always some cause for disappointment and sorrow. William claimed reimbursement for sundry travelling expenses at different times and this added up to a tidy sum. There had never been any question at the time and, even supposing that he had the right to demand some expenses, there were others that he assuredly could not in justice claim. Such, for example, were the majority of his expenses from the beginning of January 1786, when he left Ostend for England where he stayed until towards August 1787 when he set out for Barcelona, since it was clear that his stay was more for his own business than for the affairs of the house (he had a personal law case that had to be concluded). He did not omit to charge 10 shillings sterling per day for his expenses, not including carriage charges.

Despite the limited justification for this demand, to which in all other circumstances I would never have submitted, I wished to continue to act with the greatest moderation and to make even this sacrifice, to avoid litigation and upsets which would have harmed my interests and my affairs, which were beginning to take a favourable turn. I contented myself by presenting on my side an expense account for the trips that I had made on behalf of the house, which totalled just £C 1,602-13-7, while the expenses incurred by William mounted to £C 6,093-14-5 of the same money.

I have since discovered by accident that William had already had himself credited £115 st. (ƒ1207-10 in Brabant currency) in the books of the Ostend house, under the date of 17 June 1782, for some travel expenses during the preceding seven months; at Barcelona he was paid these same expenses, the majority of which were not admissible.

It has been seen earlier that the Ostend house owed Messrs Reed and Parkinson of London, under the guarantee of Mr E. Tupper of Guernsey, the sum of £1,500 st. I had flattered myself that the said house (to the liquidation of which Mr Kirkpatrick had been appointed) should have been able to realise at least sufficient to reimburse Reed & Parkinson. The difficulty of the recoveries frustrating that, Messrs Reed & Parkinson wrote to me, telling me to remit to them my part of the said sum i.e. $\frac{5}{12}$. William supported this, demanding immediate remittance in consideration that his father acted as guarantor to the said Reed and Parkinson.

This setback afflicted me badly, the more so as I saw that the affairs of my new establishment were looking promising and I feared that the least thing might be damaging. Everything depended on my reputation and industry. Thinking that I had come to the last obstacle, I applied to Mr Samuel Dobrée of London (who had placed much confidence in me). I drew on Dobrée 7 November 1789, in my own name, to the order of Reed & Parkinson, £900 st, for the sum of $\frac{5}{12}$ of what was owing to them from the Ostend house, with interest, and for my share of the small balance owed to them by Reserson, Tupper & Co of Barcelona. I hoped that I would be able to repay Mr Dobrée with what came to me from the liquidation at Ostend and that when payment became overdue, I could satisfy Dobrée by paying him interest for the time that he was out of pocket.

The bond signed at Ostend by Jean Kirpatrick and me in favour of Mr E. Tupper, and delivered to Mr D. Tupper, was immediately remitted by him (with his endorsement by proxy of his father) to his brother William at Barcelona, who did not fail to let me know that he had the said bond. He did this particularly during the course of the summer of 1790, informing me that I would have to repay him by the settlement date the share that I owed, at the same time making me understand that he would not accord the least delay.

Seeing the nasty trick prepared for me, I could not help writing to my father in the most pressing terms, representing to him that it would be absolutely impossible for me to pay my share of the bond. I did this, despite the trouble I felt that I would cause my father and the realisation that he would not be able, by himself, to help me; but I could not hide from him the danger to which I was exposed. My father did all that depended on him, he spoke about the matter to Mr E. Tupper, William's father. He replied that he would write to his son William to leave me in peace. As I well understood that that would not be enough, and that I would find myself in great trouble, I was obliged to repeat again my fears to my father who wrote to me that if William absolutely wished to hold me to the payment of the bond in question, I just had to draw on Mr Samuel Dobrée in London and that he would get Mr E. Tupper to write to Dobrée so that the drafts were cleared. Effectively Mr E. Tupper gave his guarantee to Mr Dobrée in consideration of my father's.

It might seem odd that this bond was sent immediately by Mr D. Tupper to his brother at Barcelona. Following the ordinary course of events, it should have been sent to Mr E. Tupper who, before the settlement date, would have used it as he judged suitable. This shows quite clearly that William and his family, or at least his brother, had already agreed to sacrifice me. Doubtless it must have been with unhappiness that they saw the huge sums advanced for the houses ending in pure loss and they wanted to save at least part of it at whatever price. To achieve that there was no other means than by getting rid of me. For in pursuing me vigorously, if I paid, they would achieve their main aim; if, on the other hand, I could not clear my obligations I would be unable to continue in business. This would have given William a controlling interest in the company and he could always rely on his family for support. This conjecture gains strength from what Tupper wrote to Jean Kirkpatrick after the separation, the tenor was thus: *'My purchase will always be made on equal, if not better terms, than any one as my Agent never buys but with hard cash in hand, to tell you plain my separation from Mr R has been of infinite advantage to me, as it has given me an opportunity of getting a large Capital in my possession, which I should never have had, as he and his Father were loath to part with their Cash, and obliged me to save the House to draw on mine, this you easily perceived by our last unfortunate concern.'*

It is extraordinary that the man who caused all the ill should have had the effrontery to speak in such fashion and wish in some way to cast the blame on someone else. It is quite clear that, if he had not plunged the Ostend house into so many disasters, there would not have been any need to run back to his father for help. The profits that the Ostend house made before the management of William, and those that it would have made if he had had the prudence to follow the initial plan, could have poured into the Barcelona house. By this means the latter house would have been comfortably off and able to operate with advantage and ease. Finally, it is pointless making further remarks about this, but it is *à propos* to observe that when Mr Daniel Tupper went to Ostend with me, visiting Dunkirk he said to someone, referring to me, 'I don't know what he thinks he'll do'. This, along with the brusque manner in which the separation was demanded by William, without any particular reason, and the sending to the latter of the bond as soon as it was signed, leads to the suspicion that a plan had been formed against me.

When the settlement date of the bond arrived, 20 November 1790, William did not grant a moment's delay for the payment, despite the fact that Barcelona usage is to give at least a month in parallel cases. As I saw that it would be difficult for me to negotiate immediately as large a sum, having moreover much to draw for merchandise that I was buying and dispatching, I proposed to William to give him in payment drafts on London. This he refused, saying that he wanted money, not drafts. William was not as strict with Kirkpatrick over his share of the bond. When Kirkpatrick asked, he was granted quite a considerable delay, undoubtedly in the expectation that Kirkpatrick would get William commissions, as in practice happened. So in all this episode I was the sole victim, I who had not contributed by as much as a penny to the enormous losses brought about by the speculations of the Ostend house, since they had all taken place during my absence, and most were unknown to me.

I therefore had to make the greatest efforts to get money. I managed this with much difficulty and trouble, starting from 22 November to pay William the sum of £C 8,000. In the course of the same month I had cleared ¾ of the sum and a few days later the rest, amounting to £C 30,531-8-2. The sums drawn (from the 24 November to 15 December following) on Mr Samuel Dobrée to meet this were £3,358-19-6 st or £C 30,582-10-7. To facilitate the negotiation, the money was drawn under the name of Reserson & Co. but the proceeds were paid into my personal account and I was debited for the sums paid to William.

Having thus completed the matter of the bond it is time to pass to other events. During the first year of the establishment of Reserson & Co, and following our balance of accounts on 31 August 1790, there was quite a fat profit. However, in the course of the summer of the same year there were several bankruptcies at Barcelona and we (Reserson & Co) found ourselves unhappily involved in five different failures for bills drawn on Madrid, the total sum amounted to about £C 28,000. Nevertheless this setback did not for the time-being harm the house because it had just made quite considerable profits. It continued its business quite favourably until 31 July 1791, the second balance; by that time it had recovered about £C 7,800. Money recovered, together with moneys to be received, suggested that the house had enough to cover both the considerable losses resulting from the bankruptcies and the expenses of the house during the two years of its establishment.

Day-by-day trade became more straitened, paper on Paris not being asked for, it was necessary to refuse orders coming from Dunkirk etc. unless there were credits on sound houses in London or Amsterdam. Connelly pressed me a lot to allow him to make a little trip to Dunkirk to secure orders for the house and he left Barcelona in July 1791. The success of his trip answered his plans to gather lots of orders, the majority without price limit, with credits on London and Amsterdam. The new brandies were pushed to exorbitant prices but I was obliged to follow the market, having positive instructions to buy and to despatch promptly.

So I hurried to charter ships, amongst others two Swedish vessels, one of them was already at Salou to take its cargo, when the news was received that the Dey of Algiers had declared war on Sweden. As a consequence of this it was necessary to cancel the charter parties of these two vessels (which was done) and to look for other vessels which were very scarce, for it was at a moment when vessels were much in demand. At the same time, that is to say in October 1791, Connelly returned from Dunkirk to Barcelona.

A Barcelona house which had received orders from France for a cargo of brandy that it had bought (and in part loaded at Salou) received counter-orders by reason of the high prices. This house offered to sell us the cargo and to see to changing the destination of the vessel to Dunkirk. The quantity of brandy that it offered to make over was 250 pipes and the vessel could transport 440 pipes, we would have to make good the difference from our own brandy. Connelly seemed very keen to accept this project which had been considerably disrupted by the war of the Algerians against Sweden. I pointed out that this would involve taking on more brandy than we needed at that moment but Connelly replied that he had a verbal order from his cousins at Dunkirk to ship them a hundred pipes when he found it opportune. And as for the excess, he had the means to get them accepted by some of his acquaintances. For these reasons I agreed to this purchase, although reluctantly. There was also the purchase of some extra brandy following the arrival of Connelly and his advice to help to fulfil the orders received.

News reached Dunkirk about the high prices paid in Catalonia for brandy and it became obvious that there was little chance of profit. On the contrary, there was reason to fear a loss because demand had slackened in Flanders. Almost all the houses at Dunkirk and elsewhere sent counter-orders to Barcelona, refusing to accept for their account what had been bought and partly loaded on vessels. Connelly's cousins reneged on the 105 pipes sent to them without orders, they wanted none of it. There was no question of making them take 105 pipes since they had not given an order in writing; it was on the advice of Connelly that the pipes had been bought and loaded. The matter had to be resolved by letting the pipes stand on the accounts of the house to await sale by the cousins.

The refusal of the majority of those who had really given clear, positive orders threw our house into the greatest financial difficulties, since all the brandy amounted to a considerable sum. Connelly said that it was pointless to argue with one of these houses, for which 200 pipes had been bought, seeing that it would never be possible to make that house see reason and a dispute would lead to uncertain and expensive legal processes. As demand for brandy had slackened in Catalonia in consequence of all the counter-orders, and prices being low, Connelly proposed to send these 200 pipes or thereabouts to Guernsey to be sold there for our house. I agreed to this, not knowing how to do better to get rid of the merchandise. Connelly proposed at the same time to go immediately to Dunkirk to sort out the arguments about the other brandy consignments.

So he left in December 1791 and reached an accommodation that seemed better than could have been hoped. With the exception of the 105 pipes destined for his cousins and the 200 pipes discussed, the rest of the brandy was placed and arguments were ended. However, this arrangement that appeared so favourable was not so in fact, as will be seen by what follows.

After his arrival at Dunkirk, Connelly had agreed with one of the houses (which had placed orders but had not made the same difficulties as several others) that it would also take on its account 90 pipes and 20 halves of brandy destined for another client who absolutely did not want to accept them and that the said house would undertake to clear the bills drawn on London for the total. He also made an arrangement with the same house that it would take on its account 200 pipes of brandy stored in Catalonia on condition that we would keep them for some time and that, when they decided to have them shipped, payment would be made on London. Reassured about this brandy consignment, we waited for the house to specify a destination. Finally, the house declined the brandy consignment as it did not suit them. Connelly, who had returned from Dunkirk in March 1792, represented to me that it was a house with which good business could be done in due course, besides nothing would be gained by a law suit and so it was better to make a sacrifice. So it was decided that a letter would be written to this house telling them that half their order would be cancelled - that is to say 100 pipes – but that not proving satisfactory, the house offered to give £6,000 tournois by way of damages to clear itself of the whole contract. Although the sum was trifling in comparison with the harm which hit us through the big fall in the price of brandy, Connelly again got me to agree to this proposal for the same reasons as before. So the said 200 pipes remained on our books and we had to resell them as best we could and at a great loss. If we had not regarded these 200 pipes of brandy as already placed, we would have sought to get rid of them a long while previously and in a fashion less burdensome for us.

Meanwhile no funds came in at Ostend which is why Mr Kirkpatrick made no remittance to Mr Samuel Dobrée of London for my account. We had a current account with Mr Dobrée on which we drew when we had occasion and we sent him remittances. I regarded as for my personal account the drawings that I had made on Mr Dobrée for the payment of the bond at Ostend and to repay Reed & Parkinson (about which we have already spoken); these drawings had not been passed to the credit of the said Dobrée on our books. Mr Dobrée, however, had debited the remittances to R & Co in the current accounts that he sent; I indicated that I would have wished that they should be placed separately on my personal account. Mr Dobrée replied that he thought he was doing the right thing and I answered that as I intended to cross soon to England the matter could be ironed out then. After the return of Connelly from his last trip to Dunkirk, I proposed to go and do what for some time I had planned in England, as I had written to Mr Dobrée and my parents; but, before talking about it, it is good to observe what happened before my departure, that is to say a little after the return of Connelly to Barcelona.

At Dunkirk there was a house very friendly with Connelly - that of Mr Patrick Arthur. We had done considerable business with him since setting up and our confidence in this house was great. Connelly gave assurances that one could deliver orders there in total confidence and that for the shipments we were making to him we were content to draw on the house payable in London or Amsterdam. Up to this point the house had been very correct in fulfilling its commitments, which confirmed for me the positive attitude that Connelly had generated. However, towards April 1792, Arthur wrote to us with regard to the great quantity of brandy that he had in stock, and the low demand for this liquor at Dunkirk. He found himself in difficulty to provide the funds for some bills that we had delivered on him and that he had accepted payable in Amsterdam. He entreated us to help him by discharging him from the responsibilty of funding the bills in question. It was of the greatest importance for us that the bills did not return with the protest 'failure to pay' so we wrote to Mr Pierre De Haan of Amsterdam (where they were payable and who was a friend) to get him to clear these bills, explaining to him the reasons that prevented the Dunkirk house and making at the same time a remittance to the said De Haan. For our repayment we counted on drawing on Mr Arthur, payable in Paris, as and when the opportunity presented. This would give him a bit of time and in fact we issued several bills this way on Arthur and they were accepted.

Up to this point Mr Dobrée in London had underwritten some large advances of which the principal was, as we have already seen, for the bills issued in November - December 1790 to pay the Ostend bond. In March 1792 he wrote that, needing cash, he had drawn 20,000 *piastres courantes* on us (R & Co), at 90 days from date, payable at Madrid and that he continued to draw until the following month for the total sum of 37,000 piastres. I wrote to him that it would now not be possible to provide for all these bills on settlement date. In consequence of this Mr Dobrée gave me the facility of redrawing on him at this period, this suited me.

In May 1792 G. Almgren withdrew from our house, as he did not get on with Connelly, the other partner. We had written to Guernsey to remit to Messrs Perchard & Brock of London the net proceeds of the 180 pipes and 18 half-pipes of brandy that we had sent there but we received advice from Guernsey that there was no demand for brandy and that it was necessary to wait before it could be disposed of. Messrs Perchard & Brock (on whom we drew occasionally) were out of pocket on our account because of some bills that we had drawn on them and we counted on repaying Perchard & Brock with the proceeds of the brandy.

In the shipments that we had made this season for Dunkirk we had loaded 161 pipes and 16 half-pipes of brandy for Messrs Isaac Brown & Co of the said town, close friends of Connelly and in whom he had the greatest confidence. For this reason for repayment we drew on them in Amsterdam and they accepted bills payable at the Mr De Haan already mentioned.

During the last trip of Connelly to Dunkirk, the said Brown & Co indicated to him that, overstocked, they found themselves in considerable straits. His confidence in them was such that he gave them the facility to draw £500 st. on a house in London on our account. To give flexibility for the payment of the brandy, drawn payable in Amsterdam, it was agreed between the said Brown & Co and Connelly that Mr De Haan at Amsterdam would be asked to take his repayment at settlement date of the bills in question on Mr Joseph Brown of London (brother of Brown of Dunkirk). If, on the settlement date of these last bills, the said Isaac Brown & Co still could not furnish the funds, Joseph Brown would have the facility of taking his repayment on us and we would come to an understanding with Brown & Co for repayment in the most convenient fashion. Mr De Haan of Amsterdam scarcely knew Brown & Co at Dunkirk and, purely on the recommendation of Connelly, agreed to take repayment as indicated above.

Meanwhile, to repay the bills of £500 st. that Brown & Co had drawn for their account on London (as has already been said), we drew on the said Brown & Co payable in Paris, having found opportunity to place these bills, although paper on France was very little asked for. By virtue of what had been agreed between Connelly and Brown & Co, Mr Joseph Brown of London drew on us, payable in Madrid on 20 March, at 90 days' notice, 10770 *piastres courantes* – which we accepted.

A little later, when I planned to set out for England, we received advice that Mr Arthur found himself no longer able to continue in business and had had to suspend payment. At about the same time Joseph Brown of London drew on us, for the account of Isaac Brown & Co, another sum of 13,250 *piastres courantes*, remitting the first to us for acceptance. As we were without any news of Isaac Brown & Co (although they had promised to repay the other bills of 10,770 piastres, which were already near settlement date) we did not want to accept them. We returned them to J. Brown of London, after having kept them for some days. Immediately after, we received a letter from Isaac Brown & Co to tell us the critical situation in which they found themselves and to warn us that they could not fund the bills that they had accepted payable in Paris but that all the brandy shipped to them was still in stock. We wrote immediately to Connelly's cousins at Dunkirk concerning the affairs of Arthur and Brown & Co, instructing them to take the most appropriate measures to protect our interests, and particularly to seize the brandy if necessary.

All this was the reason that I accelerated my departure by some days and left in June 1792 for Dunkirk before crossing to England. I planned to arrive in Dunkirk before Joseph Brown of London could have the time to tell his brother that we did not wish to accept his last bills. By this means, if circumstances required it, I banked on being in time to seize the brandy that I would find still in stock at Brown & Co.

On my arrival in Paris I found that Mess Boyd Ker & Co, bankers there, had already paid from our account several of the bills on Arthur (accepted as payable at the said bankers) for which he had not been able to supply the funds in consequence of his suspension of payments. Mess Boyd Ker & Co had taken their payment on us, payable in Madrid; but for those which still had to reach settlement date on Arthur and on Isaac Brown the said bankers told me that I should remit to them in good paper on Paris. We must see what had happened before I reached Dunkirk.

Arthur had proposed to give brandy and other merchandise (in which his assets consisted) in payment to his creditors, each in proportion to what he was owed, but nothing had yet been settled because not all the proxies of his creditors had arrived. As for the affairs of Isaac Brown & Co. they require a more extended explanation. Several weeks before my arrival at Dunkirk, Joseph Brown of London, knowing of the troubled affairs of Isaac Brown & Co, visited Dunkirk and came to an arrangement with his brother. The result was that, to guarantee his advances, the said Brown & Co would deliver him various goods, amongst them the 161 pipes and 16 half-pipes of brandy in stock from our shipment, the said brandy having to be deposited in the hands of another person at the disposition of Joseph Brown until his last bills of 13,250 piastres on us were accepted. Meanwhile the said Joseph Brown judged it appropriate to accept no bills that Mr De Haan of Amsterdam made on him for the account of Isaac Brown & Co.

On receiving my instructions, Connelly's cousins seized the brandy in question from the person with whom it had been deposited. Several of Mr De Haan's bills on Joseph Brown of London having been protested as 'not accepted', he wrote to Connelly's cousins to act for him against Isaac Brown and Co. I knew well that Mr De Haan only lent himself to the deal in question after the recommendation of my partner, Connelly, but I was unaware that he had also given a guarantee; I would not have believed it if anyone other than Connelly's cousins had told me and if they had not positively assured me of it.

Meanwhile, J. Brown of London, having been notified by us that his last bills on us had not been accepted, wrote to his representative at Dunkirk not to release the brandy unless we, or our representative, obliged by settling. This representative wished to persuade me that J. Brown could compel us, claiming that it was in consequence of a letter from Connelly giving him facility to draw on us for the bills of De Haan that he was involved in this deal.

Finally, seeing the sorry nature of this business, I consulted a lawyer who advised me to reach a settlement. This was also the advice of Connelly's cousins and I agreed for the following reasons. By pursuing Isaac Brown & Co I would have forced them into bankruptcy. In that eventuality it is almost certain that the brandy disputed between J. Brown and ourselves would have been awarded to the creditors of Isaac Brown and Co. The transfer made by I. Brown & Co. had not been made in accordance with the required formalities; as for us, the brandy would not have been considered our property as the bills issued for the total had been cleared and the debt of Isaac Brown was a new credit that we had willingly granted.

Our credit, then, against Isaac Brown was as follows:

1. The bills of £500 st. that Connelly had given facility to the said Brown & Co to draw on London and for which we had taken repayment on them, payable at Paris, as has already been seen. They had accepted, but they could not discharge.

2. The first bills that Joseph Brown of London drew on us for 10,770 *piastres courantes*. Co. This sum, with the £500 st. already mentioned, made a total of £88,000 tournois.

Finally, as we were considered guarantors to Mr De Haan of Amsterdam for what he drew on Joseph Brown of London for the account of the said Brown & Co of Dunkirk and which had not been accepted, there was the further sum of about £45,000 tournois.

The 161 pipes and 16 half-pipes of brandy in dispute were worth only about £86,000 tournois on the Dunkirk market, something above half what they had cost but there appeared to be a small rise in price. After several meetings between Isaac Brown & Co, the agent of Joseph Brown, Connelly's cousins acting for Mr De Haan of Amsterdam, and myself, it was finally agreed that a sufficient quantity of the brandy in question would be taken to pay Mr De Haan; the rest of the brandy would be for Joseph Brown; and in consideration of a discount of 27 ½ % that I would make for Isaac Brown & Co on the total of the bill for the brandy, the said Brown & Co would undertake to repay me the balance of the money owed to us. The greater part of the payment was to be paid in 4,6,9, 12 and 15 months' term, interest included, and part of these various payments was with a guarantee. I had difficulty in deciding to agree to this arrangement since, because of the discount, there was a loss of about £42,000 tournois. However, I entertained no hope of doing better, on the contrary, I risked coming out worse if Isaac Brown were driven into bankruptcy. Besides, I was advised by Connelly's cousins to accept this offer and I had to concede.

I would have liked to end the business of Patrick Arthur but the proxies of several of his creditors were slow to come forward so I left it in the hands of Connelly's cousins (to whom the matter had already been assigned), and I set out for London. I had to supply funds to Messrs Boyd Ker & Co at Paris for the approaching settlement date of the bills on Arthur and on Brown & Co. I obtained bills on Paris which I remitted to Boyd Ker & Co but, in order to pay for the said bills, I was obliged by the London house which had obtained them to draw on our house, payable in Madrid.

Immediately after my arrival in London I received a letter from Connelly in Barcelona, telling me that several individuals had spread rumours very prejudicial to the credit of our house, so that he could hardly negotiate his paper. This occurred at a very critical moment, since our house had to supply funds to Madrid for the bills rendered by Mr Dobrée, Boyd Ker and other houses. I did not find myself in a position to give our house the help that I would have wished, all the less now that I believed I noticed that the rumours complained about by my partner had already got as far as London. Mr Dobrée hinted to me that it was his wish that our house should cease drawing on him (which the house had been doing since my departure from Barcelona, to balance what he drew on the house) but, on the contrary, to be repaid for his advances.

I went to Guernsey in August and counted on talking to my father and Mr E. Tupper about what Mr Dobrée had said. However, having received very alarming advice from Connelly about the extreme difficulty he was experiencing in remitting to Madrid to cover the various acceptances of the house for the reason indicated, I did not know how to proceed. Every letter from Connelly heralded imminent danger for the house. Even if I had had the means to furnish every possible help, I would have feared it could not arrive as quickly as necessity demanded.

Meanwhile I made some remittance from Guernsey to Mr Dobrée on another house in London. Absolutely not knowing which way to turn, I opted to go as quickly as possible to Ostend, supposing that Mr Kirkpatrick would have realised something from the old house there and that thereby I could make a remittance to our house in Barcelona.

As I was leaving Guernsey I received a letter from Mr Dobrée informing me that he could not accept the last bills that our house had drawn on him. At the same time a house at London with which we were in correspondence, and to which we had remitted some of these bills on Dobrée, saw that they were not accepted and heard the rumours spread about our house. In consequence one of the partners crossed to Guernsey to see me and to demand a guarantee for the business that his house had with ours. Very embarrassed by all of these inconveniencies which multiplied every moment, yet still with some hope, I agreed with the partner to give him a share of the brandy held at Dunkirk, I mean Guernsey, and of which not a single pipe had been sold.

Having arranged this business, I set out towards the middle of October for England. In the course of the trip, having had the leisure to reflect on the situation in which I found myself, I regretted not having spoken to Mr E. Tupper about my situation in regard to Dobrée. As soon as I landed in England I wrote to Mr Tupper to put him in the picture. Not stopping in London, I crossed immediately to Ostend. Mr J. Kirkpatrick gave me a statement of what he had received and paid out on the account of the old house. According to this there was a balance to be shared between the partners of ƒ7,392-1-9, making my $\frac{5}{12}$ share ƒ3,080. Kirkpatrick paid me this, a poor sum in return for what should have been hoped for. After having deducted what I needed for my travel expenses and other things, I remitted the rest, that is to say a draft for £200 st. on London for our house, and determined to make my way to Barcelona.

The war between the Emperor and France disrupted the frontier-crossing at several places. For that reason I went by way of Ghent. Hard on my arrival there, French troops entered the city; it was then easy for me to go to Lille and from there to Paris, where I arrived at the end of November. I had written to Connelly to address letters to Montpellier because I counted on passing that way, but having arrived at Lyons I decided to go to Marseilles in the hope of finding some favourable opportunity to cross by sea to Barcelona. On my arrival at Marseilles on 20 December I wrote to Montpellier, asking for letters that might have been addressed to me there to be forwarded. I received correspondence from Connelly saying that Mr Dobrée had sent his proxy to William to proceed against our house; Tupper had not wished to undertake anything. He wanted me to return as quickly as possible to Barcelona, assuring me that he would do all that depended on him to serve me. In another letter, dated at the beginning of December, Connelly informed me that there was nothing new and begged me to speed my return to Barcelona.

Disgusted by the idea of a voyage because of the bad weather, I decided to travel overland, leaving Marseilles on 10 January 1793. On my arrival at Montpellier I received a letter from Connelly announcing that some of the bills that our house had drawn on London had come back protested 'failure of acceptance'. William, as proxy for Dobrée, had opposed guarantees (unlike the earlier practice) and so our house had found itself compelled to suspend payments. This sombre event did not stop me continuing my travel the next day. When I arrived at Perpignan I found further letters from Connelly cofirming the misfortune that had befallen the house. I received also the same day a letter from a young man of the house announcing that he was going to set out at once to meet me with a safe conduct. Having hired a carriage I set out the next day from Perpignan and the same day I encountered the person coming to meet me. I journeyed with him to Barcelona where we arrived on 22 January 1793.

I was immediately urged by some of my friends and by Connelly to make a proposal to my creditors. For this I needed a little time to consider carefully the state of affairs. However, I was pressed to such an extent, even by those who passed for my best friends, about the necessity for an immediate resolution, that 4 February was fixed for the creditors' meeting to deal with my proposal. Someone to whom such a disaster has befallen, who has made a long journey, who has not had time to examine everything, cannot make a reasoned decision.

My chief aim in making a proposal was to try to ward off a lawsuit involving Mr Dobrée and the rest of the creditors, which would take away everything there was. The main body of creditors refused to admit Dobrée as a creditor of our house since, according to the books, he did not appear to be such. In reality Dobrée ought not to have been considered as a creditor of our house but of me, on my own account. It is true that the bills on Dobrée in November and December 1790 of £3,358-19-6 st to clear the Ostend liabilities had been drawn by our house; but they were on my account, or my father's (who had allowed me this, as has already been seen). For the total of these bills Dobrée had recourse against Mr E. Tupper and he against my father.

The credit of Dobrée against me at the time of the disaster that hit our house was about £4,800 sterling. That is why I considered that I should enter Dobrée as a creditor for about £1,500 st. in the calculation of what I proposed to pay to the creditors of our house.

After my hasty examination of the situation, it appeared that I could offer about 42% and that is what I offered at the meeting of 4 February to satisfy various payments:

12% in one month

10% in four months

10% in eight months

10% in fifteen months

However, after much discussion, and to end the matter, I found myself obliged to pay 8% extra, payable in two years after the last payment.

It has been seen that the creditors did not want Dobrée admitted as a creditor of our house and, as a consequence, at the signing of the agreement. Nevertheless, I had told William, Dobrée's proxy, that I intended to pay him a dividend (as to the other creditors) on the sum of £1,500 st. William, not having the power to allow this offer, opposed the signing of the agreement. A little later he received the proxy of my father for the sums advanced to me. This entirely stopped the signing and cast me into the greatest difficulty, disqualifying me from taking any part, so that I found myself without other resource than that of deciding to quit Barcelona and to flee to some other country. From the point of view of my personal interest it was the only thing left for me to do, but I believed that I was obliged not to adopt this course until the last extremity. It would take too long to relate everything that I tried from the beginning of my return to Barcelona. I was constantly under pressure to clear several privileged debts of the house, such as duties owed to the customs, the rent on warehouses, not to mention clerks' salaries &c for which I was approached, without my having the means to pay them. Before my arrival the principal assets that could be realised had been sold to settle several bills that had been protested. Finally I succeeded, with much difficulty, by selling various items of furniture.

At about the period of my arrival in Barcelona news came from Edmond Connelly & Son at Dunkirk of the arrangement that they had made with Patrick Arthur for the credit of our house @ 50% loss and taking brandy in payment at current Dunkirk prices. On my return to Barcelona I was always energetically sollicited by Connelly to speed up the conclusion of my arrangement with my creditors by signing the agreement. It assuredly was not friendship nor attachment that prompted him. From all appearances it seems that his attitude was dictated by pure egoism, his main aim being to free himself from the trouble and to cast the whole weight of it on me. He did everything to achieve this goal as soon as possible. He drew up a paper in my name, maintaining that I considered him discharged of any responsibility towards the creditors of the house, regarding him simply as a clerk and that, besides, I perfectly approved his whole conduct in the management of affairs. He presented this paper to me and did all that he could to obtain my signature but I refused for the simple reason that I could not declare that I approved of Connelly's conduct since I had not yet had time to examine whether it was blameless. However, I promised that I would not oppose Connelly's being cleared of responsibility as he wished. By his exertions Connelly succeeded in obtaining from the majority of the creditors a discharge of all responsibility for his past.

It was understood by the creditors that Connelly would give every assistance possible to me to put matters in order but no sooner had he got the discharge than he arranged no longer to meet me and left me the work of sorting out the affairs as best I could. I discovered that, quite a long time before my return to Barcelona, Connelly had contracted an understanding with the house JM & Co of Barcelona to enter its service. Our house, a little before its disaster, received some orders for brandy. Connelly judged it appropriate to have them carried out by JM & Co without any profit accruing to me. It is apparently for these reasons - and for other things for which he felt guilty - that he was so anxious to want a testimonial signed by me. Having carefully examined the state of affairs, I found that the total of losses that I had sustained in 1792 exceeded £C 60,000 of which the entirety – apart from some bagatelle – arose from the business transacted with Connelly's friends and relatives at Dunkirk.

My confidence had not been fooled about the people involved in the negotiations since I did not sufficiently know any of them, that is to say their abilities, to give my trust. My total confidence was in Connelly, who used to give me repeated assurances of their soundness. I thought Connelly must have had a complete understanding about them since he had the opportunity to collect information on the standing of these correspondents during three trips that he made to Dunkirk in the space of less than two years. This is the table of losses sustained by our house in 1792.

Recapitulation of losses sustained by Reserson & Company during the course of 1792

Losses on the resale of various consignments of brandy upto 31 July			£C 9662-12-00
" " to the end of the year			13463-11-08
In these two entries is included the loss on the two hundred pipes of brandy that the Dunkirk house made difficulty about taking after our house had kept them several months by its orders.			
Idem on the consignment of 105 pipes of brandy bought and shipped on Connelly's instructions for the account of his cousins who refused to accept them and who sold 25 pipes for the account of our house, the loss on which was		2864-2-2	
The other 80 pipes not being easily able to sell at Dunkirk were sent to Ostend and Amsterdam and produced a loss of		6638-18-0	
			9503-00-02
			£C 32629-03-10
Loss with Patrick Arthur			8273-18-00
Idem by the arrangement with Isaac Brown			7383-05-07
Idem on the 180 $\frac{18}{2}$ pipes of brandy sent to Guernsey valued at about			12000-00-00
Idem on a consignment of muslin taken back from the buyer In respect of his failure		1037-10-0	
On several other merchandises		406-11-3	
			1444-01-03
			£C 61730-08-08

N.B. This was calculated counting on receiving from Arthur & Brown what had been agreed but which has not been audited.

When I had to make an arrangement with the creditors, it was made clear to me that I should propose prompt payment. William indicated to me his desire that I should arrange my affairs as quickly as possible. He assured me that he would help with all he deemed appropriate. So, when I had made my plan, I was willing to let William see it. However, he did not want to see it, saying that it was not necessary and assuring me that I could always count on him. William excused himself, however, from attending the creditors' meeting, although his presence would have been very useful to me. He made the excuse that he was ill but later avowed that it had been a ruse. What is certain is that he gave me not the least help when I badly needed a little money to settle some customs duties. I had the means to repay this sum with the rental of a house that I had let out. All that William did for me was to give a bill of exchange on London for the sum in question. For this he demanded the guarantee of the broker who negotiated it and who, seeing that there was nothing to lose, gave it to him. A few days later the rent of the house was recovered and the sum rendered.

I have an idea that I was obliged to suffer a loss in this transaction, the broker not having been able to negotiate it at the rate that William had judged appropriate to fix. There should be mention of a circumstance which will clearly show that all the promises and assurances of William were words in air and that he gave me no quarter. It was William who had been most interested to secure my return to Barcelona, after my disaster, it was he who dispatched the young man to meet me and who lent a horse for this purpose, he had even advanced a small sum to this young man to cover his travel expenses - but he grabbed the first opportunity to get his money back from me soon afterwards, when I was quite without resources.

It must be observed that, when I made my proposal, affairs had not come to the crisis to which they were carried afterwards. Peace still existed between France and Spain and England and thus I flattered myself that I could soon succeed in drawing back the funds held by Connelly & Co Dunkirk. I wrote them several letters telling them what had happened, begging them to give me a precise summary of the affairs of the house under their management but I could not ever obtain a word of reply. War breaking out some while after, I was necessarily obliged to break off correspondence and abandon hope of being able to retrieve anything from that quarter while the troubles lasted; it should also be added that, because of the war, several letters drawn on Edmond Connelly & Son (Dunkirk) came back protested, contrary to every expectation.

I was equally unfortunate in my realisation of several other assets of my house in Spain, the recovery of these could not take place as quickly as could be wished because of several, unfavourable circumstances. This, joined to the obstacle set up by Perchard, Brock, Dobrée and my father, absolutely prevented me from being able to make any payment whatsoever to my creditors. As for the brandy at Guernsey, a share of the produce had already been remitted to Perchard and Brock, and Dobrée had had the remainder arrested.

Eventually, on 12 August 1793, there was another creditors' meeting to explain the extreme difficulties into which I had plunged and the impossibility of my being able to fulfil my agreement by making payments on the terms stipulated. The creditors in general displayed the most favourable attitude towards me but I then clearly saw the mistake that I had made in counting in any way on William's help. The joy that shone on his face at seeing me in distress succeeded in bringing to its climax the extreme grief with which I was already engulfed and prevented my uttering a word. Nevertheless the majority of the creditors present still had the goodness to have consideration for my situation and they granted me a delay fixing the first payment to start in eight months and the others following on the dates already laid down after the first payment. The following month – September – the agreement was signed by the majority of creditors, except however by William as proxy for Perchard, Brock, Dobrée &c., not having instructions in this regard.

A little after my return to Barcelona, proposals had been made to me to enter a good house there and I was led to understand that this would be on an advantageous footing. I could not decide immediately to accept this offer, hoping first that my own affairs could be completely concluded before making any decision about my future destiny. The same motive equally made me refuse William's proposal to receive me into his house to help him in his business and to give me an annual salary of £200 st. with food etc. I rented an apartment and, by way of the commission on the sale of a cargo which came to the address of my house, and several other things, I managed to exist for nearly a year, i.e. to December 1793.

Eventually, William came one day to find me and earnestly solicited me to enter his house, giving to understand that, if I accepted his proposal, he would do all that he could to settle my affairs and even led me to hope that that would take place promptly. I then found myself without any resource and saw I would be obliged to make some decision in a few days in order to subsist. So I allowed myself to be persuaded and gave myself entirely to William for what he wanted to pay me, I counted that that would be at least the £200 st. which had been offered me several months earlier but it appeared that William wanted to profit from my situation which, in fact, was not brilliant. He said that he would pay me 1,000 *piastres courantes* annually at the start and following that he would increase the sum. However, during the three years or thereabouts which followed from that era until the war between Spain and England (which brought about the departure of William from Barcelona), there was no question of any increase, no measure to try to arrange my affairs, I received no help in this matter from William who, during this time, showered his largesse on various people, especially on several French émigrés and others whom he had never previously known. To some he would give money, to others he lent quite considerable sums without any security of being paid back, but for me there was absolutely nothing, despite so many repeated promises.

In the course of 1798, remaining all the time at Barcelona, I received a letter from William, by now in England, that he had heard from Kirkpatrick, the old partner in charge of the liquidation of the Ostend house and who now lived in Liverpool in England. It appeared that some time previously Kirkpatrick had received a quite considerable payment of a debt from someone in Tobago but he had given no news of this in time. William told me that he had energetically pressed Kirkpatrick to give him some money and had got £500 st. He asked me if I had also received anything for my share and, if not, or if only a part, to tell him and to furnish him a note so that he could act for me and demand what would come from Kirkpatrick. I replied to William that I had received nothing, but, owing Kirkpatrick £120 st. for an old transaction, to be on the same footing as William there would come £380 from Kirkpatrick. I received no reply from William to this letter for he, finding himself in Guernsey and having been in some scuffle with an officer, had the misfortune to fall in a duel, dying immediately from his wound. So I wrote to Kirkpatrick about this request by way of a friend. When I failed to receive a reply from Kirkpatrick to two or three letters, my friend advised me to send a proxy to challenge Kirkpatrick. I did this, remitting at the same time all the necessary documents. Having waited several months, I received news from my friend about the bankruptcy of Kirkpatrick, which I had already learned about by another route. My friend indicated the little hope of recovering anything, so there again I was the victim of that cursed house at Ostend. I had been obliged, as we have seen, to pay out my share to underwrite the enormous losses to which I had not contributed in any way. I was unable, like the others, to salvage what came from the flotsam of the shipwreck. William could have saved me this last loss if, in soliciting for himself, he had been willing to interest himself also for me. But I was doomed to be overwhelmed by every possible misfortune and, as misfortunes never arrive alone, the house of Connelly at Dunkirk failed at the end of 1798. They were debtors of mine, for they owed for the brandy that they had remitted in payment of Arthur's debt to our house and I awaited the return of a general peace before asking for anything, to avoid being paid in *assignats* or *mandats*.

The acceptance of Isaac Brown & Co for their debt to our house, following the arrangement made between them and me, had rested in the hands of Connelly & Son but I had not been able to learn anything about these matters. I considered that they must be very bad, for if Isaac Brown & Co paid their acceptances, even with some delay, they would be included in the failure of Connelly & Son; and, if they had not paid during so long a time, this would indicate that they were in financial straits and incapable of paying.

It seems, then, that a tangle of misfortunes brought about my ruin and afterwards prevented me fulfilling my agreement towards the creditors. After the account of all that happened I admit that I made mistakes and I reduce them to four main ones:

1. Of having continued my partnership with William after getting to know his character well and the losses to which he had exposed the house. My main motive, as I have already said, was not to break a relationship arranged by my father and, besides, when this partnership was

formed I was very young and consequently not as mature in my judgment as I would have been if older.

2. When I saw the disastrous state of the Ostend house in 1788 I should have forced it into bankruptcy. I have already spoken of the reasons that encouraged me to act otherwise.

3. I placed too much confidence in Connelly, it is true, but I thought him worthy of it, the more so having seen on several occasions that Connelly refused to grant credit to some old friends of mine; this gave me a higher view of his prudence.

4. The arrangement that I made with my creditors was too hasty, I agree. All that I can say to excuse myself is that I have always wanted to act properly, I went wrong but my aim was never to wrong anyone. Finally, misfortunes overwhelmed me. What can I do except exercise patience and hope that one day fortune may favour me to the extent of showing that amidst so many shameful events I have always maintained the principles of an honourable man and the wish to be able to render to each his due.

CONCLUSION

Reserson's account appears reliable whenever it can be checked against independent evidence. The character of de Vic Tupper was described by De Havilland as follows:

> He was a man in his forty-second year, strong and built like a Hercules, with a very violent and passionate temper, not knowing how to submit to anyone, excessively jealous on a point of honour, unable to stand the least contradiction, and unfortunately when he was drunk (which happened often, as he was always in company) one had to leave him to avoid quarrels. Thus he had had countless duels. He may have fought – here, in Ostend, where he went for two years 20 years ago, in Barcelona, where he was established as a merchant for 24 years (he was in partnership as a very young man with your cousin, Nicholas Reserson), and in London, where he went occasionally – he may, I say, have fought 30 to 40 duels and it is not to be supposed that he had right on his side on every occasion. (Hocart, 1997, p. 63).

Nicholas worked on in Barcelona until July 1824. The consular ledger (see p.65) seems to indicate that he issued himself a passport (perhaps an indication of the respect in which he was held at that date). He returned home to Guernsey and died soon afterwards.

JOHN GUILLE

John Guille became one of the most successful of the St Peter Port merchants. We know quite a lot about his activities thanks to the survival of family papers, including letterbooks.

John traded in a variety of commodities: rum, shipped principally from St Croix; gin, from Rotterdam; brandy from Charente, Cette, Toulon, Catalonia; wine, sometimes from France, but much more often from the Spanish coast. He bought tea through agents at the East India Sales at Rotterdam, Copenhagen, Gothenburg, and Lorient. He sold his cargoes both to English smugglers and to legitimate merchants in Britain and Canada. He also had private clients in England. For example, he sent best port, best sherry, best claret, vinegar, Frontignac, cognac brandy, and tea to a Captain John Urry of Yarmouth. This appears to be Captain Sir John Urry, who lived in the Isle of Wight and was renowned for his hospitality. He was reprimanded by the Admiralty for continually delaying HM ships which were anchoring off his property whilst the officers and crews were ashore making merry (www.marcireau. fr/urry, 2 June 2008).

John Guille also traded in textiles. He had an interest in the traditional stocking-knitting industry and employed a considerable number of islanders in this work. He imported, under licence, an annual quota of fleeces from Crew & Tatham (London). In Guernsey the wool was washed by workmen, combed by men, and spun by women. When finished, the stockings were packed in bundles, two dozen pairs of stockings per bundle. In at least one instance the bundles were arranged in seven rows, eight bundles in each row, and this made up one bale. Between May 1777 and June 1779 Guille dispatched a bale on nineteen occasions by the regular packet boats (*Montague, Providence, Susanna, Queen*) to Southampton. There Seward arranged for delivery of the consignment to Crew and Tatham in London. Tentative calculations suggest that Guille was organising the production of about 11,000 pairs of stockings annually, for which he received approximately £750 from Crew and Tatham.

Guille kept a shop in St Peter Port. There he sold, *inter alia*, bandanoes, bengals, bonnets, buttons, camlots, cardinals, chag, chelloes, chemises, *cotton fleuri*, cravats, *crêpe*, Damascus, *épilles, fil d'angleterre, fil d'holande*, flannel, garters, *grisailles*, guinea stuff, hats, *indien*, irish cloth, *lachez*, linen, looping cord, mirrors, molton, *mouchoirs des indes*, muslin, nankeens, pekin, *plumaches, pontivin, russilla*, satins, *serge de nisme, soie blanche, soie de barcelone, soie noire*, stockings, swanskin, *tabliers, velours* (IAS, Stevens-Guille papers (new), inventory, 1772). The stock was valued approximately at four thousand pounds. Guille's letterbook identifies his suppliers (see opposite). Guille was catering for a prosperous urban clientele in St Peter Port.

In London William De Jersey and Peter Perchard acted as his bankers. We find Guille asking de Jersey to arrange extra insurance on the *Lord Chatham*; to cover a cargo from Gothenburg; to guarantee extra financial backing when good opportunities for buying presented themselves; and to arrange for a school. Guille asked Perchard to insure his goods in trade for £2,000 and his household goods for £200. London was also the base of one of Guille's most important correspondents – Mark Gregory (see p. 190). Gregory was in partnership with John Guille's brother Nicholas at Barcelona, trading as Gregory & Guille (see pp. 66-67). John Guille jr (Guernsey) was thus linked to a successful partnership in Barcelona and to a powerful merchant in the city of London. Guille participated in a virtuous triangle with flows of orders, information and credit passing between the three houses and their satellites. Gregory (London-Cowes) was well positioned to co-ordinate the organisation of the businesses by securing orders, arranging shipping, delivering cargoes. He had direct access to the English market and understood international price movements. Guille (Guernsey) was able to exploit the advantages of St Peter Port as an entrepôt. He arranged shipping and solicited orders from othe Guernsey merchants to be placed with Gregory & Guille (Barcelona). During wartime Guille became especially valuable as he gave news to Gregory (London) about the sales of captured prizes at St Peter Port.

London was also the home of many businesses with which Guille traded (see tables). However, not all of Guille's correspondents were in the capital. He bought coal from John Baker of Newcastle. In the south-west he had contacts in Southampton (John Wise, Seward), Bristol (Thomas Perkins), Plymouth (Peter Tonkin), and Newlyn (William Hichens). He corresponded with Thomas Le Cocq in Alderney.

Guille maintained very good relations with a number of French *négociants*. In 1777 he advised Canel, Meslé & Bernard of Nantes and the Johnston house at Bordeaux about the impending visit of William de Jersey (jr). William was on a wine-buying expedition to France and represented Guille and other Guernsey merchants (Jean Brock & Le Marchant, Richard de Jersey, Pierre Bonamy). As war approached, Guille wrote long and friendly letters to St Malo, expressing his desire for peace and his wish to maintain goods relations even if war broke out between France and Britain. He reminded his correspondents of the ways in which neutral shipping could be used to continue trade and he even went as far as outlining how the navigation laws could be circumvented.

Clients receiving wine from John Guille during the years 1777-1779:

Messrs Abel & Macaulay of London.

Samuel Ballard of Portsmouth, taking Spanish wine; G gives advice *re* Sitges wine.

William Baynes & Co of London taking wine (some for Quebec).

William Damon of Southampton.

Davies, Strachan & Co.

James Davies of Cowes.

Benjamin Heame, (West Country), taking wine for Gill & LeMarchant, Quebec.

Messrs James Ireland & Co of Bristol.

George Knowsley of Hull, one hogshead of Malmsey at ten guineas; Guille sends sample of Teneriffe wine (which could be entered as Spanish).

James Mackenzie & Co of Cowes.

Messrs Read of Cowes.

Tulk & Lovelace of London.

Table 5.8 Hose shipped by Guille to Crew & Tatham, London

bale	date	Value (£ st)	Quantity
67	May 1777	89-15-1 ½	
68	June	17-14-3 ½	
69	July	89-1-10 ½	112 doz pairs
70	August	93-9-7	
71	September	86-17-7	
72	November	92-19-11 ½	112 dozen pairs men's, 2 dozen women's
73	January 1778	100-18-4 ½	
74	March	96-13-8	
75	April	107-18-1	
76	May	87-12-1	
77	June	67-15-11	
78	August	91-19-2	118 dozen pairs
79	September	88-12-7	
80	November	77-6-7	
81	December	81-12-11	
82	March 1779	75-17-10	
83	March	65-18-4	
84	April	79-9-8 ½	
85	June	59-19-0	

Table 5.9 English Merchants supplying textiles to John Guille, Guernsey, 1777-1779

ENGLAND

Alsop & Ashby, of London: supplying scarlet & white lettered garters, scarlet garters.
Beachcroft & Co: supplying plain dark brown camblets, black calamanco, sarsnett, superfine buff shalloon bombazeen, dark brown camblets.
Thomas Bowerbank: supplying black & brown cloth.
Paul Cooper & Co: supplying scarlet bevor, blue cloth dyed in the wool & not in the piece.
Messrs Crew & Tatham: supplying wool fleeces.
Thos. Huckell Lee: supplying blue, dark brown serge; woollens.
John & Thomas Puckle: supplying yellow breast oval buttons; black knee garters; scarlet silk; white oval buttons with a star; white silk stay braid; white narrow worsted binding; corduroy.

Table 5.10 John Guille's principal correspondents abroad, 1777-1779

CANADA - Quebec: *Gill & Le Marchant; Gregory & Woolsey.*

DENMARK - Copenhagen: *Fabritius & Wever* (Bohea tea).

FRANCE - Bordeaux: *Wm & Nathaniel Johnston* (wine).

Nantes: *Canel, Meslé & Bernard.*

St Malo: *Brillantais Marion:* Guille held Marion in high regard: 'My friend is as honest as any in Europe & would rather loose (sic) anything than be guilty of sacrificing a friend's interest for the sake of a small commission' (Journal, p. 135). Guille tried to get him admission to the *Société des Veuves* in St Peter Port but ultimately failed. Guille received chestnuts from Brillantais and possibly bought timber from him.
Chenard, Giraudais & Le Page : Guille requested this house to obtain tea at the Lorient sales for him. The tea was to be shipped supposedly to Dunkirk and no-one at St Malo would know about the arrangement (Journal, p. 33).
Dupuy Fromy: Guille received wine from this house.
Menais Robert fréres & co: Guille tried to get orders for this house but the Guernsey merchants had sent orders to Copenhagen and Gothenburg (or had old friends at Lorient whom they do not wish to leave). Guille was happy with the idea of their supplying taffia *blanc* from Martinique but did not like the idea of taffia *jaune.*

HOLLAND - Amsterdam: *Messrs Pye Rick & Wilkiesons; Berghaus.*

Rotterdam: *James Le Marchant* (supplying gin, iron hoops, tea).

SPAIN - Barcelona: *Gregory & Guille.*

SWEDEN - Gothenburg: *Arfwidson & Sons* (bohea, congo, tonkay tea); *John George Eckmann* (tea).

WEST INDIES - St Croix: *Abraham Le Mesurier* (rum); *Shirrett Tucker & Co.*

Source: Priaulx, Guille letterbook

6
Ships

Fig. 6.1: Types of sailing vessels (from *The Art of Rigging* by D.Steel, London, 1818).

SHIPS

'Three major decisions: the purchase of the right ship, the determination of what to do with it, the choice of a master; these were the management decisions which, though made only a rare intervals, were primarily responsible for settling the success or failure of the enterprise' (Davis, 1972, p. 174).

The merchant buying a ship looked for a number of features. He wanted a vessel that carried a large cargo relative to its size. Simultaneously he required a small crew in proportion to the tonnage transported; a good manning ratio kept his costs low. It was obviously desirable that the vessel should sail well and be able to respond quickly to changes in the breezes (particularly in local Channel waters). A boat that required only a small amount of ballast was preferable to one that needed much. Besides these general principles the merchant also considered his individual requirements. He had to think of the cargoes to be carried, the routes to be travelled, the ports entered. In many instances a swift vessel was an advantage. The first ship to arrive with the new crop could command higher prices in the market. Several of the criteria that we have mentioned were mutually exclusive. For example, 'Flat floors for stowing and carrying great burthens, or sharp floors for sailing fast' was the dictum of William Hutchinson in 1794 (cited by Davis, 1972, p. 74). The merchant could not buy a vessel that simultaneously carried a maximum cargo and sailed very fast. There was the further, local, consideration that sharp floors would not sit on the harbour bottom at St Peter Port when the tide was out. Sharp-floored vessels unloaded outside the harbour, in the roads. The merchant had to compromise.

The Guernsey merchants built up a fleet to service their requirements. The size and nature of the fleet directly reflected the trades in which they engaged. This chapter examines the composition of the Guernsey fleet at four different times. First, we shall examine the situation in 1680, when the merchants were involved in the Newfoundland trade and in carrying cargoes between St Malo and England. Secondly, we shall look at the fleet c. 1712 – c. 1740, when the merchants were beginning to develop St Peter Port as an entrepôt. Thirdly, we turn to the 1780s, when St Peter Port was coming to its zenith as an entrepôt. Finally we shall examine the vessels employed in the 1820s when the merchants were much engaged in the South American trade. I have selected years of peace. War brought privateering and the acquisition of ships appropriate for that activity. I am concerned to identify the vessels used for purely commercial purposes. It is fair to admit, however, that if a merchant felt that war was looming, his thoughts may have strayed to the idea of buying a ship that would function both as a merchantman and as an *armed* merchantman

1680

When Legge (BL King's Ms 48) made his survey of Guernsey in 1680 he included details about the Guernsey fleet. He recorded eighteen vessels: one ship, five pinks, eight barks, two ketches, a small hoy and a double shallop. Pinks and barks predominated. The pink was a small, square-rigged vessel with a narrow, overhanging stern. It was often of the fly-boat type with hull form of the Dutch fashion. This achieved a high carrying capacity in relation to the ship's main measurements. The term bark (barque) generally denoted a small sailing ship (until the mid-nineteenth century) and properly described a vessel with three masts (square-rigged on the fore and main sails and fore-and-aft rigged on the mizzen). Barks and pinks were well suited to the carrying of cargoes between St Malo and England. The ship was a three-masted vessel, square-rigged. The rigging was usually kept as simple as possible, because owners could not afford the size of crew required by a full (naval) rigging. The ketch had two masts (square-rigged); its main use was as a small coastal trading vessel. The hoy was a small coasting vessel; it 'had no definite characteristics as such, being any small coasting vessel which might, in other places, be called a sloop or smack' (Kemp, 1988, p. 404). The shallop was a light, small vessel. Eleven of the vessels were English-built; the remaining seven were French. The details can be re-classified as follows:

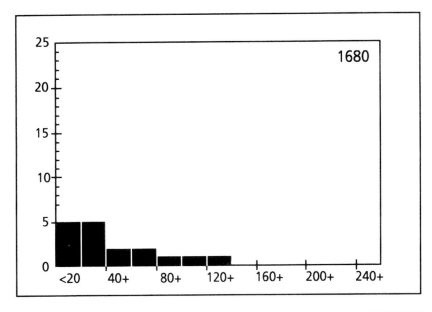

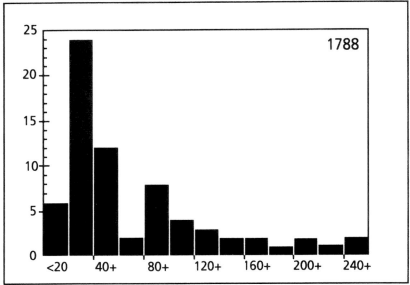

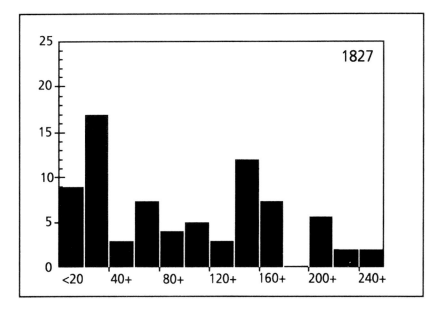

Fig. 6.2: The composition of the Guernsey fleet, 1680 1788 and 1827
(vertical axis = number of ships; horizontal axis = tonnage).

Table 6.1 The Guernsey fleet, 1680

Type	Number	Total Tonnage	Average Tonnage	Construction
Pinks	5	410	82	English
Ketches	2	65	32.5	English
Barks	8	223	27.9	Two English, Six French-bulit
Double shallop	1	8	8	English
Small hoy	1	8	8	English
Ship	1	?	?	French

The owners were: Daniel de Beauvoir, Thomas Bevis, John Bouillon, Peter Carey, Michael Falla, Thomas Fiott, Peter Gosselin, - Harris, James Haviland, Peter Le Coc, William Le Marchant, Abraham Mesurier, Nicholas Pellay. The masters were: Aron Anley, Thomas Bevis, Nicholas Blondell, John Bonamy, Samuel Gainpaine, Peter Herivell, Peter LeCoc, Francis Le Hay, Thomas Le Marchant, Nicholas Major, William Mansell, James Oliver, Daniel Palott, Eleazar Palott, Lewis Russell, Michael Thomas, and Peter Vallet. In this list we find surnames that were prominent in Guernsey's eighteenth-century mercantile world: Bonamy, Carey, Le Coc (=Le Cocq), (de) Havilland, (Le)Mesurier, Le Marchant, Major (=Mageur).

1712-1740

There are three principal sources for information about the Guernsey fleet in the period 1712-1740: the records of the *Cour d'Amirauté;* Admiralty passes; and colonial shipping returns. Vessels are frequently mentioned in cases that were heard at the *Cour d'Amirauté*. Table 6.2 gives a summary of such ship references for the years c. 1712 - c. 1730. Some caution is necessary in the use of these records. First, there is the problem of vocabulary. *Navire* may have been used in its specific sense (denoting a three-masted vessel rigged in a particular fashion) or it may simply be a generic term meaning little more than 'vessel'. Secondly, it is unlikely that every vessel in the Guernsey fleet figured in a court case; we glimpse part of the maritime scene, not the entirety. Thirdly, I have included only those references which seem to relate unequivocally to island vessels. Court cases sometimes involved ships from outside Guernsey and the archives usually ignore details about 'home ports'. I have done my best to exclude 'foreign' (i.e. non-Guernsey) shipping; in that endeavour I may have excluded some craft that actually belonged to the island. Fourthly, these boats were almost certainly not all in operation at the same time. In 1701 the island owned thirty-two vessels (of 1,260 tons, the crew strength was 180 men). By 1788 the island fleet had grown to sixty-nine vessels. We do not know the size of the fleet in the intervening years.

The court details are slight but precious. They reveal a world of ships, sloops, brigs/brigantines and ketches (*caches*). The brigantine was a two-masted vessel, square-rigged on the foremast and fore-and-aft rigged on the mainmast. The sloop had a single mast, fore-and-aft rigged. The court records are also helpful in identifying owners: André Bonamy, Jean Bonamy, Pierre Bonamy, Pierre Carey, Jean Dobrée, Samuel Dobrée, Jean de Jerzey, Daniel Le Febvre, Jean & James Le Ray, Abraham Le Mesurier, William Le Mesurier, Daniel Mauger, Josué Priaulx, Daniel Tupper, Pierre Tupper, Nicholas de Sausmarez. The surnames are those of the great families of *négociants*. Whereas small vessels were often owned outright, or with one partner, larger ships were generally owned by a group of merchants, each with a stake of one quarter or one eighth. This spread the risk in case of disaster; and the merchant with an interest in several ships had better prospects of success in at least some of his enterprises.

Other owners included ship-masters. 'The ship's master could have no better investment than the ship he commanded, if he were confident of his own abilities, and when the way was open masters constantly strove to increase their holdings' (Davis, 1972, p. 85). Prominent masters of this period included: Jacques Bienvenu, Jean Bonamy, Pierre Brock, William Cook, Jacques Cormier, Jean Dobrée, Jean Guignon, William le Mesurier, Philipe Luce, Daniel Mauger, Edouard Mauger, Helier Palot, Elie Picot, Richard Robinson, Robert Robinson, and William Warren. It will be noted that some of these came from merchant families (e.g. Bonamy, Brock, Dobrée, le Mesurier, Mauger, Robinson). Davis has a relevant comment: 'To be the master of any but the smallest ship was a worthwhile and profitable profession, which attracted a small but continuous flow of youths from much higher levels of society. These were the sons of minor merchants and prosperous ship-masters, men with influence and connections in maritime circles, able to dispose of a few hundred pounds at need to further a boy's career' (Davis, 1972, p. 117). And there was a further consideration in appointing a master from a mercantile family, shipowners had a direct interest in appointing a master who could be trusted: 'This is one reason why owners so often sought to appoint masters who would be bound by more than mere financial ties; a reason for the frequent employment of sons, brothers, nephews or cousins of the owners or their business associates' (Davis, 1972, p. 159). I would further observe that there can have been no better education for an apprentice merchant than the experience of directing the transport of cargo from the port of origin to the final destination.

The second source for this period is the Admiralty series of Passes. By definition we are dealing here with vessels sailing the high seas; small craft plying between St Peter Port and the English coast did not require a pass. So, again, we are getting a partial picture. And, just as with the *Cour d'Amirauté* cases, it should be understood that not all of these vessels were in operation at the same time. Nevertheless, the source does reflect the types of vessels employed by the merchants during the 1730s and early 1740s. We find some nineteen brigs (50/50, median and mode tonnage), fifteen sloops (35/40), ten ships (85/80), six snows (75/80), three pinks (80/80), one galley (60), and one ketch (40).

Pinks were in decline, the ship, snow, brig and sloop were becoming the preferred type of vessel. The snow was a two-masted vessel, with square sails on both masts, similar in several respects to a brig, a two-masted vessel, square-rigged on both fore and main masts. Davis comments that the snow and the brig were almost identical and both were used for all purposes, but the snow was more commonly the ocean voyager while the brig could be found most often in home waters, and particularly those of the North Sea. 'One of their best-known characteristics was the small crew they required' (Davis, 1972, pp. 77 – 78). Davis' distinction of usage does not hold for Guernsey. In practice many island brigs ventured across the Atlantic.

The colonial shipping returns, our third source, often provide useful information about construction. They show that several Guernsey-owned vessels were built in the American colonies (see Table 6.3). American-built shipping was frequently cheaper. 'According to contemporary observers, the building price per ton for a colonial vessel was often £2 to £4 less than a British-built one' (Goldenberg, 1976, p. 95). Most of the Guernsey-owned vessels had been built in New England. Goldenberg comments: 'All the colonies exported shipping, but, once again, New England was the chief contributor. Specifically, New England shipyards supplied about half of the American-built tonnage in Great Britain at the end of the colonial period. Within New England, Massachusetts and New Hampshire were the leading producers; Pennsylvania, followed by Virginia and Maryland, launched most of the remaining tonnage' (Goldenberg, 1976, p. 99). Most of the American-built vessels appear to have been purchased second-hand. However, the Cour d'Amirauté archives record that Le Sr James Le Ray actioned Pierre Ougier to go to Virginia to collect a vessel that Le Ray had ordered to be built (following the dimensions given by Ougier) and to bring the vessel back to Guernsey (CdA vol. 13, 24 Aug. 1751).

Some vessels were built in Guernsey: the snow *Charming Nancy*, the sloop *Two Brothers* (TNA CO 33/16 part 2 f 64 r, f 75 r); the *Fox*, the *Lottery* and the *Speedwell* (Raban, 1986, p. 142; Raban, 1987, p. 322).

Table 6.2 Guernsey-owned vessels 1712-1730s

Name	type	[master] owner(s)
Anne & James	navire	le Sr James Perchard
Aventure		Jacques Bienvenu, le Sr Simon Rivoire
Benediction	sloop	le Sr Josue Priaulx
Cheval de la Mer	brigantine	(carrying tobacco from Bristol for le Sr Jean le Ray)
Cheval Marin		Nicolas Brouard 1/3 interest
Daniel	cache	[Thomas Martin]
Daniel & Catherine	navire	le Sr Daniel Mauger master/part owner; le Sr Jean Luce 1/4 interest
Daniel & Philipe	barque	Daniel Queripel and Philipe Bot, half shares
Defiance		le Sr Andre Bonamy previously interested and Pierre Tupper
Deux Soeurs	barque	Jean & James Le Ray
Deux Soeurs & Marie		[le Sr William Le Mesurier]
Edouard & Jean		Etienne Broyer and le Sr Jaques Cormier
Elizabeth & Philipe		le Sr Jean Le Mesurier
Esperance	navire	Jean Le Cocq
Fidélité		le Sr Daniel Tupper armateur, Nicholas Breton interest
Fleur de la Mer	sloop	[Daniel Paint]
Flying Fish	sloop	Jean Hessy owner; Marie Godion and James le Ray interest
Guillaume	sloop	[Philip Luce]
Hirondelle		Mr Jean Dobrée and le Sr George Pellew involved in sale
Jean	brigantine	Jean Luce
Jean & Henry		[le Sr Jean Bonamy] le Sr Andre Condamine
Jean & Marie		[le Sr Daniel Mauger] le Sr Jean de Jersey had 1/2 interest
Jean & Thomas	sloop	Thomas Rogers and le Sr Jean de Jerzey 1/2 interests
Judith		[Richard Robinson]
l'Union		Mr Jean Dobrée & le Sr George Pellew involved in sale
Madelene	barque	le Sr Elie Picot master and half owner
Mairmayde	sloop	[Josue Corbin]
Marie	sloop	Samuel Dobrée
Marie	brigantine	Philipe Luce
Marie Catherine		[Philipe Luce]
Marie Elizabeth		[Pierre Pariolo]
Marie-Jane	barque	[Louis Lambert] Jean Le Ray part-owner
Mathieu Mills	sloop	Mr Daniel Le Febvre
Mauve de la Mer		Mr Nicolas de Sausmarez holding 1/4 of vessel belonging to John Inglish
Michel	navire	le Sr Jean Bonamy des Caches 1/6th interest
Paix	brigantine	Mr Pierre Careye
Prince George	sloop	Pierre Brock master and owner
Providence	cache	[Helier Palot]
Providence	sloop	[Jean Guignon] le Sr Jean le Ray 1/2 interest
Rachel		James Le Ray owner
Revenge	barque	Mr Samuel Dobrée
Richard & Judith	sloop	Richard Robinson
Societe		[le Sr Pierre Bonamy]
Southampton	navire	Mr Pierre Careye de la brasserie
Speedwell	navire	[le Sr Edouard Mauger]
Success		[Estienne Godet] Mr Nicholas Dobrée previously armateur
Susanne		[le Sr Jean Perchard junr]
Trois Amis		[le Sr Abraham Le Mesurier]

Source: Greffe, CdA, volumes 7 – 11

Table 6.3 Some Guernsey - owned vessels built in America

Name	Type	Built	Date	Registered in Guernsey	Tons	Crew	Owners
Dolphin	sloop	New England	1743	5 May 1749	30	7	James Le Ray
Dolphin	brig	New England	1743	23 Jun 1752	70	10	James Le Ray
George Galley	ship	Philadelphia	1740	19 April 1745	130	14	James Le Ray
Mary	ship	New England	1736	6 Oct 1737	130	12	Robert Gover
Mary	ship	Virginia	1750	13 Apr 1751	150	17	James Le Ray
Matthew	snow	New England	1734	21 Aug 1736	60	9	James Le Ray & Jonathan Perchard
P/Wales	ship	New England	1731	29 Jan 1735	150	15	Isaac Carey & Co
Rodney	schooner	New England	1762	14 Mar 1763	50	6	Lewis De Fraise

Source: TNA CO 5/509, CO 5/1446

1780s

By the 1780s there was considerably more official recording and it becomes easier to understand Guernsey shipping. In 1788 the island was credited with sixty-nine vessels of 5,074 tons and in the following year with seventy-seven vessels (5,861 tons). (BL Add Ms 38376 f85r - f88r; Jamieson, 1986, p. 323). There were both more – and larger – vessels. The transporting of bulk cargoes (such as wheat across the Atlantic, from Quebec to Barcelona) became profitable if there were economies of scale. The easiest way to cut costs was to achieve a good manning ratio. Small vessels required heavier manning per ton than large ships. There was thus a move towards larger vessels. Ralph Davis observed that English shipping then became progressively more efficient as the crew size in large ships was reduced. The Guernsey fleet seems to have followed the English pattern.

The Foreign Passes show that there were more **ships** during this era: *Ceres* (300 tons), *Pomona* (274), *Bell* (241), *Three Sisters* (222), *Charlotte* (196), *Fancy* (185), *Hudibras* (170), *La Monique* (150), *Mary* (148), *Ospray* (143), *St Peter* (130), *Lark* (111), *Mary* (100), *Young Mary* (70), *Flying Fish* (34). There was the occasional **schooner** - *Friendly James* (60); but the **brig** continued to be the most popular type of vessel: *Crescent* (270), *Mary* (200), *Peggy* (180), *Sophia* (145), *Industry* (140), *Hope* (134), *Eagle* (132), *Daphne* (118), *Friend's Adventure* (110), *Two Brothers* (110), *Friendship* (108), *Prince of Orange* (100), *Betsey* (89), *Patty* (81), *Anne & Mary* (80), *Two Brothers* (70), *Gaspé* (60), *Harriott* (41). The brig had the carrying capacity of a small ship but could be run by a smaller crew. Although the manning ratio may not have been quite as efficient as that achieved by a ship, in practical terms it was easier to raise a smaller crew for a voyage. Moreover, it could take longer to secure cargoes to fill a larger vessel, with the ship lying idle in port. Boats are only truly productive when they are at sea. The great danger for shipowners is under-utilisation of their vessels. A brig with a fast 'turn-around-time' offered advantages.

These vessels were mainly English-built. Some were French (often vessels that had been captured in war-time as prizes); others came from the North American colonies. Ownership was generally arranged by partnerships. Peter Mourant emerged as a significant owner (see p. 111).

1827

In 1827 the Guernsey fleet numbered seventy-seven vessels (7,723 tons) and one pleasure vessel. The composition of the fleet can be reconstructed from details presented by Jacob:

Table 6.4 The Guernsey fleet, 1827

Type	No	Tonnage
ships	6	1,328
brigs	29	4,586
schooners	6	515
sloops and cutters	36	1,294
pleasure vessel	1	14
	78	7,737

Source: Jacob (1830)

Sloops and cutters were employed in Channel trading; ships, brigs and schooners made voyages to the Mediterranean, South America and northern Europe. The brig was the most favoured type and was extensively used in the Mediterranean – South American trade.

Almost all of the vessels in the Guernsey fleet in 1827 were Guernsey-built. It seems logical to infer that the local boat-builders constructed vessels that satisfied the criteria of the shipowners. Experience taught, perhaps, that there was an 'ideal' design for a Guernsey brig. If vessels are standardised, there are cost savings. For one generation the Guernsey fleet succeeded on the South American run. But by 1840s the vessels were proving to be too small and of the wrong design: 'of little burthen from their size and sharpness' (see p. 14). The shipowners seem to have paid too much attention to speed; and they probably lacked the capital to invest in larger ships.

In the eighteenth century we are conscious of *merchants*, the ownership of vessels being a matter of partnerships and shares. By the 1820s this had changed and the *shipowner* - and the shipping firm - were recognised as such. After 1807, and the demise of St Peter Port as an entrepôt, energetic Guernsey merchants were to be found abroad; Guernsey remained the home base of the shipowners.

Fig. 6.3: Types of sailing vessels
(from *The Art of Rigging* by D. Steel, London, 1818)

7
Voyages

THE VOYAGES OF THE *POMONA* (1786-1792)

In this chapter we follow Captain Le Lacheur (a Guernseyman) in a series of voyages that took him from England to Spain with a cargo of wheat; from Spain to Guernsey with brandy and wine; to Canada with spirits; and from Quebec to Spain with wheat. This pattern changed when the Pomona *was switched to a trans-Atlantic run and brought tobacco from the Chesapeake.*

The letters written by Le Lacheur are full of interest. He was directly involved in the trade routes that were of most significance to the Guernsey merchants in the late eighteenth century. We see the Guernsey 'network' in action, at port after port Le Lacheur dealt with Guernsey merchants, or with agents and factors closely tied to the St Peter Port entrepôt.

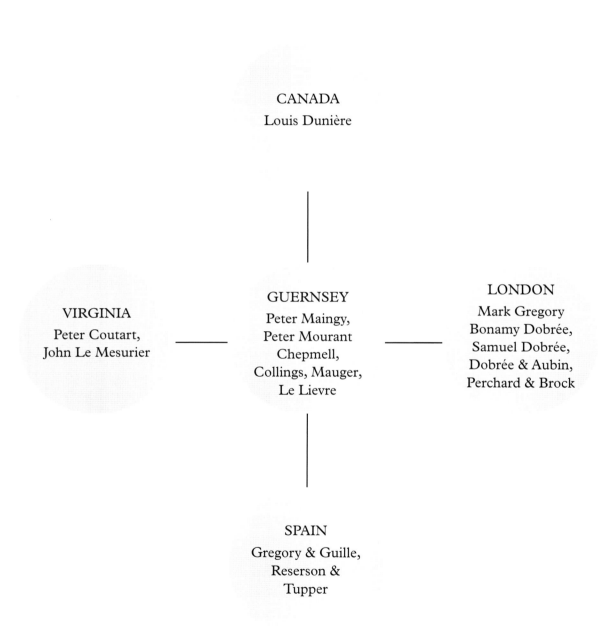

CANADA
Louis Dunière

VIRGINIA
Peter Coutart,
John Le Mesurier

GUERNSEY
Peter Maingy,
Peter Mourant
Chepmell,
Collings, Mauger,
Le Lievre

LONDON
Mark Gregory
Bonamy Dobrée,
Samuel Dobrée,
Dobrée & Aubin,
Perchard & Brock

SPAIN
Gregory & Guille,
Reserson &
Tupper

Fig 7.1: 'The network' - *the merchants and bankers
with whom Captain Le Lacheur corresponded.*

The letterbook of Captain William Le Lacheur, master of the *Pomona*, survived into the twentieth century. There are occasional published references to it but enquiries have not revealed the present location of the manuscript. However, typed transcripts were made in the early twentieth century and there are copies of these in the Priaulx Library and in private hands. The typescripts are not a complete transcript of the original document. There are places where lists have been omitted (for example, several pages of tobacco prices were left out). The Priaulx transcript has a number of manuscript corrections, indicating that it was checked against the original document. Some of the corrections suggest that the original handwriting may, at times, have been difficult to read. For example, the typed *Reno* is correctly revised, in places, to *Reus*. Some mistakes apparently stand uncorrected. For example, a letter written at Quebec, 13 Oct 1787, is addressed to Messrs Mourant & Chessmell. It is just possible that Le Lacheur made the mistake originally. However, it is more likely that the error is that of the transcriber who was unaware of Mourant's partnership with Chepmell. The transcriber seems to have been diligent in trying to achieve accuracy. In the absence of the original manuscript the corrected typescript is an imperfect but, nonetheless, useful substitute. The authenticity of the document has been confirmed by cross-referencing with independent evidence (e.g. the arrivals of the *Pomona* at Barcelona can be checked against British consular records).

The letterbook is of considerable interest. It documents a sequence of voyages made between the years 1786 and 1792 by the *Pomona*. This ship was built in 1784 at Teignmouth. She was of 250 tons, sheathed, with fourteen feet draught of water when loaded. Lloyd's Register (1784) records that she was rated A1 'Lo Tobag' (London Tobago) and her owner was given as P. Maingy, her captain as 'le Lacheur'. The 1786 Register indicates that she was inspected 'Lo Md'ra' (London Madeira) and the 1787 Register records her 'Grnda Lo' (Granada London) A1. This last inspection, published for 1787, will have taken place in 1786, for in a letter to Messrs Peter Maingy & Co (Guernsey) sent from London, 21 Oct 1786, Le Lacheur refers to his 'last passage from Granada' (his cargo was, in part at least, sugar).

The first, second and third voyages involved the transport of wheat to Spain, with a return cargo of brandy/wine to Guernsey/England. Most subsequent voyages saw the *Pomona* carrying tobacco from Norfolk, Virginia, to Europe; the cargo outwards to Norfolk sometimes consisted of brandy and gin.

In 1791 *Pomona* was refitted at Bursledon (Hampshire). Before the refitting she was capable of carrying a full cargo of ten thousand bushels of wheat (second voyage) or 465 pipes of brandy and wine (third voyage). After the refitting she was able to carry 458 hogsheads of tobacco but the eighth voyage may have been a larger cargo: 8778 white oak staves, 212 barrels of tar, 28 barrels of pitch, 20 barrels of turpentine, 395 hogsheads of tobacco, 125 barrels of flour.

Le Lacheur addressed many of his letters to the ship's owners in Guernsey – Peter Maingy & Co. From 24 August 1788 onwards the addressees are Maingy & Dunière, from which we may infer that Peter Maingy had formed a *société*. Who was Dunière? On the 21 Aug 1788 Le Lacheur, off the Kamourasca, addressed a letter to Mr Louis Dunière, Quebec. This Louis Dunière is well documented in the *Dictionary of Canadian Biography online*. Born in 1723 at Quebec, the son of Louis Dunière, he became a merchant, landowner, militia officer and politician. In 1769 he entered into partnership with Henry Boone in the grain trade. He made a business trip to London in the early 1780s and returned to Quebec in 1782 with several merchants.

There are references to a Louis Dunière in Guernsey. Louis Dunière is recorded in the HCA archives as being a Guernsey merchant-shipowner at the time of the American War. And on 20 December 1792 Le Lacheur sent a letter from Norfolk, Virginia, to Mr Louis Dunière in Guernsey. It is possible that the Quebec merchant straddled the Atlantic. However, we may be dealing with two people called Louis Dunière. In his letter of 21 Aug 1788 Le Lacheur states: 'I sail'd from Guernsey the 9th of June last, where I left your cousin & other friends very well'.

One of the more striking aspects of the letterbook is the way in which the master of the *Pomona*, Captain Le Lacheur, operated in a world of Guernsey connections. In London the four banking houses that he used (to clear bills-of-exchange and similar tasks) were all of Guernsey/Channel Island origin: Bonamy Dobrée, Samuel Dobrée, Dobrée & Aubin, Perchard & Brock. Le Lacheur carried many cargoes for Mark and Thomas Gregory of London; they were intimately linked to Guernsey merchants as Mark was a member of the *Société des Veuves* (Guernsey) and a correspondent of John Guille (Guernsey). Further, Mark Gregory was in partnership with Nicholas Guille in Barcelona (see pp. 66-67) and Le Lacheur took delivery of brandy and wine from Gregory & Guille in Barcelona. He also took cargoes in Barcelona from Reserson, a Guernseyman. In Virginia Le Lacheur collected tobacco from Coutart & Le Mesurier. Peter Coutart 'of the town of Petersburg' was of Guernsey origin. He made his will on 13 April 1804, appointing John Cendamine [*sic*, should read Condamine] of the Island of Guernsey as one of his two executors. The will was witnessed by John Chepmell (of Channel Islands) origin. Coutart's partner John (Le)Mesurier was also of Guernsey origin.

Table 7.1 The principal correspondents addressed by Captain William Le Lacheur

---

ENGLAND

London

Mark and Thomas Gregory:	merchants
Bonamy Dobrée	merchant bankers of Guernsey origin
Samuel Dobrée	" "
Dobrée & Aubin	" "
Perchard & Brock	" "

GUERNSEY

Peter Maingy & Co, Maingy & Dunière: owners of *Pomona*

Peter Mourant: leading merchant who owned a share in *Pomona*

Mourant & Chepmell: a short-lived Mourant partnership

Collings and Mauger: merchants

Richard and Thomas LeLievre; merchants

CANADA

Louis Dunière	Quebec merchant with Guernsey link
Mathew Lymburner	Quebec merchant (of Scottish origin)

SPAIN

Gregory & Guille	merchant house
Reserson	merchant
Pratt & Co	merchant
Vergetti	merchant at Reus

VIRGINIA

Peter Coutart, John (Le)Mesurier, Coutart and LeMesurier, R. and Walter Colquhoun, Wm & James Douglas, R. Harrison, Patrick Hart, George Hope (at Harnton), Walter Peter (at Hoods).

FIRST VOYAGE

[Le Lacheur shipped a cargo of 260 tons of wheat for Mark and Thomas Gregory (London) from Wisbech to Barcelona; and a return cargo from Salou of 463 pipes of brandy and one pipe of wine for Peter Maingy and others (Guernsey).]

In October 1786 Captain Le Lacheur's departure from London was delayed:

for one Mr. Roper, merchant here, for which I had 55 hogsheads of sugar last passage from Grenada, refused to pay the freight, 2 of them being very trifling damaged.

Le Lacheur lodged a protest (21 October 1786) and set sail. Progress was slow. By 24 October the Pomona *was lying, wind bound, at the Hope, about two or three miles from Gravesend. The voyage resumed on 25 October and* Pomona *reached Harwich on 30 October. From there Le Lacheur reported to the charter party, Mark and Thomas Gregory (London):*

I have had easterly wind every day since I left London, it now blows a gale of wind from the east. I hope you have been very particular in making the assurance of the ship. I hope it is mentioned that I am to load at Wisbech Old Eye (& not at Lynn) for sometimes, after an accident has happened the underwriters find difficulties from a mere trifle. I once had a Prize insured from Falmouth to Guernsey, & instead of Falmouth she lay'd at Mounts Bay which is near Falmouth, she had the misfortune to be taken off the Lizard, and we lost the insurance.

On 5 November Le Lacheur sent a report from Harwich to his owners, Peter Maingy & Co. (Guernsey):

I have gone out once since I have been here but obliged to come in again, and a great many others, this harbour is most full of light colliers & other ships, I suppose there was no less than 60 sails came in yesterday besides all them was in before, there has been one English ship wrecked on one of the sands near this port, but I don't know what she was – nor where she belonged to, though some of the masts, yards and sails are took up by a Cod Smack.

Pomona *eventually reached Wisbech on 14 November and Le Lacheur wrote to the charterers and to the owners the following day. A cargo of 260 tons of wheat was loaded relatively quickly and Le Lacheur sailed on 2 December from Wisbech Old Eye for Barcelona. Contrary winds detained the ship for several days at Yarmouth Roads. Off the Downs he dismissed a boy called Bowship from service on* Pomona. *Le Lacheur explained in a letter to Mr John Crawford, of the Cock & Bottle, Canon Street, London:*

I find your boy Bowship a very honest young lad, & everything very well, except that he is rather young & weak, and careless as almost all other boys are, (without it is to oblige my owners) I shall never carry any boys hereafter, therefore having an opportunity of sending Bowship to you, or his other friends, I send him with Mr. Lorence my pilot, which live in London, and he promised me to take the boy under his protection till he is among his friends. I have given Bowship a guinea for travelling money. I hope it will be sufficient, he can get an outside berth on the coach.

Pomona *came through the Downs on 17 December. Le Lacheur wrote two short letters advising the shipowners and the charter party of this fact and he gave instructions to the latter to pay the pilot seven pounds and nine shillings. The next letter that Le Lacheur wrote was from Barcelona, on 27 January 1787, to Peter Maingy & Co. (Guernsey):*

I arrived here the day before yesterday and had pratique this morning. I wrote you from the Downs the 17th of Decr. last, and the 27th. I made Cape St Vincent from which I have had foul wind all the way here from the 22nd to the 26th of December and had a very hard gale of easterly wind, which occasioned some part of our cargo to shift (though everything was very well secured) after the gale the ship had 3 or 4 strakes heel to starboard. We got her upright by having two hundred bags of wheat between decks that we trim her with. During the storm we received so many bad seas that broke most of our quarter rails and carried away a great part of our quarter boards, started some planks from our long boat, and I suppose we shall have some of the cargo damaged, for after the gale we got our starboard tacks aboard, & carried sail as much as possible to get her upright, & shift the bags, then the water that laid in her bilge produced at the pumps eighteen inches and we pumped out some wheat for two days after, besides the ship has made more water ever since, than ever she had before. She sprung a constant leak that obliged us to pump her every hour. I hope we shall find it out, when unloaded. I have received no letter from you, but Mr Gregory told me that I am to load at Salou, the cargo is all ready. I hope to be there soon to receive it. I pray for a few lines from you.

By 7 February Le Lacheur was able to report from Barcelona to Maingy & Co that Pomona *was half unloaded. When fully unloaded he would sail in ballast to Salou. Le Lacheur gave Maingy the news that Captain Giffard had arrived at Salou from Alicante. In fact the unloading went slowly. Some nine or ten ships loaded with wheat, all consigned for Gregory & Guille, had arrived before* Pomona:

They could not clearly unload us before, but for all that I hope they will pay me 4 or 5 days demurrage that I have been detained (for more than my 12 lay days). I finish to unload this day. Will take on ballast as fast as possible & sail for Salou.

On 23 February Le Lacheur sailed from Barcelona, having taken on board only twenty-four pipes of brandy. He arrived at Salou on 24 February from where he reported to Maingy that he had left in Gregory & Guille's hands £278-19-0 sterling to be placed to Maingy's account. He sent a duplicate of this letter by a brig bound to Guernsey. Le Lacheur's bad luck with the weather continued. On 11 March he wrote to Maingy:

I am sorry to inform you that I have received nothing this last week, that the weather has been very bad. I have on board only eighty-five pipes of brandy. Mr Moulins tells me that my cargo will be on the beach as soon as I can take it in, when the weather is fit, which I wish may be soon for I think everything have been against me ever since I left London, in regard of making a long voyage; hope for better luck the time to come.

This letter was sent overland, by way of St Malo. By 29 March 1787 Le Lacheur was able to report from Salou to Maingy:

I am entirely loaded, have on board four hundred and sixty three pipes of brandy (counting hogsheads & all) and one pipe of wine. I hope to sail this evening, if wind & wr. permits.

SECOND VOYAGE

[Le Lacheur shipped a cargo of brandy, wine, etc, from Falmouth to Quebec; wheat from Quebec to Malaga; brandy to Guernsey.]

On 29 July Le Lacheur wrote to his shipowners, Maingy & Co in Guernsey, reporting his safe arrival at Falmouth on 28 July. About one hundred and twenty tons of brandy were almost ready for loading. The charter party had not yet arrived in Falmouth from Mr Gregory (in London) but Mr Fox was going to write about this matter and Le Lacheur hoped that he would be ready for sea in about a week.

On 6 August Gregory & Co (London) sent an agreement – but no charter party – to Le Lacheur. He felt unable to sign it and explained to them:

…I am sorry I cannot sign it for it differs from that we made in London. I was to have fifteen pence per bushel if delivered at Marseilles or Italy & in the last agreement you put only 14d. You likewise put in this agreement only thirty five sh. per ton for the oil & lumber or other goods in proportion if for London. In the agreement made in London I understood oils only at forty shillings per ton or other goods in proportion to it, and in the same time I think I ought to be sure of a full cargo of wheat or other goods equal to oil if for London. You mention in the last agreement oil & lumber, or other goods in proportion, but I understood oil or other goods in proportion equal to it, for I don't know how the tonnage of lumber can be ascertained unless it is as I made you understand when I signed the copy of the letter you sent my owners, therefore I beg you'll be so good to send one agreeable to what I sign in your letterbook.

Eventually Le Lacheur reported to Maingy & Co:

I have signed the agreement, but made a reserve signed by Messrs Fox as you'll see on the back of the copy enclosed, it has not been in my power to do anything better. Mr Peter Le Mesurier's here & have furnished me with one hundred & twenty five pound sterling, for which I have given him receipt. I have on board (besides your wines) one hundred & thirty one tons of goods, that is brandy, rum & gin. I have one passenger for Quebec which shall give me twenty guineas & furnish himself in stock of all kinds. I am to sail the very first opportunity.

On 26 September 1787 Le Lacheur wrote a short note from the St Lawrence to Peter Maingy (Guernsey); the letter was sent to Maingy & Co 'by the friendship of Capt. Richard Richards bound to Wales':

I have the pleasure to tell you that we have at last got the length of this, it is 6 ½ weeks that we left Falmouth. We have had hardly any fair wind, it is now calm, hope we shall have a fair wind next. All the ship's company is in good health.

On 29 September Le Lacheur was able to send a second note to Maingy & Co., reporting that he had reached the island of Bic and had a pilot on board:

I am in hope I shall load of wheat, for the pilot tells me that there is more wheat at Quebec than can be exported this year, for they have not shipping enough. We have a light air from the eastward, and in hopes it will continue.

This note was sent by Captain Charles Guille (a Guernseyman) on the brig Wight, *bound for Cadiz. Le Lacheur explained the circumstances in his next letter to Maingy & Co., 5 October:*

I passed this island of Bic six days ago, got a pilot. I did not stop a moment, we had a fine little breeze of easterly which took us; then came to anchor on the first instant in the morning, our cable parted, the pilot would not let go another anchor for fear of losing it too, but kept under sail, the wd. blowing from the W.S.W. very hard has obliged us to bear away from the Isle Bic, where we lay at present, I did not know when I wrote mine of the 29th inst. that it was to go by Capt. Charles Guille but the brig that was then in sight happened to be him bound to Cadiz, it began to freeze very hard, when our people wash the decks the water freezes on it almost as soon as it is down. I pray to God the wind may change very soon & that we may not be freezed in the River before we can be ready to sail from it.

Le Lacheur also sent a brief note on the same day to Bonamy Dobrée (London) summarising his situation – windbound and lacking one anchor. Le Lacheur reached Quebec on 8 October and reported his arrival to Peter Maingy (Guernsey) and Bonamy Dobrée (London):

I am just arrived and the ship by which I send this is under sail, but I have seen the gentleman that is to load me, & he told me that he will load me here with wheat for Malaga. He have not enough to load me entirely by him, but he'll try to raise it, therefore I can depend on going to the Straights, he told me that wine is quite a drug, it sells only for about 4 pds per hogshead, if it is so, I suppose I shall be obliged to leave it unsold, but I shall be able to let you know better in a few days. I am hurried.

By 17 October Le Lacheur was able to report to Maingy (Guernsey) and Bonamy Dobrée (London) that he was almost unloaded:

I am almost unloaded, in hopes to begin to lay the dunnage in 2 or 3 days. I have lodged your wines with Mr Louis Dunière, for there is no such a thing to sell it even to the invoice price, the reason it is so cheap (I learn) is that there has been a cargo imported of which the remise must be made by the 25th of the month, & they sell it at any price they can get; after that time it will rise again; last year it sold for thirty & 32 dollars per hogshead now it sells only for 18 or 20 at the most, I believe we shall be here late, for all the wheat is not yet come from the country, but I hope we shall be in time enough to get away before the ice sets in.

Le Lacheur also reported back to the Guernsey merchants Mourant & Chepmell:

According to your desire I have called on Mr John Antrobus, which told me he had received your letter of the 27th April last, yet there is nothing done, but he is in hopes that he'll furnish me the necessary papers for you to receive your money in London before I am ready to sail. I have likewise been to Mr Woolsey with your letter for him, he told me he was sorry that it was not in his power to make you the remise according to your demand but he had on 8th positively made it to Messrs Gregory & Co in London, in order that they should remit it to you; he says he has no orders from you to remit the same to you direct, nor had no letters from Messrs Gregory & Co to remit it to them, he acted only as he thought was right, but he told me that he is trying to settle with Mr Gregory's agent here, and as soon as he has settled, he will send you the necessary papers for you to receive it from the London house - & he is in hopes it will be before I sail.

On 22 October Le Lacheur wrote from Quebec to Bonamy Dobrée (London), explaining that he would not be able to sail until about the 10 November for Malaga. He continued:

Enclosed is a bill of two hundred pounds sterling on Messrs Turnbull Macauley & Mr Gregory which I have received of Messrs Davidson & Lees of this place, for part of my freight from Falmouth to Quebec; please to credit Messrs Peter Mourant & Co & Peter Maingy & Co owners of the ship *Pomona* for the above two hundred pounds when received.

By 23 October the ship was half-loaded with wheat. Le Lacheur reported this to Maingy & Co. (Guernsey) and recorded his remittance to London:

I remitted yesterday to Messrs Bonamy Dobrée & Co of London two hundred pounds sterling in one bill which is part of the freight from Falmouth here. I have sent the first and second by different ships and kept the third to myself. Send a duplicate of the above by another ship. P.S. I am obliged to leave your wines in Mr Dunière's hand for I cannot sell them so high as the invoice price.

Le Lacheur was ever mindful of the business interests of Maingy & Co. On 28 October he wrote:

I have learned since I wrote you that if I could sail this day, I would save the two per cent upon the insurance. I have done my endeavour to get ready. I am now short of 130 bushels of wheat of my complement. I have on board 9870 bushels. I think it is not worth while to stay for them and lose the advantage of the insurance, in the same time I think the ship deep enough, therefore I will sail this day for Malaga. I have put your wines in Mr Louis Dunière's possession & given him orders to sell it to the most advantage & remit the proceeds to Messrs Bonamy Dobrée & Co. I have remitted a bill of two hundred pounds sterling to the said gentlemen being part of my freight from Falmouth here. Please to tell Messrs Mourant & Chepmell that it has not been in my power to do anything towards their business.

Le Lacheur sailed from Quebec on 28 October and arrived in Malaga seven weeks later, 15 December. The following day he wrote to Maingy & Co:

I am arrived here of last evening. I am going to sail again this evening for Barcelona. We left Quebec this day seven weeks. We have had a very rough passage, pumped out wheat all the passage, carry'd away part of our quarters near boards, no material damage otherways.

Le Lacheur arrived in Barcelona, 20 December, and after pratique in the morning of 21 December he went directly to Gregory & Guille:

…where I have received yours of the 15th ultimo, with the enclosed letters. I have asked Mr Guille whether he could procure me any freight for Guernsey, he told me he could not. I have likewise asked Messrs Reserson & Tupper, they told me they had none, & they expect the *Emilia* every day – you mention'd in the beginning of your letter to me to wait on the different shippers, whose address you was to put at foot, but you did not, or else I should have seen them all today. I shall enquire soon who is the principal shippers for Guernsey, & write you again to let you know whether I have found any freight or not, it is not very likely I shall find any, but if I was to find part of a cargo, then I would not know what to do because I have enquired of Mr Guille what price brandy might be at present. He told me at the least 47 dollars & that it was 50 not long ago. I fear you would not wish to give any more than 45 (at the most). I don't think at that rate I can do anything till I hear from you again or find a good freight for some other part which I shall not hurry about.

On 17 February Le Lacheur updated Maingy & Co (Guernsey) about his progress. He had sailed from Barcelona on 9 February 1788 and arrived in Tarrogona the next day. There he took on one hundred pipes of brandy 'by desire of Mr Guille'. He then sailed to Salou, arriving 15 February. The following day he took in 24 pipes of brandy. Le Lacheur had some difficult decisions to make. He had given all of Maingy's orders to Gregory & Guille, who had orders for only 50 pipes besides that of Maingy & Co.

… but Mr Guille promised me he'll put the remainder on his own accts. on these conditions, that is, if he receive orders while I am loading he will place them to it, but if not & he lose by these brandys which will be about 70 pipes I shall be obliged to lose the freight, therefore sooner than go short of being full I think it my duty to run that risk, seeing that I cannot do anything better – before I left Barcelona Mr Guille told me they had bought 200 pipes for you & that he thought they would not come to 46 piastres per pipe, but near it. I now understand that the whole is bought on an average of 45½ in board.

On the same day Le Lacheur wrote a short letter to Bonamy Dobrée, informing them of the purchase of the 124 pipes of brandy to date. He also wrote to Gregory & Guille, expressing his pleasure that the price of the brandy was fixed as it was, asking to be informed whether they had received orders for the remainder of the cargo, and complaining:

I did not find things at Tarragona as I expected for I lay'd there three times as much as I expected the whole of the brandys not being ready to ship but I am in hopes now we shall go on very fast if the wr. permits, depend on my getting home as fast as possible.

On 20 February Le Lacheur, in Reus, forwarded to Reserson & Tupper (Barcelona) a letter from Mr Peter Mourant (Guernsey). Le Lacheur expressed his willingness to accept freight consigned by Reserson & Tupper:

Enclosed is a leter from Mr Peter Mourant, I have no doubt the hundred pipes are ship'd off, but whether or not if you have anything to send to Guernsey, I shall thank you for it, as I understand the *Emily* has as much freight as she can take, if you have any orders I could take as far as seventy pipes at least, please to let me know whether you have or not by the return of the post.

Le Lacheur informed Gregory & Guille (Barcelona) of his correspondence with Reserson & Tupper:

The enclosed was a letter from Mr Peter Mourant desiring Messrs Reserson & Tupper, if I wanted freight to fill up the *Pomona*, and the Swede by which they was to send him one hundred pipes that he had ordered some time ago was not to take them, he desired they would not give them to anybody but me; but as far as I understood they are shipped off. I wrote them by this post desiring them if they have that or anything else to send by me to speak with you about it, in order that you may not meet with any disappointment.

Earlier, Le Lacheur had, apparently, taken a passenger (from Barcelona to Tarragona, perhaps). His hamper was damaged. Le Lacheur wrote to Reserson (Barcelona) expressing his willingness to compensate for the damage:

Please to desire the passenger to send the acct. of what the hamper of things in it cost him. I shall gladly pay any person you'll appoint here for the amount of it. My boy has been so careless that some of the bottles are broke in it, for what I am sorry, but let him send the acct. & I'll pay it.

Bad weather hindered the loading at Salou, as Le Lacheur informed Maingy & Co in a letter written 28 February:

We have had amazing strong gales from the South & S.W. particularly last Sunday the 24th when the *Emily*, Capt Deputron, parted her cable, and had parted one before. Very lucky her sheet cable & anchor brought her up, we have received no damage – the 19th I had the pleasure of Mr Peter Mourant's letter of the 22nd ultimo, the hundred pipes he mentioned was shipped off long ago as Messrs Reserson & Tupper writes me, & that they had the hundred & 40 pipes to ship on board the *Emily*, if she cannot take them all, I might have the remainder.

The weather remained bad. On 1 March Le Lacheur wrote to Bonamy Dobrée & Co (London), recapitulating what he had previously done and then getting them up to date:

I had the pleasure to remit you from Quebec a bill of £200 st. which I hope you have received. I send the first & second by different ships, kept the third on board. I likewise have remitted you from Barcelona, the 9th January last a bill of £250 stg & the 12 Dec. another bill of £200 stg. I sent you the two second bills from Barcelona the 19th January last I hope you have had them all in hand. You'll be pleased to give credit to Messrs Peter Mourant & Co for one half of the whole & Messrs Peter Maingy & Co for the other half being for freight of the ship *Pomona*. I have now on board one hundred & 78 pipes of brandy of which I took one hundred at Tarragona. I am to take the remainder of my cargo here to Guernsey as soon as the weather permits. I have took nothing on this 12 or 13 days past, being continually bad weather, it now continues, but I hope for an alteration.

The next day he penned a letter to Gregory & Guille (Barcelona):

I am much obliged to you for giving your consent to my taking Messrs Reserson & Tupper's parcels but as it happens it was too late what I hope will make no difference to my owners, but being employed by other people I would wish always to take the surest (if possible) though far from giving room for your meeting with any disappointment, we have not took in anything these 13 days & now the W. is as bad as ever for what I am sorry.

By 8 March the ship was loaded. Le Lacheur sent a short letter to Bonamy Dobrée (London) and a longer version to Maingy & Co (Guernsey):

I have the pleasure to inform you that I have received this morning the remainder of my cargo, we have had good weather five days of this last week. I have on board in all the value of four hundred & sixty pipes, the freight is only 32 shillings per ton and ten per cent. I have wrote you several times before about having agreed to take some to fill up of Messrs Gregory's & Guille which I am to lose the freight of if any lost on the brandys, or if they received no order to which they might place it – being rather short of cash, I gave a receipt to Mr Moulins. I will sail Monday the 10th inst. if wd. & wr. permits in hopes to have the pleasure of seeing you soon.

THIRD VOYAGE

[Le Lacheur delivers 6200 bushels of salt to Canada; loads a cargo of wheat for Spain; and returns to Guernsey with 454 pipes of brandy and 11 pipes of wine.]

Le Lacheur arrived at Quebec on 24 August 1788. On 25 August he wrote a long account to Maingy & Dunière (Guernsey):

I had seven weeks & two days passage from Guernsey to Gaspe, at my arrival there I met with Mr Thomas Le Mesurier. Mr Ohara was not at home, I understood that salt was scarce but they had wrote to Quebec for some. Mr Le Mesurier was in want of it for present use till he had his supply from Quebec he stood a long time for 18d a bushel till I threaten'd to go away again, if he did not choose to give me 2/- per bushel for at least 2000 bushels and he at last consented. While unloading that quantity Mr Ohara arrived which was not in want of any being not concerned in any fishery, and he could not recommend me any person that he could trust upon & told me that commodity was quite a drug at Quebec. I understood by several other persons the same and Mr Le Mesurier offering me 15d for the remainder at last when he saw that I was going to take my papers from the Custom House he offered me 17d; he left me take out my papers & when he saw I was going he would give me 18d sterling per bushel for the remainder the above two thousand at 2/- per bushel are likewise sterling. We measured the whole by the bushel put on board when we come to finish to deliver we was six hundred & 55 bushels short of the quantity you mentioned in your orders what gave me great uneasiness. I went and got a proper Winchester bushel from Mr Ohara and tried it with our own and found that it was four gallons upon every six bushels that our bushel was larger than Mr Ohara's. I then went to Mr Le Mesurier to rectify the measure. We had some little difficulty but as he had the matter explained Winchester bushel and all sterling, he could not be off paying me accordingly – A lucky thing it was that I did not sell it by the hogshead for you thought six Winchester bushels made one hogshead, but it is six minots, which makes a considerable difference. Even the little difference between your bushel & the other, made four hundred & seventy eight bushels difference upon the whole, which Mr Le Mesurier paid me more than we had measured out by your bushel, & then after all we have been one hundred & twenty seven short of what we had received in Guernsey. We have delivered in the whole 6200 bushels for which Mr Le Mesurier has given me the draft on Messrs Paul Le Mesurier & Co. Yesterday at my arrival here there was a ship getting under sail called the *Ann*, Capt. Ratcliffe, bound to Bristol by which I enclosed the first bill to Messrs Bonamy Dobrée & Co. the amount of it is five hundred and nine pounds thirteen shillings & fourpence sterling, there is another ship going to sail tomorrow called the *Four Brothers*, Capt. Mills by which I shall send the second bill to Messrs Bonamy Dobrée & Co. I have seen Messrs Lymburner & Co they would wish me to go to Montroyal with the ship. I told them it was impossible that she draw'd too much water & the most particular reason was that she was not insured to go any further than Quebec, therefore I could not think about it, they show'd me the letter I brought them by which Mr Hunter tells them that I must go to Montroyal if they think proper. I told them that there never was such a thing, for it stood to reason if the agreement had been such the ship would certainly have been insured accordingly, they told me they could not help it, that if I did not chuse to go, that I must at least pay part of the expenses of bringing it down, I told them it was more than I can consent to – sooner than to have any further dispute I shall be obliged to pay back about twenty pounds towards it, & in the same time to be paid back to you if your agreement don't mention that I was to go to Montroyal; if I deny paying them twenty pounds I am afeared (in short they have told me) that they was under no obligation to load me having been after the time which is only one or two days. I told them I hoped they would not mind a trifle of that kind, that it was wind and wr. that occasioned my detention, I was ten days at Gaspey to unload the salt & ballast the ship and a fortnight to come up the St Lawrence but they seem to be inclined to load me, for they have given bond at the Custom House this morning, I believe I shall be here longer that I could wish, the corn being not all come down – I have found, as I understood at Gaspey, that salt was quite a drug here – it sells for a shilling currency, if I had brought it here I must have stored it, or give it for 10d by a large quantity. Some people tells me that they would not take salt now for the storage. Capn. Breadthaft & Captn. Giffard are sail'd. I have seen nothing of them. Capt Guille is still in Montreal. Capt. Allez in Messrs Le Lievre's brig that sailed a week before me from Guernsey arrived at Gaspey two days after me. Captn Giffard has our anchor aboard to my sorrow if you please to write to him at Barcelona to leave it there, I shall be obliged to you; though it is uncertain whether I shall go or not, Salou would be the best place to leave it.

Quebec, the 2nd of September, 1788, to Messrs Maingy & Dunière:

I have wrote you twice since my coming here, which is of the 24th of last month. I have likewise wrote to Messrs Bonamy Dobrée & Co of London to which I have enclosed the first and second bills which I had at Gaspey of Mr Thomas Le Mesurier for all your salt which amounted to five hundred and nine pds. thirteen shillings & four pence sterling. I am not yet sure when I shall go from here, but however Messrs. Lymburner & Co. are going to load me with wheat. I shall let you know for what part as soon as it is in my power. Messrs. Lymburner & Co. have refused to load five brigs which had arrived here after the limited time, & I did not know at first whether they would not serve me the same, but I believe I did a very good thing, for when I saw there was no likelyness of getting up in time, I send up an express by land soon as I could which arrived at their house on the 22nd in the evening or on the 23rd, in the morning. I had likewise wrote them from Gaspey, but they had not received it, what I mistrusted by sending the express. I think we have been pretty lucky both in selling the salt at Gaspey and saving the wheat freight though I believe

I had two strings to my bow, if I had lost that one, Mr. Dunière told me he would not have let me go in ballast and would have procured me one of his own; Messrs. Lymburner & Co. wanted me to go to Montroyal, but I have refused it, knowing that the ship is not insured for it.

I suppose they will make me pay about 20 Pounds for part of the expenses of bringing down some of the corn, but in condition, that it will be paid back to you, if your agreement is not for Montroyal. I would never advise anybody to send any ship of our draft there (even in ballast) for it is very dangerous coming down, the current being amazingly strong, and no rise or fall of the water. Capt. Guille come down the other day, which got aground & was obliged to unload some of the wheat before he got off again, he has received but little damage though he will be obliged to shift two ends of plank, he says he would be near Barcelona now if he had not gone to Montroyal, Captn. Breadthaft & Giffard was both sailed before I arrived here. Unluckily Capt. Giffard took our anchor not knowing I would come or not. We are to write to him to let him know that I would be glad he would leave it at Salou, if I get an opportunity I will write to him myself.

P.S. All the ship's crew is very well.

Le Lacheur reported on 1st October 1788 to Maingy & Dunière that he was fully loaded:

I have the pleasure to inform you that I am fully loaded with wheat, bound to Barcelona direct. I will sail in two days the 3rd inst if wind & weather permits. Messrs Mathew Lymburner & Co have made me pay twenty pounds currency for part of the wheat freight from MontRoyal, I having refused to go to Montroyal with the ship, but the said sum is to be remitted if the agreement or charter party is for Quebec only. Mr Louis Dunière having as I understand still some money in hand of goods of yours, I have desired him to pay my charges & expenses here – for Messrs Mathew Lymburner & Co would not advance it on the freight without charging commission. Counting the above twenty pounds the ships part of dunnage, pilotage, wharfage, butcher's bill, baker's bill, brewery's custom, house charges &c &c comes to one hundred & thirty four pounds six shillings & ninepence currency.

On 13th December 1788 Le Lacheur wrote to Maingy & Dunière (Guernsey), reporting his arrival at Barcelona:

Sirs, I have the pleasure to inform you of my safe arrival here the 5th inst. I was obliged to lay 4 days quarantine Thos. Priaulx one of the sailors having died on the passage. At my arrival I was favoured with yours of the 7th & 13th Oct last, as soon as I had pratique, I immediately went to Mr Guille, which told me he had no more in all to give me but 400 pipes; & a little after I saw Mr Tupper and asked him for some, he told me if I would take 250 pipes I might have them, but otherwise he could not give me one, & since that he has freighted an English brig. I have seen Mr Pratt which sometimes ship some for Guernsey, he has no orders nor can I find anybody that can give me any – but as I wants but a small quantity (which is about 60 pipes) I hope some of them'll receive orders before I have took in the others, & brandies have fallen lately, what put me in hopes that they wont let me go short of freight. I shall be unloaded this evening and as soon as I am will dispatch to Salou. I am sorry I was so long at Quebec but it could not very well be helped they not being warn'd of my coming & the wr. being often wet could not load the wheat & I have had a long passage of 62 days what has occasioned my being so late. If the *Pomona* is to go to Quebec again next year, I would be very particular in the agreement (or charter party) for I believe there will be few wheat freights; the old wheat having been drained out this year & the crops not extraordinary & the ship should never be obliged to go to Montroyal. I am rather uneasy about the 60 pipes that are wanted for my homewards cargo.

P.S. Enclosed is a letter for the widow of Thos. Priaulx I shall be obliged to you if you'll put the direction to it. I suppose she'll go or send to you to settle what may be due to him. I have advanced her at Quebec ten shillings 8 pence sterling, he died the 27th October.

Mr John Sachy is very well, he has received a letter from his father by which he seem to reprimand him for not writing from Quebec, but to my knowledge he wrote by Capt. Mourant of Jersey.

A short letter to Maingy & Dunière, written 20 December 1788, explained details of the cargo to be loaded:

I wrote you the 13th inst by which I informed you of my arrival here the 5th inst (after a passage of 62 days from Quebec) likewise of having received your favors of the 7th & 13th October last & that Mr Guille told me at my arrival that he had four hundred pipes in all to give me, & I then could not get any more, but yesterday Mr Guille told me that he had received an order by which he is limited to certain price, & if it is no higher (next Monday) he will buy 50 pipes which he'll give me, so after I am sure of that I'll think myself well off – since I wrote my last we have had very indifferent weather, being mostly rainy, & a bad sea tumbling in, we are not much better than half out. I wish for good Wr. & remain.

P.S. Capt. Charles Guille is here still & cannot get a cargo for Guernsey. I believe he is going for harbour de Grace in France. The King of Spain is dead.

On 30 December 1788 Le Lacheur remitted a short letter to Maingy & Dunière:

I have the pleasure to inform you that we are quite unloaded & half ballasted. As soon as I can get the remainder of my ballast I shall sail for Salou, but we have a great difficulty in getting it, the sea being amazingly bad.

I remit by this post to Messrs Bonamy Dobrée & Co of London a bill of four hundred pounds sterling which I have of Messrs Gregorys & Guille for part of my freight from Quebec here. Mr Guille told me that they would have my cargo quite compleat for Guernsey, what I am happy to hear.

I send one by St Malo & one by London. Both copy of above.

In fact Le Lacheur was detained at Barcelona by bad weather. He wrote from Salou on 20 Jan 1789 to Messrs Peter Maingy & Co. (Guernsey):

I left Barcelona the 18th inst. The evening before Mr Guille told me that Mr Pratt had received an order to ship fifty pipes on board of me, but as Mr Guille had told me before he would compleat my cargo, I did not go to Mr Pratt, the same time he must have had your letter of the 16th December in hand, which I did not receive till I got to Salou, it is a wonder to me he did not give it to me the same day he received it, when I arrived at Reus (which was the 19th) I received a letter from him in which yours was enclosed & broke open, they make an apology to me for having done it through mistake, but I think curiosity opened it, when they found that I could not take their order. I shall put the copy of their letter the other side – I have been detained at Barcelona for 12 days by bad weather and a bad sea on the Bave and now I am at Salou the sea is so bad that we cannot load, but it is to be hoped that the weather will alter soon, for we have had uncommon bad weather lately Captain Sims by which I send a copy of this has been ten days to take on eleven pipes, Capt. Chas Guille is loading here for Havre de Grace. I have remitted from Barcelona to Messrs. Bonamy Dobrée & Co of London four hundred & thirty five pounds sterling the remainder of my freight from Quebec to Barcelona goes for port Charges & expenses.

By 30 Jan 1789 Le Lacheur was able to report to Peter Maingy & Co. that he was ready to sail:

I have the pleasure to inform you that I am quite loaded & will sail the first opportunity. I have on board the value of four hundred fifty four pipes of brandy, shipt by Messrs Gregory's & Guille, ten pipes of wine by Messrs Reserson & Tupper & one pipe of wine other ways, which is in all four hundred & sixty five pipes. I have been very lucky in regard of the weather since I wrote you of my arrival at Salou, it is tomorrow fortnight I left Barcelona. I wish I may have as good weather on my passage home as I have had loading.

On the same day he wrote to Gregory & Guille (Barcelona):

I have had the honour of yours of the 24th inst. by which I find you had consented I should take the ten pipes of wine Messrs. Reserson & Tupper has offered. (I have them on board) and I have took on likewise from Mr. Moulins four hundred & twenty seven pipes & fifty four hogsheads of Brandy, & I am now at Reus to clear out; I hope to go to sea tomorrow if wind & weather permits.

FOURTH VOYAGE

[Le Lacheur ships a cargo of tobacco from Virginia, together with staves.]

After a gap of six months Le Lacheur wrote a letter on 10 June 1789 from Norfolk, Virginia, to Maingy & Dunière:

I have the pleasure to inform you of my safe arrival here the 31st of last month after a passage of six weeks & six days. I have been to Petersbourg & Richmond, & have delivered the sundry letters I had for the shippers, they seem to have no objection to my loading at Norfolk, but they seem to be inclined to load Capt. Le Ruez & another brig which is bound for Guernsey before they begin upon me, the said brig I understd. will load partly for you, Capt Le Ruez arrived here a week before me. Capt. Rolings is not arrived – I am all ready to take in when they please but I am afear'd I shall lay here most part of my lay days.

P.S. All the ship's crew is very well. Enclosed is a letter for my wife by the *Molly* Capt. Watson bound to Jersey.

Le Lacheur experienced some frustrations, as he explained to Maingy & Dunière, writing from Norfolk, 19 June 1789:

I had the pleasure to write you by a brig bound to Jersey the 10th inst. by which I informed you of my safe arrival here the 31st of last month after six weeks & six days passage. Capt. Le Ruez by which I send this is quite well loaded, & will sail tomorrow, there is another brig that will sail for Guernsey in a day or two. I have only 75 hogsheads of tobacco on board I suppose I shall not be ready to sail much before the middle of next month. It is a great pity that we had so many lay days, for I might be near loaded now (but patience) you may depend I shall be after Le Ruez as fast as I can, I have not heard anything of Captn Rolenge, I suppose he shall soon be here, the hogshd staves are from 80/- to 100/- per thousand, and the barrel staves from 40/- to 50/-. All the crew is very well.

By the *General Eliott* Capt. Philip Le Ruez.

The next letter to Maingy & Dunière was despatched by Le Lacheur from Norfolk on 3 July 1789:

I am sorry to be detained here when I might be despatched, there is only Mr Peter Lihou's friend has not sent down his tobacco. I cannot take the 15 for Mr Peter Mourant, & I am afeared I shall be obliged to leave a few more, the hogsheads being so very large (I believe) is the occasion of it. I hope Mr Hart wont detain me longer than from the 10th to the 15th for my lay will be out. I am in hopes to sail about that time. Capt Ruez sailed 12 days ago in company with the brig *Diana* Capt Cave which I am told is partly on your acct. I pray for a short passage home.

P.S. Capt. Rolenge is not come. All the ships crew is very well.

By the 9th July 1789 Le Lacheur had better news for Maingy & Dunière:

I have the pleasure to inform you that I am quite loaded. I have on board three hundred & sixty three hogheads of tobacco & 3929 hogsheads staves & 3591 barrel ditto. I have not been able to take Mr Peter Mourant's fifteen hogsheads & I have been obliged to leave two of Mr Peter Lihou's. I have drawn a bill of fifty pounds one shilling & one penny sterling, which I have desired Messrs Bonamy Dobrée & Co to place to acct. of Messrs Peter Mourant & Co, the difference between that bill & the cash you gave me being so trifling that I thought it not worth while to do otherwise. You can settle that between Mr Mourant & you I shall sail this evening if wind & weather permits.

FIFTH VOYAGE

[Le Lacheur ships a cargo of tobacco and staves from Virginia.]

Le Lacheur, Norfolk (Va), to Maingy & Dunière, 6 Dec 1789:

I am safe arrived here of the 16th ultimo after a passage of nine weeks & two days. I am told Richmond tobacco keeps up to 24/- and Petersbourg 22/- or 23/- per hundred. I have not one hogshead on board and I suppose will not have any, till my lay days are near out, for the shippers don't like to make a beginning (I suppose) having all orders not to put in the bottom, staves are dear & scarce they are at five pounds for hogsheads, & 50/- for barrels, the great number of ships here occasions the scarcity of them. I have not yet order'd Mr P Mourant's parcels to fill me up, for I am in great hopes to have a parcel that the fancy have been waiting for and at last going without it. I therefore must have patience till she is sailed, when I immediately will apply to Mr Reed (who mean to ship them) and ask him whether he can assure me that I shall have them. If he says that he cannot assure me of them I shall in that case be under the necessity to give orders to Mr Coutart to buy 30 or 35 to fill me up. The planters seem to complain of the frost having kill'd about one quarter part of their crop, but it is very common that planters & farmers complain, it will not be well known how it is till a few months are passed. If you don't mean to have the *Pomona* lengthened soon, I think it would be very necessary to have her sheeded as soon as there is an opportunity.

From Norfolk (Va), 13 December 1789, to Mr Peter Coutart (Petersburg):

I have been waiting all this time in hopes of having Mr Reed's tobacco, if Capt.Pirvaux did not wait for it, he got out of patience & is gone without it. Mr Reed now promises it to me therefore there will be no occasion to buy for Mr Mourant (unless they would deceive me) I have not received one hogshead yet, I suppose the shippers are all asleep, but I shall be away as soon as my lay days are out what is to be in 12 or 13 days. I don't think any honour to the shippers to detain me in this manner when tobacco is plenty, was there any substantial reason I would think nothing of it but there is none that I can think of. Our friends at home are not well used. You'll do me a favour if you'll be so kind to tell them (if you see them) that it will be disagreeable to me to protest for it is not any advantage to anybody, their friends at home would thank them more for having no demurrage to pay & in the same time for having these goods dispatched to market.

From Norfolk (Va), 20 December 1789 to Mr Peter Coutart (Petersburg):

I had the pleasure to write you the 13th inst telling that Mr Reed had promised me the tobacco he had to send to Guernsey, he tells me now that his sloop (after being away for a month) is returned without one single hogshead, therefore I am at last under the necessity of desiring you to purchase thirty hogsheads of tobacco for Mr Peter Mourant's account which I'll thank you kindly for being dispatched as quick as possible. For I would be very uneasy if them there was to detain me, what I hope wont be the case. I understand that tobacco has fallen to about 20/- therefore it is lucky for Mr Mourant. I have on board and alongside about one hundred & eighty hogsheads, & I am now in hopes will have the remainder very soon.

From Norfolk (Va), 29 December 1789, to Mr Peter Coutart (Petersburg):

Yesterday morning I had the honour of your favour of the 23rd inst. I have not yet received any of Messrs Harrison, nor Peter's tobacco. I am sorry to hear that the Inspectors leave the town for so long, but as (I have no doubt) you'll look out for a craft beforehand & in the same time buy the tobacco beforehand, that it may be turned out as soon as they come in town, I am in good hopes it will not detain me long, as I am sure you'll spare nothing toward my being despatched – I have received the parcel you mentioned, directed to Messrs Perchard & Brock, London, you may be sure I shall take particular care of it according to your directions. I wish you a happy New Year & many of others

P.S. My compliments to Mr Le Mesurier.

In case you could not find a craft to your liking please to send only twenty hogsheads sooner than have sent by two crafts, for one that would be only partly loaded from you might detain me by stopping for more from other people & I shall be very deep therefore I shant mind having ten less than thirty, & above all things sooner than to be detained.

From Norfolk, 30 December 1789, to Walter Peters:

Last evening I had the pleasure of your esteemed favour of the 28th instant & the letter directed to Mr Samuel Dobrée. I shall according your desire enclose one bill of lading of each set in it, & the other two of each set I shall enclose in this & send it by the Captn of your sloop who has delivered me forty five hogsheads of tobacco this day, but I was at first rather uneasy for most of them look'd very wet, but after hearing his reason (which I thought very good) I have took them in without any further difficulty – I would have been very happy to see you down here in good health, & am very sorry to understand that you have been ill, & glad you are getting better. I wish with all my heart you may get quite well in a little time & that you may be drove from your Chimney Corner before half the winter is over. I have remembered you to Mr Brunet & remain

To Maingy Dunière, from Norfolk (Va), 10 January 1790:

I have the pleasure to inform you that I am at last quite loaded. I have on board three hundred & forty five hogsheads of tobacco, and six thousand six hundred & seventy two hogsheads staves, and one hundred & eighty barrel staves. I shall sail the first opportunity, the wind is at present contrary. I hope it wont last long.

By the *Thomson* Capt. Bell for Whitehaven.

SIXTH VOYAGE

[Le Lacheur ships a cargo of wine and brandy for Guernsey/England; and a cargo of bricks from England to Guernsey.]

Le Lacheur (Barcelona), 6 April 1790, to Maingy & Dunière:

I have the pleasure to inform you of my safe arrival here the 4th inst after a passage of 18 days but I am sorry to say that things are not to my expectations in regard to freights. I immediately at my arrival delivered Messrs Reserson & Co's letter, they had nothing worth while and advised me to enquire of the other merchants. I then delivered the sundry letters (or to speak of) except Gregory's & Guille, that had a brig lost the same day I arrived & on the Bave, called the Grampass from America loaded with wheat for which they had 600hhds of wine bought, which they offered me to carry to Cowes in the Isle of Wight at 35/- per ton, & ten per ct. primage, & the same from Cowes to Quebec, but as it was not a full cargo for me, I told them I could not unless they could compleat my cargo & assure me of a good freight from Quebec to these parts, they would not do that, but they then offered me to fill me up for Guernsey & then go & deliver the said wines to Cowes. I told them I would do that provided that it would be to your or my option, either to take or leave in regard of carrying said wines to Quebec but they would not consent but said they made no doubt but I would have the preference, I have asked Messrs. Reserson & Co's advice about it, they told me (though I had a letter from Cette which gave me some encouragement towards a Baltic freight) they would advise me to make sure of what I could get, for freights was falling very fast within this fortnight past, therefore everything considered I have thought it best to engage this day to take in six hundred hogsheads of wine for Cowes, & the remainder of wine or brandy for Guernsey at 35/- per ton & 10 pr cent primage, if you would wish that I would continue the voyage to Quebec & try to get a freight for those parts you'll be so good as to write to Mr. Gregory of London (with which I suppose it will be difficult enough to make an agreement to your advantage) at any rate I am not engaged & will not engage to go further than Cowes unless I should be assured of a full cargo, and a freight of wheat. I shall be obliged to go and load to 4 different places Matero, Vilenova, Salo & Benicarlo; that is the only freight offers here; for if any other ship was to offer to take a freight for the channel at 30/- he could not find one, all the ships are gone or going higher up to try their luck, they had a long easterly winds lately what has kept out the ships, but by all acts. there is an amazing sight gone up since the wind has vary'd. What has induced me to take this certainty & leave an uncertainty I have been advised by every thing (that I think are friends of both you & me to take it or do it) I hope it will be for the best, wish you may be pleased with it.

P.S. I left Captn. Isemonger in sight of Alicant on the 30th march, we have been in sight of one another all the passage except 2 or 3 days, we sail much alike, if any difference it is in our favour. All our crew is very well.

Send one copy of this by St. Malo, & the other by London.

From Barcelona, 20 April 1790 to Maingy & Dunière:

At my arrival at Barcelona there was only one freight that offer'd which I have accepted of. Messrs Gregory & Guille have charter'd me; I am to take in six hundred hogsheads of wine for Cowes, & the remainder of my cargo of brandy for Guernsey; at thirty five shillings per ton & ten percent primage. I have took in at Mataro 300 hogsheads of wine. I am to take in here 150 hogsheads of wine & then proceed to Salo where I am to take in 160 pipes of brandy, & lastly I am to go to Benicarlo to take in one hundred & fifty hogsheads of wine. I hope I shall be dispatched, for those gentlemen that charter'd me, would wish the wines to go to Quebec this year – if you would wish that I should carry it there you'll be so good to make the agreement with Messrs Mark & Thos Gregory's & if you or they would furnish something to fill up going & a good freight of wheat back, I think the ship might make a good voyage; if nothing can be done to your wishes towards it, the ship at any rate is at liberty when we're discharged at Cowes, therefore, if the Quebec voyage don't take place I make no doubt you'll find another by the time she'll want it, before I charter'd I had a letter from Cette, another just after, and one I received from Toulon while loading at Mataro, they all gave me some encouragement in regard of a Baltic freight, but if I had refused this first offer, I might have remain'd without any and as I found freight was on a great decay, I thought it my duty to accept of it, I wish you may be well satisfied with it.

P.S. I believe I mention in my former letters 300 hhds of wine instead of 600 – all the crew is very well.

Send one copy of the above by St Malo & one by London.

From Villanova, 20 April 1790, to Messrs Reserson & Co (Barcelona):

I took the liberty to take up what money I wanted from your friends, which amounted to one hundred & seventy nine livres twelve sous & four deniers Catalan, for which sum I have given them a double receipt.

I return you a thousand thanks for the attention has been paid me, through your good recommendation, likewise for the wine you have been so kind to order me, which I have received & remain with the greatest respect Gentlemen, your true humble & obt. Servt.

From Benicarlo, 13 May 1790, to Messrs Reserson & Co (Barcelona):

I have had for the use of the ship *Pomona*, from your friends Messrs Renaud McDonnell & Co the sum of fifty five piastres six sous one denier what you'll please put to acct. with what I took before from your acct. I have the pleasure to inform you that I am quite loaded & dispatched & will sail the first opportunity for Guernsey.

Le Lacheur returned via Guernsey and continued on to Cowes with wine. He arrived 1 July 1790, after a voyage of 20 hours from Guernsey. He found nobody at Cowes with instructions about his six hundred hogshead of wine.

From Cowes, 10 July 1790, to Mr Samuel Dobrée (London):

I have received your brother's favour of yesterday. Mr Gregory instead of sending down orders to unload us, he has send orders not to unload us till further orders, and if I insist on demurrage that he will come upon us for what he has done for the ship in former times (or voyages) he has wrote the above threatening to his agents here with orders to communicate his letters to me, he mentions likewise that my owners and myself has used him very ill but I don't think we have. I see very plain he means to hurt us somehow or other, I wish to God one of my owners was here that they might do as they thought proper, for I am afear'd of something disagreeable with him before we have done with Mr Gregory. Your brother mentions that I'll do well to ask the agents at Cowes before I begin to unload whether they are to pay me the freight, and that they must assure me they will, otherwise that I cannot deliver the wines, but I think I am obliged to deliver the wines and then call upon them for the freight, for the charter party says on arrival at the mention'd port & upon faithful delivery of the goods according to the tenor of the bills of lading the freighters oblige themselves, the heirs, executors or assignees to pay or cause to be paid unto the said master or his order for freight and hire of said ship so much per ton. Therefore I look upon it that I am obliged to deliver the goods and then sue the receivers of the goods for freights; if other ways, please give me positive orders to stop the goods on board till the agents here have promised to pay me the freight.

I had wrote your brother in my last that I beg his opinion what I was to do after the ten days that I am to lay on demurrage was out. Please to give me your opinion about it. I shall kindly thank you.

On 15 July Le Lacheur wrote from Cowes to Maingy & Dunière (Guernsey), with alarming news about the naval press gang :

I am sorry to inform you that Captn Peter Le Lacheur of your brig *Peggy* has been impressed by Lieut Young and carry'd to the Rendezvous at Cowes and delivered over to the *Romulus* frigate, Captn Thos Lenox Frederick, they prest last night from all protections, they kept all our people except Capt Dykes and the two boys, they have pressed all the other mates. Mine (which I have shipped since I have been here) was ashore at the moment that they came to take Captn Le Lacheur and the rest of our people, and now he won't stay on board. The Captn of the frigate will not even look at Captn Le Lacheur's register nor hark to anything. I have been on board and spoke to him. He told me that he had orders to do what he did, & if Captn Peter Le Lacheur had a brig in Guernsey he had no business here. I begged his pardon and told it was very common that a master of the vessel left his ship & went elsewhere to look for a freight, and it was the case with him, but a body might as well talk to a dead horse as to speak to him. I have in consequence wrote to Mr Samuel Dobrée begging the favour of him to write to the Lords of the Admiralty for his clearance & to spare no trouble nor expense. I would gladly repay him.

We have not yet begun to unload. I have been four days on demurrage & noted a protest, they expect a brig from London. If you'll insist on the demurrage to be paid you'll be good enough to let me know.

Please & try to get Captn Peter Le Lacheur clear I shall go to the Admiral at Spithead, and see whether I shall be of any service. I hope, if Mr Dobrée exercises himself, he will get him clear, or else no master is safe.

Le Lacheur sent further news about Peter Le Lacheur in a letter from Cowes, 20 July, to Maingy & Dunière (Guernsey):

The moment after I had wrote you mine of the 13th inst I went away for Portsmouth, where I enquired for Admiral Roddam, being late I could not be admitted to speak to him that evening, but I went to the secretary which told me (after representing him Captn Peter Le Lacheur's case) to get his papers by next morning & come to him again. What I did & delivered them to him. Then I was put off till noon, when I was admitted to the said admiral which told me that the Captn of the man-of-war had told him that we was all captains on board of our ship. I told him that they was such captns, that their ages & infirmity (I thought) could protect them except this Captn Le Lacheur which had come over on purpose to charter his vessel & that he did not belong to our ship and as brother master of a vessel I thought it my duty to apply to his honour for his release, which I hoped he would grant, and he immediately wrote an order to his secretary, to give me an order to go on board the ship that he thought he might be on board of, & get him out. When I came on board of the frigate, he had been sent on board the *Royal William*, where I found him & got him away. I have sent him away for Guernsey, thinking it is the best way. James Steward and Samuel De La Rue I hope will come back again. Thos Guilbert, I believe, will be kept (though it is uncertain). I have my mate that I have shipped since I have been here, for which I have took an affidavit before a Justice of the Peace, as he is my mate. They have pressed some mates out of this port that are not return'd & it is supposed they will keep them – if it had not been for this affidavit my mate would have been positively carry'd away last evening, they have pressed a captain of a sloop of about 70 or 80 tons, for which his owner is now gone to London to try to get him clear but he may be shipped away before the owner comes down again. I don't know how we shall do to get the ship home, there is here now laying several brigs that has merchants goods on board, bound for Lisbon & other places, and not a man to be got for love nor money. We have not yet begun to unload. Yet they shall be obliged to begin in a few days, for if they don't the custom house will take the wines for the security of the duties, and my lay days expire today. I now enter a protest for all costs and damages, my charter being fulfill'd.

On 22 July Le Lacheur reported that the brig scheduled to carry the wines to Quebec had arrived the previous day. Enquiries had produced a quote of 22 shillings per 1000 bricks 'took at the place they make it, & it would cost 2 or 3 shillings more to bring it alongside'. He then turned to more immediate problems:

What I am most uneasy about now, is how I shall be quite clear of Mr Gregory, for it seems as if they would not pay me any demurrage for detention since our people was pressed & so on, always some difficulty or other, then I don't know how I shall get people to work the ship home, for we are now but five in all – myself, mate, one man & two boys. Samuel de la Rue nor no other is returned, though I expected two of them – the press is as hot as ever, the brig that is charter'd to carry the wines to Quebec has all her hands pressed in the Downs & Man of War's man put on board to bring her here. Many others are laying here for want of hands, they put almost every King's ship in commission, by what I can learn. I wish I may be put in commission too.

From Cowes, 26 July 1790, to Mr Samuel Dobrée (London):

James Mackenzie & Co refuses to pay me my demurrage money. I beg you will settle that point with Messrs Mark & Thos Gregory & Co of London; enclosed is the demand I make on them for freight, demurrage etc., if you can have them to pay you the whole so much the better but sooner than go to law I think it would be better drop the 4 days detention & the charges for noting protest (though the whole is due) if they would agree with you, please to give me your advice of what steps I must take to make them pay me. If they chuse to pay you please to receive it & place it to acct. of the owners of the ship *Pomona*. I have had of their agents here some money and I shall want more, you can leave them about 50 pounds, what shall pay my expenses or thereabouts, there's no bricks to be got here. I am obliged to go to Southampton to get some, but I shall be back here to receive your answer to this –

Enclosed a copy of account to James Mackenzie & Co on behalf of Messrs Mark & Thos Gregory & Co of London

To William Le Lacheur master of the ship *Pomona*

Dr for freight of six hundred hogsheads of wine from Mataro, Villa Nouva & Benicarlo.

	£ st
To 150 Tuns of wine at 35/- per tun	262-10-0
To Primage ten per cent	26- 5-0
To Demurrage from the 9th of July to the 20th following, ten days at 52/6 per day	26- 5-0
To 4 days detention after the charter party was fulfilled at 52/6 per day	10-10-0
To charges for noting protest	10-0
	£326-00-0

A copy of the above was rendered to Messrs J. Mackenzie & Co and, at their request (being unwilling to pay demurrage) was sent to London to Mr Gregory. Le Lacheur reported this to Maingy & Dunière on 28 July 1790. He was also able to report progress in buying bricks:

I have bought forty thousand Bursledon bricks at 25/- per thousand and have agreed they'll have the debenture for the freight to carry them on board at Cowes. I could have had some cheaper, but being the very best quality, and they sells the same to other people, I have got that sort, for if I had took what I have seen otherways more than one half would have broke before they would have been out of the ship, and the difference in price is only a shilling or 18 pence per thousand. I hope I shall get them all on board about Monday or Tuesday next. Sam de la Rue & James Steward are returned. We are now in all 5 men & two boys but I don't know how to do for others. I would advise you to insure for good men are not to be had, let the number be ever so great we shall never be well mann'd, I am sorry we are here so long. I never was so uneasy in my life and have been since I left you last, for I have had always something going contrary to my wishes, if they had unloaded me, as they might have, I would have been back to Guernsey in less than a fortnight after I left it. I have not heard from you lately. I should be glad to have a few lines of you if possible before I sail.

On 29 July 1790 Le Lacheur wrote to Samuel Dobrée at London, rehearsing the problems about demurrage and opining that Mark and Thomas Gregory would pay:

for I have regularly noted protests as a guard against them. I lay'd five days in Guernsey, to unload part of the cargo, after being admitted to pratique and after arriving there & reporting the ship at the Custom house I lay'd four days more, which made the ten days for unloading and then I protested for the demurrage on the 9th inst., the 20th do. The demurrage day being out, I then again for further demurrage, & all costs & charges the 24th do. I got out the remainder of my cargo, & I can prove that when they desir'd me to unload, I did it with as much dispatch as could be wished, having unloaded all 6 hundred hogsheads in 3 days, therefore they can't say that any thing has been neglected for want of men, and I think I have fulfill'd my charter party as well as can be done considering the times. I have delivered according to your advice the copy of my demands to Messrs James Mackenzie & Co and I am going to protest the non payment. I return you many thanks for the attention is paid me & Captn Peter Le Lacheur & beg you'll send me the amount of your trouble & expenses that you was at I shall gladly pay you.

On 29 July 1790 Le Lacheur gave instructions to James Mariette of Southampton to send on board six chairs ordered by Samuel de la Rue. On 4 August he wrote to Samuel Dobrée, London, acknowledging receipt of his letter. Le Lacheur considered that he might bring an action against Gregory & Co, not least because he would soon be ready to sail and wanted the matter settled before he left. On 6 August Le Lacheur reported to Mr Samuel Dobrée, London, that he had visited two attorneys-at-law:

they both told me I ran no risk in taking my freight and primage, and give a receipt accordingly, that I can afterwards recover the demurrage the same as if I had not received the freight etc. I therefore think I'll do better to take the freight as I am almost ready to sail to Guernsey. I suppose (and the Attorney told me so) that Messrs Gregory's can settle the demurrage by arbitration if not by action, please to discourse with Mr Gregory about it, the attorney says that Messrs James Mackenzie & Co has no obligation to pay it, as you told me, the action of course must be brought against the party named in the charter party, which is Gregory & Guille of Barcelona. Therefore Mr Mark Gregory being one of the House (as far as I understand) I think you may bring the action against him & oblige him to pay it. If you think it will do, please to let me know and I can send you the charter party or the copy of it, which you'll think best, & the different protests extended (if you think it necessary to send them) Mr Davis to whom I am recommended here tells me that he thinks I'll do right to take the freight etc & then sue the charterers for the demurrage, in taking care the receipt is made in a proper form (what I'll do) & remain.

On 8 August Le Lacheur reported to Maingy & Dunière, Guernsey. He was anxious to proceed as advised by the attorneys, not least because he wanted the money to pay for forty thousand bricks and the ship's expenses ('which are but too heavy'). Le Lacheur was desperate to set sail 'I think I cannot do anything better than take the ship away from this shirk hole'. *However, he still lacked a full crew. He had sacked the new first mate* 'for he did not like to work when the first bricks came alongside, I was obliged to hire men to take them on. I then begged him to help to take them in, he told me he was not used to handle bricks, I told in answer he must use himself to it or leave the ship, which he did'. *By 10 August Le Lacheur was able to report to Samuel Dobrée that he had received his freight and primage in the form of a bill of £169-9-0 drawn by James Mackenzie & Co on Messrs J. Strahan & J. Mackenzie of London. Le Lacheur sent a similar report to Maingy & Dunière (Guernsey) with the further details that he had kept back a bill of £50 to pay for the bricks etc.:*

If possible I shall haul in the Road tomorrow to be in readiness to take the first fair wind, we have had nothing but westerly winds since I left Guernsey. I am in hopes to get a few old men to help the ship over. Please God, as I come near the Island, I shall hoist a Jack at the main top gln masthead – I'll be obliged if you send me a few hands to help us in.

LATER VOYAGES

During the summer of 1791 the Pomona *was lengthened at Burlsedon by Mr Peter Parsons. In the course of the work several parts of the vessel were refitted. The ship was painted and had a bright new appearance. After the refit the* Pomona *sailed to Guernsey. She sailed for Virginia in September and Le Lacheur arrived at Norfolk, Virginia, 27 October 1791, after a passage of six weeks. He reported to Maingy & Dunière, Guernsey, that the ship had performed well, apart from a leak when the ballast was out.*

On 13 November he wrote to Mr John Mesurier, Petersburg, reporting that he had on board 142 hogsheads of tobacco, with 116 alongside. The ship was 'as light as possible'. The leak had been detected 'We have hove her down keel out, the leak was in the scaff of her keel'. By 24 November 1791 Le Lacheur was in Petersburg, sending a letter to Dobrée & Aubin, London, explaining that he was drawing on them at sixty days' sight a bill of exchange, order Coutart & Le Mesurier for £79-5-2 sterling.

On 28 November 1791 Le Lacheur wrote to Louis Dunière (Guernsey):

...it has been wet weather lately and the most of the tobacco that comes in now is cut but as I was obliged to come down again I have contracted with Messrs Coutart & Le Mesurier, they oblige themselves to furnish me New Petersbourg on demand at 14/6 (*American currency*) to the amount of the money I have left in their hands which amounts to two hundred and sixty pounds thirteen shillings and four pence Cy (or two hundred pounds sterling). I have likewise paid them one hundred and ninety five pound sixteen shillings and ninepence currency, which sum is to be passed to your credit, I will give you an acct. of the whole on the other side; I want about 50 hogsheads of being loaded. We shall take about 465 in all. We have hove the ship down keel out & found the leak right under the keel, it was in the scarf, now the ship is as tight as can be, and she look well light, but has rather better look loaded. Captain Lauga & Captain Pirvaux has both begun to take in, they both arrived the same day just a fortnight after me. I am sorry you gave me so much money, for it would have been advantageous to draw.

On the same day Le Lacheur wrote to Collings & Mauger, (Guernsey), enclosing an invoice for 27 hogsheads of tobacco, for which he was drawing on Dobrée & Aubin of London; there was also a bill of lading for the 27 hogsheads. Le Lacheur was pleased with the ship:

She is now as tight as can be, she sails faster than she did before she was lengthened & answers a helm as well as any ship can do. I hope she'll soon repay the expenses which has been put on her at Bursledon.

On the same day Le Lacheur remitted an invoice for 20 hogsheads of tobacco to Maingy & Le Mesurier, (Guernsey), together with a bill of loading. There was likewise an invoice for ten hogsheads of tobacco for Richard & Thomas Lievre, Guernsey.

On 10 December 1791 Le Lacheur reported to Maingy & Dunière that he was at last quite loaded, having on board 458 hogsheads of tobacco and some staves.

GAP OF FOUR MONTHS

On 13 April 1792 Le Lacheur wrote from Richmond (Va), reporting to Maingy & Dunière, (Guernsey), that he had arrived after a passage of 7 weeks and one day. He had news of other Guernsey captains:

Captn Rollinge & Deputron are loading fast, the *Liberty*, Captn Guerin, I spoke to & gave a letter the 6th inst in Harnton Roads as she was coming out and I was going in, therefore I suppose you'll hear of my arrival before this reaches you.

Le Lacheur quoted the tobacco prices:

Richmond tobacco is at 14/- & 14/6 sterling. Petersburg I cannot get under 12/- sterling but has been lately something lower. Lowland is about 10/- or 11/- sterling & Smithfield something cheaper. I go in sterling, the exchange is amazingly low, has been as low as 25 and now about 30 the reason of which is that the merchants that has imported goods has been pushed to raise money to pay the duties and no indulgence is shown them. I wish you send money for the whole cargo.

Le Lacheur drew on Perchard & Brock (London) and Dobrée & Aubin (London) to settle bills for Nicholas Maingy, Louis Dunière, Peter Mourant, William Combe, Thomas Lihou, all of Guernsey. Eight pages of tobacco detail for May 1792 were omitted in the transcript.

In October 1792 Le Lacheur was back in Virginia, after a passage of five weeks and six days. He informed Maingy & Dunière that brandy was a drug on the Virginian market and that tobacco had become amazing dear.

It has sold lately viz:

For   Richmond from 23 to 24 shillings currency per ct

   Petersburg from 20 to 20/6 shillings currency per ct

   Lowland from 15 to 16 shillings currency per ct

His brother Peter served as captain of the Pomona *while William Le Lacheur moved around purchasing tobacco. By 24 December 1792 Le Lacheur was able to inform Maingy & Dunière (Guernsey), that he was at last loaded:*

I have on board on the ships acct 8778 white oak hogshead staves at £ Co 5.10.0 per mille, 212 Barrels Tar @ 16/- Currency, 28 Bls pitch at 15/- Currency & 20 Bls of Turpentine at 12/6 per barrel.

In a P.S. Le Lacheur summarised: I have in all on bd 395 hds tobacco 125 barrels of flour and the above Staves, Tar, Pitch & Turpentine.

William Le Lacheur seems to have been an exceptionally fine master. He had a wealth of experience; he understood ships and the sea; he knew the worlds of commerce and maritime law; he helped those in need but had little time for shirkers; he was punctilious in attending to the interests of the shipowners. Maingy & Dunière were fortunate to have his services.

8
Register of
Merchants

The methodology adopted in compiling this Register has already been outlined on p. 92. Nine sources are discussed there. It is appropriate at this juncture to note some further sources. First, the records of the Cour d'Amirauté (CdA) shed light on disputes. This court sat more frequently than any other in Guernsey. It therefore became an avenue for swift justice and it heard many cases that had nothing to do with maritime matters. Moreover, it should be understood that it was in no way an admiralty court. By its nature this source tends to mention the litigious and the errant. Well behaved merchants (who paid their bills promptly) do not feature often. The source is valuable in giving insights into the types of trade conducted by individuals.

Almost every year the town of St Peter Port raised a *taxe* to cover a variety of administrative measures. From the records kept by the town constables, it is possible to discover the assessment and residential area (*vingtaine*) of a town taxpayer. The poor did not pay taxes but this source includes most merchants and traders. This source has already been used once (pp. 97 – 98). In compiling the Register I have occasionally used the *taxe* records. Their evidence is helpful when dealing with merchants with 'foreign' names, the *taxe* assessment can prove that such a merchant was a resident (rather than a friendly *négociant* on a visit).

The wills held by the Ecclesiastical Court sometimes furnish details about merchants. The estates of deceased islanders were dealt with by a traditional law of *partage*. In consequence many 'locals' did not leave a will and Guernsey is not rich in probate evidence in the manner of England.

When letters-of-marque were issued by the High Court of Admiralty (HCA), there was a mention of the shipowners towards the end of the document. This regularly took the form: '*name*, merchant of Guernsey'. My designation 'merchant-shipowner *temp*. Seven Years War' therefore means, *inter alia*, that the said person had an interest in privateering. Occasionally 'merchant of Guernsey' sounds as though it was a convenient (rather than an accurate) appellation. There may be the odd rentier or captain lurking beneath the terminology.

Family files exist at the Priaulx Library for the following 'merchant families': Ahier, Bonamy, Brock, Carey, Chepmell, Collings, de Carteret, de Garis, de Havilland, de Jersey, de Lisle, de Sausmarez, Dobrée, Falla, Fiott, Grut, Guérin, Guille, Hubert, La Serre, Lauga, Le Cocq, Le Febvre, Le Lievre, Le Marchant (includes material about William Bell), Le Mesurier, Le Roy, Lihou, Lukis, Maingy, Mansell, Martel, Mauger, Métivier, Mourant, Perchard, Reserson, Rivoire, Robilliard, Robinson, Rolland, Rougier, and Tupper. The quality of these files is very mixed. Some contain family trees painstakingly compiled by Victorian genealogists (who were working within living memory of some of their Georgian ancestors). Sometimes family scandals are concealed (the full story of the Métivier family in the early nineteenth century is one such case). On other occasions the files contain family trees with internal contradictions.

I have not attempted any original genealogical research (one family can involve a lot of research, one hundred families are too many!). I have sometimes used a 'grid' which helps to sort the members of a family into generations (and, consequently, into the years in which they were active). I have briefly recorded family legends. These are important. The historical veracity of such legends is not here germane. What is significant is an understanding of the ways in which families saw themselves, and the *personae* that they projected. The Tuppers revelled in the medal won by John in 1692. Huguenots rejoiced at their escapes from the dragonnades of Louis XIV. The Collings had proved themselves staunch royalists. The Bonamys were descended from Crusaders…. The Guernsey merchants belonged to a frontier society in which confidence, courage and enterprise assured their survival and independence. Their family and island 'myths' sustained them. (I employ the word *myth* in a technical, not a pejorative, sense.) At a personal level many of the merchants enjoyed good relations with their French neighbours. But, at another level, they were implacably hostile to the Catholicism and autocracy of French monarchs and the atheism and republicanism of revolutionaries.

REGISTER OF MERCHANTS

Canary wine petition, 1776	Signatory to TNA T 1/520/59-61, petition, 20 March 1776.
CdA	Cour d'Amirauté records (Guernsey, Greffe; these are in no way related to British Admiralty Court records).
CO (Taxe)	Tax records, Constables' Office (St Peter Port; the records are now kept at the Island Archive Service).
Dealer in wine brandy	Cambridge University Library, Cholmondeley papers Ch (H) 3D 'A list of ye dealers in wine brandy: in Guernsey' *circa* 1732.
Dobrée Protest Book	Record kept by the notary Isaac Dobrée; housed at the Priaulx Library, Guernsey
EC Wills	Ecclesiastical Court Wills (Guernsey Greffe)
HCA	High Court of Admiralty - records of, at TNA
H.E.I.C.(S.)	Honourable East India Company (ship)
IAS	Island Archive Service (Guernsey)
Jacob II	Volume 2 of Jacob, J. *Annals of the British Norman Isles*, Paris, 1830 (issued posthumously as a supplement).
Job, Zephaniah	Perrycoste F.H, *Gleanings from the Records of Zephaniah Job of Polperro* (1929)
leading merchant 1752	Signatory to BL, Lansdowne ms 657 ff 57, 58; letter to Lord de la Warr about wine duty, 15 Sept 1752
leading merchant -trader 1779	Signatory to petition to Lord Amherst, TNA SP 47/10, 13 March 1779.
Livre de certificats	Register of wine shipped in British bottoms for British merchants. Housed at the Greffe, Guernsey.
Lukis	Priaulx Library, Lukis ms. listing Guernseymen trading overseas.
Martell	Jean Martell, leading brandy and wine merchant in the Charente-Bordeaux regions in the 1715-1730 era. See de la Rogerie 1931.
merchant-shipowner *temp.* American War	Person thus described in a letter-of-marque (TNA HCA series)
merchant-shipowner *temp.* Seven Years War	Person thus described in a letter-of-marque (TNA HCA series)
Société des Veuves	A club founded in 1764 to pay the widow a pension on the death of a member. A pamphlet issued at the time of the foundation gives the names of the members and their occupation. A copy of the pamphlet is at the Priaulx Library, Guernsey. See Bibliography, p. 220, *Articles of the Friendly Society...* 1764, 1769.
Sun	Sun Fire Insurance Company (the policies regularly designated the occupation of the party covered. Housed at the Guildhall Library, London). All the references in this Register are to the 1720s (except those for Gregory & Ludlam)
TC	Town Church (i.e. St Peter Port parish church, Guernsey).
TNA	The National Archives, Kew, England (formerly Public Record Office)

ADAM

Mr Adam, German merchant in Guernsey (TNA WO 34/108, 14 Jan 1782, Irving to Hillsborough). =? Mr Jaques Louis Adam acting for Jean Cornelissen, master of the brigantine *Vrouw Elizabeth* of Ostend, against Nicolas Dobrée Ec, over freight on merchandise from Bordeaux (CdA, vol. 17, 23 Feb 1782).

AFFLECK

Andrew, vintner, from Hampstead, Middlesex. Will proved 19 Jan 1743 (EC Wills, 1738-54, p. 91).

AHIER

The Ahier family had Jersey roots. Captain **William** Ahier was plying between Southampton and Guernsey in 1720 (see p. 184). **John**, commander of *Hope* (privateering vessel of Guernsey, Priaulx, Dobrée Protest book, 20 July 1747). In August 1759 (CdA, vol. 13) **Elizabeth** Ahier was named as the owner of the brigantine *le Hope Well*; she was described as separated in respect of possessions ('femme separée quant aux biens'). In 1762 Elizabeth Ahier was recorded as living in the Mont Durand/ Hauteville vingtaine and was listed as 'femme de Campbell' (CO Taxe; see under Campbell). **Peter** merchant-shipowner *temp*. American War. **Joshua** designated a leading merchant/trader in 1779. **Peter** (b. 1775) entered the East India Company in 1791 and wrote to his mother in Guernsey (see p. 46).

ALLAIN

'Mons **Thomas** Allain négociant à Guernesey' – this was, apparently, a pseudonym (or nom-de-guerre) of le Sieur Thomas Allez (Priaulx Library, Dobrée Protest Book, 11 Nov 1749).

ANLEY

Edward was designated merchant-shipowner *temp*. Seven Years War and American War. He belonged to the *Société des Veuves* (listed as merchant). In 1762 he was resident in the Grande Rue and assessed at 70 quarters (CO Taxe). 'Mr Anley of Alderney' receiving brandy from Gregory & Guille (Barcelona) *via* Peter Bonamy (IAS, Guille letterbook 6 March 1773). Mr Anley 's'est retiré à Jersey après avoir fait mal ses affaires à Auregny où il s'étoit établi' commented De Havilland to Fraissinet (Cette), 3 June 1784 (IAS AQ 655/312). 'We expect every day **John** Anley from Holland where he has been to purchase a cargo of Gin' (Priaulx Library, Le Mesurier papers, Le Mesurier to Frederick Le Mesurier, 17 Dec 1771).

BELL

See Chapter 5, pp. 103-106.

BETT(S)

A family of Scottish origin.

James, of Inster, settled in Guernsey and married (1768) Mary Andrews by whom he had three sons:

> (1) James, lost at sea, 179-
>
> (2) William, died at St Domingo 179-
>
> (3) George, of Antigua, lost at sea while returning from Antigua, Jan 1808. (He added s to the surname and this was adopted by the family subsequently).

In 1787 James Bett married, secondly, Catherine Rabey, by whom he had:

> (1) **John** Betts (1788-1876) who married (1814) Martha, daughter of Frederick Price and Marguerite de Guérin. John Betts entered the firm of Métivier, Betts, Carey at Trieste (functioning during the 1820s). (de Guérin, 1890).

BONAMY

An aristocratic family much involved in commerce and shipping in the eighteenth century.

'The Bonamys are [an] ancient family of Norman extraction….A legend exists that they are the descendants of two brothers, who, returning from the Crusades, were wrecked on the island; during their hour of peril they vowed if spared they would devote their lives and fortunes for the advancement of the people among whom they might be thrown.

'From the earliest records the family have held a prominent position in the island, and were landowners under the Crown, in St. Martin's parish in 1331. Peter Bonamy, of St. Martin, was one of the heroic band of eighty-seven men who strove to expel the French, who had taken possession of Guernsey, in 1338. They were defeated in their intrepid attempt, and their leaders, Peter Bonamy, Peter de Sausmarez, and others fled to Jersey.

'The Bonamys were strong partisans of the Parliamentary cause, and their name is mixed up with the history of the island for many centuries, they have given one Bailiff, three "Juge Délégués" besides fifteen or sixteen Jurats to the Royal Court; also one Dean and several Rectors of the name have been appointed to the different parishes, and they have inter-married with most of the influential families around them' (de Guérin, 1890, p. 21).

There were several branches of the family and it is not always easy to identify individuals. The genealogical notes of de Guérin (1890) are helpful but the family tree he presents is not complete. **Hellier** served as harbour supervisor in 1704, 1715, 1732, 1747 (=? Helier, Seigneur de Mauxmarquis, jurat 1705, died 1753; de Guérin, p. 23). **Jean** Bonamy des Caches corresponded with Martell (= John Bonamy des Caches, 1694-1730, de Guérin, p. 22). In the 1720s **Samuel** had insurance cover 'for goods and merchandise in his apartment belonging to Mr Dobrée at the lower end of Cornet Street; and for goods and merchandise in his cellar under the dwelling house of Mr Nicholas Naftell, the upper end of Cornet Street' (Sun: 12/212, 213/19679,19680). This could be Samuel, 1700-1781, son of Peter of the Grand Carrefour (de Guérin, p. 24); or Samuel 'Under the Arch', who was elected jurat in 1721 and died in 1729 (de Guérin, p. 22). There was yet another Samuel, of the Mauxmarquis branch, who died in 1784. Samuel 'dealer in wine brandy' c. 1732 (CUL). We find Samuel, master of the snow *Matthew*, owned by James Le Ray, on voyages to South Carolina, 1739 (TNA CO 5/510, f <31>v, passim) and Virginia, 1744 (from Barbados) (TNA CO 5/1446 f <31>). Samuel served as harbour supervisor, 1745 (probably = Samuel fs Samuel 'Under the Arch'; he was elected jurat in 1744 and bailiff in 1758; he died in 1770; de Guérin p. 22). Samuel, son of Peter, leading merchant 1752 (the designation 'son of Peter' fixes him as a member of the Grand Carrefour branch, de Guérin,1890, p. 22). **Elisha, Peter, Peter the younger, Samuel**, were designated merchants-shipowners *temp*. Seven Years War (Elisha b. 1706, was a member of the Grand Carrefour branch). **Peter and Andrew** belonged to the *Société des Veuves*. Peter signed the Canary wine petition in 1776. (There were at least two Peters: i. Peter 1697-1777, des Mauxmarquis, who married Mary Reserson; ii. Peter b. 1722, who belonged to the Grand Carrefour branch and married Elizabeth Bowden in 1750, de Guérin, p. 25. The second Peter is, perhaps, the Peter who served as second lieutenant on *Mary Galley* 'of this island', Samuel Thoume commander, Priaulx Library, Dobrée Protest book, 21 July 1746). **John** and **Andrew** merchants-shipowners *temp*. American War. (John =? John 1716-1791, de Guérin, 1890 p. 25). John 'of Guernsey merchant', owner of cutter *Idas* (West Sussex Record Office, Add Mss 2611, 26 Dec 1807).

BOUCAULT

Hillary Boucault & Co dealt with Zephaniah Job, 1800-1806.

BOWDEN

James and **John** were designated merchants-shipowners *temp*. Seven Years War. James belonged to the *Société des Veuves*. One member at least of the Bowden family was in partnership in Rotterdam in the house of Collings and Bowden (see under Harvey).

BROCK

An ancient Guernsey family, several members of which were *négociants* in the eighteenth century.

Henry, 'dealer in wine brandy' c. 1732 (CUL). Henry knew a *négociant* at Dunkirk, an *armateur* at St Malo, and a banker at St Malo, any of whom might be a useful contact in wartime (Sausmarez Manor archives, box 68K, letter, Nov 1747). **John, William, Henry** listed as leading merchants, 1752. At this time John lived in the Cimetière-Beauregard vingtaine and was assessed at 200 quarters; Henry lived in the same area and was assessed at 100 quarters; William sr & fils were in the Grande Rue, and were assessed at 600 quarters. **Henry elder, Henry, John elder, John, William & sons** were designated merchants-shipowners *temp.* Seven Years War. 'When Spanish brandy made its appearance in growing quantity, in 1760 the merchant house of Brock in Guernsey quoted a price for Spanish brandy to the County Kerry smuggling business of the O'Connells, who had formerly drawn their brandy from Nantes' (O'Connell papers, Trinity College, Dublin, quoted by Cullen, 2000, p. 15). John sr and John jr belonged to the *Société des Veuves*. H. Brock and Brock & Co traded in wines from Oporto (*Livre de certificats*). Henry was included in the list of leading merchants-traders in 1779. Henry dealt with Zephaniah Job, 1779-1786; the partnership of **Brock, La Serre, Maingy** dealt with Zephaniah Job 1806-1807. De Havilland wrote to Fraissinet (Cette) in June 1784 and commented that Henry Brock (fs William) was 'fort riche mais avec une nombreuse famille' (IAS AQ 655/312).

Daniel de Lisle Brock b. 10 Dec 1762, third son of John Brock Esq and Elizabeth de Lisle (whose father was Deputy-Bailiff of Guernsey). Received his early education in Guernsey; went to Alderney to study French under M. Vallatt, a Swiss protestant clergyman; then to school at Richmond; and finally to Dinan with his father, who died there. Soon afterwards he entered the counting house of his uncle Mr John Le Marchant. In 1785 he went on a voyage with Mr Herzel de Lisle, spending upwards of a year visiting Spain, Malta, Sicily, Italy, Switzerland and France (Gentleman's Magazine, 1842, pp. 546-7). He was a privateering *armateur* during the French Revolutionary wars. He was a champion of Guernsey liberties. See Marr, 1984, pp. 16-17.

His brother **William** was born in 1764. He became a merchant banker in London and with his brother Irving 'was engaged in trade with Russia, Sweden and Prussia. Because of shipping disasters William's company went bankrupt in 1811' (www.uppercanadahistory.ca/brock/brock13.html)

BUDD

Henry Budd, merchant of Guernsey, cleaned naval sloop the *Happy* (Captain T Burnett) and supplied necessaries for the sick of the sloop (TNA ADM 106/1118/150, Burnett to Navy Commissioners, 24 Sept 1756, voucher received 28 Oct 1756). **Henry** and **John** were designated merchants-shipowners *temp.* Seven Years War. Henry merchant-shipowner *temp.* American War.

CAMPBELL

James, merchant, TNA CUST 62/66, p 184, 1 Feb 1747/1748, Southampton customs to London. (See also under Ahier; this Campbell =? Elizabeth Ahier's companion).

CAREY

'The Carey family have always ranked with the ancient leading families in Guernsey' (Jacob II p. 130). The family possibly came of Norman stock and was established in Guernsey by the thirteenth century. A senior branch of the family became landowners in St Martin's and a junior branch engaged in trade in St Peter Port. Between 1522 and 1830 the family supplied Guernsey with no fewer than twenty jurats. There was hardly a year during that period when there was not a member of the family serving thus. The office of harbour supervisor was discharged on an annual basis by a jurat. In the early eighteenth century we find **James** Careye serving as harbour supervisor in 1709 and 1719; **Pierre** Careye fs Pierre in 1724 and 1736; and **Pierre** Careye fs Jean in 1726, 1737 and 1748.

The genealogy of the family is clearly delineated in *The History of the Careys of Guernsey* by W.W. Carey, E.F. Carey and S. Carey Curtis, London, 1938 (Carey, 1938). The table below gives the branches and identifying numbers used in that work. Useful additional information is to be found in some notes entitled *A short history of Le Vallon* by L.F. Carey, C.B., C.B.E. (Priaulx

Library, family files - Carey).

Pierre Careye 'de la Brasserie', fs Pierre (1689-1744) [F. 35]. In the 1720s Pierre Careye/ Peter Carey owned a house 'late the dwelling house of Peter Martin Esq in the Great Street' (=High Street, St Peter Port) which he insured with the Sun Fire Assurance Company, together

	1	2	3	4
B	Pierre (1688-1759) [B.35]	Marthe [B.43] m. John Cornelius (d.1760) ---------------------- William (b.1712) [B.44]	John Cornelius m. Marie Careye [F.52] ---------------------- William (1737-1770) [B.52]	
C	Darrel (1697-1746) [C.31]	Darrel (ob. 1760) [C.35]	Darrel (1752-1805) [C.47] William (b.1753) [C.48]	
E	Pierre des Halles/ du Marché (1690-1754?) [E.14]	Jean Careye (1714-1779) [E.16]	Jean (1740-1810) 'of Bigoterie' [E.21]	James- (1768 1845) of Bigoterie' [E.31]
F	Pierre de la brasserie (1689-1743/4) [F.35]	Pierre (1714-1770) [G.4] Laurent (1723-1769) [G.9]		
H	Isaac (1697-1757) [C.31]	Thomas (1724-1780) [H.4]	John (1748-1821) 'of Choisi' [H.6] Isaac (1758-1828) 'of Hauteville ' [H.9]	Thomas (1772-1849) [H. 10] John (1774-1855) [H.12] John (1786-1850) 'of Castle Carey ' [Hc.5] Tupper (1788-1867) [Hc.6] De Vic (1790-1876) [Hc.7] Sausmarez (1794-1879) [Hc.9] Frederick Charles (1798-1886) [Hc.11] Havilland (1799-1870) [Hc.12]

with 'his goods and merchandise in his warehouse near his brewhouse' (Guildhall, Sun Fire, 11/3/16815, 16816). Pierre was rich. In 1724 he was assessed in the St Peter Port tax list as worth 600 quarters. In terms of wealth this placed him alongside Nicholas Dobrée and Thomas Le Marchant. Apart from the warehouse and brewery, he owned the Moulin de Haut de la Ville. He was a correspondent of Martell (in the Cognac brandy industry). He owned vessels and had an interest in the Newfoundland fishing industry. In 1720 Pierre was selected as Deputy of the States of Guernsey to the Privy Council to protest against Customs House officers being sent to Guernsey. It was argued that this was contrary to the customs and privileges of the island. In 1722 he asked to be relieved of this post. In 1739 he was again selected to discharge the same office, on this occasion to protest against an act of navigation. Eventually his efforts were successful and certain clauses of the act were redrafted (Carey, 1938, pp. 183-4). Peter Careye ye brewer listed as 'dealer in wine brandy', c. 1732 (CUL).

Contemporary with Pierre Careye 'de la Brasserie' was **Pierre** Careye (1690-1754?) [E.14], fs Jean. He was sworn in Jurat of the Royal Court in 1725. To avoid confusion this Pierre was often called '**des Halles**' or '**du Marché**'. Like his namesake he was a merchant with an interest in shipping and the Newfoundland trade.

Pierre 'de la Brasserie' (1714-1770) [G.4] served as Constable of St Peter Port in 1740. In 1764 he was a member of a deputation from Guernsey to George III which sought to defend the privileges of Guernsey in sending wine from the island to England (Carey, 1938, p. 187).

John, Laurence, and **Peter** were designated merchants-shipowners *temp.* Seven Years War. John and John jr, designated as merchants, belonged to the *Société des Veuves*, as did Laurence, who was designated 'brewer'. John and John jr signed the Canary wine petition, 1776. John Carey (1714 – 1779) was listed in 1779 as one of the leading Guernsey merchants; he was living in the Grande Rue (=High Street, St Peter Port) and was assessed at 1900 quarters, indicating that he was one of the wealthiest of the Guernsey merchants. He had married Judith Dobrée, daughter of Mr Nicolas Dobrée, in 1732. Two of their daughters made significant marriages: Judith (1736-1791) married Abraham Le Mesurier of London, the merchant banker; and Caroline (1747 – 1781) married Mr Nicolas Guille of Barcelona (partner in the firm of Gregory and Guille). Carey's eldest son was also called Jean (1740 – 1810), styled 'of the Bigoterie', a house in Berthelot Street, St Peter Port. There are frequent references in the *Livre de certificats* to wine imported by Jean sr and Jean, between 1769 and 1777, from Barcelona, the Canary Isles, Cadiz, Lisbon, Malaga, Oporto. John was a merchant-shipowner *temp.* American War.

William is referred to in an official investigation into the wine business as 'resident in Bordeaux for eighteen years, eleven of which in business' (BL Add Ms. 38389 f 1444r, 15 Mar. 1786). This is almost certainly the Carey who, in 1785, was a member of the influential Hennessy group in Bordeaux (Cullen, 2000, p 123). On 27 Oct 1786, Dobrée (Guernsey) wrote to his son Pierre-Frédéric Dobrée in Nantes explaining that Paul Le Mesurier had approached the Marquis of Carmarthen in favour of Mr William Carey 'who is soliciting the place of Consul at Bordeaux' (Nantes, *Archives Municipales*, fonds Dobrée). This Carey was, surely, William [C. 48], the son of Darell Careye and Marie Le Marchant, born 29 Apr 1753, who married 'a French lady and settled at Bordeaux' (Carey, 1938, p. 129).

There was also an earlier William Carey who gave interesting naval intelligence to the British authorities:

'Yesterday about noon, one Wm Carey of the Island of Guernsey came to me voluntarily & acquainted me, that he left Brest the 2d inst., at which Time there was a ship of war of 74 guns, with five or six sail besides, from 40 to 34 guns, which, by the intelligence he had from the person he had lodged with, were bound to Guinea; & he also acquainted me that there are now near six hundred English shipwrights working in the yard, & in the merchant service at Brest; which I pray to signify for their Lordships information.' (TNA, SP 78/246, Hughes to Cleveland, Portsmouth, 13 Jun 1753).

In 1766 we find William Carey as master and owner of a snow called *Kitty*. It had been built at Southampton in 1764 and was registered in Guernsey on 7 June 1765. In 1766 Carey sailed to Madeira and took on board a small cargo of 10 pipes and one hogshead of wine. He arrived in Virginia on 9 June. That part of the story is to be found in the colonial shipping returns (TNA, CO 5/1450 f <20>). What happened subsequently is partly recorded in a letter written on 3 October 1766 by Le Gros and Le Cras of Threadneedle Street, London, to the Commissioners of the Navy:

'About ten Days ago we delivered into this office a tender from Mr Thomas Treeve of Penryn of 100 barrels of Pitch, 10 Barrels of Tar, & 10 Barrels of Turpentine, arrived into that Port per the snow *Kitty* Captn. William Carey from Virginia, the said naval stores the property of the Owners of said vessel, which is now bound to Guernsey, and Capn Carey wants to reship said stores or parts thereof if your Honours do not chuse to accept of said Tender, which he supposes to be the Case from your not having made an answer thereto; But the Officers at Falmouth will not permit him to reship 'em without first having your answer, therefore to beg the favour that you will be pleased to give an Answer, whether you will or not accept of said stores.' (TNA ADM 106/1146/185).

Thomas Carey (1724-1780) [H. 4] lived at the Vrangue Manor and owned some four hundred acres in St Peter Port, Vale and St Sampson. 'In a fit of pique because his ships laden with wheat had been taken or sunk by French privateers, Thomas sold all his Guernsey property in 1778 and moved to Southampton where he died in 1780.' By his marriage to Michelle Falla there were three sons (John, Thomas, Isaac) and two daughters, Rachel and Marguerite (Carey, L. F.).

Isaac Carey (1758-1828) [H. 9], son of Thomas Carey, was a merchant-shipowner *temp*. American War; he returned to the island on his father's death and purchased no 16, Hauteville, St Peter Port, in 1785. He prospered and nineteen years later bought Le Vallon, 'then no more than a substantial farm house. He used Le Vallon as a country house to be occupied only in the summer; the country roads at that time were little more than cart tracks and in the winter virtually impassable to anything but pack horses' (Carey, L. F.). In 1779 he married Marguerite, daughter of Elisha Tupper, Jurat of the Royal Court and a leading merchant. There were three daughters and ten sons.

One of these, **deVic** Carey (1790-1876) [Hc. 7], was 'a man of means for besides owning a wine business – he imported wine from Tarragona in Spain which I understand was only drinkable because it had been stored in sherry casks obtained from some Sandeman cousins – he married Frances Priaulx daughter of Thomas Priaulx of Montville, the most successful owner of privateers in the island who on his death left nearly half a million. De Vic spent a part of every year in Spain and much of the embellishment which went into the north side of the house can be attributed to sketches made of various houses on his travels to and from Spain. These sketches were given to Jim Le Page, a local builder, to interpret and incorporate in the house during my great-grandfather's subsequent absences from the island with results, I feel sure, that bore little resemblance to the originals.' (Carey, L. F.).

DeVic and his brothers were very active in Spain in the nineteenth century. In 1819 Devic Carey, 'negociante', was recorded as having been resident in Barcelona for four years and was living in Calle de la Merce (TNA, FO 639/8). He was signing documents there as British proconsul by 1824 (TNA, FO 638/3). His brother **Frederick Charles** (1798-1886) was listed on 30 Dec 1818 as 'clerk of the house of Messrs Kennet Carey & Co merchants in this city' (i.e. Barcelona, TNA, FO 639/5) and in the 1819 enumeration of British subjects living in Barcelona he is shown as resident in Calle de la Merce. He later served in the firm of Métivier, Betts and Carey at Trieste. Other brothers of DeVic – **Tupper** (1788-1867), **Sausmarez** (1794-1879) and **Havilland** (1799-1870) – were also involved in the Spanish enterprise. Sausmarez's son **Julius Alphonso** (1836-1893) joined the house of Carey & Co, Alicante, and became the manager in 1860. Members of other branches of the family were involved in the Alicante firm (e.g. Thomas [H.25], who joined

Carey & Co, returning to Guernsey in 1861. His children were born in Alicante between 1841 and 1856).

CHEPMELL

William started life in Jersey, the son of an English mother and father. He was 'a rather pretty little boy and very charming'. He was sent to Caen at the age of ten to learn French. He disappeared on 29th September 1765. Eventually it was discovered that he was held at the Convent of the Nouveaux Convertis. It transpired that the nuns had been in the habit of giving him bonbons as he passed the convent and one day they enticed him into the building, where he remained for some nine months. He was rescued (Ozanne, 1928). He spent at least part of his adulthood in Guernsey, in partnership for a time with Peter Mourant (and also with Le Marchant). He was designated merchant-shipowner *temp.* American War. He married Elizabeth Effard (only daughter and heir of William Coutart). On 3 June 1784 De Havilland wrote to Fraissinet (Cette) and commented that Chepmell was in partnership with young Mr Le Marchant; Chepmell was young and 'assez riche' (IAS AQ 655/312).

COLLIN[G]S

Three Collins brothers, Royalists, 'refusing to take the oath of allegiance to Cromwell…were conducted under a strong escort to the castle of Pendennis, from which they made their escape by night, and after procuring a small sloop, reached St Malo in safety, from whence they embarked for Jersey' (de Guérin, 1890, p. 37). Edward Collins (1712-1758), son of Thomas Collins (one of the three brothers), was born at St Brelade, Jersey, and founded the Guernsey branch. At the Castel Church, on 16 Feb 1734, by licence, he married Anne Smith (daughter of Andrew Smith of Limerick, Ireland). Edward was the first to adopt the additional g. His son **Edward** (1739-1820) married Anne Barbier in 1762 and there was issue: **Thomas** was born in 1773, **Edward** in 1779.

Edward was designated as merchant-shipowner *temp.* American War. Edward Collings kept a manuscript notebook entitled *Livre touchant la Distillation 1784* (private collection, Guernsey). Internal notes suggest that he used the book between 1784 and 1802 (and possibly later). There are recipes for spirit-based cordials such as Anniseed, Angelique, British Liberty, All Fours, Cinnamon Water, Coriand Water, Celery, Doctor John, Cream of Barbadoes, Clove Water, Fennel Water, India Cordial, Ladies Favorite, Lady Mary, Mint Water, Nutmeg Water, Pernicot Water, Shrub, True Love, Vespetro, White Ratafia, Worm-Wood. A note records: 'Cordials most sold here viz Uscuba, Cinnamon, Wormwood, Clove, Shrub'. Collings also noted that 'Cette Brandy (clean tasted) is much better than Salou brandy for making cordials'. After the recipes Collings wrote down observations about the strength of spirits 'The fairest manner to sell London proof Brandy, Geneva or Rum is to sell it at so much per gallon warranted to be 106, 107, or 108 degrees in strength by the dicas, & if over that strength the buyer to pay, for every degree the same as he's to pay for by ye gallon, and if under above strength, to deduct to the buyer – same proportion &c. &c.' He included methods of turning yellow Geneva white; a recipe for beer or cider turn'd sour; and recipes for curing sundry disorders. A loosely inserted notebook of eighteen pages entitled *1806 for Dutch Calculation* showed how to convert guilders, stivers and groots into pounds sterling. Edward Collings presented the notebook to his son Thomas: *I have given this Book to my Son Thomas. Witness my hand Edward Collings.*

On 6 June 1791 the Guernsey merchant Harvey ordered gin from **Collings and Bowden** at Rotterdam (private collection). The Collings involved was probably **William** (b. 11 Jan 1769), for we find reference to a contract of marriage, and conditions of marriage, at Rotterdam, 30 Nov 1803, between William Collings and Ann Smith (Priaulx Library, Maingy file). There was a daughter Maria Collings, born at Rotterdam 3 May 1814 (ms ref to birth certificate, Priaulx, family file, Maingy file). She married James Bowden-Maingy (b. Rotterdam 25 May 1813, son of Thomas Maingy and Margaret E. Smith). William and Ann had sons: William, who married a cousin, Maria Collings (son of John Collings); and George.

Thomas' brother Edward Collings (b. 1779) was also out in the Netherlands, for in 1799 he married Juliana Louisa Deutzer of Weilburg at Amsterdam (ms note in de Guérin *Our Kin* at Priaulx Library). This Edward had a son William (b. 23 Jan 1808).

By a letter of contract dated 25 April 1837, because of his bad health, William Collings of Rotterdam disassociated himself from the firm of Collings and Maingay (Albert Maingay and George Collings in Antwerp and James Bowden-Maingy in Rotterdam; Priaulx Library, family file, Maingy).

COMBE(S)

William, partner of Peter Mourant (q.v.).

CORNELIUS

John married Marthe Careye (1710-1762, B.43) in 1734, died 1760; their son Jean/John (1737-1784) married Marie Careye (1736-1779, F.52) in 1756. John, leading merchant 1752, refers to John Senr. The John who belonged to the *Societé des Veuves* and who signed the Canary wine petition 1776 was John Jr (John Senr having died in 1760).

COUTART

Peter Anthony Coutart, merchant, insuring in the 1720s, together with Elisha Le Marchant (presumably a business partner), goods and merchandise in their warehouse by itself in the upper end of 'la profonde rue' near Mr de Havilland's gardens – not exceeding £500 (Sun 22/148/38530). Peter Coutard, (sic) 'dealer in wine brandy' c. 1732 (CUL). **William**, commander of *Royal George* (owners Laurence Carey and Co), HCA 26/5/40. William, master of the *Alexander* (brig, 90 tons, 'prize this war', registered at Guernsey, 9 Mar 1759, owners Isaac Dobrée & William Coutart), arrived South Carolina, 15 Mar 1760, in ballast, from Guadeloupe (TNA, CO 5/510 f <82>v. June 1748). Capt William Coutart recorded as resident in Fountain Street, 1762, and assessed at 40 quarters (CO Taxe). William belonged to the *Société des Veuves*. William was included in the list of leading merchants-traders, 1779. William and **William Peter** designated merchants-shipowners *temp.* American War.

Will of **Peter** Coutart of Petersburg proved by oath of John Chepmell (estate left to mother/sisters), 6 Oct 1806 [Will Book 2, page 10, Hustings Court, Petersburg, Virgina. Will proved in London 18 Aug 1809, PROB 11/1501, see *North American Wills registered in London 1611-1857* by Peter Wilson Coldham].

CROUSAZ DE PRELAZ

Isaac came of a distinguished Swiss family (see *Dictionnaire historique géographique et statistique du canton de Vaud* by D. Martignier and Aymon De Crousaz, Lausanne, 1867) and settled in Guernsey. Some of his papers survive in private hands. They show that he handled port (1784, 1785); Mataro and Benicarlo wine from Barcelona (supplied by Reserson & Tupper, 1783; red wine and brandy, 1786); burgundy from Beaune (Poulet Père & fils, 1784) and brandy from Sète (S.A. Falconnet, Porta, Guirard & Porta, 1785-6). In 1793 Airesquay Glass Works, Sunderland, shipped 780 dozen champagne bottles to him. In 1796, in war conditions, Zimmerman & Gordon of Bordeaux suggested: 'your orders should come under cover of your friends in Hamburg'. On 12 April 1791 J. C. Métivier (Guernsey) wrote to William Guille (London) explaining that he had gone to taste the wines of Mr Martin 'chez M de Prelaz' and had there met Mr Thompson (IAS, Stevens-Guille letters).

De BEAUVOIR

'The family of De Beauvoir flourished in the island of Guernsey and were ornaments to the place for upwards of seven hundred years' (Jacob II p. 173). Three members of the family (Daniel, James, James) served as jurats and harbour supervisors in the early eighteenth century. I have heard it stated that they were merchants but I have not so far found clear evidence.

De CARTERET

Charles designated merchant-shipowner *temp.* Seven Years War. Messrs Charles de Carteret & compagnie actioned *re* freight on brandies, 5 Jan 1760 (CdA, vol. 13). Messrs De Carteret, De Jersey & Co importing brandy from Salou (CdA, vol. 14, 27 March 1762). Charles belonged to the *Société des Veuves*, as did **Mathew** and **Peter** who were designated 'timber merchants'. Charles in partnership with Peter Lihou (q.v.). The house of **de Carteret & Lihou** was disappointed by brandy sent from Gregory & Guille, Barcelona (IAS, Guille letterbook, Guille to Gregory & Guille 18 August 1772). Charles included in list of leading merchants-traders, 1779. Charles and Mathew designated merchants-shipowners *temp.* American War.

On 1 January 1783 **Pierre & Jean** De Carteret entered into a partnership (*société*) with Jean Guille and Isaac De Lisle. The partnership was to last three years, until 31 December 1785 but it was renewed and lasted until 2 January 1789. The capital invested in the beginning was £2,500, Jean Guille supplying brandy from Salou and gin to the value of £2,000; Isaac De Lisle supplied brandy to the value of £500. The purpose of the partnership was to deal in brandy, rum, gin, and tea. Isaac De Lisle was to superintend the warehouses, the loading and unloading of cargoes and the coopers' work; he was to furnish two boys/apprentices. There was to be a book recording the entry and exit of all commodities at the warehouses. Profits were to be shared in the proportion $\frac{4}{8}$ to Jean Guille; $\frac{2}{8}$ to Isaac De Lisle; $\frac{2}{8}$ to Pierre & Jean De Carteret. The De Carterets were to keep the account books of the partnership. (IAS, Stevens-Guille papers).

P(eter) shipping wine 1784 (*Livre de certificats*). 'De Carteret' dealt with Zephaniah Job, 1783-1799.

On 22 February 1786 Nicholas Guille (Barcelona) wrote to George Guille (Guernsey) that he had engaged Messrs Welther & Porte of Alicante to take cousin **George** De Carteret to work at their house. Nicholas recommended that George should first improve his English 'it being a thing of the greatest consequence'. George should spend three or four months in England and then travel straight to Spain, without returning to Guernsey. The firm required a young man to write the English correspondence. Nicholas was of the opinion that Alicante was a very proper place to learn Spanish and contrasted it with the 'coarse' tongue of Barcelona (i.e. Catalan).

In 1792, on the death of Henry Le Mesurier, George de Carteret wished to become the Danish consul in Guernsey. George Guille was in London at the time and the De Carteret family asked him to approach the Danish Consul General in London (George was appointed). Evidently de Carteret corresponded with Messrs George Ernst Wolf (of America Square, London) for his Danish business (IAS, de Carteret to George Guille, 28 February 1792).

DE FRAISE

Lewis 'of Guernsey', owner of the schooner *Rodney* (50 tons, built in New England 1762, registered at Guernsey, 14 Mar 1763) carrying 68 cases claret and 23 barrels of brandy, one case necklaces, one cask beads British etc, to South Carolina (from St Augustine) arrived 20 Aug 1763 (TNA, CO 5/510 f <121>v). It took a cargo of 11,000 staves and 8 hogsheads of rum back to Guernsey (TNA, CO 5/510 f <133>v). M Louis de Fraise recorded as living in the Pilori/Eglise vingtaine in 1762 and assessed at 20 quarters (CO Taxe).

De HAVILLAND

Jean served as harbour supervisor in 1729, 1740, 1751. John (merchant) belonged to the *Société des Veuves*. John signed the Canary wine petition, 1776. John merchant-shipowner *temp.* American War. (We are dealing with two generations of John (1706-1770) and his son John (1734-1810) – see Hocart, 1997).

Peter was trained to be a merchant but became an advocate (see p.51, *supra*).

De JERSEY

'The name of De Jersey is of long standing in the Island of Guernsey' (Jacob II, p. 182). **Henry**, merchant, insured his goods and merchandise in his dwelling house in Fountain Street in the 1720s (Sun 10/212/15593; see also 10/421/12230). **Daniel, John, Richard** designated as merchants-shipowners *temp.* Seven Years War. **Richard** (merchant) belonged to the *Société des Veuves*. In 1771 Richard de Jersey, Jean Guille jr and Nicholas Corbin formed a partnership. The agreement contained 23 clauses. The following is a summary, translated from the French.

> *Société* to sell tea, rum, brandy, geneva etc. for three years, starting 1 October 1771 and finishing on the same day in 1774. The fund capital £1900 sterling; Richard de Jersey to furnish £1000, Jean Guille jr £400, Nicolas Corbin £500. Each partner to supply the money on 1 October. Profits and losses to be shared in the proportions Richard de Jersey $\frac{5}{12}$, Jean Guille jr $\frac{2}{12}$, Nicolas Corbin $\frac{5}{12}$. The partners to keep two warehouses to lodge the merchandise of the partnership, one for Richard de Jersey, the other for Jean Guille, each to consign goods to the warehouses in their own name (after approval of the majority of the partnership). De Jersey and Guille to keep accounts of everything sold. Corbin to watch over the warehouses and the coopers employed to make barrels and Corbin to supply one of his apprentices to work in the warehouses (the apprentice to receive an allowance of 7 sous per day when working in the warehouses). Corbin allowed £6 per annum for usage of his coopering, for storing hoops etc and a room for lodging empty barrels. No partner to sell nominated products wholesale or retail while the partners wish to sell at the same price. Partnership funds not to be used for personal account. William de Jersey chosen as London agent, Gregory & Guille as Barcelona agent (to keep accounts in the name of Jean Guille). Nicolas Corbin to go to England to receive payment of debts owed. After the dissolution of the partnership Corbin to make a trip to England lasting one month (winding up affairs). Richard de Jersey makes over to the partnership, at cost price, 30 *bottes* of rum (which he has ordered to be bought and loaded on the *Marquis of Granby*). Guille to supply 30 *bottes* of brandy at cost price (ordered per Capt Williams) and 50 *bottes* at current price. The partnership to pay for the warehouses. The partners not to join with anyone else to sell the commodities in Guernsey. In the event of a dispute the matter to be adjudicated by a panel of three, each partner selecting a Guernsey merchant. The partners to abide by the articles of the agreement, a penalty of a £300 fine for contravention.

The partnership clearly proved successful as it was extended for four years, to terminate in 1778 (IAS, Stevens-Guille papers).

Daniel and Richard signed the Canary wine petition, 1776. Daniel was included in the list of leading merchants-traders, 1779. **Richard, Peter, Peter jr, Daniel, William** designated as merchants-shipowners *temp.* American War. **Jersey** and **de Lisle** dealing with Zephaniah Job 1778-1789; **De Jersey Guille & Co** dealing with Zephaniah Job 1779-1781; **De Jersey** and **Corbin** dealing with Zephaniah Job 1783-1788. On 3 June 1784 De Havilland commented to Fraissinet (Cette) that De Jersey & Corbin were a 'maison très solide'. He further observed that De Jersey had spent one or two years at Mr Falconnet's house at Montpellier; his father, Richard De Jersey, had left a fortune 'fort considérable' (IAS AQ 655/312).

De LISLE

'The family of De Lisle is one of the most ancient of those to be found in the Island of Guernsey' (Jacob II, p. 109). **Daniel** was appointed jurat in 1742 and served as harbour supervisor in 1744. Daniel was designated merchant-shipowner *temp.* Seven Years War. **Peter** signed the Canary wine petition, 1776. Peter and **Isaac** designated merchants-shipowners *temp.* American War. Isaac De Lisle in partnership with Jean Guille and De Carterets – see under De Carteret. Peter dealing with Zephaniah Job 1788-1799. De Havilland commented to Fraissinet (Cette) that the firm of Jersey & De Lisle was a 'maison fort solide' (IAS AQ 655/312, De Havilland to Fraissinet, 3 June 1784).

De QUETTEVILLE

Nicholas corresponded with Martell. Nicholas, 'merchant', insured his dwelling house (Sun: 10/362/16308, 18 Jan 1720).

De SAU[S]MAREZ

'Certain it is that the De Sausmarez families have always been considered among the oldest and principal inhabitants of Guernsey' (Jacob II p. 15). In the late 17th century **Mathew** and **Michael** were among the leading merchants of Guernsey. They ran a successful export trade, selling Guernsey-knitted stockings in Paris. **Henry** de Saumarez claimed not to have engaged in trade, although a Henry de Saumarez did provide cellars in which Elie Perchard stored tobacco (CdA vol. 7, f 11v, 1715). Even if not a merchant, Henry's career is interesting for its maritime focus. He gave a few facts about his early life when, in 1715, he presented a petition:

> That your Petitioner being the only Son of the Deceased Reverend Doctor John De Saumarez, who was Chaplain to His Majesty King Charles the Second, Prebendary of Windsor, and Dean of Guernsey, he never applied himself to any Trade or Profession, (though he was bred in Holland to learn Commerce,) but in an easy and quiet Enjoyment of his small Estate, he took his Diversion in the Parts of Mathematicks, his Genius or Inclination being that way, for Machines and Inventions, wherein he spent about Twenty-two Years last past, confining himself to a retired sort of Life within his little Elaboratory: And of late he fixed his Projects upon a particular Invention towards the Improvement of Navigation, which your Petitioner could not bring forth to Effect in the said Island for want of able Workmen; but being lately come over to London on purpose, he hath actually begun, and hopes (with the Blessing of God) to bring it to some Perfection.

Henry's petition was submitted to the Royal Society and concerned one of his inventions:

> The making of a Dial, which being placed any where on Board of a Ship, will by Correspondence with a small Wheel moving under Water, and a little Bell striking with the said Dial, curiously demonstrate the Geometrical Paces, Miles, or Leagues, which the Ship hath run; which being applied in a proper manner, will be of little or no Hindrance to the Course or Sailing of the Ship. The said Wheel shall turn in any Depth of the Sea, so that no Storm, nor rough Sea, nor the violent Motion of the Ship, will alter, hinder, nor stop the regular Working thereof, but the Swiftness and Slowness of the Ship shall be seen and heard by the striking of the little Bell in the said Dial.

Henry had hopes of winning the prize offered by the Board of Longitude. He petitioned not only the Royal Society, but also the King, Trinity House, and the Admiralty. Isaac Newton considered the matter and reported that Henry's invention was much like an earlier device of Mr Savery, which had been found less exact than the log-line. In 1717 Henry published an account of his efforts to get his invention accepted. He continued his campaign into the 1720s. The following is an account of an experiment that he conducted in the autumn of 1720. It is of interest for the details that it gives about masters and sailors of the era:

> Here follow the affidavits of some expert seamen, who made trial of Mr. De Saumarez's instrument, as taken under the seal of the Royal Court of Guernsey.
>
> William Ahier, about 40 years of age, who commanded several privateers in the late war, particularly, that call'd La Chasse, of about 150 tun, 16 guns and 140 men, and then master of the ship call'd the Eagle, made oath, that on October 9, 1720, he parted from Southampton with several gentlemen passengers on board, for the island of Guernsey; that he had fixed at the stern of his ship, a new invention, call'd the marine-surveyor, projected to the best of his knowledge, by Mr. Henry De Saumarez, a gentleman of the island of Guernsey, for correcting the log; &c. that after they had left the Needles, they had a fast gale of wind, attended with a rolling sea; notwithstanding which, the machine worked as regularly as if it had been smooth water, the little bell of it striking with great exactness to every mile the ship run; and that having thoroughly viewed and examin'd the experiment of this new invention, he found it to be not only practicable, but preferable to the common methods, used at sea, for finding the ship's distance sailed; that therefore for the public good, he attests the truth of the above mentioned particulars.

Abraham Le Mesurier, of about 48 years of age, formerly the captain of several ships; Peter Bonamy, of about 58 years of age, formerly the captain of several ships, and who had used the sea upwards of 40 years; John Hardy, of about 38 years of age, formerly the captain of several ships, the abovesaid William Ahier, and James Hubert of about 27 years of age, who had also been master of several vessels, made oath, that on October 19, 1720, they set sail in the morning out of Guernsey pier, with a fresh gale of wind, in a sloop, called the Dolphin, in company with several Gentlemen of the said island, in order to make an experiment at sea of a machine, called the marine-surveyor, projected, to the best of their knowledge, by Mr. Henry De Saumarez of Guernsey, which invention is intended to correct the many errors of the log, &c. And they farther declare, that they have not only thoroughly viewed, considered, and examined the said machine; but also made several experiments of it in a rough sea, sometimes sailing right before the wind, then quartering, and at other times turning to windward, and then lying by, in order to know the drift of the ship, both with and against the tide; that having tried the same invention all manner of ways, they find it much preferable to the log, or any of the methods in use for obtaining the ship's distance run, having nothing to object against it, as to its being a clog or hinderance to the sailing of the ship, &c. That being fully satisfied of the great usefulness of this invention for the improvement of navigation, and the service it may be of to all the maritime powers, they publickly attest the truth of the above-mentioned particulars.

The Marine Surveyor was not Henry's only achievement. He carried out a survey of local waters; made measurements of the tides in the River Thames; and made a chart of Alderney and its waters (see Plates I, II and XIII).

Bibliography:

'An account of a new machine, called the Marine Surveyor, contrived for the Mensuration of the way of a ship in the Sea, more correctly than by the Log, or any other method hitherto used for that purpose; together with several testimonials, setting forth the usefulness of this invention' by Mr Henry de Saumarez of the Island of Guernsey, *Philosophical Transactions of the Royal Society*, vol. 33 (1725), pp. 411-432.

'Observations upon the tides in the River Thames' by Mr Henry de Saumarez, *Philosophical Transactions of the Royal Society*, vol. 34 (1726), pp. 68-72.

'A further account of a new machine, called the Marine Surveyor, designed for the mensuration of the way of a ship at sea, more correctly than by the log, at present in use, or any other method invented for that purpose', *Philosophical Transactions of the Royal Society*, vol. 36 (1729), pp. 45-58.

Later in the eighteenth century **Mathieu** de Sausmarez was designated as a merchant-shipowner *temp*. Seven Years War; and imported wine (*Livre de certificats*). Several members of the family turned away from trading and became deeply involved with the Royal Navy. Captain Philip de Saumarez (1710-1747) served as a lieutenant in the *Centurion* under Commodore Anson. He was killed in command of the *Nottingham*, in 1747, in Lord Hawke's action. Captain Thomas Saumarez, younger brother of Philip, also accompanied Anson around the world. He became Commander of the ship *Antelope* and 'was employed in convoying the trade between the West Indies and Bristol, during which service he was greatly distinguished' (Jacob, 1830, vol. 2, p. 38). Sir James, who became Admiral the Right Honourable Lord de Saumarez (1757- 1836) was the nephew of Philip and Thomas. He entered the Royal Navy at the age of fourteen and had a long and brilliant career. He distinguished himself during the Napoleonic wars by his naval victories and by his diplomacy in the Baltic. (There is an excellent new work on Admiral Saumarez: - T. Voelcker, *Admiral Saumarez versus Napoleon*, Woodbridge, 2008 – which provides a helpful background for understanding the maritime/mercantile issues of the era).

DOBRÉE

'This family have from an early date numbered with the ancient leading families of Guernsey, and have been connected with most of them in marriage' Jacob II p. 254. The Dobrée family came from France and settled in Guernsey in the sixteenth century. They were very active in Guernsey trade in the eighteenth century as the following list demonstrates:

Samuel and **Nicholas** corresponded with Martell. **Peter, Isaac, Thomas fs Nicholas** leading merchants 1752. **Isaac, Nicholas, Nicholas younger, Peter elder, Peter younger, Thomas, Thomas fs Nicholas** designated merchants-shipowners *temp.* Seven Years War. **Nicholas, Thomas,** and **William** members of the *Société des Veuves*. **Peter** and **Thomas** signed the Canary wine petition. Thomas imported wine (*Livre de certificats*). Thomas listed among leading merchants-traders, 1779. **Nicholas, Thomas,** and **John** merchant-shipowners *temp.* American War. **Harry** vice-consul [in Guernsey] for Hanover, Naples and Sicily, Denmark and the Grand Duchy of Mecklenburgh 1820s (*Guernsey Almanacs*).

[A] The branch of John (1597-), the 'Beauregard branch'

Peter (1722-1808) nicknamed 'the Cardinal' – his sons were much involved in trade:

    a. (Peter) Bonamy (1755-1825) married into the Mourant family.

    b. Elisha (1756-1845)

    c. Samuel (1759-1827) married into the wealthy Hankey family.

    d. Peter (1760-1843) merchant, Gracechurch St, Clapham.

    e. Helier (1761-1846) 'of Hauteville'- his sons became merchants

        Henry (1794-1875) merchant, Naples.

        John (1799-1879) merchant, Palermo & Naples.

    f. John (1766-1812) joined H.E.I.C.

[B] The branch of Samuel (1635-1691), shipowner, one of the principal stocking manufacturers in Guernsey in the 1670s. His sons entered trade:

a. John (1665-1728) of the Pollet, a woollen merchant.

b. William (1674-1760) merchant-banker in London (by 1701), agent for Guernsey privateers with shares in twenty-five privateers by 1709. In 1712 he opened an account with the Bank of England; principal banker to Guernsey for the next forty years. O.s.p.

c. Peter (1676-1715) merchant and agent to Prince George of Denmark. Married Martha Carey.

        His son, Peter (1714-1754) was a 'merchant of Monument Yard, London'.

d. Nicholas (1678-1751) If any one person may be seen as the founder of St Peter Port as a successful entrepôt, that person is Nicolas Dobrée. He advocated the completion of the north pier project; this rendered the harbour more sheltered. He supported the building of the 'hospital'; this helped to solve the problem of urban poverty and the hospital inmates laboured at tasks useful to the port (such as rope-making). Finally, he published a series of charts of Guernsey, Alderney, Sark, Herm, and Jethou based upon his personal survey. The charts were issued with an accompanying pamphlet of *Observations*, which described and discussed the maritime hazards around the islands. In his preface he explains:

> The Author, who has been for many Years in Trade, having observed the Fear as well as the Danger to which all Ships, unacquainted with the Island of Guernsey, are exposed, when they come there, for want of a correct Chart (all those that have hitherto been published being very faulty, and of dangerous Consequence to those who might sail by them) endeavoured to persuade several Masters of Ships and Pilots to undertake such a Work; but none of them being willing, he at last resolved, for the publick Good, to

	1	2	3	4	5	6
A	[Branch of John]	Elisha (1663-1727)	Elisha (1698-1729)	Peter (1722-1808)	a.(Peter) Bonamy (1755-1825) b.Elisha (1756-1845) c.Samuel (1759-1827) d.Peter (1760-1843) e.Helier (1761-1846) f.John (1766-1812)	Peter Bonamy --------------- Henry John
B	Samuel (1635-1691)	a. John (1665-1728) b.William (1674-1760) c. Peter (1676-1715) --------------- d. Nicholas (1678-1751)	Samuel (1686-1719) --------------- Elisha (1692-1758) --------------- Peter (1714-1754) --------------- Nicholas (1703-1746) Peter (1707-1773) William (1718-1741) Isaac (1719-1763) Judith Elizabeth Mary	Elisha (1715-1767) --------------- Elisha (1723-1798) --------------- William (d.1784) --------------- Thomas (1728-1798) Nicholas (1732-1800)	--------------- Peter Paul (1782-1825) Pierre-Frédéric (1757-1801)	
C	Thomas (1640-1715)	Thomas (1676-1738) Samuel (b.1689)	Nicholas (1715-1768) Thomas (1725-1784)			

make and perfect the Charts now published. To which Purpose he has been on all the Rocks and dangerous Places, has taken all the Soundings, and examined the Ebbings and Flowings of the Tide, in order to place them all in the most exact manner; and that Strangers might the more easily come to, or go from Guernsey or Alderney, he has drawn the following Instructions, by the help of which they may come to these Islands without the least Fear.

Dobrée printed a testimonial in the *Observations*:

We the under-signed Commanders, and Masters of Ships, as well as Pilots and Fishermen, belonging to this Island of Guernsey, do hereby certify, that the Maps or Charts of the said Island, and Dangers adjacent, drawn by Nicholas Dobrée, Senior, of this said Island, Esq; have been examined by us, and that we find them very correct; and Strangers observing the Marks and Directions placed therein, may come safe, and without Danger into the Road and Harbour thereof. Given under our Hands at Guernsey aforesaid, this first Day of February, 1745-6.

Abraham Le Mesurier, Michael Robinson, Elias Pitton, Junior, Ab. Le Mesurier, Son of Abr. Daniel Roland, Stephen Mourant, Andrew Naftel, Michael Thoume, Andrew Naftel, Junior, Peter Ougier, Philip Bott, Elizee Henry, Jean de France, Pierre Herivel.

Nicholas (1678-1751) had seven children:

1. Nicholas (1703-1746) trading on his own account by 1737; trading with Barbados; his son

    a. Thomas (1728-1798), a Guernsey merchant; and son

        Pierre-Frédéric went to Lorient and then to Nantes (see pp. 107 – 110).

    b. Nicholas (1732-1800) 'of Bellevue'; visited Canton (see p. 45) and became a merchant.

2. Peter (1707-1773) merchant, trading on his own account by 1741.

3. William (1718-1741) buying wine in Provence 1737; stayed in Cognac with his cousin Anthony Le Mesurier who had settled there. Misbehaved. Went on Anson trip; died of scurvy 1741.

4. Isaac (1719-1763): staying with uncle William in London at age of 14. He travelled in the Low Countries and France (from Rotterdam to Cognac). Back in Guernsey he was both a merchant and notary public. Importing wine, in partnership with Jean Careye (CdA, vol. 14, 5 Feb 1763).

5-7 And three daughters:

Judith, who married John Carey, 1732.

Elizabeth.

Mary, who married Henry Le Mesurier of Alderney, 1742.

[C] The branch of Thomas (1640-1715)

Thomas (1676-1738), merchant of Guernsey, greffier, married (1) Esther Hampton (2) Elizabeth Careye de la brasserie (widow of Elisha Dobrée of Beauregard). This Thomas probably = the Thomas who insured with the Sun Fire Company his 'dwelling house situate between the houses of Aaron Guillaume & the heirs of Elisha Saumarez' (Sun: 10/421/-).

Samuel (b. 1689) married Mary de Quetteville (member of a merchant family).

Bibliography: Hocart 1983; Priaulx, family files.

DOUGLAS

Ninian, merchant, 'in the island of Guernsey', mentioned in the will of Benjamin Douglas, s. of George Douglas of Jedburgh; will proved 30 Dec 1796 (EC Wills 1795-1803, pp. 70-72).

DUNIERE

Louis, merchant, from Quebec; see P.L. Wickins, 'The Economics of Privateering: Capital Dispersal in the American War of Indepenence', Journal of European Economic History, vol. 13, no 2 – Fall 1984, p 389. For Dunière see *Dictionary of Canadia Biography* vol. 5, 1801-1820, Toronto, 1982, pp. 283-284. Merchant-shipowner *temp.* American War. See pp. 155-156.

FALLA

Michel, correspondent of Martell. Michael and John, 'dealers in wine brandy' c. 1732 (CUL).

FIOT(T)

Thomas Fiott, harbour supervisor in 1705, 1716, 1733. **Fiott and Martell** partners, Bordeaux, 1724-5, 'buying Margaux at 350 livres per barrel: in other words they had dealings at the top end of the London market (Haut Brion and Margaux). Wine was consigned directly to Elisha Dobrée in London. The brandy business in Cognac was handled on his behalf by his fellow Channel Islander, Le Mesurier. The partnership with Fiott ended in 1725, apparently as a result of a falling out among the circle of Guernsey men who provided the custom for the business' (Cullen 2000, p. 31).

Laurens Fiott, harbour supervisor in 1743. 'A letter dated 20.i.1749 from Mr. Matt. Perchard to Mr. Laurens Fiott states that a certain Mr. Patrick Wood, "painter" used to frequent the "White Hart" in Abchurch Lane. This Mr. Wood had in his possession "Camden's MS.", and at the request of Mr. Perchard he copied therefrom the arms of a family of a name which was near enough to that of Fiott to suit the heraldic ambitions of Laurens Fiott. Hence the Fiott arms' (Rybot 1928, p.348).

FRECKER

Abraham, vintner, from Gosport, Isle of Wight; will proved 19 Sept 1761; EC Wills 1754-62, p. 208.

FRERE

Pierre imported wine from Barcelona and Oporto between 1774-1788 (*Livre de certificats*). He had links with Le Fort at La Rochelle and with P.C. Lambert at Paris (Priaulx Library, Guille journal of French tour, 1787). PF had been in the West India trade (Priaulx Library, John Guille letterbook, p. 124). The Frère family was prominent in Barbados in the eighteenth century (H. Beckles, *A History of Barbados*, Cambridge, 1990, p. 43). Guille recommended PF: 'you run no risk in accepting Mr Frere's bills as I know he does not out run his capital in his affairs and is a very honest man I mention this being acquainted with the greatest part of his transactions (Priaulx Library, Guille letterbook, p. 133).

GOGUET

Jean, merchant-shipowner *temp.* American War.

GOVER

Robert, master and joint owner (with James Le Ray) of the snow *Princess of Wales* (90 tons, 11 crew; plantation-built 1734, registered at Guernsey 3 Aug 1736) shipping wine and European goods to South Carolina (arrived 15 Nov 1736); and taking rice, pitch, tar, turpentine, mahogany planks to Falmouth. CO 5/510 ff<10> , <36>.

Master and owner of *Mary* (ship, 130 tons, built in New England 1736, registered at Guernsey 6 Oct 1737), carrying rum and sugar from Barbados to Virginia, arrived 2 June 1739 (TNA CO 5/1446 f <80>). *Mary* visiting Virginia, 1740, 1741 (TNA CO 5/1446 *passim*).

GREGORY

Mark Gregory was not a Guernsey merchant but he has been included because he was a member of the *Société des Veuves* and had very close ties to the Guernsey merchants, especially the Guille family. We first find him operating as a merchant at Cowes, I-of-W. In December 1764 there was Petersburg hemp lying at Cowes with Mark Gregory that could be delivered to Portsmouth (TNA ADM 106/1136/179, 12 Dec 1764). In 1765 he subscribed to *The American Negotiator: or, the various currencies of the British Colonies in America*. He then makes London his centre and through directories we can chart his progress: merchant at Will's Coffee House, Cornhill, 1768-1772; later at 12 Castle Court, Holborn in 1779, 1780; then at 8 King's Arms Yard, Coleman Street, where, in August 1781, Gregory insured his 'brick, small part timber' house for £550, utensils, stock and goods for £1500, printed books for £50, wearing apparel for £50, china and glass for £100 (Guildhall, Sun Fire Insurance Policy: vol 295/policy 447133). In August 1784 he was returned as M.P. for Newtown, I-o-W. and represented the seat until 1790. Holden's London Directory for 1790 lists him as 'His Majesty's Consul Abroad for Spain at Malaga for the protection of trade'. According to Namier and Brooke (1964) vol.2, p. 536, Gregory was 'a London corn and flour merchant with correspondents at Leith, Liverpool, and Lynn. He also traded with Spain and Turkey, and was partner in a commercial house at Barcelona'. Gregory 'seems to have gone to the Continent some time in 1791 or 1792; spent a considerable time touring French industrial towns; and died in Paris 1 May 1793'. For terms of Barcelona partnership *vide supra*, pp. 66 - 67.

GRUT

Paul, signed the Canary wine petition, 1776.

[de] GUERIN

A Huguenot family. Young **Daniel** escaped the persecutions. A family servant 'concealed him, provided him with a suit of clothes to disguise him as a shepherd, and supplied him with money. Daniel made his escape over the Pyrenees, worked his way through Spain and Portugal, and after much suffering and privation, reached Lisbon in a state of destitution. He hastened to the quay, where, whilst speaking to the sailors belonging to a vessel flying the English ensign, he was accosted by Mr. Peter Martin, of Guernsey, who perceiving, in spite of his condition, that he was a gentleman, kindly took him to his house, fed and clothed him during his stay, and gave him passage in the vessel to Guernsey, also a letter of recommendation to the Messrs Carey, of the Brasserie, in whose office he remained several years. On his arrival in Guernsey, Daniel de Guérin was admitted to the sacraments of the Protestant Church' (de Guérin, 1890, pp. 84-85).

Daniel's descendant **Elias** was a leading merchant/trader 1779. Elias' son **Thomas** was in partnership with Abraham Naftel and Thomas Corbin (IAS, letterbook AQ 276/11 letter to J Le Marchant, 24 July 1781).

GUILLE

'This is a very ancient Guernsey family' (Jacob II p. 150). **John jr** and **Thomas** belonged to the *Société des Veuves*, listed as merchants. **Jean senr** and **jr** imported wine (*Livre de certificats*). Thomas leading merchant/trader 1779. **Richard**, John merchants-shipowners *temp*. American War.

A notebook /diary for the years 1714-1721 kept by **Jean** (1674-1721) reveals a countryman

Jean Guille (1674-1721) Elizabeth	Jean senr (1712-1778)	John Jnr (1733-1820) Thomas (b.1737) Nicholas (1742-1797) Charles Richard (1745-1818)	William (1766-1792) George (1768-1792) John

who also had shipping interests. In 1712 he was involved in the purchase of *La Fidélité* (250 tons), commanded by Peter Tupper and owned by Jean Tupper. In 1713 Guille went to St Malo to engage crew for *la Fidélité*, to go fishing at Newfoundland (Priaulx; ms. discussed by Moullin, TSG 1950, pp. 44 - 58; but see now Hocart 2007).

His sister Elizabeth married Andrew Lovic, from England, and the couple emigrated to the West Indies, to Basseterre, St Christopher. Jean (1712-1778) tried to arrange for his aunt to visit Guernsey. She was very isolated and his letters to her travelled *via* Mr Wm Le Mesurier merchant in Barbados (IAS 4 May 1749; 7 Aug, 3 Mar 1750). Jean suggested that his son (Jean jr), being a seafarer, could go to help her to voyage across the Atlantic. He described his son as a 'pretty & lickly Boye; he was 'near seventeen' and had been two years at sea. Jean explained to his aunt that he had 'a large familie & am resolved with ye blessing of God Allmighty to send them all abroad, no doubt America must be the lot of some'. He actively encouraged his children to travel. Jean (1712-1778) is sometimes referred to as Jean senior to distinguish him from his son, Jean junior. Jean senior imported wine, as did his son (*Livre de certificats*). Some correspondence dating from the 1750s is difficult to attribute and may relate to father or son. Given that they seem to have worked together the confusion is not serious. A letter to Jn Omnanney Esq., agent victualler of His Majesty's Navy at Plymouth, 14 Feb 1757 asked for a sample to make cordage 'there are often vessels loading limestones in Plymouth for Guernsey' (which could bring the sample, or it could be sent *via* Seward of Southampton). Jean Guille wrote to Mr James Le Marchant at Rotterdam 'il y a quelque temps que j'exerce la profession de cordier mais le chanvre a haussé tres considerablement en Angleterre' (21 Aug 1760). He subsequently ordered hemp, cloth, timber and iron from St Petersburg for himself, Messrs Le Rey, Carteret sons. He received 6 hogsheads of rum shipped by the snow *Friendship* from Barbados; Mr Abraham Le Mesurier drawing on Messrs Peter & Peter Perchard of London, 16 Sept 1761 (Priaulx, Guille papers). There are also letters at the Island Archive Service which show John Guille in correspondence with James Le Marchant of Rotterdam about hemp (Stevens-Guille, 29 Apr 1762; 2 Nov 1762; 20 Jan 1764).

Jean senr wrote to Miss Guerdeon (apparently the inheritor of a Jamaica estate) on 21 Jan 1761 (Priaulx Library), suggesting that she should marry his son *Nicholas*, aged eighteen, 'gallant, bienfait & fort sobre, bien conditionné', presently at Alderney, working for the Governor 'pour lui assister dans le commerce', the Governor treating him like a son and giving him £20 st per annum ('le regarde comme son enfant & lui donne 20£ sterling par an pour les salaires'). On Guille's death Nicholas will have 'une honete fortune'. Nicholas did not marry Miss Guerdeon, he moved to Barcelona and traded with Mark Gregory as Gregory & Guille. In 1774 Nicholas journeyed to Stockholm and 'got the place of Swedish Consul at Barcelona' (IAS Guille letterbook, 20 June 1774, 31 July 1774). On 8 June 1775 he married Caroline Carey (b. 8 Jan 1746/7), sister of John Carey 'of the Bigoterie'.

Nicholas' brother *Richard* was a merchant and traded on his own account. He was a prominent privateering agent *temp.* American War. Brother *Thomas* also was a prominent merchant. He married, first, Mary Sutton Mauger, daughter of Charles Mauger; and, secondly, Elizabeth de Beauvoir. Brother *Charles* served as a ship captain for many years, plying between Guernsey and England, on transatlantic routes, and to-and-from Spain. In 1770, for example, we find him as master of the snow *St George*, shipping wine from Gregory and Guille (loaded at Villanova) to Jean Guille, Guernsey (*Livre de certificats*); Charles was shipping wine from brother Nicholas in Catalonia to brother John in Guernsey, in a vessel named after the Guille estate. **John jr** became one of the most successful of the St Peter Port merchants. We know quite a lot about his activities thanks to the survival of family papers, including a letterbook covering the years 1777-1779. He went to sea at the age of fifteen and sailed to the Straights (IAS, Stevens-Guille, letters of Jean Guille to Elizabeth Lovic, 4 May 1749, 7 August 1749, 3 March 1750). In the 1760s he was involved with Mathew de Carteret, *armateur* of the snow *St George* (master Capt Charles de St Croix); he had, apparently, a one-fifth share (IAS Stevens-Guille papers, 21 June 1764). The snow was in the

Newfoundland trade. See pp. 137-139 for a discussion of his trade in the 1770s.

John had two sons, **William** and **George**. They helped him in his work. See pp. 55-60.

HARRIS

John George, merchant-shipowner *temp.* American War.

HARVEY

Benjamin	Henry Benjamin (in Falmouth) Sampson (in Philadelphia) John (1736-1778) (in Guernsey)	Thomas (1764-1783) John jr (1771-1820)

Benjamin, and his wife Jane, came from Cornwall and settled in St Peter Port. There were sons: Henry; Benjamin, who lived in Falmouth; Sampson, who lived in Philadelphia (USA); **John**, (1736-1778) who lived in Guernsey. John had a son Thomas (1764-1783) and a son also called John (1771-1820). In 1790 **John jr** married Elizabeth Guille (daughter of Richard Guille and Mary Mourant). According to reminiscences in a family album 'the family built up a good business as merchants during the American and the French Wars, when these islands were dependent upon armed vessels for their supplies'. There were 'friendly relations with the Cornish and American branches of the Harvey family'. In the late 18th century the family house was in the Pollet. The Harveys corresponded with S. Dobrée (London), Messrs Dobrée & Aubin (London), Messrs Perchard & Brock (London), Messrs Collings & Bowden (Rotterdam, supplying gin), Messrs Arfwidson (Gothenburg, supplying Bohea and Congo tea). John Harvey bought brandy from Gregory & Guille, Barcelona (IAS Guille letterbook, 6 Dec 1773). The Harvey family of Guernsey may have been related to the Harveys who developed the Bristol sherry company. Thomas Harvey (fl. 1807 - 1819) 'had come to Bristol from Hayle in Cornwall' (Harrison, 1955, p. 79).

HUBERT

Michael, former commander of the *Cambridge*, captured on passage from Barbados to London (Priaulx, Dobrée Protest book, 21 March 1745/6). **James**, merchant-shipowner *temp.* Seven Years War. **Peter**, signed the Canary wine petition, 1776.

ICEMONGER/ISEMONGER

Anthony, signed the Canary wine petition, 1776. Le Sieur Antoine Isemonger master of *The New London Packet* (CdA, vol. 16, 31 Aug 1776). Antoine shipping paving stones to London (CdA, vol. 16, 23 Nov 1776). Le Sieur Anthony Isemonger master of *la Princesse d'Orange* (CdA, vol. 16, 20 May 1780).

JENNINGS

John, merchant, member of the *Société des Veuves*. **George**, merchant-shipowner *temp.* American-War.

JEREMIE

John, merchant-shipowner *temp.* American War.

KENNETT

William, merchant-shipowner *temp.* American War.

His son, **Daniel Vardon** Kennett (b. 1781), was trading in Spain in the early 19th century. He entered into partnership with John Carey and was based at Tarragona and Barcelona. While Carey and Kennett worked in the north, their colleagues Métivier and DeVic Carey operated further south, in Valencia and Alicante. See p. 64.

KEYT

Richard, vintner, TC burial 9 Feb 1743.

LAGE[R]MAN

Mr Lagerman, merchant, TNA WO 34/108 f 31r, 5 Jan 1782 Irving to Amherst: 'German merchant who has resided here some years'; TNA WO 34/108 f 39r, Irving to Hill: L 'from Morlaix'. Importing wine (*Livre de certificats*). Messrs **Biggs Lageman & Co** trading in tobacco (CdA, vol. 17, 19 Aug 1780). Messrs Biggs Lageman & Co actioned by Mr Thomas Priaulx over brandy and gin supplied by TP (CdA, vol. 17, 26 Apr 1782). Messrs Biggs Lageman & Co acting for Mr Christian Lageman of Bremen, *affreteurs* of the Ostend vessel *le Vriendship*, Jean Jones master (CdA, vol. 17, 21 Oct 1782). Messrs Biggs Lageman & Co renting a vault ('voute') near the public quays, owing £12:10:0 st to Dame Marie LePatourel for two quarters' rent (CdA, vol. 18, 30 Jun 1783). Lageman agent for Gibbs of Fowey, Laurence of Cornwall (IAS Stevens-Guille letters, Wm Guille to John Carey Métivier, Guernsey, July 1791).

La SERRE

John (1682-1774), of Ville Magne in Languedoc (France), was a Huguenot doctor who found religious refuge in St Peter Port. He married Esther Whitehead (1690 – 1774) on 23 February 1725. There were three sons: William, John and Thomas. **John** was born in 1730 and became a successful merchant, accumulating a large fortune. In 1751 he married Anne Bisson, his cousin. He left no descendants and died in April 1815. The obituary in the *Star* records his death 'at his residence, in the Pollet. This gentleman was ever humane, tender, and affectionate to all around him; he never suffered any to want a blessing that he could bestow; he instructed by his life, and taught by his example, being sensible that piety is the source and foundation of every virtue'. John La Serre jr belonged to the *Société des Veuves*. John leading merchant/trader, 1779. John merchant-shipowner *temp*. American War. Mr Jean jr actioned Robert Foster master of the vessel *l'Anne* about a missing *ballot* of wool in a shipment from Southampton to Guernsey (CdA, vol. 17, 16 Nov 1782).

LAUGA

There are frequent references to the Lauga family in the second half of the eighteenth century: **John** merchant-shipowner *temp*. Seven Years War; **Solomon** belonged to the *Société des Veuves* (designated tobacconist); John Solomon and Solomon signed the Canary wine petition 1776; John Solomon leading merchant-trader, 1779; Solomon merchant-shipowner *temp*. American War.

The Lauga family were Huguenots from Clairac in Agenais (France). The family tree is not well established and is further complicated by the usage of the Christian names Solomon (often spelled Salomon) and John, generation after generation.

Solomon Lauga came to Guernsey as a religious refugee. His son John was probably the John referred to as a merchant-shipowner *temp*. Seven Years War. John's son Solomon married Jane Mansell (1735-1773). He was, perhaps, the Salomon who had owned a brigantine (*les trois frères*, CdA, vol. 14, 22 Jun 1761) and a *chasse marée* (*la Paix*, CdA, vol.14, 11 Jun 1763). In 1776 we find Mr Salomon Lauga and Mr William De Jersey acting against Mr Isaac Moses of New York *re* Teneriffe wine (CdA, vol. 16, 27 Apr 76); in 1780 Mr Salomon Lauga was in an action *re* merchandise from Cette (CdA, vol. 16, 22 Jul 1780); and in 1780 Mr Salomon Lauga was importing brandy (CdA, vol. 17, 12 Aug 1780). In June 1784 De Havilland commented to Fraissinet (Cette) that Salomon Lauga, despite having made some losses in the war, 'passe pour un homme d'une fortune aisée' (IAS AQ 655/312). In 1795 Dobrée commented that R.P. Le Marchant and Mr Lauga had imported a large quantity of wine from Bordeaux (see p. 110).

LeCOCQ

Peter and **Thomas**, merchant-shipowners *temp*. Seven Years War. le Sr Pierre Le Cocq in action *re* rum from Barbados (CdA, vol. 14, 24 Oct 1761). le Sr Pierre Le Cocq formerly part-owner (¼) of the snow *l'Aventure* (CdA, vol. 14, 7 Apr 1764). **John**, leading merchant/trader 1779.

Samuel, merchant-shipowner *temp*. American War.

Le FEBVRE

William correspondent of Martell. **Samuel** and **Daniel**, 'dealers in wine brandy' c. 1732 (CUL). Daniel, shipowner, see p. 147. Daniel Frederick Gould of Cork delivered a cargo of beef and pork on the *Friendship* to Mr Daniel le Febvre 'of this island merchant'; le Febvre was actioned because 'he has not thought proper as yet to unload ye said vessel which now remains in ye Harbour with her full loading on board' (Priaulx Library, Dobrée Protest book, 7 June 1748). Daniel, leading merchant 1752. **Nicholas** merchant-shipowner *temp*. Seven Years War.

Le LIEVRE

Peter signed the Canary wine petition, 1776. **Nicholas, Richard, Thomas** merchants-shipowners *temp*. American War.

LeMARCHANT

'This ancient noble Norman family has long been resident in Guernsey' (Jacob II, p. 201). The family dominated Guernsey in the eighteenth century. They served as harbour supervisors, e.g. Josué in 1722; Eleazar in 1723 and 1735; William in 1703, 1713, 1731, 1742, 1754; Thomas in 1727, 1738, 1749. For most of the century the bailiff was a Le Marchant: Joshua was appointed in 1728; Eleazar in 1752; William in 1771; Robert Porret in 1800 (resigned in 1810).

There were several branches to the family and it is not always easy to tease out identity. There were two prominent members of the family named **William**. The earlier (1681-1758) was sometimes distinguished by the appellation **'de l'Hyvreuse'**. He was the author of a treatise about the harbour, published in 1755. He married, first, Elizabeth (daughter of Jean Careye); and, secondly, Elizabeth (daughter of Dan Perchard).

The other **William** (1721- 1800) was appointed jurat in 1754 and sworn as bailiff in 1771. He imported wine from Lisbon, Malaga and Oporto (*Livre de certificats*). He also dealt in brandy: Mr William Le Marchant actioned for freight on 97 pipes & 6 bariques brandy from Salou (CdA, vol. 14, 16 Jun 1761). Le Marchant supplied alcohol to the Royal Navy during the Seven Years. He owned shipping (e.g. a half share in the schooner the *Oporto Merchant*, (CdA, vol. 16, 5 Apr 1777). He wrote an important defence of the privileges and liberties of Guernsey (reprinted on several occasions). William was of an autocratic disposition and became involved in a series of political disputes with leading Guernsey families. The English official Stiles visited Guernsey in 1800 and met Le Marchant:

> 'This gentleman has much power and influence; he has long been the Chief Magistrate of the Island, is a native thereof, and being allowed to possess more knowledge of its concerns than any other inhabitant, is constantly referred to on all occasions of importance, but being near eighty years of age he has lately procured from government the appointment for his son, Mr Robert Le Marchant to be his successor, who was accordingly sworn into the office of bailiff on the day I left the island. The father received me with much cordiality, and having (as he told me) been previously informed by Mr Alderman Le Mesurier of London of the nature of my mission, declared he should act openly and candidly with me, and speak his sentiments on the subject without reserve.....The substance of what passed at this interview having been communicated by the Bailiff to the jurats and merchants, the same became instantly known to all the inhabitants, and so far from receiving any insult afterwards from the lower ranks of people, I was treated by them with respect'. (TNA T64/153 pp. 5-6).

His son Robert Porret signed the Canary wine petition, 1776, and was listed as leading merchant/ trader in 1779.

James, William, Thomas leading merchants 1752. Thomas and William merchants-shipowners *temp*. Seven Years War. **John** and **Josias** were members of the *Société des Veuves*. John and Thomas imported wine from Lisbon, Malaga, Oporto, Teneriffe; William imported from Lisbon, Malaga, Oporto (*Livre de certificats*). William, John, Thomas merchants-shipowners *temp*. American War. Jean in partnership with Jean Brock (CdA, vol. 18, 17 July 1784). Cargo loaded

Quebec July 1775 by Mr **Charles** Le Marchant acting for Thomas Dobrée Ec to Barcelona to Messrs Curtoys & Co agents of Mr Dobrée (CdA, vol. 16, 14 Jun 1777).

The Rotterdam branch

At some time in the mid-eighteenth century **James** settled in Rotterdam. He was certainly established there by 3 March 1758 when he wrote to the Guernsey merchant Thomas Priaulx, addressing him as 'cher frère' (Priaulx Library, Carteret Priaulx papers). James' sister Rebecca was married to Thomas Priaulx (fs Thomas); and his sister Marie was married to the Guernsey merchant Pierre Lihou (fs James). James married twice, his second wife being Jeanne Thomas of Rotterdam. There was a daughter Jeanne, who married her Guernsey cousin **James (fs Jean)** (1760 – 1817). The nephew joined his uncle's firm in Rotterdam and they traded as **James & James Le Marchant**. The firm supplied large quantities of gin to the Guernsey merchants. The letterbook of Thomas Priaulx (Priaulx Library) shows that in 1778 the Rotterdam house was supplying Henry Brock, Carteret & Lihou, John Guille & Co., Jersey & De Lisle, John Le Marchant, Nicholas Maingy, Peter Mourant, and Thomas Priaulx (and probably others).

James (1760 – 1817) had two sons: John (b. 1785) and William (b. Rotterdam 1791 – 1835). They continued the business: a Gosselin account book (Priaulx Library) refers to John Le Marchant, Louis Wm Le Marchant and Charles Lauga trading as James & James Le Marchant of Rotterdam, supplying gin, staves and hoops to Jaques Mauger of Cherbourg, Monsieur Andrieux of Morlaix, Monsieur Lesquin of Roscoff, Monsieur Seranne of Alderney, and Jean Bouabert of Cherbourg.

LeMESURIER

'The Le Mesurier family have had lands and hereditaments in Guernsey as far back as any authentic records extend, and for nearly three hundred years members of the Le Mesurier family have held important positions in the Royal Court of Guernsey' (Jacob II p. 123). The family was deeply involved in trade in the eighteenth century.

Antoine in Cognac region, 1720s (see p. 51). **Abraham** 'dealer in wine brandy' c. 1732 (CUL). **Henry, John** and **William** were designated as merchants-shipowners *temp.* Seven Years War. John, 'merchant', was a member of the *Société des Veuves*. Henry signed the Canary wine petition, 1776. **E.** & **J.** Le Mesurier, and H. Le Mesurier, imported wine into Guernsey (*Livre de certificats*). H. Le Mesurier was a leading merchant/trader, 1779. **Havilland**, Henry, John, **Nicholas**, and **Peter** Le Mesurier were merchants-shipowners *temp.* American War. De Havilland refers to Nicholas Le Mesurier (fs Nicolas des Maumarquis, deceased), aged twenty years, as being in partnership with Jean Le Mesurier. De Havilland considered that this firm would flourish but that it did not have much capital at the time of his writing (IAS AQ 655/312, De Havilland to Fraissinet, 3 June 1784).

The *Rough Index to Le Mesurier or Le Messurier papers* privately printed (compiled by A. Le Mesurier, 1910, copy in 'Family Files' at Priaulx Library) helps with identification. I have used the numbering system of the Rough Index to assist cross-referencing.

There were two branches of the family that were particularly involved in trade: the sons of Abraham and the sons of Jean.

[A] The sons of Abraham Le Mesurier had strong connections with Barbados and London.

(a) Elizée (1712 – c.1777, 230), merchant, sometime in partnership with his brother Jean.

(b) Jean (1713 – 1792; 231), plantation owner in Barbados; in his will he gave to John Spooner of Barbados and James Butler Harris of Powis Place all his plantations, lands, tenements, etc., and all his houses, slaves and their offspring, cattle and utensils in trust for Mary, the widow of his brother Nicholas for her life, and after that to her sons William and Samson. Will proved in London 8.xi.1792.

(c) William (b. 1716; 233) was in Barbados in the 1730s-1750s and then returned to Europe; *circa*

[A] Abraham	a. Elizée (1712-1777) [230] b. Jean (1713-1792) [231] c. William (b.1716) [233] d. Abraham (1718-1802) [234] e. Mathieu (1728-1750) [239] f. Nicholas (1730-1780) [240]	Peter (1769-1832) [299]
[B] Jean (1682-1722) [205]	a. Henry (1713-1779) [274] ------------------------------ b. John (1717-1793) [284]	Martha m. (1744-1787) Benjamin (1767-1836) ------------------------------ Peter (1750-1803 [357] Frederick (1753-1783 [358] Paul (1755-1805) [359] Havilland (1758-1806) [364]

1756 he was established in London, where he died some years later.

(d) Abraham (1718 – 1802, 234), married Judith Carey and established himself in London where he acted as banker. Abraham's son

> Peter (1769? – 1832, 299) was appointed a writer in the East India Company; he married Harriet Bond (daughter of Charles Bond, Commodore E.I.C. Marine and Naval C. in C 1798-1803. Harriet's sister Hannah was married to John Ravenshaw, E.I. Director). In 1800 Peter became Factor and Deputy Secretary Public Department, Bombay; in 1804 he was Senior Merchant; in 1805 Civil Paymaster and Assistant to the Collector of Bombay and Salsette. In 1806 Collector of Bombay, Salsette and Caranja and Custom Master at Tanna and Caranja. During the years 1817-1826 he was at Manilla.

(e) Mathieu (1728 – 1750, 239), died at Guinea (i.i. 1750) *en voyage*. He was, presumably, involved in a slaving expedition.

(f) Nicholas (1730 – 1780, 240), married a West Indian lady, Mary Nicolls, in Barbados, in 1769; he died in London.

[B] The sons of Jean Le Mesurier (1682-1722), Governor of Alderney. His sons Henry (1713 – 1779) and John (1717 – 1793) both traded in Guernsey at various times.

(a) Henry (1713 – 1779, 274) succeeded as Governor of Alderney.

> (i) Henry's daughter Martha (1744 – 1787) married Peter Perchard in 1768; Peter subsequently became Sheriff and Lord Mayor of London, 1804.

> (ii) Henry's son Benjamin (1767-1836) succeeded his patron and brother-in-law Peter Perchard in business under the name of Brock and Le Mesurier. He resided in the Triangle, Hackney. The business failed in 1811/ 1812; he eventually retired to Guernsey.

(b) John (1717 – 1793, 284) Governor of Alderney (by exchange) in 1744. He married Martha, daughter of Peter Dobrée. Although based in Alderney, John frequently visited Guernsey. His son Peter wrote to brother Frederick 17 Nov 1773: 'My father has taken lodgings at Mr Vardon which he has furnished with some of my grandmother's old things. It is much better to have lodgings than to trouble a friend every time we go there' (Priaulx, Le Mesurier papers, Peter Le M. to Frederick Le M.). John corresponded with his son Frederick about business affairs and involved him in some. On 22 Dec 1777 he wrote: Mr Bell 'can always get it [*claret*] ready in time when we can be sure of a vessel for Madeira. We have wrote to Cherbourg to know if we can send Capt Caubisson (Falaise) which I suppose will meet with no difficulty. As soon as we are sure of that you may send any articles from London you'll think proper.' On 15 Jan 1778 he wrote again: 'Before I left Guernsey I agreed with Messrs Thomas Dobrée that we should freight Captn Caubisson (that is Thos Falaise's sloop) to go to Madeira, altho' Mr Dobrée's friend in London should refuse to be concerned with us, and we propose that we shall sail for Madeira about the middle of next month…You'll do well not to speak to any body about this expedition…'. Two weeks later John explained that the *Falaise* would be sent to Madeira. The sloop had gone to Lorient but would soon be back. John added: 'There are two other young fellows who will most likely go with Mr Hocart to London to enter in your ship; one is Pierre Martin, a cooper, and the other, Wm Batiste, a brother of our chambermaid. Neither of them have been to sea; but they are stout young fellows, and you know that these islanders become sailors much sooner than those born at a distance from the coast' (Priaulx, Le Mesurier papers, John Le M. to Frederick Le M., 29 Jan 1778).

John's sons prospered.

(i) Peter (1750 – 1803, 357) in turn became Governor of Alderney (1791). When the British government investigated smuggling in the Channel Islands, Peter enlisted the services of his brother Paul [(iii) below]. Stiles records:

'On the 4th of September he [*Peter Le Mesurier*] did me the honour to call upon me, accompanied by his brother, Mr Alderman Le Mesurier of London. He began the conference by acknowledging the receipt of my letter and its inclosure, to which he assured me he would return an answer: but said as he had written to the Duke of Portland, submitting his claim to an indemnification, in case smuggling should be abolished, something like what was done in the case of the Isle of Man, he therefore requested leave to delay his answer, until he should be honoured with one from His Grace, adding at the same time, there was no doubt but that every order government might think proper to give, would be duly carried into effect.' (TNA T64/153 p. 40).

(ii) Frederic(k) (1753 – 1783, 358) served in the H.E.I.C., eventually becoming captain of the *Ponsborne* (804 tons, built 1780; principal owner Thomas Lane). In 1779/80 Frederick took the *Ponsborne* on a voyage to Madras, Bombay and China (Farrington, 1999).

(iii) Paul (1755 – 1805, 359) was sent to London to take up a business career under the auspices of his relative Peter Perchard. He made a good marriage to Mary Roberdeau, daughter of Isaac Roberdeau, and niece of Noah Le Cras Esq., merchant of Walbrook, London. The firm of Le Cras and Le Mesurier made large sums of money during the American War by acting as prize agents. By 1784 Paul was a director of the H.E.I.C. and served intermittently until 1804. He became an alderman of London in 1784 and was MP for Southwark, 1784 – 1796. He spoke on a variety of subjects 'but most often on East India Company affairs'. He supported Pitt's India bill (1784), sometimes spoke in defence of Warren Hastings; and voted for Pitt's parliamentary reform proposals. He was in partnership with Frederick Samuel Secretan (b. 1750, Lausanne - 1837) from 1789 to 1796. The partners 'owned a whaling vessel, the 220-ton Guernsey Lily built 1789 in Bristol and commanded by Captain Folger, an American from Nantucket. It fished both in the Bering Straits, and off Grenada and Barbados' (Turner, 1989, p. 3). When war came the partners provided bonds for privateers and acted as ships' agents. Le Mesurier was appointed colonel of the Honorable Artillery Company 1792; Sheriff of London, 1796, then Lord Mayor, 1797. He took his brother Havilland into partnership in 1797, trading under the name of P & H Le Mesurier of no 3 Austin Friars. His funeral was particularly grand. (See Meyer 2004 B).

(iv) Havilland (1758 – 1806, 364). Born in Guernsey; scholarship to Winchester 1770; spent the next few years as a merchant with his father and brother Peter. In 1782 he married Elizabeth Dobrée. He was joint deputy (with John Dumaresq of Jersey) in presenting a humble memorial from the merchants of the islands of Jersey & Guernsey to the Lords Commissioners of His Majesty's Treasury, making representations about the trade of the islands (TNA, PC 1/3465B, 26 Jan 1785). He joined a large mercantile firm at Le Havre; engaged in the slave trade (see p. 215); then moved to London. Early in the war he was appointed adjutant commissary-general of stores, supplies and storage with British forces on the continent. He returned to England in 1795 and traded with his brother Paul as 'P and H le Mesurier, of Austin Friars, Merchants'. He was appointed Commissary-General. (See Meyer 2004 A).

Le RAY

James 'dealer in wine brandy' c. 1732 (CUL). James was trading to Virginia and South Carolina in the 1730s onwards. He owned several vessels (see p. 80), one of which (*Two Brothers*), owned jointly with his brother John, was seized in the port of Halifax in 1761 for smuggling wine etc. at Isle of Bic (see p. 78). James was one of the wealthiest merchants in St Peter Port in the mid-eighteenth century (IAS, CO Taxe).

Le ROY

Rybot comments: '**James** Le Roy, son of Jean, member of a family of landowners in the Castel Parish. He and his partners were owners of successful privateers and succeeded in amassing a considerable fortune. This branch of the family is now extinct in the Island, but they were undoubtedly originally of the same stock as the country family of Le Ray who still spell their name as pronounced in the vernacular' (Rybot, 1928, p. 343).

James, merchant-shipowner *temp*. Seven Years War. James, merchant, member of the *Société des Veuves*. In 1772 Guille (Guernsey) reported to Gregory & Guille (Barcelona) that Mr James Le Roy had found the brandy that he had received from them 'seedy' (IAS, Stevens-Guille collection, letterbook, Guille to Gregory & Guille, 31 December 1772).

LIHOU

James Lihou imported wine (*Livre de certificats*). James Lihou Ec. acts for Messrs Robert Foster & Co Bordeaux (CdA, vol. 16, 10 Aug 76); Mr James Lihou, constable of St Peter Port, in action over part of a cargo of wheat loaded by Messrs Reserson, Tupper and Kirkpatrick at Ostend (CdA, vol. 18, 3 Apr 1783). **Thomas** Lihou signed the Canary wine petition, 1776.

Peter, member of the *Société des Veuves*, listed as 'yeoman'. Leading merchant/trader, 1779; designated merchant-shipowner *temp* American War. The letterbook of Peter (1766 to 1780) is housed at the Priaulx Library. Initially Peter was in partnership with Charles de Carteret and traded as **Carteret & Lihou;** but de Carteret, feeling unwell and suffering from gout, made way for Lihou (July 1780). Lihou was the brother-in-law of James Le Marchant, Rotterdam; cargoes were sometimes carried from Rotterdam to St Peter Port on the brig of 'notre neveu James Le Marchant'. In November 1773 PL joined with Richard de Jersey, Charles de Carteret, Nicholas Maingy and Pierre Bonamy, to buy tobacco from Mr John Blan, Blandford, Virginia; the partners drew on William de Jersey (brother of Richard); the order was for 160 hogsheads of 'your very best long strong leaf sweet scented upland tobacco of a black brown colour & none of your white pale short leaf'. The order was later (27 Dec 1773) increased to 200 hogsheads and twenty thousand of hogshead and barrel staves. Apart from tobacco, Lihou also traded in gin and brandy.

Peter Lihou's Correspondents			
England	London	William de Jersey	banker
	Southampton	William Seward	agent
	Cawsand	John Borlase; Anthony Plumleigh; Peter Tonkin	smuggling accounts
Denmark	Copenhagen	John Brown	tea
France	St Malo	Sebire l'aîné	
Holland	Rotterdam	James Le Marchant (brother-in-law)	gin, tea, staves, hoops, sling stuff
Spain	Barcelona	Gregory & Guille Courtys Barry Aguals & Co	brandy, wine
Sweden	Gottenburg	Arfwidson; John George Eckmann	tea

LUDLAM

Peter Ludlam 'merchant' insured his dwelling house 'brick, stone & tiled' for £320, wearing apparel not exceeding £40, plate not exceeding £40 (Sun: vol. 267/399905, July 1778); listed as a leading merchant/trader 1779. Mr Pierre Ludlam selling cloth and silk handkerchiefs (CdA, vol. 17, 6 Mar 1783).

LUKIS

The Lukis family came to Guernsey in the late seventeeth century. William moved from the centre of St Peter Port to a more salubrious site in the Grange. His son, John, prospered. **John** (1753-1832) was a merchant and supplied Cornish smugglers (Zephaniah Job, 1790-1808). He married Sarah Collings of the merchant family; and two of his daughters married into the Collings family. (E.F.Lukis, 'The Lukis family of Guernsey', Review of the Guernsey Society, Winter 1974, vol. xxx, no. 3, pp. 79-82; H. Sebire, *From Antiquary to Archaeologist: Frederick Corbin Lukis of Guernsey*, Newcastle 2007).

McBRIDE

Duncan imported wine (*Livre de certificats*).

MACHON/MASHON

Daniel Mashon of Guernsey, merchant and owner of the sloop called *Judith* of Guernsey, in action concerning threatening words used by Charles Norris (Southampton Archive Service SC/9/4/283 31 Dec 1742). *Judith*, 'sloop of this said island', (Dan Machon owner, Peter Boucaut sailor) was loaded at Scotch Warf on the River Thames with a cargo of 86 chests of soap for the account of Mr Peter Dobrée 'of this island merchant' and 14 bags of wool for the account of Darel Carey 'of this island merchant'. There was a problem loading the fourteenth bag but the authorities insisted on it being taken as it had been cleared (Priaulx, Dobrée Protest book, 22 Feb 1745/6).

MACULLOCK

John James Macullock importing from Barcelona (see p. 63).

MAINGY

Nicholas Maingy '& fils' involved in a court action *re* rum shipped from St Croix on *le Lord North* (master le Sieur Leonard Jehan, CdA, vol. 16, 7 Dec 1776); actioned *re* freight on 198 pieces of merchandise from Rotterdam loaded by Roche & Lihou (CdA, vol. 16, 21 Feb 1778); importing brandy from Cette (CdA, vol. 16, 22 July 1780). Nicholas Maingy and brothers dealing with Zephaniah Job, 1778-1808. **Pierre** Maingy to purchase 40 *bottes* rum for Guille at St Croix (IAS Guille letterbook, 12 March 1773). Messrs Pierre Maingy & Co importing gin from Rotterdam (CdA, vol. 16, 14 Nov 1778). Nicholas and Peter leading merchants/traders 1779; Nicholas and Peter merchants-shipowners *temp*. American War; Nicholas, Peter senr, Peter junr, Thomas, John - privateering, French Revolution Wars.

London Gazette, Tuesday 23 June 1840, no 19868, p. 1495: '...the Queen has been pleased to grant unto Thomas Maingy of the Isle of Guernsey, William Maingy of the City of St Petersburg, Bonamy Maingy of the Isle of Guernsey, son of Thomas Maingy of the same island, Peter Maingy, Commander in the Royal Navy, Anthony de la Combe-Maingy, late in the Civil Service of the East India Company on the Madras establishment, son of Peter Maingy, John Maingy of Guernsey, Henry Maingy, Commander in the Royal Navy, Charles Maingy of the City of Naples, merchant, John Maingy of Guernsey, her Royal Licence and Authority that they and their issue respectively may henceforth take the surname Maingay...'

MANSELL

Several members of this family served in the East India Company. **James Perchard** Mansell, commander H.E.I.C. navy 1776-1810. **John** served in H.E.I.C. navy 1798-1805. **William** (1780-1869), surgeon H.E.I.C. **Samuel** (1788-1819), lieutenant H.E.I.C. (*The Mansell Family a brief sketch of the career of some of its members*, Guernsey, 1895).

MARTEL[L]

Jean, of Jersey origin, served an apprenticeship in Guernsey and then moved to France. He played an important role in developing the Cognac brandy industry and exporting wine from Bordeaux. See Cullen (1998) and Cullen (2000); see also pp. 22, 51.

MARTIN

Pierre served as harbour supervisor in 1714. **Laurent** set up Martell in business and encouraged him to go to Cognac. 'Martell retained a sense of indebtedness to him' (Cullen 2000, p. 3). Madame **Jeanne** Martin was a correspondent of Martell. See also p. 190 under Guérin

MAUGER

Rybot refers to the arms of the Mauger family blazoned on china plates and comments that the same arms 'are also borne by the family of Major or Magor of Southampton and the Isle of Wight, and there is reason to believe that these families came from Guernsey' (Rybot, 1928, p. 343, citing letter from MacCulloch to Mauger, 3 July 1871).

Elias, merchant, insured his dwelling house in the High St (Sun: 13/56/22374). Le Sieur **Daniel** Mauger master/part owner of the vessel *Daniel & Catherine* (see p 146). **Charles** correspondent of Martell. Charles, merchant, insured a house 'called the Grand Boscq now empty' and goods and merchandise in a house 'called Bosse' (Sun: 10/201/15538; 10/436/16680). Charles & Elias Mauger 'dealers in wine brandy' c. 1732 (CUL). Charles knew merchants/bankers who might be useful in wartime: Bordeaux (Feger père), La Rochelle (Wooywerf), Nantes (Delaunay Montaudoin), Brest (Raby), Vannes (Desniseaux), St Malo (Leynte l'ainé, *armateur*), Cherbourg (Creste Valval), Rouen (Le Vieux, banker), Le Havre (Piquier) Letter, Nov 1747, Sausmarez Manor archives box 68K). **John**, merchant-shipowner *temp.* Seven Years War. Le Sieur **James** Major (=Mauger) part-owner of a cargo of merchandise loaded at Guernsey on *The Two Brothers*, master Nicholas Le Mesurier, for delivery to Quebec (CdA, vol. 18, 26 Apr 1783).

METIVIER

Jean Gabriel Métivier, native of France, to give the Receiver a full and exact list of wines and brandies discharged in this island for his account, also a list of wines and brandies received in Guernsey for other strangers since 28 Sept 1753 down to this day (CdA, vol. 13, 30 Aug 1755).

Revd Jean Métivier came to Guernsey in 1752. His son **Jean-Carey** Métivier (d. 24.ix.1795) married Esther Guille (1762-1787) and there were five sons. **William** was in partnership with Kennett and the Careys in Spain by 1814. In the early 1820s he moved to Trieste (partnership of Métivier, Betts and Carey).

MOLLET

Charles lived at The Woodlands, Castel. He was of gentry status, often mixing, at home and in town, with the island aristocracy. On his estate he produced cider, some of which he sold. He signed the Canary wine petition, 1776. During the American revolutionary war he bought small shares in privateering ventures (28 Jan 1778, 9 May 1778, 5 Oct 1778, 16 Oct 1778, 18 Dec 1779). In January 1788 Mollet entered into a *société de commerce* with Mr Marett for six years. By the end of the month the partnership had taken possession of two stores at Braye (Alderney). Mollet records that on 29 January 'nous avons commence aujourd'hui a vendre ayant vendu 183 ½ gallons' of gin and brandy. Although it is nowhere explicitly stated in the diary, there can be no doubt that Mollet was supplying English smugglers. On 17 April 1789 the Governor explained to Mollet that he could no longer officially receive him because of the 'illuminations', a reference to the signals between the smugglers and their suppliers. Mollet obtained alcohol from Holland, Cette, Barcelona, Toulon and St Croix. The partnership also seems to have handled wine, sugar and chocolate. In some instances the goods were supplied directly to Alderney; otherwise they were sent on from Guernsey (and occasionally from Jersey). In mid-October 1788 Mollet paid a visit to Cherbourg where he saw brandy warehouses. At the end of the month he crossed to England. His peregrinations in Devon and Dorset (and in Hampshire in 1789) suggest that he was visiting customers. He dissolved his partnerships in May 1790 and early in June was appointed ADC to the Governor of Guernsey. (Priaulx Library, Mollet papers).

MOREAU

Henry, merchant-shipowner *temp* American War. De Havilland commented to Fraissinet (Cette) that **Jean** Moreau was an ironmonger who traded in various branches, that he was in happy circumstances, but De Havilland did not know his associates (IAS AQ 655/312, De Havilland to Fraissinet 3 June 1784). Jean Moreau & Co owe £3295:11:1 st to several merchants (CdA, vol. 19, 21 Aug 1784).

MOURANT

The family originally came from Jersey.

[i] Stephen: master of *Expedition* (Dobrée Protest book, 12 Aug 1746).

[ii] Robert: ¼ interest in sloop *le Franc-Macon* (auctioned on chaussée, CdA, vol. 14, 18 Jun 1763). Robert Mourant pilot (TNA ADM 106/1127/130, 5 Aug 1763).

[iii] Peter: 'upwardly mobile' and very successful in commerce. See pp. 110-114.

[iv] Stephen in Demerara in the early 19th century (see p. 86).

PELLEW

George had shipping interests (see p. 145) and was probably a merchant.

PERCHARD

'I find record of the Perchard family having been early numbered among the ancient resident families of Guernsey, and having been connected in marriage with the families of Le Marchant, Saumarez, Le Mesurier, La Serre, and De La Condamine' (Jacob II p. 117).

Daniel commander of Guernsey privateer (Dobrée Protest book, 29 July 1747). **John** (son of John Perchard and Thomasse née Bouillon) b. 1720, m. Elizabeth Coutart 1750, d. 1780. =?John merchant, member of the *Société des Veuves*. =? John leading merchant/trader 1779.

Peter (d. 1763) 'of London', son of Peter Perchard of London, in partnership as a jeweller, goldsmith and banker with his brother **Matthew** Perchard in Hatton Gardens, both of whom lived in Abchurch Lane, Cannon Street; married Marie de Beauvoir (d. May 1794).

Peter (1729-1806) apprenticed to his uncle Matthew (*vide supra*); installed as Prime Warden of the Goldsmith's Company (1786-87); Sheriff of the City of London (1793); President of St Bartholomew's Hospital (1804); created Lord Mayor of London, 1804. He married Martha, daughter of Henry le Mesurier and their daughter Martha married John le Mesurier. (T.F. Priaulx, QRGS, summer 1961, vol. xvii, no. 2).

PRIAULX

Pierre was harbour-supervisor in 1706, 1717. **Joshua** was a merchant-shipowner *temp.* Seven Years War; and **Joshua St John**, merchant, was a member of the *Société des Veuves*. In July 1774 we find Josué St Jean Priaulx & James Le Ray, part-owners of the *Nancy*, in an action against le Sr Nicholas Massy, formerly master, over brandy hidden on board the vessel in Guernsey and seized in London (CdA, vol. 15, 16 July 1774). Joshua was perhaps the Priaulx involved with Le Ray in sending brandy to Havana in October 1763 on the snow *la Perle*, Captain Bacchus master (CdA, vol. 14, 15 Oct 1763 'Messrs Priaulx, Le Ray & Co').

In another branch of the family **Thomas,** and **Thomas, the younger,** were merchants-shipowners *temp.* Seven Years War. Thomas jr, merchant, was a member of the *Société des Veuves*. Thomas was a leading merchant/trader, 1779. Thomas and **Carteret** merchants-shipowners *temp.* American War. Carteret, Thomas, and **Anthony** were involved in privateering in the French wars.

Thomas Priaulx (d. 1771) was linked to the de Carteret family, who formed a banking partnership in London with Richard de Jersey; the house was styled Carteret, Jersey & Co. Priaulx banked with them and in the mid-eighteenth century we find the partnership of Carteret Priaulx trading. Thomas Priaulx the elder died in Alderney in 1771. His son **Thomas** began his career as captain of his father's privateer *La Marie*. He prospered and married Rebecca Le Marchant and had three sons: Carteret, Thomas and Anthony. We can see the nature of his business from a letterbook covering the years 1774-1780 (see below).

At his death in 1784, the business passed to his two elder sons **Carteret** and **Thomas**, who traded as Carteret Priaulx & Co. and, at one time, owned no fewer than twelve privateers. Carteret Priaulx were energetic in the 'new' trades with the West Indies and South America. The firm also cooperated closely with the Janvrin family of Jersey, particularly in the Newfoundland cod trade. Carteret, who married Marie Le Marchant, predeceased his brother. Thomas was influential in founding the Guernsey Chamber of Commerce in December, 1808. In 1818 Carteret Priaulx & Co. were the leading shipowners of Guernsey, with a fleet of seven vessels (of 1458 tonnage; Jamieson, 1986, p. 325). Thomas was a partner in the Guernsey Banking Company (Priaulx, Le Marchant, Rougier & Co.), founded 18th of June, 1827.

Thomas Priaulx's principal correspondents 1774-1780

England: Anthony Delacombe and Thomas Bartlett were important correspondents in Cornwall. In London Le Mesurier usually acted as Priaulx's banker.

Zephaniah Job: TP dealing with 1778-1782.

Northern Europe

Gothenburg: Arfwidson supplied bohea and congo teas; George Bellender also supplied tea.

Copenhagen: Priaulx sent orders to David Brown for teas and enamelled china.

Rotterdam: James Le Marchant was his brother-in-law and Priaulx refers to 'mon epouse votre soeur' in his correspondence. Priaulx placed orders with Le Marchant for bohea tea from EI sales, and for gin.

France

St Malo: Sebire l'aîné acted as Priaulx's agent at the E.I. sales at Lorient.

Lorient: Mons Daniel.

Toulon: Laurent Caine supplied brandy.

Spain

Catalonia: in 1775-1776 Pratt Marti supplied Priaulx with brandy, hankerchiefs and wine (Benicarlo, Mataro, Grainache). Priaulx was not happy with the firm and also placed orders with Gregory & Guille, Thomas Barry & Co, Reserson & Tupper.

West Indies

St Croix: Tennent & Ross; Macklen, Tucker & Ross; Abraham Le Mesurier

Source: Priaulx Library, letterbook of Thomas Priaulx.

Correspondents of Carteret Priaulx c. 1802-1805

Barcelona Nicolas Guille

Demerara Mourant & Delisle (taking Madeira wine, supplying sugar, coffee, cotton, rum). See p. 86.

Gibraltar Robinson and Lihou.

London Brock and Le Mesurier (bankers).

Montpellier Brock Rigaud & Co; Fred Brock & Co supplying Roussilon.

Naples Rigaud, Brock & Maingy
Rotterdam J & J Le Marchant
Valencia Price, Tupper & Co
Sources: Priaulx, Carteret Priaulx papers; see White 1963.

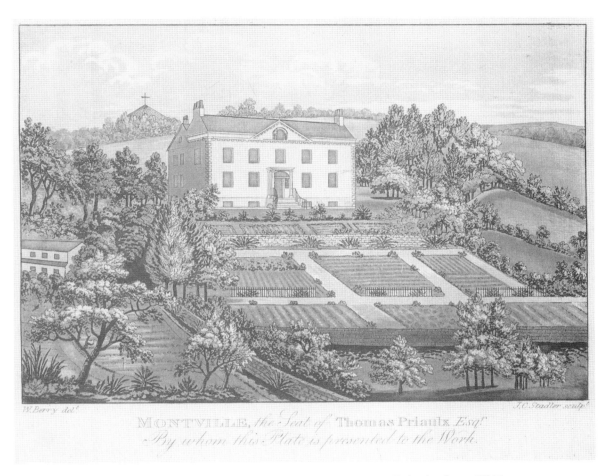

Fig. 8.1: Montville, the home of Thomas Priaulx, from W. Berry,
The History of the Island of Guernsey, 1815.

PRICE

The family was possibly of Welsh extraction and came to Guernsey *circa* 1700. **Thomas** Price (1708 – 1766) married Marthe Solbé (the Solbés were a maritime/merchant family). Thomas and Marthe had two sons – **Thomas** (1736-1800) and **William Pierre** (1755-1815). William Peter Price was designated a leading merchant/trader in 1779 and merchant-shipowner *temp*. American War. William Pierre married Eleonore Sheppard (daughter of Hannibal Sheppard q.v.). Their two sons **Thomas** and **Hannibal** established themselves at Jacmel in Haiti in 1805/6. A beam engine and sugar mill were introduced into Haiti c. 1818 thanks to a Price. See pp. 84-85 for Price in Haiti.

On 6 March 1773 Guille (Guernsey) reported to Gregory & Guille (Barcelona) that Thomas Price was trying a Spanish house (rather than ordering from Gregory & Guille). The letter appears to indicate that Price would be working in concert with Peter Bonamy (acting for Mr Anley of Alderney), Messrs Brock, Peter Mourant, Jersey & De Lisle, Elisha Tupper, James Le Ray, and Thomas Priaulx 'for they are very great together' (IAS, Stevens-Guille, Guille letterbook).

British consular records show a **Charles** Price at Barcelona in December 1785 (see p 65). Lukis records a Price at Valencia (Carteret Priaulx corresponded with *Price, Tupper* there in the early 19th century). Bibliography: R.Price *Les Price dans la Trace des Batisseurs de Société* Haiti n.d; M.R. Doret *Les écrivains Price d' Haiti* France/Haiti 1993.

RESERSON

Nicolas (b.1727) married Elizabeth, daughter of Rev Thomas Fiott, Rector of St Martins, 12 Oct 1752. He was designated merchant-shipowner *temp.* Seven Years War. In 1772 Guille (Guernsey) reported to Gregory & Guille (Barcelona) that Mr Reserson had complained about the brandy received from them, it was seedy (IAS Guille letterboook, Guille to Gregory and Guille, 31 December 1772). De Havilland commented to Fraissinet (Cette) in June 1784 that Reserson had retired (IAS AQ 655/312). **Nicolas** (son) was born 8 Nov 1753 and went to Spain *circa* 1771 to work for Gregory and Guille. He entered into a partnership with William DeVic Tupper in 1775. The partnership was unsuccessful and Nicholas ended up bankrupt. The story is related at length on pp. 116-136. The following is a résumé.

In 1775, at the wish of their respective fathers, Nicholas Reserson and William de Vic Tupper entered into a business partnership. Quite soon Nicholas discovered that William had a wild character. The house traded until 1778. When war broke out between Spain and Britain,

Rollfsen took over and William went to England. Nicholas remained at Barcelona until 1779 and then made his way to Guernsey, where he met up with William. In 1780 they employed a house at Ostend to carry on their business. Then, in September 1781, they established their own house there. The partnership was made up of Reserson ($\frac{5}{12}$ share), Tupper ($\frac{5}{12}$ share) and Kirkpatrick ($\frac{1}{6}$ share). Reserson and Kirkpatrick worked hard (in Tupper's absence) and by June 1782 a profit of thirty to thirty five thousand Brabant florins had been built up. Nicholas went to Guernsey to have a holiday and to sort out a cargo of brandy that had been dispatched from Barcelona by Rollfsen. Nicholas then returned from Guernsey to Barcelona *via* Ostend. There he started to learn about losses sustained by the Ostend house thanks to some imprudent speculations of Tupper. When Nicholas arrived back in Barcelona he discovered that the house there had done well during the war, but Rollfsen had taken the profits.

In December 1784 Tupper went to Ostend and ended up in prison. Eventually he was extracted and at the beginning of 1786 he went to England; after a long absence he arrived back in Barcelona in September 1787. In May 1788 Nicholas journeyed to Ostend to sort out the affairs of the house there. He gave a bond payable to Elisha Tupper. In December Edmond Connelly approached Reserson. Connelly had worked for two years in Barcelona and wished to join the house of Reserson & Tupper. In April 1789 Connelly and Almgren joined the firm but on 31 July the partnership was dissolved on the insistence of Tupper. On 1 August Nicholas founded his own house – Reserson & Co – with Almgren as a partner for three years and Connelly for six to nine years.

In November 1790 Reserson managed to discharge his bond to Elisha Tupper. The following July Connelly went to Dunkirk to secure orders; he returned in October 1791. Brandy was shipped to Dunkirk but the market fell; merchants there repudiated their orders and Reserson & Co found themselves in difficulties with some of their correspondents. The house of Patrick Arthur failed; Isaac Brown (Dunkirk), Joseph Brown (London), and de Haan (Amsterdam) experienced difficulties with bills-of-exchange; Reserson & Co were damaged by assurances that Connelly had given. Matters came to a head in the summer of 1792 and at a meeting terms were agreed. Nicholas made his way to London and Guernsey; Dobrée intimated that Nicholas should no longer draw on him. In Guernsey Reserson accomplished little. During December 1792 – January 1793 he made his way back to Barcelona. In 1792 his losses amounted to £C 60,000. He met his creditors on 4 February 1793 and terms were fixed. Connelly left the partnership. There was another creditors' meeting on 12 August 1793. After his failure Nicholas lived in penury for a while. He then worked for his erstwhile partner, William De Vic Tupper (who died in 1798). In July 1824 Nicholas returned to Guernsey and died not long after.

Nicholas' brother Thomas (b. 10 Apr 1755), became Rector of St Peters, married Marie Guille, and died at Montpellier where he had gone for his health, 13 Feb 1789. Another brother, Pierre, b. 30 Apr 1760, died 8 May 1786 at Ostend, unmarried. There were five sisters.

RIVOIRE

Simon Rivoire m. Anne Marsault	Simon Peter (b.1705) m.(1732) Esther Roland	Jean William
	William (b.1706) m. (1730) Mary Le Ray	Anne m. William Solbé Elisabeth m. Louis Dunière Margaret Marie m. Peter Maingy

The Huguenot **Simon** Rivoire seems to have emigrated to Guernsey from St Foy in Savoy *circa* 1700. He married Anne Marsault in 1701. Their second son, **Simon Peter**, was born in 1705. He married Esther Roland in 1732 and there were two sons, **Jean** and **William**, who became merchants. They died without offspring. Simon Peter's brother **William** (b 1706) married Mary Le Ray (1730) and there were four daughters: Anne, Elisabeth, Margaret and Marie. Three daughters married merchants: Anne married William Solbé; Elisabeth married Louis Dunière (q.v.) and Marie married Peter Maingy (Priaulx, Rivoire family file).

Le Sieur Simon Rivoire part-owner of vessel *Aventure* (see p. 145). *The Economist*, a brigantine of 100 tons, William Rivoire master, John Rivoire owner, arrived at Virginia (in ballast, from Madeira), 9 June 1766 (TNA CO 5/1450 f <20>). On 6 March 1773 Guille (Guernsey) wrote to Gregory & Guille (Barcelona) that Wm Rivoire had cheated 'our merchants of about £500 sterling when he went to Martinico which was not discovered till lately when the accounts arrived from the West Indies'. Guille declared that the merchants would oblige John Rivoire to give up 'his all, therefore keep your silver secure, for he has not a farthing'. Rivoire had made over his effects in Quebec to Mr John Carey. (IAS Stevens-Guille papers, Guille letterbook). John signed the Canary wine petition 1776. John, merchant-shipowner *temp*. American War. A letter from Carteret Priaulx (Newton Bushell, 17 Jan 1785) to John thanks him for what he has done; if Brown 'desires to put his tobacco in our lower cellars, let him do it'; presumably Rivoire was acting in partnership with Priaulx (Priaulx Library, Rivoire file).

Dames **Elizabeth & Mary** Rivoire actioned the master of a Danish vessel for missing merchandise (loaded by Messrs E. Fabritius & Wever, Copenhagen; CdA, vol. 20, 11 May 1786).

ROBILLIARD

Nicholas, merchant-shipowner *temp*. American War. Goods from Copenhagen shipped to Richard Guille & frères (Guernsey) for re-shipping to Messsrs Robilliard & frères, Alderney (CdA, vol. 20, 13 May 1786).

ROBINSON

The Robinson family originated in Sunderland and were in Guernsey in the early eighteenth century. Edith Carey has a reference to **Richard** fs Thomas, captain of Henry Brock's privateer (Priaulx, Robinson family file).

Richard, sometime owner of the sloop *la Marguerite* (CdA, vol. 11, 15 July 1737).

Michael, leading merchant/trader 1779. Merchant-shipowner *temp*. American War. On 3 June 1784 De Havilland observed to Fraissinet (Cette) that Michel Robinson was the brother-in-law of G. Knapp and had served as second-in-command on his ship; Robinson had a large fortune and was continuing in commerce (IAS AQ 655/312).

ROCHE

Peter, moved to Holland in 1776 to establish a firm there with a Mr Lihou; see p. 47. See also under Coutart, (above).

ROL[L]AND

Mr **Daniel** Rolland 'formerly commander of vessel, now merchant' inspected a Portuguese schooner in the harbour and its cargo of French wine and molasses (Priaulx Library, Dobrée Protest book, 6 March 1748/9). Capt Daniel Roland recorded as resident of Fountain Street, 1762, and assessed at 50 quarters (CO Taxe).

ROUGIER

Hilary (or Helier), (1765-1852). In his career Helier was variously a sailor, merchant, shipowner and banker (one of the founders of the Guernsey Banking Company, May 1827). See T.M.H. Hugo 'Hilary Rougier, Sailor, Merchant and Banker' QRGS vol. xvi no. 2, Summer 1960.

ROWE

John, of Guernsey, purchase of brig for wine trade (East Kent Archives Centre EK – U1453/B5/4/1115).

SHEPPARD/SHEPHARD

Hannibal 'son of a Plymouth merchant who had shared two privateering ventures in 1747/8, one with Samuel Dobrée and the other with John de Jersey. Shephard had settled in Guernsey and had been taken by the French on a vessel (chartered by Isaac Dobrée and other Guernseymen) which was on a smuggling venture to England in August 1756.' Shephard, along with a Captain Arthur, three English ships' masters and four Jerseymen, escaped from Dinan, stole a boat at Cancale and escaped to Jersey (Raban 1986, p. 138). In a court case, Jeanne Goguet was referred to as 'femme d'Annibal Shepard, femme marchande' (CdA, vol. 14, 18 Sept 1762). Hannibal listed as leading merchant/trader 1779; designated merchant-shipowner *temp*. American War. Sheppard & Co. shipowners in the 1820s.

SOLBE

'This family, originally from Normandy, are traditionally of Huguenot descent' (de Guérin, 1890, p. 157). **William**, designated merchant-shipowner *temp*. Seven Years War. William, master and owner of brigantine (120 tons) *United Society*, built Liverpool 1755, registered Guernsey 26 Jan 1765. The *United Society* arrived at Virginia on 16 September 1765 (in ballast from Guernsey); and left Virginia for Falmouth with a cargo of 95 hogsheads of tobacco and five thousand staves on 23 Dec 1765 (TNA CO 5/149 f f<96>, <97>v De Guérin's genealogy does not easily accommodate this Solbé. He gives a William born in 1687, married to Mary Guille (1703), by whom there was issue: Henry, Mary and Catherine. Capt **Richard** Solbé was recorded as residing in the Pollet in 1762 and was assessed at 30 quarters (IAS, CO Taxe).

STEPHEN

Peter Stephen /Pierre Etienne, merchant, insured goods and merchandise in the 1720s to the value of £1000 [Guildhall, Sun Fire Insurance, 10/355/16274, 16275. *Vide* also 12/395/20565 and 26/230/44851]. Peter owned property in London, where his son traded. Peter Stephen 'of the Island of Guernsey, merchant,' granted power of attorney to his son John Stephen of London, merchant, to treat with Theophilus Salloway, 26 July 1732 (London Metropolitan Archives ACC/0349/295; see also ACC /0349/296, 18 Aug 1732, for articles of agreement *re* Snow Hill, St Sepulchres without Newgate called the Queen's Head abutting upon the Pied Bull, occupied by P. Stephens).

TAYLOR

John, vintner, TC burial 9 Nov 1742.

THOM[P]SON

David, merchant, probably from Montrose, Scotland. Member of the *Société des Veuves*. Shipping wine 1769 - 88 from Cadiz, Lisbon, Malaga and Oporto (*Livre de certificats*); leading merchant/trader 1779; merchant-shipowner *temp*. American War; shipping Bordeaux wine to Guernsey (CdA, vol. 16, 30 May 1780); nuts brought on a Danish vessel (CdA, vol. 18, 17 Apr 1784). At a wine-tasting held 'chez Mr de Prelaz' Thompson indicated to John Carey Métivier that he was thinking of disposing of his capital (valued at £4,000 st). Métivier communicated this to William Guille (in London). The success of Bell and Thompson suggested that the wine business could be profitable (IAS Guille letters, Métivier to Guille, 12 April 1791). Guille replied that he had met Thompson who did not mean to leave off business entirely. If Thompson was merely in search of a partner, Guille would be happy to join him. In fact Thompson was joined by a Mr Brown (IAS, Guille to George Guille, 4 May 1792). Thompson left £5,000 to his sister, nephew and nieces at Montrose in Scotland; £1,000 to his servant Ann Fraser; £100 to Elizabeth Bayne, his cook; £500 to Peter De Jersey, his cooper; one hundred pounds to his servant John Cooper; and £1,500 to his executors. Will proved 8 Feb 1796 (E.C. Wills 1795-1803, pp. 44-46).

THOUMINE

Thoumine Moullin & Co dealt with Zephaniah Job, 1804-1806.

TUPPER

The Tupper family originated from Cassel in Germany. They fled from religious persecution in 1522 and arrived in England *via* the Low Countries. According to family tradition John Tupper (ob. 1602) of Chichester, while on his way to Bordeaux, was shipwrecked on the coast of Guernsey. He remained, purchased an estate, married and became the common ancestor of the Guernsey Tuppers.

The branch of John (1668-1720)	Daniel (1689-1741)	Daniel (1714-?) Elisha (1726-1802)	Daniel William de Vic John Elisha Emilia Elizabeth Margaret	Ferdinand Brock (the historian)

In 1692 his descendant **John** Tupper (1668-1720) took news to the British fleet about the location of the French fleet, intelligence which led to the Battle of La Hogue. After the resounding British victory William and Mary presented a massive gold medal and chain to Tupper as reward for his patriotic service. Thereafter the chain and medal were incorporated in the coat-of-arms of the Tupper family (see above, and Plate XI). John's son Daniel (1689-1741) married Elizabeth Dobrée. Their eldest son, **Daniel** (1714-?) settled in Barbados (and died in St Vincent). The second son, **Elisha** (1726-1802) became a jurat of the Royal Court and was one of the leading *négociants* of his day. He was the most prominent member of the family for several decades. Along with his cousins **John** and **John jr**, Elisha was a merchant-shipowner *temp.* Seven Years War; he imported wine from the Algarve, Barcelona, Benicarlo, Cadiz, Faro, Figueira, Lisbon, Malaga, Mataro, Oporto, Salou (*Livre de certificats*). Elisha (and John jr and Daniel) signed the Canary wine petition in 1776. Elisha (and John jr) were designated leading merchants-traders, 1779. Elisha, Daniel, **William de Vic, John Elisha**, and **John jr** were all designated merchants-shipowners *temp.* American War. Elisha's daughters married well: Emilia married Sir Peter de Havilland (who became bailiff of Guernsey); Elizabeth married William Le Marchant; and Margaret married Isaac Carey. His son William De Vic entered into partnership at Barcelona with Nicholas Reserson and was killed in a duel in 1798.

Peter Carey Tupper (1785-1825) highly distinguished himself during the Peninsular War (1808-1814) in encouraging the Spaniards to resist the invasion of Napoleon. In May 1808, when not quite twenty-four years of age, he was appointed a member of the supreme Junta of the kingdom of Valencia; and soon after, during the massacre of the French residents in the city, he was exposed to personal danger in his endeavours to save them – many were rescued by him. During the siege of Valencia, 1811-2, Tupper helped to organise the gun direction. After serving as British Consul at Valencia, Tupper was moved to Catalonia (see p. 64). In 1816, the King of Spain conferred upon him the title of Baron, at the solicitation of the municipality of the city of Valencia. He had a pension of six hundred pounds a year for his services. He died at Madrid, April 13, 1825. (See Duncan, 1841 p. 615; *Sarnia: or brief memorials of her many sons, (civil, military, and naval)* Guernsey, 1862, pp. 32-34 See p. 64 *supra* for commercial activities of P.C.T.).

Thomas Tupper (died 11 May 1841): 'Having assisted his brother, the Consul for Valencia, during the Peninsular War, he was appointed in 1823, when British Consuls were first sent to the Spanish South American revolted colonies, consul in Caraccas with a salary of £1,000 a year; and afterwards in Riga, with a salary of £800 a year. As he was travelling alone in a carriage to Alicante during the war, he was met near that town by a band of robbers, who ordered the driver to stop, but on learning that "Don Tomas" was the brother of the consul, they not only warmly greeted him, but sent two or three of their party to accompany him to the gates of the town, so as to secure him from further danger, thus exemplifying the maxim that there is honour among thieves, and showing the influence which the Consul had acquired over the peasantry of the kingdom of Valencia' (*Sarnia: or brief memorials of her many sons, (civil, military, and naval)* Guernsey, 1862, p. 52, abbreviated). **John Elisha** Tupper & Co at Reus (TNA 638/3 f 202 v, British Consulate to J. E. Tupper, 10 Jan 1824).

UT[T]ERMARK

Mr Rudolph Utermark of Hamburgh married Elizabeth Dobrée 1779 (Dobrée family files).

VARDON

'Daniel Vardon, a native of Caen, Normandy, together with his wife Marie Marchand, escaped to Guernsey and during their flight to the coast they were fired upon and their son Daniel an infant only a few weeks old, (b. 1715), narrowly escaped being shot, the bullet lodging in the bible which the mother held before her babe as a screen. As may be imagined this bible was preserved in the family as a precious relic. The son, **Daniel**, afterwards married Charlotte, (b. 1719) only child of Jean Le Marchant, who settled in Guernsey, by his wife Jeanne Sale, both Huguenot refugees. Issue

1. Mary, b. 1746, ob. 1796, m. 1767, William Kennet, by whom she had a family.

2. Martha, b. 1756, ob. 1830, unmarried.

3. **Daniel**, b. 1759, m. at Lisbon, Sarah Cole.

    1. Daniel, b. 1790, ob. 1802

    2. Charlotte Anne, b.1783, m. John, son of Thomas Mansell and Martha Price.

    3. Maria Martha, m. Frederick, son of Frederick Price and Marguerite de Guérin.

    4. Isabella, m. John, son of John Bonamy and Mary de Guérin.' (de Guérin, 1890, p 25).

Daniel, leading merchant/trader 1779. Daniel and Daniel jr merchants-shipowners *temp.* American War. Daniel's will indicates that he settled over two thousand pounds of debt incurred in trading by his son Daniel; hence little was left to the son (referred to as being in America). Will proved 25 July 1793 (EC Wills, 1780-1795, pp. 302-308).

WANGREEN

Andrew, merchant, member of the *Société des Veuves*. Capt André Wangreen residing in Fountain Street, 1762, and assessed at 60 quarters (IAS, CO Taxe).

WATKINS

Le Sr **Daniel** Watkins recorded as resident in the Pilori-Eglise vingtaine, 1762, and assessed at 20 quarters (CO Taxe). Daniel signed the Canary wine petition, 1776.

WILLIAMS

Thomas, merchant, member of the *Société des Veuves*.

WOOD

John, merchant-shipowner *temp.* Seven Years War; and *temp.* American War.

WRIGHT

M., importing wine from Naples (*Livre de certificats*).

GLOSSARY

acte	law created by the States of Guernsey.
armateur	shipowner; ship husband; orgaiser of a privateering expedition.
Bailiff	in the eighteenth century the Bailiff (by tradition a Guernseyman) presided both in the Royal Court and in the States of Deliberation.
barrique	barrel containing almost sixty gallons of wine.
botte	butt (usually 126 gallons of wine).
boucaut	hogshead (63 gallons).
cabotage	coastal trade (as opposed to 'le grand commerce' – international trade.
charter party	contract between shipowner and merchant whereby a ship is hired out for a voyage or a stipulated period of time.
chasse-marée	usually a fast lugger employed in cabotage.
demurrage	time during which the charterer of a vessel retains possession beyond the period allotted for unloading the cargo.
hogshead	measure of wine, half a pipe.
jurat	'judge' sitting in the Royal Court, Guernsey.
lay time	period allowed in charter party for loading/unloading cargo.
livre tournois	monetary system (of Tours) used in France and Guernsey. One *livre* =20 *sols* = 240 *deniers*. French and English scholars vary in their conversion values.
marchand	trader.
mercantilism	economic theory that discouraged the 'leaking' of money abroad to buy foreign luxury goods.
Navigation Acts	British laws designed to limit the shipping that could carry cargoes, especially between Britain and her colonies.
négociant	merchant operating at national/international level, on a higher scale than the *marchand*.
ordonnance	regulation issued by the jurats of Guernsey.
pipe	wine cask = two hogsheads; a measure of 105 – 132 gallons.
pratique	permission granted to a vessel to enter port when it has been established that the vessel is free of contagious disease.
primage	payment made to the master of a vessel over and above the freight charge.
société d'assurance	partnership for a maritime/commercial venture, spreading the risk.
taxe	tax levied in Guernsey
tod	measure of wool, regularly 32 lbs.
tonneau	one tonneau = four barriques.
tun	measure = four hogsheads = two pipes.

END NOTES

CHAPTER 1

1. A. L. Simon, *The History of the Wine Trade in England* (London, 1907), vol. 2, pp. 39–42.
2. I. K. Steele, *The English Atlantic 1675–1740* (Oxford, 1986), p. 23.
3. *The Case of the Inhabitants of the Island of Guernsey, in Relation to several Orders of Council obtained by the Commissioners of the Customs, for setting Custom-House-Officers in the Island, and subjecting the Inhabitants to the Laws relating to the Customs in Great Britain.* [n.d., Priaulx copy marked c.1708/1709].
4. BL Add Ms. 38463 f 208v, 17 Aug. 1764, Southampton Customs board to London Customs House.
5. C. M. Andrews, *The Colonial Period of American History* (New Haven, 1943), vol. 4, pp. 66–67. However, a copy of an Order-in-Council, 20 March 1675, permitted trade between Guernsey (and Jersey) and British plantations in America, without ships having to journey via an English port. Island Archives Service, Price Collection, AQ49/1 It is not surprising that the English customs felt confused at times.
6. C. M. Andrews, *op.cit.*, vol. 4, p. 68.
7. Priaulx 18459 p. 18, 7 June 1777, Guille to Knowsley (of Hull).
8. Greffe, Original Correspondence, vol. 1, no. 99, 18 Nov. 1667, Atkins to Andros.
9. Northampton Record Office, Finch Hatton papers, 278.
10. A. Croix, *La Bretagne aux 16e et 17e siècles* (Paris, 1981), vol. 1, p. 62. A. Lespagnol, *op. cit.*, p. 192.
11. C. M. Andrews, *op. cit.*, vol. 4, p. 68: 'This traffic was carried on in defiance partly of the acts of trade and navigation and partly of the acts passed in 1678, 1689, 1693 and 1704 prohibiting trade with France.'
12. PRO SP 47/3, copy of extract of letter 29 Sept. 1712 from Mr John Sherwood.
13. Greffe, Depositions, 23 June 1713.
14. C. M. Andrews, *op. cit.*, vol. 4, p. 67. See also Priaulx Library, Guille (Jean Snr) account book, pp. 6–7: Guille engaging crew in the St Malo – Dinard region, Nov.–Dec. 1713.
15. BL Sloane Ms 4053 f 239 r, 1 July 1734, Carey to Sloane [' … about 18 years ago …']. A. Lespagnol, *op. cit.*, pp. 541–646 for trade of St Malo with the South Seas.
16. *Vide infra.*
17. PRO CUST 62/59, 10 Sept. 1719, Eyre to Southampton Customs board.
18. Cambridge U L, Cholmondeley (Houghton) Papers, 41/29.
19. BL Lansdowne Ms 657 f 17r, 25 Sept. 1750, Strahan to Governor.
20. T. Dicey, *An Historical Account of Guernsey* (London, 1751) p. 33.
21. Royal Court, Legge survey.
22. *Actes*, vol. 1 pp. 145, 165.
23. *The Case of the Town Parish versus the Nine Country Parishes … 1759* (Guernsey, 1843), p. 19. E. W. Sharp, 'The Evolution of St Peter Port Harbour' TSG XVIII, part iii, for 1967 (Guernsey, 1968), pp. 226–255. R. Hocart, *An Island Assembly The Development of the States of Guernsey 1700–1949* (Guernsey, 1988), p. 5.
24. W. Le Marchant, *Histoire de l'Erection Originelle de l'avancement & Augmentation du Havre de la Ville de St. Pierre Port à Guernesey* (Oxford, c. 1755), Appendice pp. 4-5.
25. T. Dicey, *An Historical Account of Guernsey* (London, 1751), pp. 195–196. There are copies of the sailing directions in the Priaulx Library, Guernsey, and the British Library. The significance of Dobrée's charts is underlined by Dicey's comment that all the others 'in any of the Books of Charts' were 'extremely erroneous and not to be depended on' (Dicey, *op. cit.* pp. 195–196).

Nicholas Dobrée (1678–1751) was one of the leading merchants in St Peter Port in the first half of the 18th century. A monument in the Town Church records that he devoted himself to the security of navigation, the improvement of the harbour and the establishment of the town hospital; text in W. Berry, *The History of the Island of Guernsey* (London, 1815), p. 148. For further details of his life see R. Hocart, 'A Guernsey Merchant and his Family in the Reign of George II' TSG vol. XXI, part iii, for 1983 (Guernsey, 1984), pp. 360–378; and C. Aptel *et al.*, *Thomas Dobrée Un Homme Un Musée* (Nantes, 1997), pp. 26–28.

26. G. Dupont, *Histoire du Cotentin et de ses Iles* Caen 1885 vol. 4 pp. 447, 471-473.

27. BL Add Ms 38463 f 199v – f 200r, 13 Aug 1764 Poole customs report.

28. *Ibid* f 200 r.

29. Information from Dr N.A.M. Rodger. See also TNA T1 381/9, 4 Oct. 1758, Cleveland to West requesting permission for 46,250 gallons of wine to be shipped from Guernsey to navy at Spithead (wartime). The importance of Guernsey in victualling the Royal Navy with brandy and wine is brought out by the French scholar Christian Buchet, *Marine, économie et société Un exemple d'interaction: l'avitaillement de la Royal Navy Durant la guerre de sept ans*, Paris, 1999 (pp.41, 134, 166-168, 172, 303). There are two passing references in D. Syrett, *Shipping and Military Power in the Seven Years War*, Exeter, 2008. In 1759 'two Navy Board transports were sent to Guernsey to procure wine for Hawke's ships' (p. 48). In the same year 'Holburne was directed to provide transports to carry to the Bay of Biscay from Guernsey enough wine for 13,000 men to last 35 days' (p. 50).

30. TNA HO 98/30, 5 Feb 1807 Doyle to Treasury.

31. TNA T1 445 f 215v, 24 Nov 1766; Wilkins 1992, 39.

32. BL Add ms 38463 f 21v, 25 Aug 1764 Weymouth Customs Board to London.

33. Priaulx, Lukis ms.

34. Priaulx, le Mesurier papers, articles of agreement.

35. Priaulx, Guille letterbook 14 Aug 1778; Gothenburg Landsarkivet, Ekman papers contain some references to the Guernsey trade B1;10 letterbook 1782-1784, pp. 129-130.

36. Priaulx, Guille letterbook.

CHAPTER 2

1. Price, 1973, vol. 1, p. 130.

2. Price, 1973, vol. 1, p. 131.

3. See p. 33 for trade with Scotland; Price 1973, vol.2, pp. 796-7.

4. TNA HO 98/23 Brown to Amherst, 23 Aug. 1791; Le Marchant to Amherst, 25 Aug. 1791.

5. TNA SP 47/3 Mauger and de Sausmarez to Duke of Newcastle, 22 July 1732.

6. TNA SP 47/4 Henry Mauger report, 18 Sept 1734. Compare Cambidge U.L. Cholmondeley (Houghton papers), 41/30 (circa 1733) 80 'tonneaux de thee' imported in one year from Nantes.

7. There are many references in TNA CUST 62/63 – 62/66.

8. TNA CUST 62/63 London to Southampton, 12 May 1737; CUST 3/44 for 1744.

9. BL Add Ms 38463 f 196v, 9 Aug. 1764 Portsmouth report; f 199v, 13 Aug. 1764 Poole report.

10. Goddio (2002) pp. 123-124.

11. Cullen 1998, 25.

12. CdA vol. 1, pp 42-3, December 1730 (13,799 gallons of rum from Antigua to Guernsey, shipped on *la Marie*).

13. TNA CUST 62/65 p. 251 London to Southampton 13 Sept 1744; T1/445 f 214r, 24 Nov.1766 Lutwidge *re* Manx traders.

14. Priaulx, Guille letterbook, Guille to Yates 21 Sept. 1796.
15. TNA SP 89/55 f 255r, 6 Apr 1762, Consul to Egremont.
16. TNA CUST 3/63 for 1763. BL Add Ms 38463 f 211v, Warren Lisle to London, 20 Aug. 1764.
17. Baldwin, S. *A Survey of the British Customs*, London, 1770, p. 182.
18. Simon 1948, 91.
19. Inglis 1834, 230.

CHAPTER 3

1. BL Lansdowne ms 657, chapter VIII.
2. Jamieson 1986 p. 314.
3. TNA T 64/153 William Stiles report, pp 40-41.
4. Leabon 1812, 69.
5. Anderson 1964, 445-451. TNA HO 98/30 5 Feb 1807 Doyle report.
6. Crouzet 1990, 414.
7. TNA CUST 3.
8. Clark 1938, 37-39.
9. James Watson, merchant, Greenock 1738-1750: Scottish Record Office CS.96/1919 (renumbered). Other information kindly supplied by Dr Keith Marshall.
10. TNA CUST 14/2 f 6r – f 6v (microfilm).
11. TNA CUST 14/13B, 3 f 12r (microfilm).
12. TNA CUST 14/1B f 282v (microfilm). CUST 14/8 f 96v (microfilm). See also Scottish Record Office GD.1/306 (Alexander Oliphant Letterbook); CS. 96/3231, Sederunt book 1803-1804, p. 33.
13. TNA HO 98/23, 14 Feb. 1782 Budd to Irving; 15 Feb.1782 Irving to Hillsborough. See Vignols 1928 for the context of this trade.
14. TNA CUST 15/86 onwards lists Guernsey trade separately. TNA CUST 15/91: 1395 yards of linen, year ending 25 Mar 1788.

CHAPTER 4

Lloyd's Lists

The Lloyd's Lists often give only a vague indication of the port of origin of a vessel: 'Newfoundland' 'Spain', 'Coast of Spain', 'Basque Road', 'West Indies' etc. In compiling Table 4.1 entries for Santander and Bilboa were aggregated under Basque Road. Similarly, entries for Arichat and Gaspé were aggregated under 'Newfoundland'. 'Spain', 'Catalonia' and 'Coast of Spain' have been combined. Under 'West Indies' I have aggregated Antigua (1755), Montserrat (1765), St Thomas (1785), St Kitts (1786, 1790).

Represented in the table under 'others' are a few rare arrivals from: Algiers, Aveiro, Bremen, Camprere, Cherbourg, Chipagan, Cognac, Dunkirk, Figuera, Grandeville, Guadeloupe, Konigsburg, La Rochelle, Laavedio, Labrador, Landernau, Le Havre, Marseilles, Mortayne, Naples, New England, Padron, Port Vendre, Rochefort, Roscoff, Stade, Streights, Tortola, Trondheim, Udewalle, Vigo, Villa Nova, Villafranca, Vivero.

The entries for Cognac, La Rochelle and Rochefort should be interpreted alongside the Charente entries (and probably relate to the shipping of brandy). Some entries relate to the unusual circumstances of wartime (Guadeloupe was temporarily held by the British during the Seven Years War). In some instances (e.g. Roscoff) we are getting an echo of the activities of Guernsey merchants elsewhere. Sometimes we are dealing with vessels that put into Guernsey after a difficult voyage –quite often, in stormy weather, St Peter Port was a harbour of refuge for ships bound elsewhere.

It cannot be overstressed that the Lloyd's Lists tell us about the entrepôt trade, about the arrival of shipping of many nationalities in St Peter Port. The lists generally fail to capture the activities of Guernsey ships trading away from Guernsey (the slave trade and the Madeira trade in particular). The entries for New England (1764, 1768) possibly under-represent links with that part of North America.

Table 4.2

Several entries are simply recorded as 'Norway'; under this heading I have aggregated Norwegian ports (such as Arundahl). Similarly, under 'Basque Road' I have aggregated Bilboa, Corunna, Gijon, Ribadeo, Santander, (St) Sebastian. Cuba includes Havana, St Jugo de Cuba, Trinidad de Cuba. Haiti includes Jac(qu)mel, Port-au-Prince.

'Other' includes rare arrivals from: Baltimore, Batavia, Bayonne, Calais, Cape of Good Hope, Elsinore, Gallipoli, Getzvhl, Greetzyl, Groundsound, Heligoland, Jamaica, La Guayra, Liebau, Longsound, Lima, Martinique, Memel, Messina, Odessa, Palermo, Passages, Pernambuco, (St) Petersburg, Porsground, Riga, Senegal, Smyrna, South Seas, St Jean de Luz, St Michael's, St Salvador, St Ubes, Surinam, Tortola, Valparaiso, Zante. In most instances these represent just one or two arrivals in one or two years. The major exception is St Petersburg. In the late eighteenth century this invariably implied an arrival from Virginia. However, in the early nineteenth century it is not clear whether Virginia or Russia was meant.

Slave trade

How many slaving expeditions did the Guernsey merchants mount? In *The Trans-Atlantic Slave Trade A database on CD-Rom* edited by D. Eltis, S.T. Behrendt, D. Richardson, H.S. Klein (Cambridge 1999) we find further details of slaving voyages connected with Guernsey. Following their identification code, nos: 24002, 24003, 24004, 24005, 24008, 24532 and 24961 departed from Guernsey (although they were not necessarily Guernsey-owned). Nos 77536 and 77581 are listed as registered in Guernsey. Eltis also gives details of *Cumberland* (27164; 24003), *Africa(n)* (77581; 24961) and *Gold Coast Galley* (24951), which can be related to Guernsey by the evidence cited on pp. 72-73. Eltis' entries (interpreted in conjunction with the Cour d'Amirauté evidence) give eleven voyages, to which it may be that the *Charles*, and Jamieson's five expeditions should be added (see pp. 72-73).

Slaving expeditions with Guernsey connections (correlating Eltis 1999 evidence with Cour d'Amirauté evidence)

Ident. no	Ship's name	Master	Date	Slaves taken	Where	Slaves delivered	Where
77536	*Ann Gally*	Ebsworthy	1741	293		239	
27164	*Cumberland*	John Mauger	1749	109		89	Barbados
24002	?	John Major	1750	320	Gambia	279	
77581	*African*	J. Mauger	1750	136		111	Barbados
24951	*Gold Coast Galley*	William Coutart	1750-1752	293		239	Jamaica
24003	*Cumberland*	Pinneaux	1752	200	Gambia	174	
24961	*Africa*	David Pineaux	1752	125	Gambia	109	Barbados
24004	*Castleton*	Lyndo	1756	189	Gambia	165	
24005	*Duke of Cumberland*	Sands	1756	189	Gambia	165	
24008	*Jenny*	John Allman	1756/7	75	Gambia	65	St Croix
24532	*Fanny*	Bareaud	1761	189	Senegal	165	Martinique

By way of comparison it may be noted that French ports mounted the following numbers of slaving expeditions between 1713 and 1792:

Nantes: 1,402; La Rochelle: 423; Le Havre: 399; Bordeaux: 393; St Malo: 214; Lorient: 156; Honfleur: 125; Marseille: 82; Dunkirk: 44; Rochefort: 20; Vannes: 12; Bayonne: 9; Brest: 8; Dieppe-Morlaix: 2 (Roman, 2001, p. 36).

The African destination (when known) was usually Gambia. Some Guernsey shipmasters would have known the route, as they were familiar with near-by Mayo in the Cape Verde islands (a source of salt). From Gambia the slaving expeditions went, on occasion, to Barbados. In the mid-eighteenth century William Le Mesurier and Daniel Tupper were buying slaves there (see pp. 77, 79). William was the major buyer at an auction sale held at Speight Town, acquiring slaves transported on the African, a Guernsey-owned vessel. It is interesting to note that his brother Mathieu Le Mesurier died on 1 Jan 1750 'at Guinea' while on a voyage (see p. 183). Pierre Le Mesurier, a surgeon, also died at Guinea in 1750 (*Rough Index to Le Mesurier or Le Messurier Papers*, p. 35).

On 10 June 1789 Thomas Le Mesurier wrote to Havilland Le Mesurier and replied to a query with the following observation:

> I can form no reasonable or probable conjecture what will be the event whether the trade will be abolished or regulated or what length the regulations may extend are points upon which therefore [*if*] I were to pretend to give you an opinion I should be at least as likely to be wrong as to be right. You must therefore exercise your own judgment – I have nothing but cautions to give you and to desire you to take care that your dashing disposition does not engage you too rashly or too far... (Priaulx Library, Le Mesurier papers).

Havilland Le Mesurier, working at Le Havre, was involved in the slave trade. He was the principal owner of *le Bosquet d'Or*, which made a voyage in 1788/9 from Le Havre to the Gold Coast, taking thence 374 slaves to Tobago (Eltis 1999, 32771); in 1790 his ship took 491 slaves from the Gold Coast to St Domingue (Eltis 1999, 32803).

We have seen that William Brock was an owner of the *Gold Coast Galley* (*vide supra* pp. 72-73). He may have been the William Brock who was the first of four owners of the *Peggy*, a brigantine (built at Liverpool in 1757 and registered there in 1767). The *Peggy* took 114 slaves from Africa, delivering 103 at Dominica in 1768. (Eltis 1999, 91357).

Mauger was a prominent captain in Guernsey slaving expeditions (see p. 72). He may have been the same Mauger who was captain of the *Neptune* which took 189 slaves from Senegal in 1761/1762 and delivered 165 (Eltis 1999, 75924).

There are a few further scraps of evidence about slavery in the Guernsey archives. On 20 June 1749 Henry Cook actioned James Viscount, master of a vessel 'in the road of this island' ('rade de cette Isle'). The case involved a negress left, by Viscount for Cook, with Paul Bedford, a merchant in Barbados. Cook sought the proceeds of the sale of the negress, if sold. The vessel is not named but the Viscount/Viscont family were involved locally in shipping (CdA, vol. 12, f 158, 20 June 1749). In Jan 1749/50 Isaac Dobrée stood 'caution' for James Viscount in the case brought by Henry Cook for £30 sterling 'pour le produit d'une negresse appellée Easter, que le dit Cook avait livrée au dit Le Viscount pour vendre à l'isle de Barbade, & dont le dit Viscount n'a rendu compte au dit Cook, & aux frais à peine de prendre ses biens' (CdA vol. 12 f 177).

After a voyage from Virginia, and a short stay at Falmouth, the slave Olaudah Equiano (aged about eight) arrived in Guernsey, on a vessel named *The Industrious Bee*. Nicholas Dobrée was a part-owner of this snow. Equiano's account reads:

> One night I was sent on board the ship again; and in a little time we sailed for Guernsey, where she was in part owned by a merchant, one Nicholas Doberry. As I was now amongst

a people who had not their faces scarred, like some of the African nations where I had been, I was very glad I did not let them ornament me in that manner when I was with them. When we arrived at Guernsey, my master placed me to board and lodge with one of his mates, who had a wife and family there; and some months afterwards he went to England, and left me in the care of this mate, together with my friend Dick. This mate had a little daughter aged about five or six years, with whom I used to be much delighted. I had often observed, that when her mother washed her face it looked very rosy; but when she washed mine it did not look so; I therefore tried oftentimes myself if I could not by washing make my face of the same colour as my little play-mate (Mary), but it was all in vain; and I now began to be mortified at the difference in our complexions. This woman behaved to me with great kindness and attention; and taught me every thing in the same manner as she did her own child, and indeed in every respect treated me as such. I remained here till the summer of the year 1757, when my master, being appointed first lieutenant of his Majesty's ship the Roebuck, sent for Dick and me, and his old mate: on this we all left Guernsey, and set out for England in a sloop bound for London.

Research by Vincent Carretta suggests that Equiano was mistaken about the date 1757 and that it should read 1755. See *Olaudah Equiano, The Interesting Narrative and Other Writings*, ed. Vincent Carretta, London, 2003; and the essay by Brycchan Carey 'Olaudah Equiano: An African slave in Guernsey', RGS, Summer 2003. See also in this book, under Barbados section, for the slave called Jacko taken from Barbados.

CHAPTER 5

[1] Roy Porter has some helpful material about incomes: 'in 1750 one was said to need a capital of £20,000 to set up as a banker, £2,000 - £10,000 to be a brewer and £1,000 - £5,000 to be a woollen draper; but a mere £10-£100 would start you off as a butcher.' (*English Society in the Eighteenth Century*, London, 1991, p.78). Porter also gives details of London merchants worth between £100,000 and £500,000. Some of the Guernsey merchants were wealthy, but it is misleading to refer to them as 'merchant princes' (as journalists have).

The fortunes of the Guernsey merchants were roughly of the order of those of the Dunkirk *négociants*:

Mais, en dehors des grands ports des millionaires, c'est en centaines de miliers de livres que se comptent les fortunes de l'élite négociante. Dans les années 1770-1780, C. Pfister nous donne les quatre principales fortunes de Dunkerque: J. Benoist Houelt 738 747 lt, Cornel Constantin Woestyn 404 740 lt, Olivier Houelt 323 456 lt, Jean Baptiste Morel 276 070. Dans de nombreux ports, les fortunes ne depassent pas les 500 000 livres et sont souvent plus proches de 100 à 200,000 livres' Le Bouëdec, 1997, pp. 304-305.

Bibliography

Manuscript sources

Printed original sources

        A.   Acts and Orders

        B.   Newspaper and contemporary journals

        C.   Contemporary writings

Printed secondary sources

Internet

Unpublished theses

MANUSCRIPT SOURCES

ENGLAND

Cambridgeshire

Cambridge University Library

    CUL Cholmondeley (Houghton) papers

London

British Library

BL	Add Mss 38376, 38463, 38759
BL	King's Ms 48
BL	Lansdowne Ms 657
BL	Sloane Ms 4053
BL	Dumaresq

Guildhall Library

    3291/1, 3291/2 Dobrée ledgers

    11936 Sun Fire Insurance Company

London Metropolitan Archives

    ACC/0349/295; ACC/0349/296.

The National Archives

TNA ADM 1	Admiralty and Secretariat papers
TNA CO 5	Board of Trade and Secretaries of State
TNA CO 33	Colonial Office and predecessors: Barbados, miscellanea
TNA CO 111	Colonial Office and predecessors: British Guiana
TNA CO 388	Board of Trade: original correspondence
TNA CO 390	Board of Trade: original correspondence
TNA CUST 3	Ledgers of Imports and Exports, England
TNA CUST 14	Ledgers of Imports and Exports, Scotland
TNA CUST 15	Ledgers of Imports and Exports, Ireland
TNA CUST 59	Outport records: Weymouth
TNA CUST 60	Outport records: Poole
TNA CUST 62	Outport records: Southampton
TNA CUST 105	Outport records: Channel Islands
TNA FO 638	Foreign Office, Consulate, Barcelona
TNA FO 639	Southern Department and Foreign Office
TNA HCA 26	High Court of Admiralty: Prize Court: Registers of Declarations for Letters of Marque
TNA HO 98	Home Office: Channel Islands
TNA SP 47	Secretaries of state: State Papers Channel Islands
TNA T 1	Treasury Board Papers
TNA T 64	Treasury, various

Northamptonshire

Northampton Record Office

    Finch Hatton papers (278)

FRANCE

Nantes

Archives municipales

    Fonds Dobrée

GUERNSEY

Greffe, St Peter Port

References to *List of Records in the Greffe, Guernsey*, volume 1 (List and Index Society, special series volume 2, London, 1969) are given in parentheses.

Greffe	*Cour d'Amirauté* (I.23, p. 32)
Greffe	Depositions, 1699-1715 (I.36.10, p 35)
Greffe	General Letterbooks, first series (II.46, p 40)
Greffe	*Livre de certificats* 1768-1788 (II. 50.14, p. 41)

Island Archive Service

IAS	de Havilland papers
IAS	Dobrée papers
IAS	Price papers
IAS	Stevens-Guille papers

Priaulx Library

Priaulx	Dobrée (Isaac), notary book
Priaulx	Family files
Priaulx	Gosselin account book
Priaulx	Guille (Jean senr), account book
Priaulx	Guille papers
Priaulx	Guille (George?), journal of tour of France 1787
Priaulx	Guille, letterbooks
Priaulx	Kennett papers
Priaulx	Le Mesurier papers
Priaulx	Lihou (Peter), letterbook
Priaulx	Lukis ms
Priaulx	McCulloch ms.
Priaulx	Mollet journals
Priaulx	Mourant (Peter), journal
Priaulx	Priaulx, Carteret Priaulx papers
Priaulx	Reserson, *Apologia* by Nicholas Reserson

Private

Private	Collings papers (including *Livre touchant la Distillation*, 1784)
Private	de Crousaz papers
Private	Guille journey from Guernsey to Barcelona, accounts
Private	Harvey family papers
Private	Trieste letterbook
Private	William Le Lacheur's letterbook (voyages of *Pomona*), transcript of
Sausmarez Manor	de Sausmarez papers

Royal Court Library

Royal Court Legge ms

Original Letters [List of Records in the Greffe, Guernsey, vol 1 (London, 1969) IV.77.3, p 59].

SCOTLAND

Edinburgh

Scottish Record Office

SPAIN

Barcelona

AHCB Arxiu Històric de la Ciutat de Barcelona Fons Comercial, A79, A80; B11.

Tarragona

AHP Arxiu Històric del Port de Tarragona (Port books)

AHT Arxiu Històric de Tarragona (Notarial records)

SWEDEN

Gothenburg - Landsarkivet

Ekman papers

PRINTED ORIGINAL SOURCES

A: Acts, Orders, Legal records

Statues of the Realm:

Acts 12 Car II cap 32; 4 Geo III chap. 13 sect. 11; 8 Geo III chap 23 sect.2.3

Parliamentary Papers

An Account presented to the House of Commons, of the number and names of vessels Cleared out from the Port of Guernsey, in the Months of November and December 1806, and January and February 1807, with the Amount of the excise and customs duties thereon. 21st July, 1807, p. 10, in Parliamentary ERS< House of Commons, session 27 June - 14 August 1807, iv<57>, pp.89-95.

Guernsey *Actes* and *Ordonnances*

Actes des Etats de l'Ile de Guernesey, 1605-1845, (8 vols), Guernsey, 1851-1938

Recueil d'Ordonnances de la Cour Royale de l'Isle de Guernesey, 1533-1840 (2 vols) Guernsey, 1852-1856.

Scottish Sessions Papers

B: Newspapers and contemporary journals

Almanacs

Gazette de Guernesey

Gazette de l'Ile de Jersey

Gentleman's Magazine

Guernsey Evening Press

London Gazette

Loyd's Lists

Lloyd's Registers

Philosophical Transactions of the Royal Society

The Guernsey and Jersey Magazine

The Star (Guernsey)

The Times

C: Contemporary Writings

Articles of the Friendly Society, of the Island of Guernsey, Salisbury (1764); and *An Additional Article, of the Friendly Society in Guernsey*, Southampton (1769). [Known as *La Société des Veuves*].

The Case of the Inhabitants of the Island of Guernsey, in Relation to several Orders of Council obtained by the Commissioners of the Customs, for setting Custom-House-Officers in the Island, and subjecting the Inhabitants to the Laws relating to the Customs in Great Britain (c. 1708).

The Case of the Town Parish versus the Nine Country Parishes, respecting a change in the rates and representation, appointed to be heard before the Committee of the Privy Council, at eleven o'clock, on

Thursday, April 26, 1759 (Guernsey, 1846).

[Anon.] (1787)*The Gentleman's Guide in his Tour through France*, London.

[Anon.] (1862)*Sarnia: or brief memorials of her many sons, (civil, military, and naval)*, Guernsey.

Berry, W. (1815) *History of the Island of Guernsey*, London.

Bolingbroke, H.A (1809)*Voyage to the Demerary*, London.

Dalzel, A. (1793) *The History of Dahomy, an inland kingdom of Africa*, London.

de Boisgelin, L. (1810) *Travels through Denmark and Sweden* (2 vols), London.

de Saumarez, H. (1717) *An Account of the Proceedings of Henry De Sausmarez, of the Island of Guernsey, Gent.*, London.

de Saumarez , H. (1725) '*An account of a new machine, called the Marine Surveyor...*' *Philosophical Transactions of the Royal Society, vol. 33 (1725), 411-432.*

de Saumarez, H. (1726) '*Observations upon the tides in the River Thames*' *Philosophical Transactions of the Royal Society, vol. 34 (1726), 68-72.*

de Saumarez, H. (1729) '*A further account of a new machine, called the Marine Surveyor...*' *Philosophical Transactions of the Royal Society, vol. 36 (1729), 45-58.*

Dicey, T. (1751) *An Historical Account of Guernsey, from its first settlement before the Norman Conquest to the present time*, London.

Dobrée, N. (1746) *Observations sur les cartes des Isles de Guernesey, Aureny, Sercq, Herm, & Jethou, levées & dressées par Nicholas Dobrée Ecuyer.* London.

Ham, E. (1945) *Elizabeth Ham by herself 1783 - 1820* , edited by E. Gillett, London.

Inglis, H.D. (1834) *The Channel Islands*, London.

Jacob, J. (1830) *Annals of the British Norman Isles*, Paris. [Vol. II (supplement) was published posthumously by his family.]

Le Marchant (1755) *Histoire de l'Erection Originelle de l'avancement & Augmentation du Havre de la Ville de St Pierre Port à Guernesey.*

Le Marchant, W. (1771) *The Rights and Immunities of the Island of Guernsey*, London. [Reprinted with additional material, 1805].

Leabon, G (1812) *Persecution!! A Narrative of facts, connected with the military system, and illicit trade, of a part of the Channel Islands*, London.

Mackenzie, H. (1927) *Anecdotes and Egotisms of Henry Mackenzie 1745 - 1831*, edited by H.W. Thompson, Oxford.

Malham, J (1799) *The Naval Gazeteer*, London.

Marshall, J. (1833) *A Digest of all the Accounts*, London.

Pidansat de Mairobert, M.-F. (1756) *Lettre à Madame de *** sur les Affaires du Jour, ou Reflexions politiques sur l'usage qu'on peut faire de la Conquête de Minorque, suivies d'un état circonstancié des Isles de Gerzey & de Guernezey,* (Paris?).

Richards, W. (1747) *The Complete Penman*, London.

Steele, D. (1818) *The Art of Rigging*, London.

Townsend, J. (1791) *A Journey through Spain in the Years 1786 and 1787*, London.

Tupper, F. B. (1836) '*Remarks on the slave trade at Rio de Janeiro.-1827*' in The Guernsey and Jersey Magazine, vol. 2, July 1836, 9-12.

Tupper, F. B. (1837) '*Commerce of Guernsey*' in The Guernsey and Jersey Magazine, vol. 4 November 1837, pp. 306-310; and '*Commerce of Guernsey - No. 2*' vol. 4, December 1837, pp. 359-368.

PRINTED SECONDARY SOURCES

Anonymous (1895) *The Mansell Family a brief sketch of the career of some of its members*, Guernsey.

Aldrich, R. (ed.) (2007) *The Age of Empire*, London.

Anderson, A. (1964) *'Trade between the Channel Islands and Southampton in the Mid-Eighteenth Century'* BSJ vol. XVIII, 445-451.

Andrews, C.M. (1943) *The Colonial Period of American History*, New Haven.

Aptel, C., *et al.* (1997) *Thomas Dobrée Un Homme Un Musée*, Nantes.

Beckles, H. (1990) *A History of Barbados*, Cambridge.

Bowen, H.V., Lincoln, M., Rigby, N. (eds) (2002) *The World of the East India Company*, Woodbridge.

Braudel, F. (1984) *Civilization and Capitalism* (3 vols), London.

Buchet, C. (1999) *Marine économie et société Un exemple d'interaction: l'avitaillement de la Royal Navy durant la guerre de sept ans*, Paris.

Carey, E. (1931) *'A Trip to Guernsey in 1798 by W.T. Money'* TSG vol. VIII, 237-258.

Carey, L.F. deVic *(n.d.) A short history of Le Vallon*, Guernsey.

Carey, W.W. et al. (1938) *The History of the Careys of Guernsey*, London.

Clark, G.N. (1938) *Guide to English Commercial Statistics 1696-1782*, London.

Clark, J.G. (1981) *La Rochelle and the Atlantic Economy during the Eighteenth Century*, Baltimore.

Coclanis, P.A.(ed.) (2005) *The Atlantic Economy during the Seventeenth and Eighteenth Centuries: Organization, Operation, Practice, and Personnel*, Columbia.

Coldham, P.W. (2007) *North American Wills registered in London 1611-1857*, London.

Crawford, A. (1984) *Bristol and the Wine Trade*, Bristol.

Croix, A. (1981) *La Bretagne aux 16e et 17e siècles*, Paris.

Crouzet, F. (1990) *Britain Ascendant: comparative studies in Franco-British economic history*, Cambridge.

Cullen, L.M. (1968) *Anglo-Irish Trade 1660 - 1800*, Manchester.

Cullen, L.M. (1998) *The Brandy Trade under the Ancien Regime*, Cambridge.

Cullen, L.M. (2000) *The Irish Brandy Houses*, Dublin.

Curtis, S. Carey (1929) *'The Tupper Medal'* TSG vol. X, 425-433.

Davis, R. (1972) *The Rise of the English Shipping Industry in the Seventeenth and Eighteenth Centuries*, London.

de Guérin (1890) *Our Kin*, Guernsey.

de la Rogerie, A. Bourde (1931) *'La Famille Martell'* TSG vol. XI, 259-262.

de Lemps, C. Huetz (1975) *Géographie de commerce de Bordeaux à la fin du règne de Louis XIV*, Paris.

Delumeau, J. (1966) *Le mouvement du port de Saint Malo, 1681 - 1720*, Paris.

Devine, T.M. (1990) *The Tobacco Lords*, Edinburgh.

Dickson, D., Parmentier, J., and Ohlmeyer, J. *(eds.)* (2007) *Irish and Scottish Mercantile Networks in Europe and Overseas in the Seventeenth and Eighteenth Centuries.* Ghent.

Duncan, J. (1841) *The History of Guernsey*, London.

Duncan, T. (1972) *Atlantic Islands*, Chicago.

Dupont, G. (1885) *Histoire du Cotentin et de ses Iles*, Caen.

Farrington, A. (1999) *A Biographical Index of East India Company Maritime Service Officers, 1600-1834*, London.

Feldbaek, O. (1963) *India trade under the Danish Flag 1772-1808*, Denmark.

Fisher, H.E.S. (1971) *The Portugal Trade*, London.

Foucqeron, G. (1999) *Saint-Malo 2000 ans d'histoire*, St Malo.

Francis, A.D. (1972) *The Wine Trade*, London.

Goddio, F. (2002) *Griffin: On the Route of an Indiaman*, London.

Goldenburg, J.A. (1976) *'Shipbuilding in Colonial America'*, Charlottesville.

Guilbert (1901) *'Recollections of an old sailor, Captain Guilbert, aged 92'*, The Star, 2 February 1901.

Hancock, D. (2000) *'A revolution in trade: wine distribution and the development of the infrastructure of the Atlantic market economy, 1703 - 1807'* in McCusker & Morgan, 105 - 153.

Hancock, D. (2005) *'Self-Organised Complexity and the Emergence of an Atlantic Market Economy, 1615 - 1815'* in Coclanis (ed.) 30-71.

Harris, L. and Fisher, K. (2004) *Guernsey on the Map*, Guernsey.

Harrison, G. (1955) *Bristol Cream*, London.

Haudrère, P. (1989) *La Compagnie Française des Indes au XVIIIe Siècle (1719-1795)*, Paris.

Haudrère, P. (1997) *Le Grand Commerce maritime au XVIIIe siècle*, Paris.

Hocart, R. (1983) '*A Guernsey Merchant and his Family in the Reign of George II*' TSG vol. XXIV, 360-378.

Hocart, R. (1988) *An Island Assembly The Development of the States of Guernsey 1700-1949*, Guernsey.

Hocart, R. (1997) *Peter de Havilland Bailiff of Guernsey - a History of his Life, 1747 - 1821*, Guernsey.

Hocart, R. (2007) '*Jean Guille and the Management of the St George Estate*', TSG vol. XXVI, 252-275.

Huetz de Lemps, C. (1975) *Géographie du Commerce de Bordeaux à la fin du règne de Louis XIV*, Paris.

Hugo, T.M.H. (1960) '*Hilary Rougier, Sailor, Merchant and Banker*' in QRGS, *vol. xvi, no 2, Summer 1960*, Guernsey.

Jamieson, A.G. (ed.) (1986) *A People of the Sea*, London.

Jespersen, K.J.V. (2007) '*Scandinavia: An Outsider in European Imperialism*' in Aldrich, 112-127.

Kemp, P. (ed.) (1988) *The Oxford Companion to Ships and the sea*, Oxford.

Le Bouëdec, G. (1997) *Activités maritimes et sociétés littorales de l'europe atlantique 1690 - 1790*, Paris.

Le Mesurier, A. (1910) *Rough Index to Le Mesurier or Le Messurier papers*, (Guernsey ?).

Lespagnol, A. (1990) *Messieurs de Saint-Malo*, St Malo.

Little, C.H. (1959) *The Recapture of Saint John's Newfoundland (Maritime Museum of Canada occasional paper no 6)*, Halifax.

Lyons, M.A., and & O'Connor, T. (2008) *Strangers to Citizens - the Irish in Europe 1600-1800*, Dublin.

Marr, J. (1984) *Guernsey People*, Chichester.

Mauro, F. '*Merchant Communities 1350 - 1750*' in Tracy (1990), 255 - 286.

McCusker, J. and Morgan, K.(eds.) (2000) *The Early Modern Atlantic Economy*, Cambridge.

Meyer, J. (1969) *L'Armement nantais dans la deuxième moitié du XVIIIe siècle*, Paris.

Meyer, W.R. (2004A) *Havilland le Mesurier (1755-1806)* in Oxford Dictionary of National Biography, *vol. 33*, Oxford.

Meyer, W.R. (2004B) *Paul le Mesurier (1755-1805)* in Oxford Dictionary of National Biography, *vol. 33*, Oxford.

Minchinton, W. (1957) *The Trade of Bristol in the Eighteenth Century*, Bristol.

Minchinton, W. (1989) '*Characteristics of British Slaving Vessels, 1698 - 1775*' Journal of Interdisciplinary History, xxii (Summer 1989), *53-81*.

Mollat, M. (1987) *Histoire des pêches maritimes en France*, Paris.

Namier, L. and Brooke, J. (1964) *The House of Commons 1754 - 1790*, London.

Ommer, R. (1986) '*The Cod Trade in the New World*' in Jamieson (ed.), 245 - 268.

Ozanne, C. (1928) '*Adventures of a Channel Islander in France in the 18th Century*' TSG vol. X 275-283.

Parmentier, J. (1997) '*Profit and Neutrality: The Case of Ostend, 1781-1783*' in Starkey, van Heslinga, de Moor, 206-226.

Parmentier, J. (2007) '*The Sweets of Commerce: The Hennessys of Ostend and their Network in the Eighteenth Century*' in Dickson, Parmentier and Ohlmeyer, 67-92.

Perrycoste, F.H. (1929) *Gleanings from the records of Zephaniah Job, of Polperro*, (Polperro reprint, 2007)

Priaulx, T.F. (1961) '*Peter Perchard, Lord Mayor of London*' in QRGS summer 1961, vol. xvii, no. 2, Guernsey.

Price, J.M. (1973) *France and the Chesapeake*, Ann Arbor.

Price, J.M. (1995) *Tobacco in Atlantic Trade, The Chesapeake, London and Glasgow 1675-1775*, Aldershot.

Raban, P. (1986) '*War and Trade in the Mid-Eighteenth Century*' TSG vol. XXII, 131-161.

Raban, P. (1987) '*Clandestine Trade in the Mid-Eighteenth Century*' TSG vol. XXII.

Richard, G. (1997) *Européens et Espaces Maritimes au XVIIIe siècle*, Paris.

Richardson, D. (1986, 1987, 1991, 1996) *Bristol, Africa and the Eighteenth-Century Slave Trade to America* (4 vols), Bristol.

Roman, A. (2001) *Saint-Malo au temps des négriers*, Paris.

Rybot, N.V.L. (1928) '*Heraldry in Guernsey*' TSG vol. X, 319-357.

Sarre, J. (2007) *Guernsey Sailing Ships 1786-1936,* Guernsey Museums monograph no 8 [CD ROM format] Guernsey.

Sarre, J. and Forbrigger, L. (1991) *'Some Guernsey Connections with Cape Breton Island'* TSG vol. XXIII, 173-181.

Schumpeter, ER.B. (1980) *English Overseas Trade Statistics 1697-1808,* Oxford.

Segarra Blasco, A. (1994) *Aiguardent i mercat a la Catalunya del segle XVIII,* Barcelona.

Sharp, E.W. (1968) *'The Evolution of St Peter Port Harbour'* TSG XVIII, 226-255.

Shaw, L.M.E. (1998) *The Anglo-Portuguese Alliance and the English Merchants in Portugal, 1654-1810,* Aldershot.

Simon, A. L. (1948) *Drink,* London.

Simon, A.L. (1907) *The History of the Wine Trade in England,* London.

Starkey, D.J., van Eyck van Heslinga, E.S., and de Moor, J.A. *(1997) Pirates and Privateers New Perspectives on the War on Trade in the Eighteenth and Nineteenth Centuries,* Exeter.

Steele, I.K. (1986) *The English Atlantic 1675 - 1740,* Oxford.

Syrret, D. (2008) *Shipping and Military Power in the Seven Years War,* Exeter.

Thomas, J.H. (2002) *'East India Company Agency Work in the British Isles, 1700-1800'* in Bowen et al.

Tracy, J.D. (1990) *The Rise of Merchant Empires,* Cambridge.

Tupper, F. B. (1854) *The History of Guernsey,* Guernsey.

Turk, M.G. (1979) *The Quiet Adventurers in Canada,* (U.S.A.)

Turner, M.D.K. (1989) *Contract Unbroken: Secretan's 200 Years at Lloyd's 1789-1989,* London.

Valls Junyent, F. (2004) *La Catalunya atlàntica,* Barcelona.

Vignols, L. *L'Importation en France au XVIIIe siècle du boeuf d'Irlande'* in Révue Historique, part 159, (1928), 79 - 95.

Vilar, P. (1977) *Catalunya dins l'Espanya moderna,* Barcelona.

Voelcker, T. (2008) *Admiral Saumarez versus Napoleon,* Woodbridge.

White, M. (1963) *'The Carteret Priaulx Papers'* TSG vol. XVII, 447-488.

Wickins, L. (1984) *'The Economics of Privateering: Capital Dispersal in the American War of Independence'* Journal of European Economic History, vol. 13, no.2 (Fall 1984), 375-395.

Wilkins, F. (1992) *Strathclyde's Smuggling Story,* Kidderminster.

Yule, H., and Burnell, A.C. (1985) *Hobson-Jobson,* London.

INTERNET

Dictionary of Canadian Biography online.

Oxford Dictionary of National Biography online.

http:/ngb.cheto.org/Articles/colville-1762.shtml.

www.kuiters.org/wgi/history/botgardpaxton.html (Details about Archibald Stuart)

www.marcireau.fr/urry, 2 June 2008. (Details about Captain Urry)

www.uppercanadahistory.ca/brock/brock13.html.

www.maplandia.com/guyana/east-berbicecorentyne/vi-2-east-canjee-c-berb/port-mourant/

The references to East Kent Archives Centre (p. 207), London Metropolitan Archives (p. 207), Southampton Archive Service (p.199) and West Sussex Record Office (p.175) were taken from an archival reference system (internet) at The National Archives.

UNPUBLISHED THESES

Fernandez Diaz, R *La burguesia commercial barcelonesa en el siglo XVIII. Tesi doctoral. Lleida: Estudi General, 1987.*

Price, J.M. *(1954) The Tobacco Trade and the Treasury, 1685-1733: British Mercantilism in its Fiscal Aspects' Ph.D. Thesis (Harvard, 1954).*

INDEX

This is an index of names occurring in the main text, pp. 1 – 170. Chapter 8 - Register of Merchants (pp. 171 - 210) - lists families in alphabetical order. For the wealth and ranking of families, see pp. 97 – 98.

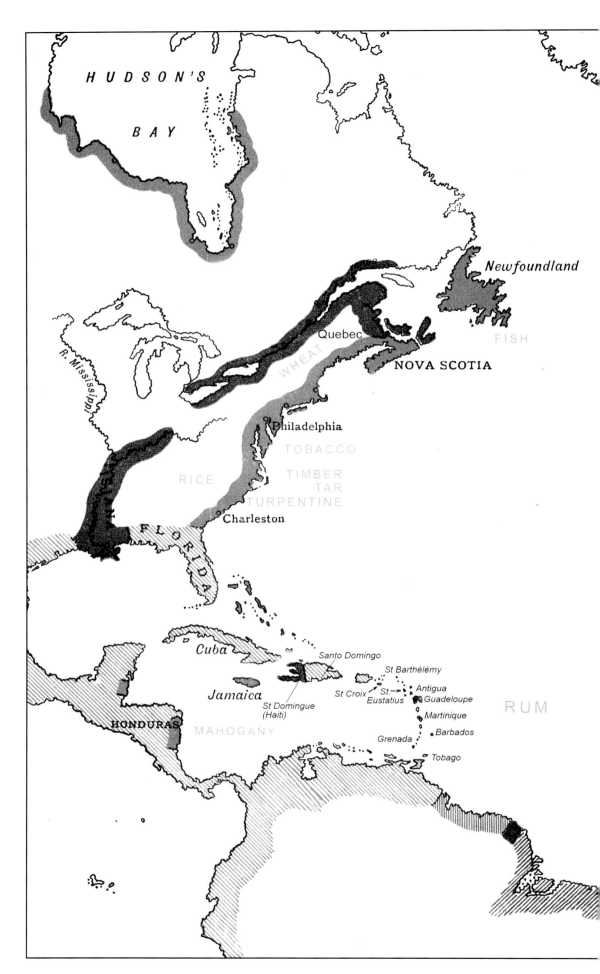

HUDSON'S

BAY

Newfoundland

FISH

Quebec

WHEAT

NOVA SCOTIA

R. Mississippi

Philadelphia

TOBACCO

TIMBER
TAR
TURPENTINE

RICE

Charleston

FLORIDA

Cuba

Santo Domingo

St Barthélémy

Jamaica

St Croix

*St.→
Eustatius*

Antigua

Guadeloupe

*St Domingue
(Haiti)*

RUM

Martinique

HONDURAS

MAHOGANY

Grenada

Barbados

Tobago

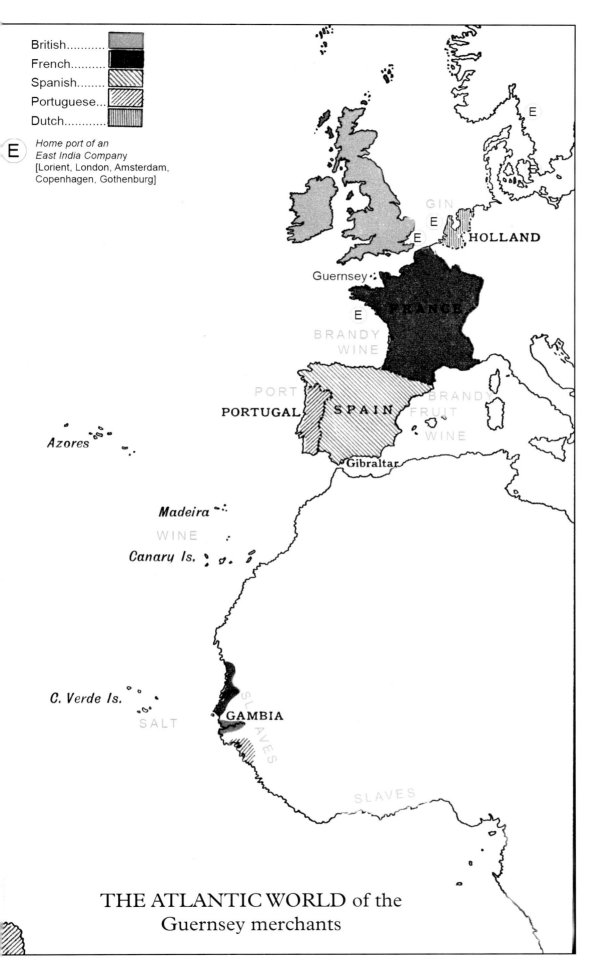

British...........
French..........
Spanish........
Portuguese...
Dutch...........

E Home port of an
East India Company
[Lorient, London, Amsterdam,
Copenhagen, Gothenburg]

E

E E

E HOLLAND

Guernsey

E

FRANCE

GIN

BRANDY
WINE

PORT

PORTUGAL SPAIN

BRANDY
FRUIT
WINE

Gibraltar

Azores

Madeira

WINE

Canary Is.

C. Verde Is.

SALT

GAMBIA

SLAVES

SLAVES

THE ATLANTIC WORLD of the
Guernsey merchants

AN
ACCOUNT
OF THE
PROCEEDINGS
OF
Henry De Saumarez,
OF THE
Ifland of *Guernefey*, Gent.

Concerning His DISCOVERY of an
Invention, by which the Courfe of a
Ship at Sea may be better Afcertained
than by the Logg-Line, *Viz.* By a Dial
placed in fome convenient Place of the
Ship, with a little Bell ftriking from
Time to Time, the Geometrical Paces,
Miles, and Leagues, which the Ship
hath run.

London, Printed in the Year. 1717.

I

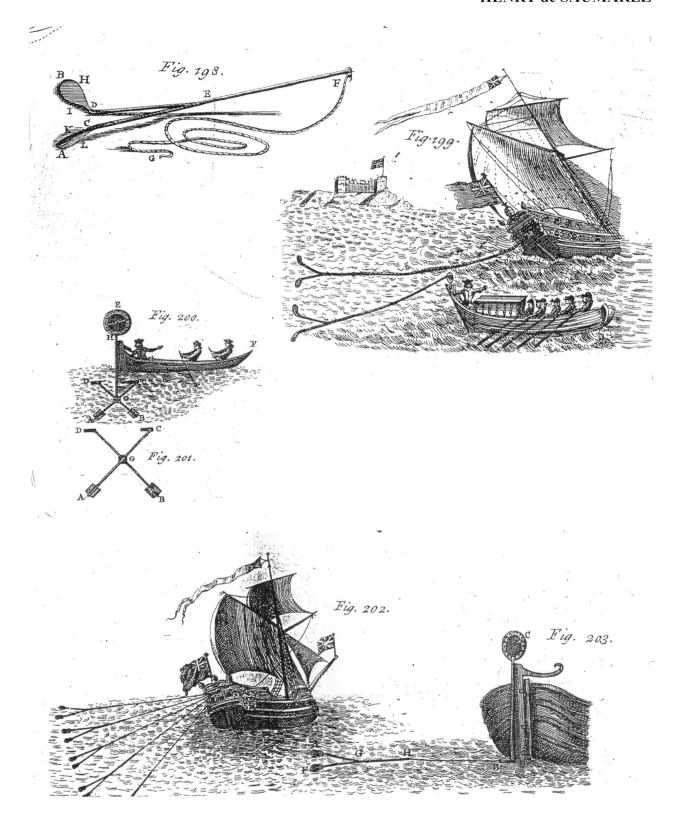

Left: Title-page (enlarged) of Henry de Saumarez's pamphlet about the virtues of his invention.

Above: Details from a plate which accompanied de Saumarez's account in the *Philosophical Transactions of the Royal Society* (abridged edition).

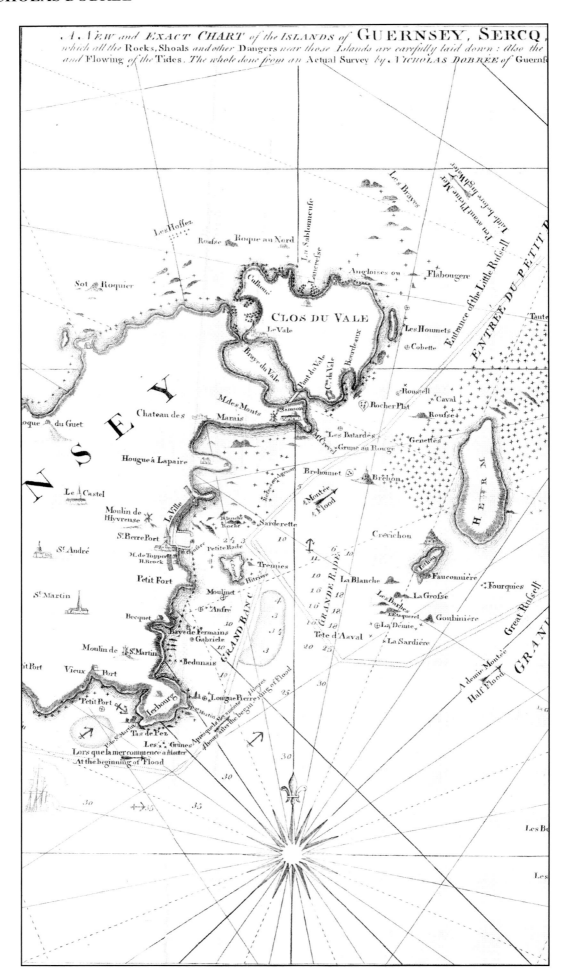

(21)

Of the little Road.

THIS Road lieth to the Northward of the said *Castle Cornet*, and Distance from the said Castle, and the Rock called *La blanche Roche ou Sardrette*, is the Place where to anchor in; and when you moor your Ship, you drop one of your Anchors near the Rocks on *Castle Point*, and the other Anchor you drop Northerly, near the said *Blanche Roche*, then is your Ship safe, was she even a Forty Gun Ship.

Of the Mole or Pier Harbour.

THIS Mole or Harbour lieth on the East Part of the Island, inclosed with two Piers made of Stone; the Entrance therein at the top Part is about an hundred Feet in Breadth, and at the Bottom about sixty-eight Feet; the Height of the Rampart or Piers is about thirty-five Feet. Here the Tide flows West, and ebbs East; and in Spring-Tides is about 28 or 30 Feet deep, and in Nip-Tides not above 12 or 14 Feet deep, neither then doth it go out of it, tho' in Spring-Tides it falls near 150 Yards below it.

An Explanation of the following Marks or Characters, which have Reference to the Charts of *Guernsey*, *Alderney*, *Serk*, *Erm* and *Jethou*, which serve to distinguish the Nature of the Banks, Shoals, and Rocks on the respective Coasts of the said Islands, as they are set down in the aforesaid Charts.

 Bank never above Water.

× Rocks which appear at Low-Water in Spring-Tides.

 Rocks which appear above Water at half Ebb.

 Rocks always above Water.

 Dangers which Strangers must avoid.

.... Channel where Ships may pass.

D   The

Left: A section of Nicholas Dobrée's chart, first issued in 1746, showing the hazards of the sea approaches to St Peter Port.

Above: Details from the book of *Observations* issued to accompany the charts.

IV

Thomas (H.4), 1724-1780, 'de la Vrangue'

John (H.6), 1748-1821, 'of Choisi'

Isaac (H.9), 1758-1828, who married
Marguerite Tupper

Pierre Careye (F.35), 1689-1744, 'de la brasserie'

The old Carey house (Town church on the right)

Le Vallon

La brasserie – the old Carey house in St Peter Port

LE VALLON.

Le Vallon was built by Isaac (H.9) and incorporated
architectural ideas from Spain

The Vrangue Manor

12. NANTES. — Quai Fosse. Station de la Bourse.

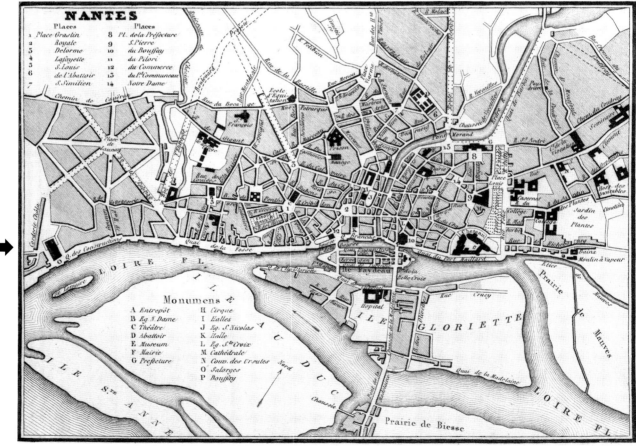

(95)

occafion pour renouveller à S. E. les témoignages de fa haute eftime & de fon refpect. (Signé) CHAUVELIN, miniftre-plénipotentiaire de France.

GUERNESEY.

Lettre Circulaire, adreffée aux Négocians des villes maritimes du Royaume de France. Par les Négocians de cette île.

Meffieurs.

Les négocians de l'île de Guernefey ayant pris en confidération les rapports calomnieux qui fe propagent, & qui ont pour but de faire croire qu'ils faifiroient l'occafion favorable des circonftances, pour s'enrichir aux dépens de la France, en armant des *Corfaires* fous le pavillon de fes ennemis.

CONSIDERANT, que le nombre de navires propres à cet armement qui eft à leur difpofition : l'activité connue des habitans dans les dernières guerres, & la fituation avantageufe de cette île fembleroit juftifier une pareille imputation, fi elle n'étoit défavouée formellement.

Confidérant, fur tout, qu'un armement contre la France, feroit aufli criminel aujourd'hui en ce qu'il pourroit compromettre la Mère Patrie, qu'il étoit autrefois légal, & une preuve de leur attachement pour cette même Patrie, quand elle fe trouvoit en guerre.

Ont réfolu de repouffer une calomnie aufli atroce par une déclaration formelle de leurs fentimens.

Qu'ils renoncent à toute efpèce d'avantage & de confidération d'intérêt, que préfentement d'une manière peut être facile, mais affurément infame, des entreprifes fur le commerce de leurs voifins.

Qu'ils s'engagent folennellement, à ne point s'intéreffer directement ni indirectement dans aucun armement hoftile contre la France, pendant que l'Angleterre fera en paix avec elle.

Guernefey 2 er. Mai 1792.

N.B. Cette lettre eft fignée de foixante-deux négocians de cette île. Nous n'avons pu les inférer faute de place.

Réponfe de Meffieurs les Commiffaires de la ville de Nantes, aux habitans de l'île.

Meffieurs,

Mr. Dobrée, l'un de nos collégues nous a remis copie de l'engagement, que vous avez pris le 1. Mai dernier de ne point vous intereffer directement ni indirectement, dans aucun armement hoftile contre la Fance, pendant que l'Angleterre fera en paix avec elle.

Les négocians de cette Place à qui nous avons communiqué, Meffieurs votre déclaration, loin de croire aux bruits calomnieux repandus contre la droiture de vos intentions, étoient perfuadés d'avance que votre générofité, votre defintereffement & votre amour pour la liberté, ne vous porteroient jamais à rompre les liens d'un bon voifinage, avec un peuple qui combat pour le maintient de fes droits; en conféquence ils nous chargent de vous faire tous les remercimens que mérite votre acte généreux & d'être perfuadés de leurs fentimens fraternels & du defir qu'ils ont de vivre en paix avec des voifins aufli jaloux du maintient des traités.

Nous nous félicitons, Meffieurs, d'être auprès de vous les interprêtes des fentimens & de la reconnoiffance de nos concitoyens. Nous fommes avec fraternité.

Mathieu Boudoüin, Orrillard, Jaillant de Chantelot, Thema, Van Neunen, Jofeph Nomeron, Le Roux de Commerquiers, François Delaville, François Noriez, Lincolu, Dobrée.

Extract of a letter dated, Bordeaux 2 nd. June 1792 : to Mr. Thomas Lauga, at Guernfey.

I have receiv'd a few days fince your favor of 17 Ultimo, with an inclofed for Mr. Marandon, which I fent him fome day after perufal : he publifhed your Letter &c. in his paper, I made it publick as I could, particularly at the Infurance offices; it had a very good effect & is much to the honor of your Ifland.

I am &c.

Signed, Nat. Johnfton.

ÇA - I R A , ÇA - I R A.

On parle beaucoup de cet air fi chéri des François, de cet air fameux qui réjouit les hommes libres, & fait trembler les defpotes,

Left: Pierre-Frédéric Dobrée lived on the Quai de la Fosse at Nantes. The Quai was badly damaged during World War 2 but the postcard (c. 1900) illustrates the handsome merchant houses of 18th century Nantes. Map – early nineteenth century.

Above: In May 1792 sixty-two Guernsey merchants expressed their pacific intentions *via* Dobrée to the *négociants* of Nantes (*Gazette de Guernesey*, 16 June 1792).

VIII

*Colour
Plates
IX – XX*

Embroidered coverlet (approx. 295 cms x 224 cms) made in India (Deccan) for the European market
(1725 – 1750). Reproduced by kind permission of Francesca Galloway (London).

Large coverlet (292 cms x 218 cms) of red satin with silk chain stitch in cream, turquoise, blue and pink. Made in Bengal for the European market. Reproduced by kind permission of Francesca Galloway (London).

X

John Tupper (1668-1720), after an oil painting by an unknown artist. This is the only known likeness of John, who brought glory to the Tupper family. Reproduced by kind permission of Guernsey Museums & Galleries (GMAG 4270).

Gold medal and chain given to John Tupper by William III and Queen Mary, 1692, for his services in bringing to the English fleet the news as to the whereabouts of the French fleet. This led to the Battle of La Hogue, a famous British victory. Reproduced by kind permission of Guernsey Museums & Galleries (GMAG 1978.99).

Daniel Tupper (1753-1808), after a watercolour by an unknown artist. Daniel was a merchant and played a small, but critical, role in the story of Nicholas Reserson. Reproduced by kind permission of Guernsey Museums & Galleries (GMAG 2006.115a).

Helier Rougier, after an oil painting, artist unknown. Helier was born at Les Eperons in 1765 and became a shipowner and privateer. He helped to found the 'Old Bank'. He died in 1852. Reproduced by kind permission of Guernsey Museums & Galleries (GMAG 3917).

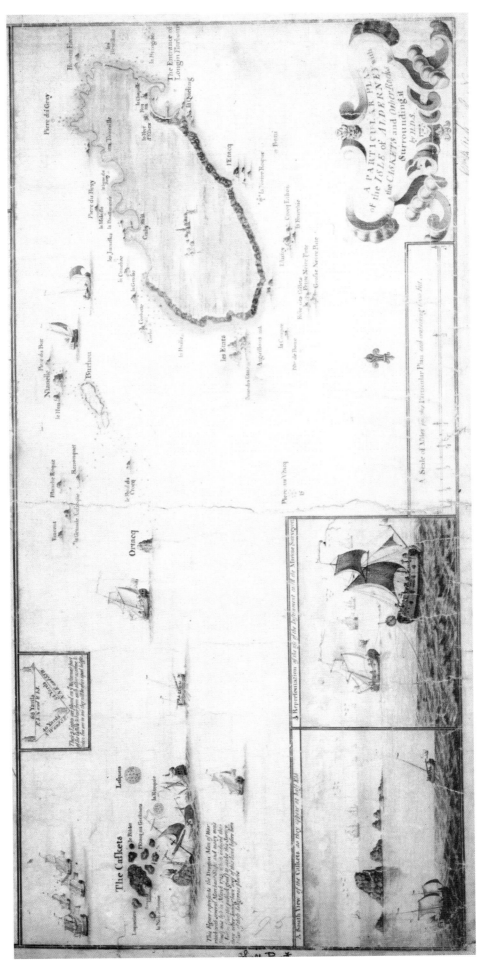

Map of Alderney and the Caskets, executed by Henry de Saumarez in 1727, with inset pictures of the Caskets (a notorious shipping hazard); and of the marine surveyor (Henry's invention). Reproduced by kind permission of the National Maritime Museum, Greenwich.

Falmouth, after a hand-coloured aquatint and etching designed by H. Mitchell, engraved by R. Pollard and published by H. Michell in Falmouth, 9 June 1805. Falmouth was frequently visited by Guernsey-bound vessels, often at the end of an Atlantic voyage. It was a port for quarantine and an important link in the communications network. A good coach service took messages to-and-from London. Reproduced by kind permission of the National Maritime Museum, Greenwich.

Algeciras, Spain. While Guernsey merchants continued to trade to the north, their fellow-islander Sir James Saumarez was fighting naval actions on the south Spanish coast. 'This plate, representing the British Squadron, preparing to pursue the Combined Squadron, of France & Spain, on the afternoon of the 12th of July 1801'. One of a series of five aquatint plates depicting the Battle of Algeciras, drawn by Sir Jahleel Brenton, Sir James Saumarez's flag captain at the battle, and published in 1802 'for the benefit of the widows & orphans of those who fought & fell on that glorious day'. For sale at Bernard Quaritch Ltd, Antiquarian Booksellers since 1847.

South view of Madeira and the city of Funchal,
after a hand-coloured aquatint by Gleader after Hopkins,
issued in *An Historial Sketch of the Island of Madeira*, London, 1819.

Trieste, after a coloured etching by Ferdinando Artana (Vienna), *circa* 1830. Reproduced by kind permission of the National Maritime Museum, Greenwich.

The brig *St George* entering Trieste, after a watercolour by Felice Polli. This vessel (of approximately 111 tons) was built in 1819 in Guernsey and was employed on the Rio-Trieste run. Reproduced by kind permission of Guernsey Museums & Galleries (GMAG 1981.680).

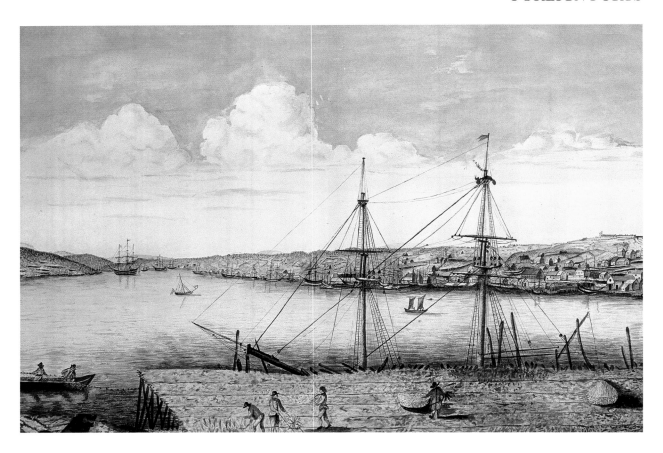

St John's, Newfoundland, the harbour looking inland. Watercolour by John Reeves (1752-1829).
Reproduced by kind permission of Messrs Christie's, Auctioneers, London (TOP 270906087A).

Quebec, after an aquatint in *Travels through the Canadas* by George Heriot, London, 1807.
(Private collection).

Custom House negroes at Rio de Janeiro, after an engraving in *The History of the Brazil* by James
Henderson, London, 1821.

Rio de Janeiro, after a hand-coloured lithograph, designed by L. Le Breton, published by J. Youds,
Rio de Janeiro, mid-nineteenth century. Reproduced by kind permission of the National Maritime
Museum, Greenwich.

The brig *Collingwood* of Guernsey, in distress, after a watercolour by Jacob Petersen. The *Collingwood* was built in 1816 at Monkwearmouth and was employed on the Trieste-Tarragona-Hamburg-Rio runs. Reproduced by kind permission of Guernsey Museums & Galleries (GML 1989.45).

The schooner *Aurora* off Naples, after a watercolour by an unknown artist. The *Aurora* was built in 1836 in Guernsey and was employed in the Mediterranean trade, carrying fruit. Reproduced by kind permission of Guernsey Museums & Galleries (GMAG 1995.141).